D0929927

LONDON IN THE AGE OF SHAKESPEARE

LONDON IN THE AGE OF SHAKESPEARE:
AN ANTHOLOGY

Edited by Lawrence Manley

Bruce R Bartlett

via mail from Barnes &
Noble / NYC

16 Sept 94

THE PENNSYLVANIA STATE UNIVERSITY PRESS
University Park and London

© Lawrence Manley 1986

First published in Great Britain by Croom Helm Ltd.
Published in the United States of America by
The Pennsylvania State University Press.

Printed in Great Britain.

Library of Congress Cataloging-in-Publication Data

London in the age of Shakespeare.

   Bibliography: p.
   Includes index.
   1. Shakespeare, William, 1564–1616 — Contemporary
England. 2. London (England) — Description — To 1800.
3. London (England) — Literary collections. 4. English
literature — Early modern, 1500–1700. I. Manley,
Lawrence, 1949–
PR2918.L66 1986   820′.8′003   86-20476
ISBN 0-271-00445-2

CONTENTS

For Brian and Judy Dobbs,
Richard and Donna Vinter,
and their children

PREFACE

Roughly speaking, the limits of this anthology extend from 1485 to 1660, though my search for good examples or revealing contrasts has led me to include a few selections that were written slightly earlier or later. The largest number of selections was written during Shakespeare's lifetime (1564–1616). With two exceptions (Chapters 3 and 8), the chapters represent individual literary kinds; and with the exception of Chapter 11, the selections in each chapter are arranged in chronological order.

My texts are based, wherever possible, on the earliest printed editions, but I have consulted the best modern editions as well. Each selection is identified by a title (those in square brackets are mine), and by author and date. Where more than one date appears, the first is either the date of composition, where it is known to differ substantially from the date of publication, or the date of first publication when my copy-text is a later edition. Fuller information is supplied in the Bibliographical References (pp. 357-63), which are keyed to the numbers heading each selection in the text. Spelling and punctuation are modernised. When capitalised, 'City' denotes the Court of Aldermen, the Court of Common Council, and their officers. In lower case, according to context, 'city' denotes either the physical extension of the City's 26 wards or, like 'London', this area plus the built-up areas of Westminster, Southwark and the other suburbs. Unfamiliar words and allusions are glossed in the notes at the end of each chapter, but I have glossed only those place names which are obscure or which carry particular connotations. For the others, readers may consult such standard reference works as: George H. Cunningham, *London: A Comprehensive Survey ... of Buildings and Monuments* (1927); Henry A. Harben, *A Dictionary of London* (1918); Edward H. Sugden, *A Topographical Dictionary to the Works of Shakespeare and His Fellow Dramatists* (1925); Henry B. Wheatley, *London Past and Present* (3 vols, 1891); and Ben Weinreb and Christopher Hibbert, *The London Encyclopedia* (1983). All of these, however, rely heavily on John Stow's monumental *Survay of London* (1598, 1603), and readers can not do better than consult it in the modern edition by C.L. Kingsford (1908).

Preface

For permission to publish or reprint material (indicated by chapter and selection number in parenthesis), I am grateful to the following: Jonathan Cape, Ltd. (1.14), Yale University Press (2.15), Harvard University Press (2.16, 2.20, 6.4, 6.5, 6.6), The Royal Historical Society (3.10), The Bodleian Library (4.11), The University of Washington Press (7.2), Ernest Benn, Ltd. (9.6), and the James Marshall and Marie-Louise Osborne Collection of the Yale University Library (13.10).

For their courtesy I thank the staff at the Bishopsgate Institute, the Bodleian Library, the British Museum, the Guildhall Library, the London Library, the Museum of London, the Folger Shakespeare Library, the Huntington Library, the New York Public Library, the Houghton and Widener libraries at Harvard University and the Beinecke and Sterling libraries at Yale.

London is a subject that affords its students many pleasures, not least of which are the many consultations it provokes. For sharing their lore I wish to thank Stephen Barney, Kimberly Benston, Lars Engle, Margaret Ferguson, Stephen Foley, Ellen Graham, Thomas Greene, John Guillory, Richard Halpern, Oscar and Lilian Handlin, Ralph Hexter, John Hollander, George and Shelagh Hunter, Thomas Hyde, Ralph Kean, Daniel Kinney, Dominic Kinsley, George Lord, Charles McClendon, Clarence Miller, Robert Shaw, Suzanne Wofford and Marjorie Wynne.

I owe a special thanks to Eugene Waith, who cannot be blamed for this book's shortcomings but who helped me to rethink the way I put it together. The resourcefulness and wisdom of my two splendid graduate assistants, Donna Heiland and Tom Bishop, has been essential. Finally, for counsel in war and sacrifice in the field, I wish to thank the Londoners named in the dedication.

INTRODUCTION

At the accession of Henry VIII in 1509, London was a thriving community of 50,000 souls located on the cultural fringe of Northern Europe; at the accession of Charles II in 1660, as its population was approaching half a million, it had become a rapidly changing metropolis, the engine of an early modern economy and society, a capital that would soon become the largest and most powerful in Europe. This growth came at great cost to the English countryside, to the realm's lesser towns, and to countless Londoners, but it had also propelled England into a role of leadership in the modern age. When the historian A.F. Pollard declared that 'Tudor despotism consisted largely in London's dominance over the rest of England', he had in mind primarily the parliamentary legislation of the English Reformation. In a broader sense, however, the cultural 'Renaissance' of England, frequently associated with the achievements of the Tudor–Stuart monarchy and its court, was supported by the wealth and stability of London's long-established mercantile community.

London, said the anonymous author of the *Apology for the City of London* (1580), was 'a mighty arm and instrument to bring any great desire to effect, if it may be won to a man's devotion'. But London's powers were not exclusively political or economic. Next to the English language, it was the largest and most widely experienced artefact in the Tudor–Stuart period. Like the language, it was undergoing rapid change, offering new possibilities for exchange and combination, evolving signs, symbols, habits and systems of order that influenced every aspect of behaviour. In London, as in other major cities of the time, the urban experience contributed to new ideas about the individual, the community, and the power to shape the human environment creatively. Many of these ideas grew out of established civic traditions and native literature, and many were adapted from the newly fashionable literature of classical antiquity and the continental Renaissance. But they were shaped, too, by the processes of urban life, by the development of new class functions (linked especially to commerce, law and court bureaucracy), by new types of economic and religious association, and by a host of problems — poverty, dearth,

1

crime, vice and disease — the causes of which were poorly understood.

All of these developments animate the materials gathered in this anthology — a body of literature which consists largely of imaginative works (lyrics, ballads, praises, satires, jests, plays, pageants) but which also includes descriptions, chronicles, sermons, speeches and official proclamations. Taken as a whole, this literature amounts to a kind of city in itself, a polemical space in which competing visions and voices exert a productive infiuence on each other. Thomas Adams, a seventeenth-century London preacher, suggested that the city might 'not unfitly be compared to certain pictures, that represent to divers beholders, at divers stations, divers forms'. In its scope, variety and richness, the literature of Tudor–Stuart London embodies much of the city's complex and tumultuous life. Yet underlying the great diversity of forms and individual visions are the threads of continuity — the enduring traditions and common concerns — that made eloquence an important part of London's institutional life. In the literature of Tudor–Stuart London, as in the city itself, variety and change emerge from common purpose and belief. That is the basis of its power.

Much of London's impact on the kingdom and on the minds of the English can be traced to a set of civic institutions evolved during the Middle Ages and well established by the early Tudor period. Long before the seven Saxon kingdoms were united, London had enjoyed a measure of independence, largely as a result of the weakness of the Saxon kings. Its parish and ward boundaries (the latter created for defensive purposes during the Danish invasions of the eleventh century) were a physical heritage from Saxon times. And although William the Conqueror cowed the city with the massive Tower he built at the eastern limit of the city wall, he also issued a charter confirming 'the laws and customs of London as they were in King Edward's time'. Henry I (1100–35) was forced to allow Londoners to collect their own taxes and elect their own sheriffs, and in exchange for the city's support, King John allowed London to be governed by its first mayor, Henry Fitz-Alwin, and in 1215 permitted the city to elect its mayor annually. Ten attempts by Henry III to restore direct royal rule over the city — each of which was defeated by the King's need for London's financial support — proved that the wealth of London was the principal guarantee of its self-determination. With the deposition of Edward II and the accession of Edward III in 1327, the City won important new charters supposed to be immune from supersession, leading the chronicler, Froissart, to proclaim that from this time on Londoners were men *'pars lesquels tout le royaume d'Angleterre se ordonne et gouverne'*. By the later fifteenth century, London's rulers had begun to style themselves 'Lord Mayor' and to receive knighthood upon successful completion of their year in office. The claim of a fifteenth-century chronicler that London's mayor 'is next unto the king in all manner thing' was no idle boast: the Lord Mayor of Tudor–Stuart London was, on the death of a monarch, the highest ranking officer in the kingdom. London was a power to be reckoned with, as Henry VIII, Elizabeth and Burghley realised, and as Wolsey, Mary and the Stuart kings learned to their cost.

The freedoms and privileges extracted from the Crown were not at first widely shared. But two centuries of internal strife and experiment gradually broadened participation and established the form of City government in place in the early Tudor period: a Lord Mayor and Court of Aldermen, the executive governing body of the City, the legislative assembly of the Court of Common Council, and an electoral assembly called the Court of Common Hall. Irregularities and changes make it difficult to fix a precise summary that is valid for the whole Tudor–Stuart period, but in principle the Court of Common Hall was the City's largest assembly, which nominated annually two candidates (usually these were senior aldermen) for Lord Mayor and confirmed the actual choice made by the aldermen. It assisted in the election of London's two sheriffs and chose the City's four Members of Parliament. The roughly 200 members of the Court of Common Council (six or eight from each ward) who were elected by all freemen at an annual meeting of the wardmote, joined the Court of Aldermen in legislating on civic order and taxes. Each of the 26 aldermen was nominated by his ward but chosen by the Court of Aldermen, and he held office for life. Together with the Mayor and sheriffs, usually chosen from their ranks, the aldermen formed an oligarchic, self-perpetuating executive and judicial body. Each alderman was responsible for order in his ward, and the senior alderman, as justice of the peace, presided over London's many courts and jails. The aldermen issued licences, heard complaints, controlled the City's resources, and sat on or appointed the City's commissions and administrative posts. London was thus a self-governing community with its own laws, police, courts, army and welfare system.

The heart of this system were the London guilds, economic associations that had evolved from religious fraternities and neighbourhood groups into bodies regulating training, production and commerce in individual trades. The freedom of London, and thus the right to trade within the city, could be inherited by birth or purchased by 'redemption', but the principal means of enfranchisement was through seven years' apprenticeship and eventual membership in one of London's guilds. The guilds thus controlled citizenship, from which were excluded foreigners, provincial craftsmen and migrants, the disabled, criminal and unemployed, and all manner of labourers, from carters and porters to watermen and domestic servants. Estimates vary, but as early as the thirteenth century, only one in three Londoners may have qualified for citizenship. In 1537, approximately 15,000 Londoners, a quarter of the city's population, belonged to the citizen class.

Despite its exclusiveness, guild membership was the main channel for the social mobility associated with London in the period (see Chapter 3). Because the rate of deaths exceeded the rate of births in London, the city's population had constantly to be replenished by fresh immigration from the countryside. Less than 20 per cent of Tudor London's merchant élite can be shown to have been born in the city and more than 50 per cent almost certainly were not. Indentured in the 'art or mystery' of London's guilds, the sons of gentlemen and yeomen from all the shires of England might rise through the guild and civic hierarchy to enjoy the advantageous marriages, royal favour and lavish ceremony that were the perquisites of London's most powerful citizens. City politics was a recruiting ground for royal officers, and the pattern of ultimate success — often crowned by retirement to a rural estate — has as much to do as constant immigration with the rapid turnover in family names at the Guildhall.

In the late fourteenth and early fifteenth centuries, the guilds began to acquire royal charters allowing them to hold property in perpetuity, and by the early sixteenth century many of London's more than 70 companies had acquired splendid halls. During the same period, the power of ruling London had been consolidated in the hands of a few powerful guilds, which came to be known collectively as the Twelve Great Companies — the Mercers, Grocers, Drapers, Haberdashers, Fishmongers, Goldsmiths, Skinners, Merchant Taylors, Salters, Ironmongers, Vintners and Clothworkers. Even in the fourteenth century, only 9 of 260 aldermen had come from the lesser guilds, and in the sixteenth century, the Grocers, Haberdashers, Merchant Taylors and Mercers alone supplied 44 per cent of London's aldermen and common councillors. The sixteenth-century cloth and drapery trades together accounted for 61 per cent of these offices. The power of the London cloth trades was epitomised by the Merchants Adventurers, a cloth-trading consortium, in existence since 1407, which drew its members from several merchant groups but was controlled by the London Mercers. Chartered by Henry VII to 'use, occupy, and exercise in all quarters and kingdoms of this world all and every kind of merchandise', this conglomerate supplied nearly all of London's Lord Mayors between 1550 and 1580, prompting the proto-capitalist Sir Thomas Gresham to ask, 'how is it possible that a minstrel player, or a shoemaker, or any craftsman, or any other that hath not been brought up in the science [of international trade] to have the present understanding of the feat of the Merchant Adventurer?'

The domination of London by the major livery companies ran parallel to a growing division within the guilds themselves between the privileged members allowed to wear the company's livery and the lesser yeomanry — usually producers rather than merchants in the craft. From the livery came the masters, wardens and court of assistants (former masters and wardens) who governed the affairs of the guild. Financed by fines, enrolment fees and quarterly dues, the guilds exercised tight control over their membership. The court of wardens in each guild oversaw production and merchandising, it heard complaints from customers, and settled disputes between the members. The guilds provided a channel through which civic orders and proclamations could be issued and enforced, and they were the main source from which the Crown could directly extract able-bodied men and money.

One of the most important guild functions was the regulation of apprenticeship. The guilds approved candidates for enrolment (often requiring the ability to read and write), drew up their indentures, and relocated apprentices whose masters had died. They dealt firmly with dishonesty, riot, drunkenness, ostentation and profligacy, but they rarely handed apprentices over to the law. The prospect of advancement and a system of deference and ceremony, in which yeomen treated journeymen much as they were treated by the livery, added cohesion to the guilds, as did their religious, fraternal and charitable functions. The guilds provided for the widows and orphans of their members and for their own almsmen and pensioners. On those occasions, such as funerals and civic holidays, when the masters, wardens, assistants, livery, clerks, beadles and yeomen met in general assembly, the conventional formula of 'the whole company of the fellowship' was presumably not without its meaning. The annual pageants for the inauguration of the new Lord Mayor (Chapter 16), sponsored by the guilds, were its consummate expression.

The foundation for this elaborate institutional life was the wealth derived from London's diverse economy. A major European port and domestic distribution centre, London combined its major trading and industrial functions with its role as capital in such a way as to withstand economic hardships, outstrip its rivals, and become the cornerstone of the economy of early modern England. The advantage of London's proximity to Westminster can be traced to the mid-eleventh century, when Edward the Confessor built a palace near the Thames in order to oversee the building of a Romanesque structure on the site of an abbey founded by King Offa. Edward's son Harold was the first English king to be crowned in the Abbey, and by the end of the century William II had added to the palace the Hall that was to be so crucial in the development of Westminster. With King John's loss of Normandy in the early thirteenth century, Westminster became an important residence of the court. Several royal residences were later established in the vicinity of London. In addition to the Tower, officially a royal residence, Henry VIII owned palaces at the former Hospital of St James for Leprous Virgins, at Bridewell inside the city walls, and at Whitehall, formerly the splendid residence of the fallen Cardinal Wolsey. Through the parsimony of Elizabeth, who abandoned many of her father's palaces in the countryside, Whitehall and Greenwich became the settled residences of the court.

Royal residence in Westminster enhanced not only London's prestige but also its economic life, especially through the establishment of the Great Wardrobe, which furnished the court, near Baynard's Castle in 1361. Henceforth, countless Londoners found employment in the many service and luxury trades the court required. The roughly 1,500 members of the Tudor royal household, located first in the palace of St James and later near the river in the palace of Whitehall, represent only a fraction of the employment generated by the court. The quest for patronage, education and marriage drew swarms of aspiring courtiers to London and Westminster; by 1560 half of England's peers owned London houses, many of them on the sites of the pre-Reformation episcopal palaces along the Strand between the city and Westminster. Their presence transformed London into a centre of conspicuous consumption, an emporium for the specialised luxury goods imported by the city's merchants and manufactured by its craftsmen. Vastly outnumbering the more than 70 chartered guilds were literally hundreds of specialised trades, many of them generated by courtly fashion. Courtiers, ambassadors and travellers from abroad were the making of countless collar-makers, starch-makers, buckle-makers, buttonmould makers, pin-makers, hat trimmers and hatband makers, gold-wire drawers, diamond cutters, minstrels and players.

Parliament, too, had begun to meet regularly in Westminster under Edward III, but even more important was the settlement of England's principal courts in Westminster at the same time. Hostels for the clerks and lawyers associated with these courts sprang up in Holborn, near Chancery Lane. Leased out to lawyers, the former property of the Knights Templar became the Middle and Inner Temple. Together with a dozen others, these Inns of Court — half law school, half youth hostel — comprised, in Stow's words, 'a whole university, as it were, of students, practisers and pleaders, and judges of the laws of this realm'. Populated by sober jurists as well as aspiring gentlemen seeking education, polish or promotion, the Inns transformed the area between Fleet Street and Holborn into a hive of lodging-houses, shops and taverns. The country-folk who trudged from all the counties of England to seek law in London carried the city's finery back with them, but more importantly, the gentlemen of the Inns helped to diversify the city's economy and its intellectual life. The pursuit of fashion and the cultivation of adversarial eloquence at the Inns added an urbane aggression to London life. The location of the Inns between the city and Westminster aptly symbolises the fluid status and sophistication of the legal sub-culture from which dozens of intellectuals and writers emerged.

London's role as a capital, however, was inseparable from its role as a commercial centre. Even the Venerable Bede had

described London as a 'market-place for many peoples, who come
by land and sea'; but the prosperity of early modern London, like
that of cities all over Europe, can be traced to the receding of Arab
influence and the re-opening of the Mediterranean in the tenth
century. The rise of the merchant cities of Italy brought to life the
towns of Northern Europe, which, though England traded directly
with such places as Genoa and Venice, were the nation's main
trading partners. Ideally situated on the Thames, London had
ready access to the textile manufactories and entrepôts of the
Netherlands, to the Rhineland cloth markets, and to the Baltic
towns of the Hansa. Consequently, as early as the thirteenth cen-
tury, London's exports had increased from one-seventh to
one-third of the nation's total. Essentially a colonial economy until
the fourteenth century, England exported such raw goods as tin,
lead, corn, hides and wool, and re-imported the wool as finished
cloth (woven in Ghent and Bruges) along with jewels, pottery, silk,
wine, spices and other luxury goods. All this began to change when
Edward III brought Flemish weavers to England and the country
began to export rough woollen cloth. Largely through the enter-
prise of the Merchants Adventurers, dominated by London's
Mercers, the export of cloth increased 17 to 18 times between
1350 and 1500; by the end of this period, it represented 70 per
cent of English exports, as against 8 per cent for raw wool.
Between 1500 and 1550, when the price of woollens doubled,
London's share of the trade increased from 70 to 88 per cent, and
while the city accounted for 50 per cent of customs revenue under
Henry VII, it was accounting for 86 per cent by 1581–82. Three
times as large as Bristol, its nearest English rival in the early four-
teenth century, London was by 1520 ten times as large as Norwich,
which had overtaken Bristol for second place. In the Loan Book of
1520, London, which contained only 3 per cent of the English
population, was assessed at £20,000, or 12 per cent of the national
total; the whole of Kent only paid half as much. In the next half-
century the gap widened tremendously: London was assessed in
the 1576 parliamentary subsidy at £12,226, while Norwich con-
tributed £493; in all, London, Westminster and the Borough of
Southwark contributed four times the total of all the other English
boroughs together.

Some of this growth may be traced to the fall of Constantinople
to the Turks in 1453, and to the subsequent shift of trade routes
from the Mediterranean to the Atlantic; as the economic initiative

subsequently shifted from the south to the north of Europe, London enjoyed the first of many benefits stemming from the problems of its rivals. Antwerp became the hub of European trade and London was its principal satellite: in 1563–64 London exported to Antwerp goods worth £700,000–900,000 wholesale, £1.5 million retail. But with the sack of Antwerp by the Spanish in 1572, and with religious wars raging in the Netherlands and France, London rose to unrivalled leadership in the economy of Northern Europe.

At the same time, London's economy was undergoing revolutionary change. A depression in the cloth market in the mid-sixteenth century had forced Londoners to seek new markets. The Russia Company, founded in 1553, was the first of several new trading companies that included the Levant Company (1581), the East India Company (1600), the Virginia Company (1606) and several African companies. Guild membership, of course, had never prevented members from dabbling in several trades, but these new joint stock companies, open to anyone willing to invest capital, far more drastically eroded the traditional forms of economic organisation. The voyages of these companies, like those of new privateering, discovery and plantation syndicates, commonly returned a profit on investment of 300 or 400 per cent and helped to widen the financial and social gap between international traders and retail merchants. Such ventures attracted noblemen and courtiers, as did the many new customs farms, collectorships, patents and concessions which were licensed by the Crown to royal favourites and relatives who sold or leased them, in turn, to London merchants and companies or to new types of sub-livery syndicates formed by merchants and speculators. The traditional economic regulation of the guilds had been, in many ways, monopolistic, but these new organisations helped to give the term 'monopoly' its pejorative cast from virtually the moment it became current in later sixteenth-century English. Along with collecting and licensing rights, and with supervising rights in certain trades and industries, the Crown granted exclusive patents over newer industries. Though intended to stabilise supply, quality and price, and to foster technological innovations, these patents were often a mere excuse for exploiting settled trades; drawing their capital from London merchants, or even from lotteries, and protected by the influence of courtly sponsors, monopolies were established over a range of products from finished cloth to playing cards. Joining the ranks of the great Elizabethan financiers — the Greshams, the Pallavicinos, the Stoddards — were the Stuart speculators, promoters and projectors who gave new meaning to words like 'venture', 'fortune' and 'security'. Sir Arthur Ingram, the son of a linen draper, for example, became a successful real-estate speculator by withholding payment from those who sold him land, thereby forcing them to ruin themselves with legal expenses. Sir Lionel Cranfield, a mercer's apprentice who married his master's daughter, became Lord High Treasurer and Earl of Middlesex through his financial acumen in administrative patents; while Sir William Cockayne parlayed an ill-advised monopoly for finishing cloth into a massive personal fortune. Sir Thomas Smythe (1558–1625) became a merchant prince by governing the Russia Company, the Levant Company, the Somers Islands Company and the East Company.

At the highest levels, commercial change brought new mobility, as the Garveys, Suttons, Hickses, Pindars, Crisps and Sandys made their way to court from London; while the aristocratic Herberts and Cecils worked the London customs. But a growing disparity between capital and labour closed off opportunity further down; the attempts of yeomen and journeymen to establish breakaway artisan guilds are only one sign of the waning life of London's older economic system. The position of the guilds was further weakened by an influx of Flemish and Huguenot refugees, many of them skilled craftsmen, who established new, unregulated industries or who challenged older ones by setting up shop outside the City's jurisdiction in the unregulated suburbs.

The new economy eventually threatened even the City's traditional loyalty to Westminster, as London's merchants, at first allied with the interests of the Stuart court against Parliament and the provinces, had come, by 1628–29, to resent the Crown's extortionate interventions in the urban economy. Stuart foreign policy was offensive to the more extreme Protestants, but it was also detrimental to trade, and the objections of Londoners to Stuart-controlled tithes and preferments were economic as well as doctrinal. The exaction of tonnage and poundage or customs duties, the abuse of monopoly grants, the royal attempts to incorporate the suburbs and thus to control the freedom of the City, all helped to alienate members of the merchant class from Crown policies. Essential to London's support of Parliament during the Civil War was a challenge to the City's aldermanic elite from the City's

Common Council, on which many lesser merchants and craftsmen were represented. Recent work suggests, however, that even London's wealthiest and most powerful citizens had grown disenchanted with King Charles, and that their supposed pro-Royalist sympathies were only the belated response of moderates who feared the excess of revolution and hoped for reforms at Court. In 1642, 100,000 Londoners turned out to ring the city with defensive fortifications, and at the sight of the 24,000 volunteers of London's trained bands, many of whom had brought their families to witness an impending battle at Turnham Green, the Royalist forces fled without a fight. It was impossible, Thomas Hobbes later wrote, for the King to resist 'the army of Parliament, maintained by the great purse of the City of London'.

Despite the strains of economic and social change, the life of London remained fundamentally orderly. Even while some guilds were dying out, they were being replaced by new ones, and to lay exclusive stress on the waning power of the guilds is to overlook the many other institutions that helped to maintain stability. Each alderman, assisted by a host of ward officers, including beadles, constables, scavengers and comptrollers maintained the order of his ward through regular meetings of the wardmote inquest, which addressed literally dozens of local matters from sanitation and public health to business dealings and social harmony. Through a system of more than 200 local precincts (each of them on the average 120 yards square) constables enforced good and decent order. Overlapping with the precincts were the boundaries of more than 100 parishes, whose vestries were a generating force in city politics. While two or three churchwardens handled the finances of the parish and the life-records of the parishioners, several vestry-men, who often sat on the ward inquest and participated in the electoral nominating process, dealt with a combination of paro-chial and civic business, including taxes, public health and vice. The paternalistic tone of this system was balanced by an openness to widespread participation in local affairs and to advancement through it.

The physical limits of this civic order extended well beyond the medieval city walls, from Temple Bar in Fleet Street and Holborn Bars in the west, across Smithfield and Moorfields to St Mary Spital beyond Bishopsgate in the north, and from there to White-chapel Bars and the Minories in the east. The inclusion of these extramural areas within the City's liberties reflects the origin of the wards as units for military defence in Saxon times, but they were already becoming well populated by the sixteenth century, as the large areas of green space within the walls, many of them church-yards or gardens and orchards owned by religious houses, had put building space at a premium. The core of the city remained, how-ever, the area defined by the old walls, which ran from the Tower in the east to the street now known as London Wall in the north, and from there to the Fleet river and Blackfriars in the west. Bounded on its outside by a deep ditch that was gradually being filled in and breached by a series of massive gates opening on to the main routes to the north, London could be sealed shut at night and in times of crisis. Its walls remained the symbol of its power as a world unto itself.

To the south, the city was bounded by the crescent lifeline of the Thames, whose tidal rhythm dictated much of London's activity. Houses fronting onto the river, which was then much wider and shallower, had steps descending to the water, giving access to the small boats which were still a major means of trans-port to the south bank or to Westminster. Though contemporaries estimated that these small boats and the people employed by them ran into many thousands, they were only part of a fleet of barges, lighters, tilt boats and ferries that off-loaded goods from larger ships harboured from the Tower and beyond and carried them up river to the series of docks and wharves where much of England's wealth was landed within a space of a few hundred yards. Spanning the river at the foot of Bridge Street was the magnificent stone bridge whose 19 arches supported the populous street that made London the crossroads of England. The drawbridge and gate at the southern end provided access to travellers from the south, and the drying heads of traitors, impaled on spikes above the gate, provided savage warning to potential insurrectionists.

Though virtually destroyed in the Great Fire of 1666, the city within the walls was recorded in lavish detail in the many maps and panoramas of the period, and in countless descriptions, among which John Stow's *Survay of London* (1598) is unrivalled in scope or particularity. The most striking visual features of the urban landscape were the towers and spires of well over 100 churches. Even after 1561, when lightning destroyed its nearly 600-foot wooden spire, the most imposing of these was at St Paul's, the massive Norman cathedral built on Ludgate Hill as a rival to the one at Winchester, the old Saxon capital. The outdoor pulpit at

Paul's Cross, angled into the north-east corner of the cathedral in the churchyard, was a centre of the religious life of the city and the nation (see Chapter 3). Within the cathedral itself was the famous meeting-place where journeymen were hired, transactions were made and gossip was exchanged. By the beginning of the seventeenth century, both the ruinous condition of the cathedral and the uses to which it was put had become a scandal of the age.

Prior to the Henrician Reformation, London's churches were only part of a religious fabric that included more than 50 religious houses and dozens of hermitages and private chapels. Among the larger religious landowners were the pre-Norman college of Augustinian canons at St Martin-le-Grand, the Dominican Blackfriars, just inside the western limit of the city wall along the Thames and Fleet river, the Carmelite Whitefriars east of the Temple, the Greyfriars or Franciscans at Newgate, the Austin friars, near Broad Street, and the priors of Holy Trinity, Aldgate. The dissolution and sale of these and other houses by Henry VIII, mainly in 1538, wrought major changes in London's life and fabric. While most members of the orders themselves were pensioned off, hundreds of Londoners who depended on the houses for employment, as well as those who received their charity, were left without support. Some charitable restitution was made when Henry, virtually on his deathbed, returned a few of the houses to the City, enabling it to establish or renew five great hospitals: the Hospital of St Bartholomew in Smithfield and the Hospital of St Thomas, founded in Southwark by the monks of Bermondsey Abbey and the friars of St Mary Overy, became medical institutions for the sick and infirm, while the small hospital of St Mary of Bethlehem became a refuge for the insane; Greyfriars, with its Christ Church, which except for St Paul's was the largest place of worship in London, became the orphanage of Christ's Hospital, an institution Londoners favoured heavily in charitable bequests. The royal palace of Bridewell, built by Henry VIII to receive the Emperor Charles V in 1522, but abandoned during the plague of 1529 because of its proximity to the noxious Fleet river, became an infamous workhouse for the destitute and unemployed. A few other properties survived, such as the church of the Priory of St Helen's Bishopsgate, which was incorporated into the parish church, and the chapel of St Thomas of Acon, which became the chapel of the Mercers' Company. Others, however, were converted to industrial purposes. Part of the Bishop of Hereford's Inn became a sugar factory; Eastminster, the Cistercian abbey, was pulled down and replaced by naval storehouses and a bakery for ship's biscuits; armour was stored and manufactured at the Minories, the convent of St Clare; St Mary Axe became the factory of a superb glassmaker, Jacob Verzelini; and Dutch watchmakers, to avoid the City's jurisdiction, set up shop in St Martin-le-Grand.

Because the original immunities granted to religious houses were extended with their sale as liberties under royal franchise, former religious properties were choice locations for high-rent, high-density tenements. Coldharbour, where Cuthbert Tunstall, Bishop of London, had once resided, was given over to tenements inhabited by debtors seeking immunity from the law, and St Martin-le-Grand became a noted haunt of costume jewellers and hucksters (pedlars). England's first indoor theatre, established in the precinct of Blackfriars where the City's writ did not run, can be traced to the 1540s, when Sir Thomas Carwarden, Master of the Revels, adapted the convent church as a storehouse for the props from court entertainments.

Meanwhile, the courtiers who replaced the bishops in residence along the Strand were far more than new tenants. With a religious zeal suitably matched to his grandiose ambition, the Protector Somerset tore down the houses of five bishops to build his own residence, drawing the materials from the charnel house at St Paul's and from the church of the Knights Hospitallers in Smithfield, which, said Stow, 'was undermined and blown up with gunpowder'. At sixpence the load, sevenpence with carriage, Sir Thomas Audley, the Lord Chancellor, pulled down and sold for paving stone the priory of Holy Trinity in the Minories. Nevertheless, amid a process of deracination and displacement that transformed the landscape, London's government and citizenry lived in essential harmony. Friendships, marriages and business dealings crossed denominational lines, and the appeal of moderate, pragmatic Protestantism to most of London's leading citizens was rooted in a communal ethic that antedated the Reformation.

The central expression of this ethic was the Guildhall between Aldermanbury and Basinghall Street, which was built in the early fifteenth century during the height of guild incorporation and was much embellished through the next 100 years. Combining the functions of court, senate house, feasting-hall and civic chapel, it was, together with the company halls, the Customs House, the hospitals and more than a dozen jails and prisons, part of an important fabric of civic structures. As their names suggest, Cheapside and Poultry, forming the major east–west axis within the city, were a focus of economic activity. In the vicinity were London's major market-places. The Stocks Market, for fish, flesh and produce, stood at the end of Poultry on the site of the present Mansion House. Further to the east, in Bishopsgate, was the Leadenhall Market, for wool, corn and dry goods; it also served as a granary and municipal armoury and contained the City's beam. To the north of Cheapside was Blackwell Hall, the cloth exchange. On the south side of Cheap lay Goldsmith's Row, 'the most beautiful frame of fair houses and shops that be within the walls of London', and opposite, on the north side, stood the hall and chapel of the mighty Mercers. Just to the east of Poultry, on Cornhill, was Thomas Gresham's Royal Exchange, erected in 1566 as a meeting-place for London's merchants and financiers. Modelled on the great Bourse at Antwerp, this magnificent structure housed on its upper level some 100 shops offering the luxury goods of armourers, milliners, apothecaries, booksellers, goldsmiths and glass-blowers. With its open courtyard, covered arcade and marble columns, the Exchange symbolised the emergence of London, after the fall of Antwerp, as the leading entrepôt of Northern Europe. Just as symbolic, perhaps, was the closing of the Steelyard, the great riverside complex of the foreign Hanseatic merchants, in 1598.

Most of London's tradesmen continued to concentrate in specific locales — drapers, for example, in Candlewick Street and Watling Street, skinners in Budge Row and Walbrook, shoemakers in Cordwainer Street and St Martin-le-Grand, butchers in Eastcheap, stationers and booksellers in Paternoster Row and St Paul's churchyard. Inns and taverns abounded. In 1574, the greater part of the 876 taverns listed for Middlesex and the 454 listed for Surrey could be found in the vicinity of the metropolis.

Nestled everywhere within the walls and among London's religious, civic and commercial structures were the dwellings of people of all ranks. Splendid merchant houses were clustered in areas throughout the city — in Basinghall and Limestreet wards, in the warehouse district along Thames Street from Baynard's Castle to Coldharbour, and in the busy commercial districts of Candlewick Street, Lombard Street and Fenchurch Street. Many of London's finest merchant houses, including Crosby Hall, Fisher's Folly, and Gresham House, stood along Bishopsgate.

From 'Crosby place up to Leadenhall corner, and so down Gracechurch Street,' Stow reported, were 'fair and large-builded houses for merchants and such like'. At the city's north-western limit, along Red Cross Street from Cripplegate out to the Barbican, and east along Beech Lane, were 'summer houses for pleasure' and 'beautiful houses of stone, brick, and timber'. The suburban summer-houses of London's elite, Stow complained, were 'like Midsummer pageants, with towers, turrets, and chimney tops, not so much for use or profit as for show or pleasure, betraying the vanity of men's minds'. Many noble families, too, continued to reside within the city's limits. The Earls of Huntington still dwelt in their ancient Inn near Paul's Wharf, and since 1546 the Herberts, Earls of Pembroke, had been established in Baynard's Castle, a former stronghold named for the lieutenant in whose hands the Conqueror had placed the city. However, while some Tudor courtiers, such as Walsingham and the Lord Lumley, occupied or built on church properties within the city, many older noble houses had given way to a swelling tide of population. The house of the Earls of Ormond, in Knightrider Street, Stow claimed, had been 'lately taken down and divers fair tenements are builded there'; the house of the Lords of Berkeley, faring less well perhaps, was 'all in ruin, and letten out in several tenements'. Northumberland House, the London home of the Percys, had given way to bowling alleys and dicing houses and then to 'small cottages for strangers and others'. Even where fair houses still stood in the main streets, the areas behind them were a honeycomb of lanes, alleys, courts and gardens, where lesser dwellings — tenements and sometimes hovels — clustered with ever-increasing density. There were, for example, 24 lanes, alleys and yards in the 600 yards along the river between Queenhithe and London Bridge. The streets themselves, paved within the city and out to Charing Cross and Clerkenwell, were crowded from first light. Especially active were the points at which public cisterns were placed — the Great Conduit and the Standard in Cheapside, the Tun in Cornhill, the Little Conduit near Paul's Gate, and others in Fleet Street, Aldermanbury, Cripplegate, Colman Street and Stocks Market. Laid down centuries before, and now inadequate for the flow of traffic, the streets were further congested by the premium on building space. Stalls erected along the side of the streets had a habit of becoming permanent structures, and as houses grew vertically, they extended outward, storey by storey, sometimes nearly joining the two sides of the street and shutting out light and air. Tile had long replaced thatch for roofing, and brick was coming into use, but timber, lath and plaster were still the mainstays in often jerry-built construction.

The increasing density within the walls was matched by explosive growth beyond the walls and in the suburbs. The river economy, aided by the building of royal shipyards at Deptford and Woolwich, had attracted development eastward. There was building from the Tower to Wapping along the river, from the Tower towards Shadwell along the Ratcliff highway, and from Aldgate along the road to Mile End. Crowding was worst nearest the city walls. The area around St Katherine's, east of the Tower, Stow said, was 'pestered with small tenements and homely cottages, having inhabitants, English and strangers, more in number than some cities in England'. The parishioners of St Botolph's without Aldgate had grown so numerous that the church was 'pestered with lofts and seats for them', and the road beyond Aldgate was 'not only fully replenished with buildings outward', but also 'pestered with divers alleys on either side to the Bars ... to Whitechapel and beyond'. Further north, near Bishopsgate, the district of Petty France had grown up on the banks of Houndsditch, built by 'citizens of London that more regarded their own private gain than the common good of the city'. Outside of Bishopsgate, in the road through Shoreditch, from Bethlehem 'northward upon the streets' side, many houses have been builded, with alleys backward, of late time, too much pestered with people (a great cause of infection) up to the Bars'. The public grounds in the northern suburbs — the Artillery Yard near Spitalfields, the archery ground in Finsbury Field, and Moorfields, a former fen laid out with walks in 1607 — were for the time being spared. But further west, northward development had pushed past the Finsbury windmills to Old Street, along the unsavoury Turnmill Street to St James's Clerkenwell, and out of Holborn past Staple Inn toward St Giles in the Fields.

Westward development, though equally intense, was somewhat different. Shops and taverns sprang up not only in Fleet Street but on the sites of former mansions along the Strand; 'Britain's Burse', a rival to Gresham's Royal Exchange, was built in 1609 on property owned successively by the Bishop of Durham, the Duke of Northumberland and Sir Walter Raleigh. But in contrast to the noxious developments in the east, the west became increasingly a district of wealth and high fashion, as courtiers, lawyers and bureaucrats were attracted by the proximity to Westminster and by the freshness of the prevailing westerly winds. The east and west ends of London began to polarise with Robert Cecil's development of St Martin's Lane, with the Earl of Bedford's development of the Covent Garden piazza, designed by Inigo Jones and laid out in the 1630s, and with William Newton's somewhat later development of Lincoln's Inn Fields.

Meanwhile, across the river to the south were the growing suburbs of the Borough of Southwark and Bridge Ward Without, incorporated into the City in 1550. The physical isolation of Southwark, together with lax jurisdiction and a tradition of liberties associated with its many earlier religious properties, had made the place a suitable location for several hospitals and jails, and for the notorious brothels and bear-baiting rings of Bankside. To these were added both the expanding industrial plants of such noxious trades as tanning and soap-boiling and the series of great outdoor theatres that began to spring up at the end of the sixteenth century — the Rose, the Swan and the Globe. Sited on the southern approaches to the city, and on the Canterbury pilgrimage route, Southwark had long been famous for its inns and hostelries, which now extended southwards from the bridge for nearly a mile along the High Street.

Even beyond these built-up areas a ring of villages had entered the metropolitan orbit. Brick kilns and stockyards were springing up at Tottenham, Islington and Hackney, and both sides of the road had been built up in Hoxton. The riverside villages of Brentford, Putney and Barnes were becoming favoured suburban resorts, and Osterley became the site of Sir Thomas Gresham's splendid country house.

Even when they were the most wretched of shanty-towns the suburbs were, of course, a manifestation of London's sometimes brutal economic might. With capital earned from luxury goods distributed through the provinces, Londoners drew an increasing supply of victuals from the countryside. This, together with a rapid rise in population, produced staggeringly inflated prices for food-stuffs, and the resultingly higher profits of agricultural landowners made their way back to London through an ever-more fashionable demand for specialist goods and services. In a cycle that continued to concentrate capital in London, a tide of immigrants increased the demand for foodstuffs, kept wages low, and provided labour for diversifying luxury and service trades. By the end of the sixteenth century, when food prices had increased fourfold while wages remained essentially stable, the mixed fruits of London's growth were evident throughout the city and its environs in a mean harvest of crime, poverty, unemployment, vice, disease and unrest.

In 1580 Elizabeth had made the first of many futile attempts — which extended through the next two reigns — to halt the growth of London by fiat. Unlicensed building was forbidden within 3 (later 5) miles of London, and restrictions were placed on the overcrowding of tenements and the partitioning of existing buildings. But corruption, lax enforcement and a profit margin that made covert building more than worth the risk of prosecution rendered these measures ineffective. The City Fathers, furthermore, were understandably reluctant to extend their jurisdiction to the suburbs, in which the problems of growth were greatly magnified. The simple provision of water, food and fuel, for example, posed staggering problems. By the early seventeenth century, the water-driven pumps under London Bridge and at Broken Wharf, installed in the 1580s to supplement the city's over-used wells, had become inadequate, and the City was forced to construct a 40-mile-long canal to bring water from Hertfordshire. Chronically poor harvests and short supplies required the city to maintain large stocks of corn in the municipal granaries, and forestallers and regraters had constantly to be reckoned with. Coal was replacing a dwindling supply of wood, but both were marketed with notorious fraudulence and careful supervision was needed. Public health was under constant threat. Both Walbrook and the Fleet river had become sewers and gradually disappeared under buildings, but human and animal waste had constantly to be removed from the streets and from the dumps and privies that formed in lanes and alleyways. Epidemic diseases like smallpox, the sweating sickness and consumption took their frequent and heavy toll, but none of these could match the plague, which visited London at recurring intervals. The major outbreaks were devastating: 17,500 died in 1563, 23,000 in 1593, 30,000 in 1603, and 40,000 in 1625; none, however, was as disastrous as the great onset of 1665, which took perhaps 100,000 lives.

The increased size and diversity of London's population meanwhile posed challenges to social order. Vagabonds, paupers, demobbed soldiers and masterless men were the subject of frequent searches and identification schemes. Alien workers were thought to pose an economic threat, and, along with Anabaptists,

recusants and religious deviants of all persuasions, they were a
concern to religious authorities, who feared the formation of secret
conventicles. The criminal sub-culture of prostitutes and thieves
took on mythical proportions, and public disorders were dreaded
but fairly common events. Early in the reign of Henry VIII,
Londoners armed with shovels and spades had attacked recently
erected hedges and ditches enclosing the common ground north of
the city, and the Evil May Day riot of 1517, when apprentices led
an attack on alien residents, was only the worst in a centuries-long
series of risings against foreigners. Extra watches and curfews were
imposed during times of political unrest, such as the rebellions of
1549 or the crisis of 1601, when the Earl of Essex rode through
Fleet Street with 200 supporters. Rowdy apprentices frequently
went on the rampage, food riots recurred throughout the sixteenth
century, and the authorities were particularly swift in revenging a
millenarian disturbance in 1593. London's field of force thus was
at once centripetal and centrifugal, inclining one poet to liken
London's suburban expansion to a lawless riot:

> The city's sure in progress, I surmise,
> Or going to revel it in some disorder,
> Without the walls, without the liberties,
> Where she need fear nor Mayor nor Recorder.

Literature was, in fact, an essential part of this changing life, an
institution, or set of institutions, in which writers attempted to
record and order a common urban experience. In the literature of
London, social, linguistic and literary forms combined to make the
city a major preoccupation of the age. In the eloquence of the
medieval officials who compiled London's records and
customaries, and in the learning of its clerks and preachers, the city
had always been an idea as well as a place, a focus for common
fears and aspirations. But it was in the sixteenth century, when
London was emerging as an economic power and Tudor capital,
that the first stages of social and economic change coincided with
the infusion of an intellectual ferment associated with the Renais-
sance, the Reformation and the spread of printing. From More's
time onward, an expanding repertoire of literary forms and ideas,
derived from ancient Greece and Rome and from writers on the
continent, gave Londoners new intellectual means by which
to interpret and shape their common life. St Paul's School,

reorganised by Colet in 1512 for 'little Londoners especially', introduced the humanistic curriculum to England and became the first in a series of London schools that were among the foremost in the kingdom — Westminster School (reorganised 1560), Merchant Taylors' School (1561), and Charterhouse School (1611). London's merchants played a leading role in founding and supporting these schools, as well as countless others in the countryside, and their openness to education and new ideas contributed to the city's high rate of literacy. Thomas More may have overestimated when he said that 60 per cent of Londoners could read, but by the early seventeenth century only 24 per cent of London's tradesmen and artisans were unable to sign their name. Related to literacy, too, was London's role as the birthplace of English printing. In 1485, William Caxton, governor of the Merchants Adventurers at Bruges, set up his press at the Red Pale in Westminster, and in one of his first books he paid tribute to the city of London, 'my mother, of whom I have received my nurture and living'. It was Caxton's apprentice Wynkyn de Worde, however, who took the crucially symbolic step of moving the press to Fleet Street in London. With the incorporation of the Company of Stationers in 1557 — a measure designed to tighten censorship — printing became a virtual monopoly of London. By 1585, there were 24 separate printers operating in London, and by 1649, following the relaxation of censorship, the number had passed 60. Demand was heavy for devotional and doctrinal works, though the coming of the Protestant Reformation had opened not just London's presses but also its pulpits to a flood of new ideas. By the 1630s, Londoners were supporting more than 100 Puritan lecturers to supplement the services of the regular clergy, and this intellectual activity was matched elsewhere by the rise of such institutions as the Royal College of Physicians, the Society of Antiquaries and Gresham College, which offered public lectures in divinity, law, astronomy, music, geometry, rhetoric and physic.

The presence of the court, meanwhile, offered patronage to many intellectuals. An important literary circle formed around Sir Philip Sidney at Leicester House, and included Edmund Spenser, a journeyman's son from the Merchant Taylors' School. Another adventurous circle, formed around the Earl of Northumberland and Sir Walter Raleigh, included the *enfant terrible*, Christopher Marlowe, and George Chapman, the translator of Homer. Together with the Inns of Court, Westminster attracted aspiring

intellectuals from throughout the realm, and their restless compe-
tition for advancement and divided loyalties added a peculiarly
urbane tone to London life. Both the court and Inns provided
major audiences for dramatic talent, though the fanciful, chivalric
tastes of the court were balanced at the Inns by a fashion for
acerbic epigram, satire and city comedy. A whole body of myth,
meanwhile, extolled the virtues and justified the civic pride of
London's merchant community, whose ambitions were also exploi-
ted in a growing literature of practical and moral advice. Popular
oral culture, furthermore, supported a tradition of urban jest and
underworld legend, while songs and ballads were peddled through
the streets and sung in alehouses. Yet the Mermaid Inn in Bread
Street could also number among its lively clientele the likes of
Raleigh, Donne, Jonson, Beaumont and Shakespeare. Interludes
had been performed at the Clerkenwell Pump in the Middle Ages,
passion plays had been enacted on the roof of St Peter in Cornhill,
and the city's galleried innyards had long served as theatres for
itinerant troupes. But the drama came of age between 1576 and
1613, when 11 permanent theatres were opened in the unregu-
lated liberties and suburbs. The life of London was itself a drama
of conflicting voices, visions, styles and purposes, and its inherently
theatrical nature was annually projected onto the streets, when the
City's leaders, guilds, artists and populace combined to celebrate
their common life in words, spectacle and song.

The experience of London, then, is not merely reflected in the
works gathered in this anthology, but embodied in their very
forms. It was, one early Tudor writer said, 'through the monu-
ments of writing' that men were 'moved ... to build cities'. Ancient
tradition held that Orpheus and Amphion, the earliest of poets and
musicians, had the power to civilise men and pile up stones with
song. They were, said Thomas Lodge, the 'first raisers of cities'.
Emerging from the varied strands and forms of London life, and
integrated with them, the London that was performed, imagined
and sung was, in many ways, the London that was lived. It was a
city, as a contemporary epigram had it, that lived on more than
bread alone:

This is that city strong to which three gifts are given by three:
By Bacchus, Ceres, Phoebus, wine, wheat, and poetry.

1

PORTRAIT OF A CITY:
PROSE DESCRIPTION

Nothing better illustrates than prose description the extent to which Tudor–Stuart London was a place of the imagination. The London to be found in prose description almost always bears the imprint of a given writer's individual style, while points of resemblance between one version of London and another sometimes owe no more to actual consensus than to a common reliance on established schemes, topics and models of city description. Inevitably, however, there remains in nearly every description a fresh and vigorous power of observation, at times, almost a sense of discovery. It would not be going too far to say that Tudor–Stuart descriptions of London reveal that a major corollary of the Renaissance discovery of man was the discovery of the city.

Like many features of early modern urban culture, the description of cities was an art developed in the Middle Ages. Greek and Latin literature provided a few examples, but a great impetus to the development of the genre was the experience of medieval religious pilgrimage. Cities like Jerusalem and Rome were the focus of descriptions meant primarily to encourage veneration and to stimulate the imagination of potential pilgrims. Such descriptions provided little in the way of accurate topography, but they served as the first models for later, more factual and secular accounts.

The description of London, too, emerged from a religious background. William Fitzstephen's *Descriptio Nobilissime Civitatis Londonia* (1173–75) was actually a part of his life of Thomas à Beckett, and its account of London was intended to bestow upon the city, where Beckett had been born, some of the prestige his recent martyrdom and canonisation had brought to Canterbury. Much of Fitzstephen's enthusiasm was reserved not for the martyr who was his former master, but for the city which was his home.

His closely observed descriptions of London's street life, its festivals and markets, and the activities of its youth served as models for John Stow, who included them in his *Survay of London* (1598). As an inspiration to Stow, the greatest of all London topographers, Fitzstephen may be regarded as a progenitor of English urban studies.

By the early Tudor period, however, several new developments had combined to make the description of cities an important literary genre. The discovery of the New World, first of all, led to a heightened awareness of the geographical environment and sharpened the techniques for describing it. While producing his monumental world atlas, the Flemish geographer, Abraham Ortelius, revived a science Ptolemy had called 'chorography', a study which combined topography with history, archaeology and, at times, anthropology. A student of the renowned map-maker Mercator, Ortelius, along with Sebastian Münster, profoundly influenced the great English topographers, Camden, Speed and Norden, whose painstaking work put the national landscape and its history at the fingertips of their countrymen. Commerce, as well as exploration, helped to fix new interest on the description of cities. Part of the appeal of geographical works was, in fact, the power of print to reduce the world to epitome. As early as 1531, Sir Thomas Elyot remarked that it was possible

> in one hour, to behold those realms, cities, seas, rivers and mountains that uneath in an old man's life cannot be journeyed or pursued. ... I cannot tell what more pleasure should happen to a gentle wit than to behold in his own house everything that within all the world is contained.

A lavish work clearly meant to satisfy this impulse was Braun and Hogenberg's *Civitates Orbis Terrarum* (1572); modelled, as its very title indicates, on Ortelius's atlas, it combined descriptions with magnificent copperplate views of Europe's cities and towns. The urban focus of this work suggests that commerce, as well as exploration, fuelled the interest in description. Indeed, its six sumptuous folios, clearly designed for the pleasure of Europe's merchant élite, were quickly reduced to a single neat octavo by Adriano Romano. Many similar guidebooks, designed for the use of commercial travellers, soon followed. It should be added, too, that the Grand Tour had begun to take its place in the education of gentlemen; the foreigners represented here include not only the pedagogue Paul Hentzner and the physician Thomas Platter, but also such aristocrats as Frederick, Duke of Wirtemberg, and Philip Julius, Duke of Stettin-Pomerania. Finally, the varieties of Renaissance statecraft are responsible for much urban description, whether in the form of status reports from ambassadors, or of hyperbole from Englishmen newly-conscious of a national identity.

Descriptions of London, like those of other Renaissance cities, have much in common with the maps and panoramic views which they so frequently accompanied. In the first place, especially early in the period, both visual and verbal images were intended less to represent reality than to convey the impression of a reality. The earliest printed view of England, in the *Nuremberg Chronicle* of 1493, was purely imaginary, as was the illustration of London in Wynkyn de Worde's *Chronicle of England* (1497), where an inspiring skyline bears no relation to physical reality. Only the addition of a river in Richard Pynson's *Chronicle of England* (1510) justifies any equation of this later image with London. So, too, in the descriptions below there is much that cannot be taken literally. References to London's Trojan origins, for example, are meant to convey an impression of the city's antiquity and prestige, just as numbers (as in Heylyn's population estimate of 600,000) are more often used adjectivally than with mathematical precision. Furthermore, just as maps and views were frequently copied and reworked without reference to topography, so many features in the description of London were the common, conventionalised property of writers. Both Paul Hentzner, who had visited London, and Braun and Hogenberg, who had not, borrowed parts of their descriptions from the same passage in an earlier writer, Paolo Giovio. William Harrison is often celebrated for his vivid and accurate descriptions of English life, yet his description of London Bridge, which he claims 'I have often viewed', is a word-for-word translation from the Latin of Polydore Vergil. Vergil also supplied Thomas Platter with his account of fish slit open and sewn up again. Harrison borrowed this story too, as did Giovanni Botero and Matthias Quadt. So different were the conventions of observing and describing that the account of London sights witnessed by Philip Julius was actually written, as was common in the case of dignitaries, in the third person by his secretary.

This is not to question the basic veracity of the descriptions below, but to note that in them, the image of London is always mediated by a variety of common motifs and assumptions. The more obvious of these, in fact, were sometimes codified for the aid of travellers and writers. One such scheme, proposed by the German humanist, Nathan Chytraeus, is the following:

Things to be noted in travelling

I.   The name of the city, and the reason for the name, if extant
     Item: the founder, augmenter (enlarger), or renewer of the place

II. 1. Rivers, each of them, their course, length, source
     2. The seaside or harbour
     3. Mountains
     4. Woods, groves, or other things of note

III. Buildings, which are either
     public

secular	sacred
palaces	cathedrals
gates	monasteries
squares	churches
arsenals	
fortresses	
towers	
means of defence	

     private, or things in the private dwellings which are of note, for example gardens, pictures, fountains, statues

IV. Method of government, and things pertaining to it
     1. The assembly, its members, and honest servants of the city
     2. Schools, method of educating and training youth
        Item: learned men and libraries
     3. Vulgar customs. Food and drink
        Item: workshops

No single scheme of this kind is exhaustive or definitive, but it may be taken as indicative of what were, for an educated observer in the Renaissance, the essential components of a city. The first of the four main topics in Chytraeus's scheme is probably the most alien to readers. It derives from the Renaissance preoccupation with

ancient origins and authority, and with a sense that cities repre-
sented heroic power and achievement. Even where Renaissance
cities had outgrown their medieval walls, their identity was still
linked to the mythical founders who first performed the ritual of
tracing out the city's limits, and to those subsequent augmenters
and renewers who added to them. These were the symbolic acts
that defined a city as an entity and ensured its preservation. Along
with a city's walls, a city's name might enfold its historic identity.
Together with gods and heroes, cities are one of the few entities to
be favoured with more than one name or to be identifiable solely
in terms of epithets of praise. The name of Troynovant figures
prominently in the description of London (see Chapter 10), but so
do impressive catalogues of epithets, in which such writers as
Camden, Speed and Lupton attempt to fix London's character as
the breviary or epitome of the nation, the seat and chamber of
kings, the storehouse and market of the world.

If a city's greatness was determined by its past it was also
determined by its site, Chytraeus's second major topic. The har-
mony between a city and its site, between the forces of culture and
nature, was a sign that both were parts of the divine creation. In
the description of London, 'most sweetly situate upon the
Thames', as Norden puts it, it is the presence of this great tidal
river that destines London to its greatness. And throughout the
descriptions below, the sight of London Bridge, arching its way
over the river's course, seems to signal the city's determined
mastery of a providential circumstance.

The bridge belongs, too, to the physical expressions of the city's
achievements, its fabric of buildings, streets and public places. In
Chytraeus's scheme, and in the passages below, architectural
monuments articulate the city's social order; they define sacred
and secular, public and private space and embody the community's
values and priorities. But they are also the means by which time is
rendered visible, by which strata upon strata of generations leave a
lasting impression upon their descendants. More than one Tudor
writer paused to trace the building of the Tower to Julius Caesar.

Finally, the character of a city was rooted in its civic and social
order. Latin tradition, which derives the word for city (*civitas*)
from the citizens (*cives*) who compose it, had taught Renaissance
writers to describe cities in terms of their human and political
resources, and this tendency was reinforced by the actual achieve-
ments of the cities themselves, which had been evolving

sophisticated means of maintaining their independence, cohesion
and stability. The plebeians of Shakespeare's *Coriolanus* echo any
number of classical writers in their claim, 'the people are the city'.
Sir Philip Sidney remarked to his younger brother Robert, who
was about to take the Grand Tour, that the knowledge of cities is
'not to have seen towns and marked their buildings, for houses are
houses in every place ... but ... the knowing of their religions,
policies, bringing up of their children ... and such like'. It is not
surprising, then, to find John Carpenter linking the city's imposing
Trojan origins to its political liberties, or to find later writers extol-
ling London's good government or the civic pride and loyalty of its
citizens. To match the courtesy, godliness, loyalty, industry,
prudence and learning stressed by native Englishmen there are, of
course, the less attractive qualities so frequently noted by
foreigners — the hostility of Londoners to strangers, the idle-
ness of their youth, and their inclination toward gluttony and
drunkenness.

The conceptual framework for urban description thus provided
for variety, subtlety and precision on the part of individual writers.
Despite certain formal resemblances throughout the period, it is
possible, for example, to chart from prose descriptions the course
of London's growth, from the 3-mile circumference mentioned by
Andreas Franciscus in 1497 to the 8-mile circumference outlined
by Peter Heylyn in 1652; or from the jostling crowds experienced
by the Duke of Wirtemberg, through the sprawl towards
Westminster recorded by Speed, to Howell's image of a city (now
populated by 600,000 according to Heylyn's inflated estimate)
thronging through its gates to the suburbs. Something of the
changes wrought by commercial expansion may be gathered from
Stow's remarkable account of London's peripatetic markets — an
account the more remarkable for being only one of several
hundred pages of similarly detailed description. And the economic
transformation of London, from a craft-based community to the
centre of an expanding maritime empire, can be traced from early
accounts of the goldsmiths' shops, which were once the greatest
symbol of London's prosperity, through Camden's later image of
the Thames forested with shipmasts, to Speed's lavish praise of a
London fleet that had 'accomplished the compassing of the uni-
versal globe'. As important as such signs of change, however, are
the many vivid impressions of London's life, its houses and its
muddy streets, its theatres and pageants, its alehouses, tobacco

shops, fishmarkets, dwarfs and snow-white swans. Images like these suggest that even when descriptions of London may have been factual, few facts of London's life failed to leave their mark upon the imagination.

1
(John Carpenter, 1419)

London was founded by Brute, in imitation of great Troy, ... whence it is that, even to this day, it possesses the liberties, rights, and customs of that ancient city Troy. For it has its senatorial rank as well as its minor magistracies. ... All persons too that come here, of whatever condition they may be, whether freemen or serfs, obtain a refuge here, as well as protection and liberty.

2
(Andreas Franciscus, 1497)

The town itself stretches from East to West, and is three miles in circumference. However, its suburbs are so large that they greatly increase its circuit. ... Throughout the town are to be seen many workshops of craftsmen in all sorts of mechanical arts, to such an extent that there is hardly a street which is not graced by some shop or the like. ... This makes the town look exceedingly prosperous and well-stocked, as well as having the immediate effect of adding to its splendour. The working in wrought silver, tin, or white lead is very expert here, and perhaps the finest I have ever seen. There are many mansions, which do not, however, seem very large from the outside, but inside they contain a great number of rooms and garrets and are quite considerable. ...

All the streets are so badly paved that they get wet at the slightest quantity of water, and this happens very frequently owing to the large numbers of cattle carrying water, as well as on account of the rain. ... A vast amount of evil-smelling mud is formed, which does not disappear quickly but lasts a long time, in fact nearly the whole year round. The citizens, therefore, in order to remove mud and filth from their boots, are accustomed to spread fresh rushes on the floors of all houses. ...

Merchants from not only Venice but also Florence and Lucca,

and many from Genoa and Pisa, from Spain, Germany, the Rhine valley and other countries meet here to handle business with the utmost keenness, having come from different parts of the world. ...

Londoners have such fierce tempers and wicked dispositions that they not only despise the way we Italians live, but actually pursue them with uncontrollable hatred, and whereas at Bruges foreigners are hospitably received and complimented ... by everybody, here the Englishmen use them with the utmost contempt and arrogance, and make them the object of insults. ... They eat very frequently, at times more than is suitable.

3
(Andrea Trevisan, c. 1500)

Although this city has no buildings in the Italian style, but of timber and brick like the French, the Londoners live comfortably, and, it appears to me, that there are not fewer inhabitants than at Florence or Rome. It abounds with every article of luxury, as well as with the necessaries of life; but the most remarkable thing in London is the wonderful quantity of wrought silver. ... In one single street, named the Strand, leading to St Paul's, there are fifty-two goldsmiths' shops, so rich and full of silver vessels, great and small, that in all the shops in Milan, Rome, Venice and Florence put together, I do not think there would be found so many of the magnificence that are to be seen in London. ... These great riches of London are not occasioned by its inhabitants being noblemen or gentlemen; being all, on the contrary, persons of low degree, and artificers who have congregated there from all parts of the island, and from Flanders, and from every other place. No one can be mayor or alderman of London who has not been an apprentice in his youth, that is, who has not passed the seven or nine years in that hard service. ... Still, the citizens of London are thought quite as highly of there as the Venetian gentlemen are at Venice.

4
(Andrew Boorde, 1548)

In England there be many noble cities and towns, amongst the which the noble city of London precelleth[1] all others, not only of that region, but of all other regions; for there is not Constantinople, Venice, Rome, Florence, Paris, nor Cologne, cannot be compared to London, the qualities and the quantity considered in all things. And as for the order of the city in manners, and good fashions, and courtesy, it excelleth all other cities and towns. And there is such a bridge of pulchritudeness, that in all the world there is none like.

5
(John Coke, 1550)

As concerning the ancient and famous city of London, ... no city in France is to be compared unto it, first for the most pleasant situation; then consider the magnific and decorate churches, the godly predications and serves[2] in them; the true and brief administration of justice; the strong Tower of London; the large and plenteous river; the beautiful palaces, places, and buildings royal, as well all along the said river as in every street of the city and round about the same; the rich merchants and other people; the fair ladies, gentlewomen, and their children; the godly bringing up of youth, and activity of their children to learning; the prudent order amongst the occupations; their beautiful halls; the great number of gentlemen there always estudying the laws of the realm; the high estate of the mayor and sheriffs, and the keeping of their sumptuous households; the Bridge of London, with the fair mansions on it; the large and mighty suburbs; the pleasant walks without every port, for recreation of the inhabitants; and the exceeding number of strong archers and other mighty men which they may make to serve their king furnished for the wars. These things well considered, sir herald, I think many of your cities is not to be compared to London.

6
(Stephen Perlin, 1558)

Their capital city is called in French 'Londres', in English London; it is a very beautiful and excellent city and, after Paris, one of the most beautiful, largest, and richest places in the whole world. One must not mention with it Lisbon, the capital and metropolitan city

of Portugal; nor Antwerp; nor Pamplona, a city of Navarre; nor
Burgos in Spain; nor Naples; nor divers others, neither for extent
nor riches: for, first, this city is rich in grocery, in cloth, linens, fish-
eries, and has one of the most beautiful bridges in the world. In it
are several streets, as the street of Blanchapton, Paternoster Street,
and the street of Sodouart. [3] There are beautiful suburbs, which are
even greater than the city itself, as the suburbs of Oisemestre, the
suburbs of Oincester,[4] and those of Sodouart. Their' principal
church is dedicated to St Paul, which they call in their language,
Paul's; and when they would say, Which is the way to St Paul's
Church? they say, *'ou es ou est goud ad Paules?'*

In London you will see the apprentices in their gowns, standing
against their shops and the walls of their houses bare-headed, inso-
much that passing through the streets you may count fifty or sixty
thus stuck up like idols, holding their caps in their hands.

7
(Georg Braun and Franz Hogenberg, 1572)

London, a most ancient city in the county of Middlesex, the most
fertile and salubrious region in all England, is situated on the River
Thames, 60,000 paces from the sea, at 52 degrees latitude and
nineteen degrees, 15 minutes longitude. Its founder is claimed by
countless chroniclers to have been Brutus. ... The noble River
Thames, which is at first called the Isis, springs not far above the
village of Winchcomb, and then, augmented by brooks and rills,
near Oxford it joins waters with the River Tame, and so the names
are joined too. After flowing by London, it empties into the sea
through a broad and navigable estuary, which, says Gemma Fri-
sius,[5] in 25 hours fluctuates 80,000 paces with the ebb and flow of
the tides. This city is great in itself, but also has spacious suburbs
and a magnificently built castle, called the Tower. It is adorned
with worthy buildings and temples, and with one hundred and
twenty churches, which they call parishes. A stone bridge leads
over to the other side of the river, a long and amazing work con-
structed on a series of arches, with houses on both sides of it,
arranged so that it does not look like a bridge but a continuous
street. ... According to Polydore Vergil,[6] London has continually
been, from ancient times, a royal seat and head of the realm, most
crowded with citizens and foreigners, abounding in riches and

goods, and most famous in its market. In London, kings are crowned in style and inaugurated in splendid ceremonies. In London the council (they call it Parliament) meets; and moreover, London is administered according to an ancient privilege of the British realm by 24 citizens whom the English call Aldermen, or elders, as it were. From whose number they elect a city 'praetor', called Mayor in their language; and two 'tribunes', called Sheriffs, in alternating years apply municipal laws and justice. It is a wonder for learned men, who shine famously among writers and who come forth abundantly, from the whole of England but from London especially.

8
(William Harrison, 1577)

I would here make mention of sundry bridges placed over this noble stream, of which that at London is most chiefly to be recommended, for it is in manner a continual street, well replenished with large and stately houses on both sides and situate upon twenty arches, whereof each one is made of excellent free squared stone, every of them being three-score foot in height and full twenty in distance one from another, as I have often viewed.

In like manner I could entreat of the infinite number of swans daily to be seen upon this river, the two thousand wherries and small boats, whereby three thousand poor watermen are maintained through the carriage and recarriage of such persons as pass or repass from time to time upon the same, beside those huge tide boats, tilt boats and barges which either carry passengers or bring necessary provision from all quarters of Oxfordshire, Berkshire, Buckinghamshire, Bedfordshire, Hertfordshire, Middlesex, Essex, Surrey and Kent unto the city of London.

9
(Lupold von Wedel, 1584-85)

I again stepped into my boat, sailing down the river thirty miles towards London, where I arrived at twelve o'clock. All the time the river was full of tame swans, who have nests and breed on small islands formed by the river. They are exclusively used for the

Queen's table, and it is on pain of death forbidden to meddle with them.

... The Thames is crossed by a bridge, leading to another town on the other side of the water called Sedorck.[7] This bridge is built of stone, 470 paces long, but its upper part has not the appearance of a bridge, being entirely set with fine houses filled with all kinds of wares, very nice to look at. ...

On the 23rd we went across the bridge to the above-mentioned town. There is a round building three storeys high, in which are kept about a hundred large English dogs, with separate wooden kennels for each of them. These dogs were made to fight singly with three bears, the second bear being larger than the first, and the third larger than the second. After this a horse was brought in and chased by the dogs, and at last a bull, who defended himself bravely. The next was, that a number of men and women came forward from a separate compartment, dancing, conversing, and fighting with each other; also a man who threw some white bread among the crowd, that scrambled for it. Right over the middle of the place a rose was fixed, this rose being set on fire by a rocket: suddenly lots of apples and pears fell out of it down upon the people standing below. Whilst the people were scrambling for the apples, some rockets were made to fall down upon them out of the rose, which caused a great fright but amused the spectators. After this, rockets and other fireworks came flying out of all corners, and that was the end of the play. ...

On 6 March I saw here in London a woman only twenty-eight breadths of the thumb high. She had very short legs, about a span in length; her steps were not longer than a cock's. She was fifty-three years old, and born in a town of Flanders called Dam.

On the 13th I saw a young fellow with red and black spots on his head, resembling a pig.

10
(William Camden, 1586/1610)

London, the epitome or breviary of all Britain, the seat of the British Empire, and the king of England's chamber, ... situate in a rich and fertile soil, abounding with plentiful store of all things, and on the gentle ascent and rising of a hill, hard by the Thames side, the most mild merchant, as one would say, of all things that the world doth yield; which swelling at certain set hours with the ocean tides, by his safe and deep channel able to entertain the greatest ships that be, daily bringeth in so great riches from all parts, that it striveth at this day with the mart-towns of Christendom for the second prize, and affordeth a most sure and beautiful road for shipping. A man would say, that seeth the shipping there, that it is, as it were, a very wood of trees disbranched to make glades and let in light, so shaded it is with masts and sails. ...

It is so adorned everywhere with churches, that religion and godliness seem to have made a choice of their residence herein. For the churches therein amount to the number of one hundred and twenty one, more, verily, than Rome itself (as great and holy as it is) can show. ... A long time it would ask to discourse particularly of the good laws and orders of the laudable government, of the port and dignity of the mayor and aldermen, of their forward service and loyalty to their prince, of the citizens' courtesy, the fair building and costly furniture, the breed of excellent and choice wits, their gardens in the suburbs full of dainty arbors and banqueting rooms, stored also with strange herbs from foreign countries, of the multitude, strength, and furniture of their ships, the incredible store of all sorts of merchandise (two hundred thousand broad cloths, beside other Antwerp alone hath received from hence every year) and of the superabundance of all things which belong to the furniture or necessity of man's life.

11
(Frederick, Duke of Wirtemberg, 1592/1602)

London is a large, excellent, and mighty city of business, and the most important in the whole kingdom; most of the inhabitants are employed in buying and selling merchandise, and trading in almost every corner of the world, since the river is most useful and convenient for this purpose, considering that ships from France, the Netherlands, Sweden, Denmark, Hamburg, and other kingdoms, come almost up to the city, to which they convey goods and receive and take away others in exchange.

It is a very populous city, so that one can scarcely pass along the streets, on account of the throng.

The inhabitants are magnificently apparelled, and are extremely proud and overbearing; and because the greater part, especially the tradespeople, seldom go into other countries, but always remain in their houses in the city attending to their business, they care little for foreigners, but scoff and laugh at them; and moreover one dare not oppose them, else the street-boys and apprentices collect together in immense crowds and strike to the right and left unmercifully without regard to person; and because they are the strongest, one is obliged to put up with the insult as well as the injury.

The women have much more liberty than perhaps in any other place; they also know well how to make use of it, for they go dressed out in exceedingly fine clothes, and give all their attention to their ruffs and stuffs, to such a degree indeed, that, as I am informed, many a one does not hesitate to wear velvet in the streets, which is common with them, whilst at home perhaps they have not a piece of dry bread.

12
(John Norden, 1593)

I thought it not unfit to begin my *Speculum Britanniae* with Middlesex, which above all other shires is graced with that chief and head city London; which as an adamant draweth unto it all the other parts of the land, and above the rest is most usually frequented with her Majesty's most regal presence. . . .

This shire is plentifully stored, and, as it seemeth, beautified with many fair and comely buildings, especially of the merchants of London, who have planted their houses of recreation not in the meanest places; which also they have cunningly contrived, curiously beautified with divers devices, neatly decked with rare inventions, environed with orchards of sundry delicate fruits, gardens with delectable walks, arbors, alleys, and great variety of pleasing dainties: all which seem to be beautiful ornaments unto this country. . . .

Many things might be spoken of this famous city which would too far exceed my purpose. It is most sweetly situate upon the Thames, served with all kind of necessaries most commodiously. The air is healthful, it is populous, rich, and beautiful; be it also faithful, loving and thankful.

13
(John Stow, 1598)

Men of trades and sellers of wares in this city have oftentimes since changed their places, as they have found their best advantage. For whereas mercers and haberdashers used to keep their shops in West Cheap, of later time they held them on London Bridge, where partly they yet remain. The goldsmiths of Guthron's Lane, and Old Exchange, are now for the most part removed into the south side of West Cheap, the pepperers and grocers of Sopers Lane are now in Bucklersbury and other places dispersed. The drapers of Lombard Street, and of Cornhill, are seated in Candlewick Street and Watling Street; the skinners from Saint Mary Pellipars, or at the Axe, into Budge Row and Walbrook; the stockfishmongers in Thames Street; wet fishmongers in Knightriders Street and Bridge Street; the ironmongers of Ironmongers Lane and Old Jewry, into Thames Street; the vintners from the Vintry into divers places. But the brewers for the more part remain near to the friendly water of Thames; the butchers in East Cheap, Saint Nicholas Shambles, and the Stocks Market; the hosiers of old time in Hosier Lane, near unto Smithfield, are since removed into Cordwainer Street, the upper part thereof by Bow church, and last of all into Birchover Lane by Cornhill; the shoemakers and curriers of Cordwainer Street, removed the one to St Martin-le-Grand, the other themselves in Lothbury; cooks or pastlers, for the more part in Thames Street, the other dispersed into divers parts. Poulters of late removed out of the Poultry betwixt the Stocks and the Great Conduit in Cheap into Grass Street, and St Nicholas Shambles; bowyers, from Bowyers Row by Ludgate into divers places, and almost worn out with the fletchers; paternoster-makers of old time, or bead-makers, and text-writers, are gone out of Paternoster Row, and are called stationers of Paul's Churchyard; pattenmakers of Saint Margaret, Pattens Lane, clean worn out; labourers every work-day are to be found in Cheap, about Sopers Lane end: horse coursers and sellers of oxen, sheep, swine, and such like, remain in their old Market of Smithfield, etc.

14
(Thomas Platter, 1599)

London is the capital of England and so superior to other English

towns that London is not said to be in England, but rather England
to be in London, for England's most resplendent objects may be
seen in and around London: so that he who sightsees London and
the royal courts in its vicinity may assert without impertinence that
he is properly acquainted with England. The town is called in
Latin *Londinium*, in French *Londres*, by the ancients *Trinovan-
tum*, and is situated on the river Thames (*Thamesis*) sixty Italian
miles or 60,000 paces from the sea, which ebbs and flows as far as
London and yet further. ... For which reason ocean-craft are
accustomed to run in here in great numbers as into a safe harbour,
and I myself beheld one large galley next the other the whole city's
length from St Katherine's suburb to the bridge, some hundred
vessels in all, nor did I ever behold so many large ships in one port
in all my life. ...

And while a very fine long bridge is built across this stream, it is
customary to cross the water or travel up and down the town as at
Lyons and elsewhere by attractive pleasure craft, for a number of
tiny streets lead to the Thames from both ends of the town; the
boatmen wait there in great crowds, each one eager to be first to
catch one, for all are free to choose the ship they find most attrac-
tive and pleasing, while every boatman has the privilege on arrival
of placing his ship to best advantage for people to step into. ...

This city of London is so large and splendidly built, so populous
and excellent in crafts and merchant citizens, and so prosperous,
that it is not only the first in the whole realm of England, but is
esteemed one of the most famous in all Christendom; especially
since the wars in the Netherlands and France it has increased by
many thousands of families who have settled in this city for reli-
gion's sake. ...

Most of the inhabitants are employed in commerce; they buy,
sell and trade in all the corners of the globe, for which purpose the
water serves them well, since ships from France, the Netherlands,
Germany and other countries land in this city, bringing goods with
them and loading others in exchange for exportation. For which
reason they allow some 10 per cent interest, because through
shipping much may be effected and attained with money.

There are also many wealthy merchants and moneychangers in
this city, some of whom sell costly wares while others only deal in
money for wholesale transactions.

In one very long street called Cheapside dwell almost only gold-
smiths and moneychangers on either hand so that inexpressibly

great treasures and vast amounts of money may be seen here.

The Exchange is a great square place like the one in Antwerp, ... a little smaller, though, and with only two entrances and only one passage running through it, where all kinds of fine goods are on show; and since the city is very large and extensive, merchants having to deal with one another agree to meet together in this palace, where several hundred may be found assembled twice daily, before lunch at eleven, and again after their meal at six o'clock, buying, selling, bearing news, and doing business generally. ...

On September 21st after lunch, about two o'clock, I and my party crossed the water, and there in the house with the thatched roof witnessed an excellent performance of the tragedy of the first Emperor Julius Caesar with a cast of some fifteen people; when the play was over, they danced very marvellously and gracefully together as is their wont, two dressed as men and two as women.

On another occasion not far from our inn, in the suburb at Bishopsgate, if I remember, also after lunch, I beheld a play in which they presented divers nations and an Englishman struggling together for a maiden. ... Thus daily at two in the afternoon, London has two, sometimes three plays running in different places, competing with each other, and those which play best obtain most spectators. The playhouses are so constructed that they play on a raised platform, so that everyone has a good view. There are different galleries and places, however, where the seating is better and more comfortable and therefore more expensive. For whoever cares to stand below only pays one English penny, but if he wishes to sit he enters by another door, and pays another penny, while if he desires to sit in the most comfortable seats, which are cushioned, where he not only sees everything well, but can also be seen, then he pays yet another English penny at another door. And during the performance food and drink are carried round the audience, so that for what one cares to pay one may also have refreshment. The actors are most expensively and elaborately costumed; for it is the English usage for eminent lords or knights at their decease to bequeath and leave almost the best of their clothes to their serving men, which it is unseemly for the latter to wear, so that they offer them then for sale for a small sum to the actors. ...

There are a great many inns, taverns, and beer gardens scattered about the city, where much amusement may be had with eating, drinking, fiddling, and the rest, as for instance in our hostelry, which was visited by players almost daily. And what is particularly curious is that the women as well as the men, in fact more often than they, will frequent the taverns or ale-houses for enjoyment. ...

In the ale-houses tobacco or a species of wound-wort[8] are also obtainable for one's money, and the powder is lit in a small pipe, the smoke sucked into the mouth, and the saliva is allowed to run freely, after which a good draught of Spanish wine follows. This they regard as a curious medicine for defluctions[9] and as a pleasure; and the habit is so common with them, that they always carry the instrument on them, and light up on all occasions, at the play, in the taverns or elsewhere, drinking as well as smoking together, as we sit over wine, and it makes them riotous and merry, and rather drowsy, just as if they were drunk, though the effect soon passes — and they use it so abundantly because of the pleasure it gives, that their preachers cry out on them for their self-destruction, and I am told the inside of one man's veins after death was found to be covered in soot just like a chimney. ...

At the fishmarket, in a long street, I saw a quantity of pike up for sale; they are very fond of this ... and feed it with needle-fish (*aiguilles*), eels, and other tiny fish. And I noticed that each of these fishermen and fishwives kept a copper or brass needle and thread in the tub, with a sharp knife. And when the purchasers desired a pike the salesmen and saleswomen slit open its belly at their bidding, placing the guts on their hands to show whether the pike was sufficiently fat, and then sewed it up again: if the pike proved fat enough, then the purchaser took it, but if the guts looked thin and poor the fishmonger kept it, throwing it back into the basin among the tenches, against which they rub themselves and recover enough to keep fresh for at least another week, in fact according to them, fish could keep fresh for some months. Indeed, they kept tench ready in the fish tanks with the pike, so that they would get used to them; all this I witnessed in London with my own eyes, nor is it otherwise.

15
(Paul Hentzner, 1600)

The streets in this city are very handsome and clean, but that which is named from the goldsmiths, who inhabit it, surpasses all the rest.

There is in it a gilt tower, with a fountain that plays; near it, on the farther side, is a handsome house, built by a goldsmith, and presented by him to the city. There are, besides, to be seen in this street, as in all others where there are goldsmiths' shops, all sorts of gold and silver vessels exposed to sale; as well as ancient and modern medals, in such quantities as must surprise a man the first time he sees and considers them.

16
(Philip Julius, Duke of Stettin-Pomerania, 1602)

On arriving in London we heard a great ringing of bells in almost all the churches going on very late in the evening, also on the following days until 7 or 8 o'clock in the evening. We were informed that the young people do that for the sake of exercise and amusement, and sometimes they lay considerable sums of money as a wager, who will pull a bell the longest or ring it in the most approved fashion.

Parishes spend much money in harmoniously-sounding bells, that one being preferred which has the best bells. The old queen is said to have been pleased very much by this exercise, considering it as a sign of the health of the people. They do not ring the bells for the dead, but when a person lies in agony, the bells of the parish he belongs to are touched with the clappers until he either dies or recovers again.

As soon as this sign is given, everybody in the street, as well as in the houses, falls on his knees offering prayer for the sick person. . . .

On the 15th his princely Grace intended to see the Exchange, where the merchants are used to assemble in a square, covered space. Round the top is a fine broad vaulted gallery, where may be bought almost everything a man may imagine in the way of costly wares.

At eleven o'clock, at noon, and at five o'clock in the evening, the lower part becomes so filled with people that only by force you are able to make your way. It is a pleasure to go about there, for one is not molested or accosted by beggars, who are elsewhere so frequently met with in places of this kind. For in all England they do not suffer any beggars, except they be few in number and outside the gates.

Every parish cares for its own poor; strangers are brought to the hospital, but those that belong to the kingdom or have come from distant places, are sent from one parish to the other, their wants being cared for, until at last they reach their home.

17
(Edmund Howes, 1611)

What is he that hath any understanding, and knows not London to be the most flourishing and peaceful city of Europe? of greatest antiquity, happiest in continuance, most increased, chief in prosperity, and most stored with plenty? ... The promised blessing unto the ancient Israelites to possess a land that flowed with milk and honey, is with seven-fold measure heaped on your heads, your city filled more abundantly with all sorts of silks, fine linen, oils, wines, and spices, perfection of arts, and all costly ornaments, and curious workmanship, than any other province. So as London well deserves to bear the name of the choicest storehouse in the world, and to keep rank with any royal city in Europe: her citizens rich and bounteous, witness their frank giving of more than twice seven fifteenths in one year, and their long continued charges and expences, as well upon all occasions by sea and land, for defence of their prince and country, as in aiding and relieving their distressed neighbour nations, and in performing many other worthy matters for their own honour, the delight of strangers, and the relief of the poor ... so as without offence it may truly be said, that the liberality of the Londoners is but half known to their common friends. Peace and plenty in the highest degree possesseth now your gates and palaces; all nations repair with willingness to be partakers of your happiness; many other glorious cities have many ways wanted these incessant blessings.

18
(John Speed, 1611)

This city doth show as the cedars among other trees, being the seat of the British kings, the chamber of the English, the model of the land, and the mart of the world, for thither are brought the silk of Asia, the spices from Africa, the balms from Grecia, and the riches of both the Indies East and West: no city standing so long in fame, nor any for divine and politic government, may with her be compared. Her walls were first set by great Constantine the first Christian emperor, at the suit of his mother, Queen Helen, reared with rough stone and British brick three English miles in compass; through which are now made seven most fair gates. ...

This London, as it were disdaining bondage, hath set herself, on each side, far without the walls, and left her west gate[10] in the midst, from whence with continual buildings (still affecting greatness) she hath continued her streets unto a king's palace, and joined a second city[11] to herself, famous for the seat and sepulchre of our kings, and for the gates of justice, that termly[12] there are opened ... No walls are set about this city, and those of London are left to show rather what it was than what it is; whose citizens, as the Lacedaemonians did, do repose their strength in their men, and not in their walls, how strong soever. ... The wealth of this city (as Isay once spake of Nilus)[13] grows from the revenues and harvest of her south-bounding Thames; whose traffic for merchandising is like that of Tyrus, whereof Ezekiel speaks,[14] and stands in abundance of silver, iron, tin, and lead, etc. And from London her channel is navigable, straitened along with meadowing borders, until she taketh her full liberty in the German Seas. Upon this Thames the ships of Tharsis[15] seem to ride, and the navy, that rightly is termed the Lady of the Sea, spreads her sail, whence twice with lucky success hath been accomplished the compassing of the universal globe.

19
(Fynes Moryson, 1617)

Now at London, the houses of the citizens, especially in the chief streets, are very narrow in the front towards the street, but are built five or six roofs high, commonly of timber and clay with plaster, and are very neat and commodious within. And the building of citizens's houses in other cities is not much unlike this. But withal understand that in London many stately palaces, built by noblemen upon the River Thames, do make a very great show to them that pass by water; and that there be many more like palaces also built towards land, but scattered, and great part of them in back lanes and streets, which if they were joined to the first in good order, as other cities are built uniformly, they would make not only fair streets, but even a beautiful city, to which few might justly be preferred for the magnificence of the building. Besides, the aldermen's and chief citizens' houses, howsoever they are stately for building, yet being built all inward, that the whole room towards the streets may be reserved for the shops of tradesmen, make no show outwardly, so as in truth all the magnificence of London building is hidden from the view of strangers at the first sight, till they have more particular view thereof by long abode there; and then they will prefer the buildings of this famous city to many that appear more stately at the first sight.

20
(Thomas Gainsford, 1618)

As for London, but that you will say my particular love transporteth me, it hath many specialties of note, eminence, and amazement; and for greatness itself, I may well maintain, that if London and the places adjoining were circumunited in such an orbicular manner [as Paris], it would equal Paris. ... From St George's in Southwark to Shoreditch south and north; and from Westminster to St Katherine's or Ratcliff, west and east, is a cross of streets, meeting at Leadenhall, every way longer — with broad spaciousness, handsome monuments, illustrious gates, comely buildings, and admirable markets — than any you can name in Paris or ever saw in other city, yea Constantinople itself. Concerning multitude of people, if you take London merely as a place composed of merchants, citizens, and tradesmen, the world never had such another; if you conjoin the suburbs, Southwark, Westminster, and Katherine's, and such like, it exceeds Paris even for inhabitants. ... But let us search our comparison a little further: instead of a beastly town and dirty streets, you have in London those that be fair, beautiful, and cleanly kept; instead of foggy mists and clouds, ill air, flat situation, miry springs, and a kind of staining clay, you have in London a sun-shining and serene element for the most part, a wholesome dwelling, stately ascension, and delicate prospect; instead of a shallow, narrow, and sometimes dangerous river, bringing only barges and boats with wood, coal, turf, and such country provision, you have at London a river flowing twenty foot, and full of stately ships that fly to us with merchandise from all the ports of the world, the sight yielding astonishment, and the use perpetual comfort. ... Instead of ill-favoured wooden bridges, many times endangered with tempests and frosts, you have in London such a bridge, that without ampliation[16] of particulars, is the admirablest monument, and firmest erected structure of that kind in the universe. ... Instead of an old Bastille and ill-beseeming arsenal, thrust as it were into an outcast corner of the city, you have in London a building of the greatest antiquity and majestical form, serving to most uses of any citadel or magazine that ever you saw. ...

We have in London such a *circo* for merchants, with an upper quadrant of shops, as must needs subject it to foreign envy, in regard of the delicacy of the building, and stateliness of the contriving. We have in London a second building[17] for the ease of the court, profit of the artisan, and glory of the city, which for any thing my outward sense may judge of, can equal the proudest structure of their proudest towns, though you should name St Mark's Piazza in Venice, for so much building. We have in London a Guildhall for a state-house, and Westminster for general causes of the kingdom; two such rooms that, without further dispute, maketh strangers demand unanswerable questions, and, gently brought to the understanding particulars, lift up their hands to heaven and exclaim, O happy England! O happy people! O happy London! ... Instead of narrow dirty streets, neither graceful to themselves, nor beautified with any ornament, we have spacious, large, and comely streets, exposing divers works of peace, charity, and estimation. Instead of obscure churches, we have first the goodliest heap of stones in the world, namely Paul's; next the curiousest fabric in Europe, namely Westminster Chapel,[18] and generally all our churches exceed for beauty, handsomeness, and magnificent building, as framed of hard stone and marble. ...

Instead of a poor provost and a disorderly company of merchants and tradesmen, we have a Podesta or Mayor, that keepeth a princely house; we have grave senators, comely citizens, several halls, and authorized corporations, all governed by religious magistracy and made famous by triumphant solemnities; so that our best gentry are delighted with the spectacle, and strangers admire the bravery.

To conclude, if you look on and in our London truly, as it is composed of men following trades and occupations, there is not such a city, such a government, such a method of conservation,

such a variety of good fellowship, such a glass to see unity and
beauty in, such a treasury of wealth, such a storehouse of all terres-
trial blessings under the sun.

21
(Donald Lupton, 1632)

She is grown so great I am almost afraid to meddle with her. She's
certainly a great world, there are so many little worlds in her. She
is the great beehive of Christendom, I am sure of England. She
swarms four times in a year, with people of all ages, natures, sexes,
callings; decay of trade, the pestilence, and a long vacation[19] are
three scarecrows to her. She seems to be a glutton, for she desires
always to be full. She may pray for the establishing of churches, for
at the first view they are her chiefest grace. She seems contrary to
all other things, for the older she is, the newer and more beautiful.
Her citizens should love one another, for they are joined together;
only this seems to make them differ: they live one above another
— most commonly he that is accounted richest lives worst. I am
sure I may call her a gallimaufry of all the sciences, arts, and
trades. She may be said to be always with child, for she grows grea-
ter every day than other; she is a mother well stored with
daughters, yet none equal to her for greatness, beauty, wealth. She
is somewhat politic, for she enlarges her bounds exceedingly, in
giving way to make cities of common gardens; and it's thought her
greatness doth diminish her beauty. Certainly she is no puritan, for
her buildings are now conformitant;[20] nor she is no separatist, for
they are united together. She hath a very great desire, 'tis thought,
to be good, for she is always mending; she may be called a great
book fair, printed *Cum Privilegio Regis*[21] She is the countryman's
labyrinth; he can find many things in it, but many times loseth him-
self. He thinks her to be bigger than heaven, for there are but
twelve celestial signs there, and he knows them all very well, but
here are thousands that he wonders at.[22] Well, she is a glory to her
prince, a common gain to her inhabitants, a wonder to strangers,
an head to the kingdom, the nursery of sciences, and I wish her to
be as good as great.

22
(Peter Heylyn, 1652)

London, seated on the Thames, by which divided into two parts, conjoined together by a stately and magnificent bridge. ... The river capable in this place of the greatest ships, by means whereof it hath been reckoned a long time for one of the most famous mart-towns in Christendom; and not long since had so much got precedence of all the rest, that the greatest part of the wealth of Europe was driven up that river. ... The circuit may contain 8 miles at least, in which space are 122 parish churches. ... It is wondrous populous, containing well nigh 600,000 people, which number is much augmented in the term time. Some compare London with Paris thus: London is the richer, the more populous, and more ancient; Paris is greater, more uniform, and better fortified. But for my part, I do not think that London is the more populous; so neither can I grant that Paris is the greater city, except we measure them by the walls. ... For uniformity of building Paris indeed doth go beyond it, but may in that be equalled also in some tract of time, if the design begun in King James his reign, tending to the advancement of such uniformity,[23] be not interrupted. ... Certain it is that London is ... increased so much in wealth and honour from one age to another, that it is grown at last too big for the kingdom; which whether it may be profitable for the state, or not, may be made a question. And great towns in the body of a state are like the spleen or melt in the body natural, the monstrous growth of which impoverisheth all the rest of the members, by drawing to it all the animal and vital spirits, which should give nourishment unto them.

23
(James Howell, 1657)

Touching the form and shape of London, it may be aptly compared to a laurel leaf, which is far more long than broad; and were London round, as Paris and other cities are, she would appear more populous, by a more often encounter of the passengers. ... 'Tis true that the suburbs of London are much larger than the body of the City, which make some compare her to a Jesuit's hat, whose brims are far larger than the block; which made Count Gondamar

the Spanish Ambassador to say, as the Queen of Spain was dis-
coursing with him, upon his return from England, of the city of
London, 'Madam, I believe there will be no City left shortly, for it
will all run out at the gates to the suburbs.'

Notes

1. Excels, surpasses.
2. Preachings and service.
3. Whitechapel, Paternoster Row and Southwark.
4. Westminster and Winchester (the district of Southwark under the jurisdiction of the Bishop of Winchester).
5. A Belgian cartographer, whose *Cosmography* first appeared in 1529.
6. An Italian humanist, attached to the court of Henry VIII, who included a description of London in his Latin history of England.
7. Southwark.
8. A family of weed, including goldenrod and vetch.
9. The concentration of vital humours in diseased parts of the body.
10. Ludgate.
11. Westminster.
12. With each law term.
13. See Isaiah 23:3.
14. See Ezekiel 27:12.
15. Tarshish.
16. Amplification.
17. The New Exchange, or Britain's Burse, built in the Strand in 1609.
18. The Henry VII Chapel.
19. Between the end of the Trinity law term, in late July, and the beginning of Michaelmas term, in early October.
20. See 8.6, below.
21. With royal licence.
22. A reference to London's tavern signs; see 6.2, below.
23. See 8.6, below.

2

IN PRAISE OF LONDON:
VERSE *ENCOMIA*

Urban *encomia* are substantially an invention of early modern
Europe, emerging side by side with the independent and eco-
nomically resurgent city-states of the Middle Ages. They are, as
one historian has said, 'a manifestation of the growth of cities and
the rising culture and self-confidence of the citizens'. Description
and praise are closely related impulses in the period. Indeed, the
earliest praises, which come primarily from Italy, are prose
descriptions, more clearly influenced by the guide literature written
for religious pilgrims than by classical rhetoric. Fitzstephen's
twelfth-century *Description of London* (1173–74), from which
Stow drew material for his *Survay of London,* is an English exam-
ple of this trend. But the rise of classical humanism in Italy,
together with the increasingly tumultuous life of the city-states
themselves, produced a more highly crafted and philosophic mode
of praise, the greatest example of which is Leonardo Bruni's
Panegyric of the City of Florence (1403–4).

The versified praise of London, however, developed through a
concatenation of several influences. Late medieval poets like
Lydgate and Fabyan had experimented with native forms of praise,
and to these were added both classical influence and the contem-
porary neo-Latin poetry through which classical influence was
often filtered. In continental Latin poetry English poets could have
found splendid praises of Venice, Ferrara, Verona, Paris, Rome,
Trier and other cities. Several of the examples included here were
originally written in Latin, often by foreigners like Wenceslaus
Clemens and Jan Sictor, who were religious refugees (see 2.17 and
2.18 below). Others, however, were written by such English
humanists as John Leland, who established an important native
tradition of topographical poetry and influenced the later praises
of Spenser and Drayton. Topographical writing, as the previous

49

chapter indicates, was congenial to the most hyperbolic forms of praise. Indeed, the topographical writings and chronicles of the period were frequently embellished with decorative poems of praise, some examples of which, by Robert Fabyan and John Johnston the Scot, are represented here (2.4 and 2.8). At the same time, a number of praises, such as those by Lydgate (2.1) and the pseudo-Dunbar (2.3), were clearly meant to celebrate state or civic occasions.

The strategies of praise are many, but we may take as a starting-point a schema proposed in a rhetorical handbook of 1563:

> Upon a city, praise may be recited, considering the goodly situation, as of Paris, Venice, London, York; considering the felicity of the land, the wealth and abundance, the noble and famous governors, which have governed the same. The first author and builders of the same, the politic laws and goodly statutes therein maintained; the felicity of the people, their manners, their valiant prowess and hardiness. The building and ornatures of the same, with castles, towers, havens, floods, temples, as if a man would celebrate with praise. The old, famous, and ancient building of the same, the coming of Brutus, who was the first author and erector of the same.

The highest compliment that could be paid to London was to say that it was old. The legendary founding of Troynovant by Aeneas's descendant, Brute — first perpetrated by the medieval chronicler, Geoffrey of Monmouth — provided the city with an imposing pedigree. In the earliest praises, the name of Troynovant is first of all a simple claim to venerability. But after 1534, when Henry VIII declared, 'this realm of England is an empire', the Trojan foundation story increasingly became a legitimising myth for England's national and imperial ambitions (see Chapter 10). In Spenser's epic *Faerie Queene* (1590–96) London thus emerges as the legitimate successor to Troy and Rome, and hence as the heir to a culture migrating westward. The myth of Troynovant naturally emphasises London's role as a national capital, and from the earliest praises onward, the city's loyalty to the Crown — celebrated in such oft-repeated epithets as 'chamber of the king' — is a major cause for praise. Nevertheless, poets just as frequently focus on the civic and mercantile institutions of the city, and in the later, more 'popular' idiom of the praise of Richard Niccols or the ballad

London's Praise (1685), the exaltation of burgherly and Puritan
virtues involves an anti-courtly edge.

One of the chief means of praise is personification. Once the
city takes on a personal identity, praising it is not unlike praising a
woman. Indeed, many praises proceed in the manner of a sonnet
blazon, listing the features of the city just as a sonneteer might
praise his lady's hair, brow, eyes, cheeks and lips. The chief physi-
cal elements in such blazons, however, are the site and the fabric,
the river and the architecture. In countless praises, the Thames is a
means of articulating the harmonious reciprocities of sea and land,
nature and culture, eternity and historic endurance in London's
life. The wondrous bridge, majestically spanning the river, provides
a foothold for the city's triumphal posture. The city's walls and
Tower often bear the weight of martial themes, and the fact that
London had been neither sacked nor occupied in historic memory
provides a point of contrast with the troubled life of such other
European cities as Rome, Antwerp and Paris. Towers, turrets and
temples repeatedly grace the facets of a crown worn by this per-
sonified lady, just as they do in the maps of the period and in a
tradition begun by Homer. The tower-crowned city, like so many
other images — the jewel, the theatre, the encyclopedia or
epitome, the pleasance or paradise, the harbour forested with
masts — is both a standard epithet and an enduring emblem, no
less moving for its frequent repetition.

There is, finally, a movement toward concretion in these poems
that perhaps reflects a major transformation in the city's life. The
earliest poems represented here, which come from the mid-fif-
teenth century, are essentially lists of splendid chivalric
abstractions — 'faithful observaunce', 'troth' or 'legiaunce' —
whose deep and subtle resonances are largely lost to us. More
accessible are the increasingly concrete images of wealth and com-
merce, which sometimes threaten to transform London's praise
into quantitative terms. Isabella Whitney's remarkable *Testament*
(2.6 below), for example, is a crowded shopping-list. At the same
time, the human resources and institutions of the city — its charit-
ies and reformed churches — remain a basic thread of continuity
with the medieval past. The ballad *London's Praise* (1685) singles
out the same values of justice and equity exalted by Fabyan in
1500, and when in a schoolboy's simple Latin the refugee Wences-
laus Clemens celebrates London as a religious haven, he builds on
a foundation praised in Fabyan's claim that 'Christ is the very

stone/ The city is set upon.' The mock praise attributed, perhaps mistakenly, to the Royalist Thomas Randolph, even while it ridicules the burgherly independence and ideals of the city, pays implicit tribute to their endurance, and their power to irritate the more fashionable court.

1
[On Henry VI's Triumphal Entry into London]
(John Lydgate, 1432)

Of seven things I praise this city:
    Of true meaning, and faithful observaunce,[1]
Of righteousness, truth, and equity,
    Of stableness aye kept in legiaunce;[2]
    And for of virtue thou hast such suffisaunce,[3]
In this land here and other lands all,
The king's chamber of custom men thee call.

2
On the Procession to St Paul's of the Reconciled Parties
25 March, 1458 (Anon.)

Of three things I praise the worshipful city:
    The first, the true faith that they have to the king;
The second, of love to the commonalty;
    The third, good rule for evermore keeping;
    The which God maintain evermore during,
And save the Mayor and all the worthy city;
    And is amiss[4] God bring to amending,
That England may rejoice to concord and unity.

3
[In Honour of the City of London]
(attr. William Dunbar, 1501)

London, thou art of towns *a per se.*
    Sovereign of cities, seemliest in sight,
Of high renown, riches and royalty;

Of lords, barons, and many a goodly knight;
Of most delectable lusty[5] ladies bright;
Of famous prelates in habits clerical;
Of merchants full of substance and might:
London, thou art the flower of cities all.

Gladdeth[6] anon, thou lusty Troynovant,
　City that some time cleped[7] was New Troy;
In all the earth, imperial as thou stant,
　Princess of towns, of pleasure and of joy,
　A richer resteth under no Christian roy;
For manly power, with craftis natural,
　Formeth none fairer sith the flood of Noy:[8]
London, thou art the flower of cities all.

Gem of all joy, jasper of jocundity,
　Most mighty carbuncle of virtue and valour;
Strong Troy in vigour and in strenuity;[9]
　Of royal cities rose and geraflour;[10]
　Empress of towns, exalt in honour;
In beauty bearing the crown imperial;
　Sweet paradise precelling[11] in pleasure;
London, thou art the flower of cities all.

Above all rivers thy river hath renown,
　Whose beryl stremys, pleasant and preclare,[12]
Under thy lusty wallys runneth down,
　Where many a swan doth swim with winges fair;
　Where many a barge doth sail and row with are;
Where many a ship doth rest with top-royal.[13]
　O, town of towns! patron[14] and not compare,
London, thou art the flower of cities all.

Upon thy lusty bridge of pillars white
　Been merchants full royal to behold;
Upon thy streets goeth many a seemly knight
　In velvet gowns and chains of gold.
　By Julius Caesar thy Tower founded of old[15]
May be the house of Mars victorial,
　Whose artillery with tongue may not be told;
London, thou art the flower of cities all.

Strong be thy walls that about thee stands;
 Wise be the people that within thee dwells;
Fresh is thy river with his lusty strands;[16]
 Blithe be thy churches, well sounding be thy bells;
 Rich be thy merchants in substance that excels;
Fair be their wives, right lovesome, white and small;
 Clear be thy virgins, lusty under kells;
London, thou art the flower of cities all.

Thy famous Mayor, by princely governance,
 With sword of justice thee ruleth prudently.
No Lord of Paris, Venice, or Florence
 In dignity or honour goeth to him nigh.
 He is exemplar, lodestar, and guide;
Principal patron and rose original,
 Above all mayors as master most worthy;
London, thou art the flower of cities all.

4

Prologue to a Chronicle
(Robert Fabyan, 1516)

Now would I fain,
In wordys plain,
Some honour sayen,
And bring to mind
Of that ancient city,
That so goodly is to see,
And full true ever hath be;
And also full kind

To prince and king,
That hath borne just ruling,
Since the first winning
Of this island by Brute;
So that, in great honour,
By passing of many a show'r,
It hath ever borne the flow'r
And laudable bruit.[17]

Of every city and town,
To seek the world 'round,
Never yet cast down
As other many have be;
As Rome and Carthage,
Jerusalem the sage,
With many other of age,
In story as ye may see.

This, so oldly founded,
Is so surely grounded
That no man may confound it,
It is so sure a stone
That it is upon set;
For though some have it threat
With menaces grim and great,
Yet hurt had it none.

Christ is the very stone
That the city is set upon;
Which from all his fone[18]
Hath ever preserved it
By mean of divine service,
That in continual wise
Is kept in devout guise
Within the mure[19] of it:

As houses of religion,
In diverse places of this town,
Which in great devotion
Bene ever occupied;
When one hath done, another begin,
So that of prayer they never blin,[20]
Such order is these houses within,
With all virtue allied.

The parish churches also to reckon,
Of which number I shall speken,
Wherein speak many priest and deacon,
And Christ daily they serve.
By mean of which sacrifice,

I trust that He in all wise
This city for His service
Doth evermore preserve.

This city I mean is Troynovant,
Where honour and worship doth haunt,
With virtue and riches accordant,
No city to it like.
To speak of every commodity,
Flesh and fish and all dainty,
Cloth and silk, with wine plenty,
That is for whole and sick;

Bread and ale with spices fine,
With houses fair to sup and dine,
Nothing lacking that is condign,
For man that is on mould.[21]
With rivers fresh and wholesome air,
With women that be good and fair;
And to this city do repair,
Of strangers many fold.

The vitail that herein is spent
In three households daily tente,[22]
Atween Rome and rich Kent
Are none may them compare.
As of the mayor and sheriffs twain
What might I of the justice sayne,
Kept within this city plain?
It were long to declare.

For though I should all day tell
Or chat with my rhyme doggerel,
Might I not yet half dospell[23]
This town's great honour.
Therefore shortly, as I began,
Pray for it both child and man,
That it may continue on
To bear of all the flower.

And so to dwell in rest and peace,
Good Lord grant that it not cease,

But ever to have more increase,
If it be Thy will;
And to continue the old fame,
The king's chamber, that the right name
London, to keep without blame
As it hath hither till.

5
Cygnea Cantio [The Song of the Swan]
(John Leland, 1542)

The streaming river bears us on
To London's mighty Babylon;
And that vast bridge, which proudly soars,
Where Thames through nineteen arches roars,
And many a lofty dome on high
It raises towering to the sky.
There are, whose truth is void of stain,
Who write, in Lion Richard's reign,
That o'er these waves extended stood
A ruder fabric framed of wood;[24]
But when the swift-consuming flames
Destroyed that bulwark of the Thames,
Rebuilt of stone it rose to view,
Beneath King John its splendours grew,
Whilst London poured her wealth around,
The mighty edifice to found;
The lasting monument to raise
To his, to her eternal praise,
Till, rearing up its form sublime,
It stands the glory of all time!

6
The Will and Testament of Isabella Whitney
(Isabella Whitney, 1573)

I first of all to London leave,
    Because I there was bred,
Brave buildings rare, of churches store,

And Paul's to the head.
Between the same, fair streets there be,
    And people goodly store;
Because their keeping craveth cost,
    I yet will leave him more.
First for their food, I butchers leave,
    That every day shall kill;
By Thames you shall have brewers store,
    And bakers at your will.
And such as orders do observe,
    And eat fish thrice a week,
I leave two streets, full fraught therewith,
    They need not far to seek.
Watling Street and Canwick Street,
    I full of woolen leave,
And linen store in Friday Street,
    If they me not deceive.
And those which are of calling such
    That costlier they require,
I mercers leave, with silk so rich
    As any would desire.
In Cheap, of them, they store shall find,
    And likewise in that street
I goldsmiths leave, with jewels such
    As are for ladies meet.
And plate to furnish cupboards with,
    Full brave there shall you find,
With purl[25] of silver and of gold
    To satisfy your mind.
With hoods, bongraces, hats, or caps,
    Such store are in that street,
As if on t'one side you should miss,
    The t'other serves you forte.[26]
For nets of every kind of sort,
    I leave within the Pawn[27]
French ruffs, high purls, gorgets, and sleeves
    Of any kind of lawn.
For purse or knives, for comb or glass,
    Or any needful knack,
I by The Stocks[28] have left a boy
    Will ask you what you lack.

I hose do leave in Birchin Lane,
    Of any kind of size —
For women stitched, for men both trunks
    And those of Gascoyne guise.[29]
Boots, shoes, or pantables[30] good store,
    St Martin's hath for you;
In Cornwall,[31] there I leave you beds
    And all that 'longs thereto.
For women shall you tailors have,
    By Bow[32] the chiefest dwell;
In every lane you some shall find
    Can do indifferent well.
And for the men, few streets or lanes,
    But bodymakers be,
And such as make the sweeping cloaks,
    With guards[33] beneath the knee.
Artillery at Temple Bar,
    And dags at Tower Hill;
Swords and bucklers of the best,
    Are nigh the Fleet until.
Now when thy folk are fed and clad
    With such as I have named,
For dainty mouthes, and stomachs weak
    Some junkets[34] must be framed;
Wherefore I pothecaries leave,
    with banquets in their shop;
Physicians also for the sick,
    Diseases for to stop.
Some roisters still must bide in thee,
    and such as cut it out,
That with the guiltless quarrel will,
    to let their blood about.
For them I cunning surgeons leave,
    some plasters to apply,
That ruffians may not still be hanged,
    nor quiet persons die.
For salt, oatmeal, candles, soap,
    or what you else do want,
In many places shops are full,
    I left you nothing scant.
If they that keep what I you leave

ask money when they sell it,
At Mint there is such store, it is
   unpossible to tell it.
At Steelyard[35] store of wines there be,
   Your dulled minds to glad,
And handsome men that must not wed,
   Except they leave their trade.[36]
They oft shall seek for proper girls,
   And some perhaps shall find
(That need compels or lucre lures)
   To satisfy their mind.
And near the same, I houses leave,
   For people to repair
To bathe themselves,[37] so to prevent
   Infection of the air.
On Saturdays I wish that those
   Which all the week do drug,[38]
Shall thither trudge, to trim them up
   On Sundays to look smug.
If any other thing be lacked
   In thee, I wish them look,
For there it is; I little brought,
   But nothing from thee took.
... I make thee sole executor, because
   I loved thee best.
And thee I put in trust, to give
   The goods unto the rest.
Because thou shalt a helper need,
   In this so great a charge,
I wish good fortune be thy guide, lest
   Thou shouldst run at large.
The happy days and quiet times,
   They both her servants be,
Which well will serve to fetch and bring
   Such things as need to thee.
... So fare thou well a thousand times,
   God shield thee from thy foe,
And still make thee victorious
   Of those that seek thy woe.
And though I am persuade that I
   Shall never more thee see,

Yet to the last, I shall not cease
To wish much good to thee.

7
From *To the Good Lord Mayor*
(Thomas Churchyard, 1580)

This city claims, by tract of time, a stately civil trade,
And is a lamp or shining sun to country's silly[39] shade;
For civil manners here began, and order root did take,
When savage swains in rubbish[40] soils did civil life forsake.
Here wit through wisdom wieldeth wealth, and world good time
        attends,
And God through traffic's toil and pain a world of treasure sends;
Here states repair[41] and laws are tried, and noble customs shine,
Here dwells the sages of the world and all the Muses nine.
The Court itself, and Inns of Court, where wit and knowledge
        flows,
Haunts here as term[42] and time commands, and people comes and
        goes;
Here are ambass'dors feasted still, and foreign kings have been,
Here are the wheels of public state that brings the pageant in,[43]
And here is now the maiden town that keeps herself so clean
That none can touch, nor stain in troth, by any cause or mean. ...
Here is the soil and seat of kings and place of precious price,
Here worthies makes their mansions still and buildeth stately
        towers,
Here sits the nobles of the realm in golden halls and bowers.
O London, look to thy renown, thy fame hath stretched thee far;
Thou art a stay in time of peace, a help in cause of war,
A fear to foes, a joy to friends, a jewel in our days,
That well may match with any town or seat of greatest praise.

8
[An Epigram on Augusta]
(John Johnston, 1586)

This city well Augusta[44] called, to which (a truth to say)
Air, land, sea, and all elements, show favour every way.

The weather nowhere milder is, the ground, most rich to see,
Doth yield all fruits of fertile soil, that never spent will be.
And ocean, that with Thamis stream his flowing tide doth blend,
Conveys to it commodities, all that the world can send.
The noble seat of kings it is for port[45] and royalty,
Of all the realm the sense, the heart, the life, and lightsome eye.
The people ancient, valorous, expert in chivalry,
Enriched with all sorts and means of art and mystery.
Take heedful view of every thing, and then say thus in brief,
This either is a world itself, or of the world the chief.

9
[Britomart's Praise of London][46]
(Edmund Spenser, 1590)

It Troynovant is hight,[47] that with the waues
    Of wealthy Thamis washed is along,
    Upon whose stubborne neck, whereat he raues
    With roring rage, and sore him selfe does throng,
    That all men fear to tempt his billowes strong,
    She fastned hath her foot, which standes so hy,
    That it a wonder of the world is song
    In forreine landes, and all which passen by,
Beholding it from farre, doe thinke it threates the skye.

The Troian Brute did first that citie fownd,
    And Hygate made the meare[48] thereof by west,
    And Ouert gate by North: that is the bownd
    Toward the land; two riuers bownd the rest.
    So huge a scope at first him seemed best,
    To be the compasse of his kingdomes seat:
    So huge a mind could not in lesser rest,
    Ne in small meares containe his glory great,
That Albion had conquered first by warlike feat.

10
[The Thames Crowned by London][49]
(Edmund Spenser, 1596)

But he their sonne full fresh and iolly was,

All decked in a robe of watchet[50] hew,
On which the waues, glittering like Christall glas,
So cunningly enwouen were, that few
Could weenen,[51] whether they were false or trew.
And on his head like to a Coronet
He wore, that seemed strange to common vew,
In which were many towres and castels set,
That it encompast round as with a golden fret.[52]

Like as the mother of the Gods, they say,
In her great iron charet[53] wonts to ride,
When to Joues pallace she doth take her way:
Old Cybele,[54] arayd with pompous pride,
Wearing a Diademe embattild[55] wide
With hundred turrets, like a Turribant.[56]
With such an one was Thamis beautifide;
That was to weet[57] the famous Troynouant,
In which her kingdomes throne is chiefly resiant.[58]

11
From *London's Description*
(Richard Johnson, 1607)

Long may'st thou live, fair London's wished bliss,
Long may'st thou reign, Great Britain's happiness!
Live, reign, and be when there no being is,
Triumphant over all that wish thee less,
   In earth adored with glory and renown,
   In heaven adorned with an angel's crown!

Of London's pride I will not boast upon,
Her gold, her silver, and her ornaments,
Her gems and jewels, pearls and precious stones,
Her furniture and rich habiliments,
   Her cloth of silver, tissue, and of gold,
   Which in her shops men daily may behold.

What mines of gold the Indian soil doth nourish
Within the secrets of her fruitful womb,
London partakes it, and doth daily flourish,

Ordained thereto by heaven and heavenly doom;
   All foreign lands whom majesty doth move,
   Do still contend to grace her with their love.

   What Seville, Spain, or Portugal affordeth,
What France, what Flanders, or what Germany,
What Crete, what Sicily, or what Naples hoardeth,
The coasts of Turkey, or of Barbary,
   The boundless seas to London walls presenteth,
   Through which all England's state she much augmenteth.

   If Rome by Tiber substance doth attain,
Or Euphrates to Babylon brings plenty,
If golden Ganges[59] Egypt fills with gain,
The Thames of London surely is not empty;
   Her flowing channel poureth forth much profit
   For London's good, yet few knows what comes of it.

   Thus by the bounty of imperious minds,
Furthered by nature with a noble flood,
Proud wealth and wealthy pride brave London finds,
Nor wants she not that[60] brings her gain and good;
   Within her walls there lieth close concealed,
   That wealth by tongues can hardly be revealed.

   London hath likewise four terms of law[61] most fit,
The fourfold year in equal parts divide,
In which the judges of the law do sit,
Depending matters justly to decide —
   The poor man's plaint, and eke the rich man's cause,
   And sentence given by justly dooming laws.

   First of the four fresh spring doth entertain,
The second is in sweating summer placed,
The third with windy harvest doth remain,
And freezing winter doth delight the last:
   When these times come, and courts of law unlock,
   'Tis strange to mark how men to London flock.

   These be the bees by which my being is,
England the orchard, London is the hive,

Their toil her triumph, and their fruit her bliss;
When most they labour, London most doth thrive:
   The lofty courtier and the country clown,
    By their expence brings London rich renown.

And thus from all sides doth much substance flow,
By Thames, by terms, by sea, and by the land;
So rich a mass whole kingdoms cannot show:
In this estate fair London still doth stand,
   Four pillar terms, and Thames be the fift,
    Which ta'en away, then farewell London's thrift.

12
[Hills of Gold]
(Anon., 1609)

... Mine eyes did draw
(With wonder) to behold afar
The brightness of the kingdom's star;
A thousand steeples, turrets, towers
(Lodgings all fit for emperors)
Lifted their proud heads 'bove the sky,
As if they had sole sovereignty
O'er all the buildings in the land,
And seemed on hills of gold to stand,
For the sun's beams on them being shed,
They showed like mines new burnished.

13
From *London's Artillery*
(Richard Niccols, 1616)

Canto VII
The Argument

London's fair arms with honour won,
And grace to her by princes done.

This queen of cities, lady of this isle,
So happy seated both for air and soil,

Famous in name from all antiquity
To keep the same unto posterity,
Upon her lap did nurse those sons of fame,
Whose deeds do now nobilitate her name. ...
For which[62] the dagger of so brave a hand,
On London's crossed shield shall ever stand,
As the fair ensign of that honour got
By merit of the noblest deed, and not
Like that, which begged and bought through every age,
To upstart gentry gives a feigned badge,
Whose scutcheons wanting colours of desert,
Are painted by the hand of bribed art,
Which truth as things of scorn shall wash away,
And future time shall laugh at their decay. ...
But many here perhaps with narrow eyes
Looking on London's glory, may despise
These things as toys, and boasting their descent
From Jove himself, will wish fame's looks were rent,
Rather than with their gentry in the same
True honour any City-born should name;
For many now the name of London scorn,
Whose ancestors were London bred and born. ...

Canto VIII
The Argument

London with light of grace endued;
Heav'n's blessings, her ingratitude.

The King of gods, Monarch of heav'n, and Lord
Of land and seas, who by His only word
Made earth our grandam's barren womb to bear,
Hath chosen London for His Sion, where
The sons of men should with true praise adore
His sacred deity, who with that whore
Of Babylon[63] themselves should not defile,
Whose witchcrafts our late fathers did beguile;
But keep that truth and that true worship teach,
Which t'our forefathers that grave man[64] did preach. ...

14
From *Poly-Olbion*, Song XVI
(Michael Drayton, 1619)

Thames his either banks, adorned with buildings fair,
The city to salute doth bid the Muse prepare;
Whose turrets, fanes, and spires, when wistly[65] she beholds,
Her wonder at the site, thus strangely she unfolds:
'At thy great builder's wit, who's he but wonder may?
Nay, of his wisdom, thus ensuing times shall say:
O more than mortal man, that did this town begin,
Whose knowledge found the plot, so fit to set it in!
What god, or heavenly power, was harboured in thy breast,
From whom with such success thy labours should be blessed?
Built on a rising bank, within a vale to stand,
And for thy healthful soil chose gravel mixed with sand,
And where fair Thames his course into a crescent casts
(That, forced by his tides, as still by her he hastes,
He might his surging waves into her bosom send)
Because too far in length, his town should not extend.
And to the North and South, upon an equal reach,
Two hills their even banks do somewhat seem to stretch,
Those two extremer winds[66] from hurting it to let;[67]
And only level lies upon the rise and set[68]
Of all this goodly isle, where breathes most cheerful air.
And every way thereto the ways most smooth and fair,
As in the fittest place by man that could be thought,
To which by land, or sea, provision might be brought;
And such a road for ships scarce all the world commands,
As is the goodly Thames, near where Brute's city stands.

15
[The City of London: A Mock Praise]
(Thomas Randolph, *c.* 1629)

O fortunate city, rejoice in thy fate,
That hast so religious a magistrate;
Oh, Jonas the 2nd[69] is sent unto thee,
As Jonas the first to old Ninvee,[70]
  Thou penitent city of London.

Divinity means to cure all souls,
And charity means to repair old Paul's.[71]
The clergy and laity lovingly meet;
Th'one sweeps the conscience, the other the street,
    In the cleanly city of London.

Each citizen unto the prison is borne
That every night will not hang out his horn;[72]
Yet spare all your candles good providence[73] might,
And hang out their wives that are surely as light,[74]
    In the delicate city of London.

Know this good magistrate hath a command
In Middlesex, London, and Charing and Strand.
Oh, with what sins, with what sins are w'oppressed,
When the Mayor on the Sabbath can take no rest,
    In Westminster nor in London.

Sobriety then shall arise some think,
That no man so late in the night shall have drink;[75]
Yet then, good fellows, retain your old crimes,
Rise early, good fellows, and be drunk betimes,
    In the temperate city of London.

Authority now smites us no more
To drink in a tavern, or speak with a whore;
The late proclamation was so good sense,
That banished away all gentlemen hence,[76]
    From the chargeable[77] city of London.

The Bankside is honest and Bloomsbury[78] chaste,
The ladies turned careful and look to the waste;
Nor can we now beershops in Turnbull Street see,
No bawdy house now but St Anth'lin's[79] shall be,
    In the Puritan city of London.

16
The Praise of London, or A Delicate New Ditty
(Richard Climsall, 1632)

All you that delight in pastime and pleasure,

Now list to my ditty, wherein I will show;
In London, they'll say, is good store of treasure,
   And that, for a certain, there is many doth know.
Great store of silver and gold you may see,
   With all things else pleasing as ever can be;
There are fine shows and glistering sights,
   Then come to the city for your delights. ...

You see how the chiefest are thither resorting,
   And chiefly are there in the cold winter time;
The city in winter is better for sporting
   Than 'tis in the country in the summer prime.
The lords and the knights and the ladies so gay,
   May there take their pleasure and go to a play;
Pleasure it flows there days and nights,
   Then come to the city for your delights. ...

17
[The Praise of a Refugee]
(Wenceslaus Clemens, 1636)

Ancient city, the vast world in epitome,
Favoured of the lands, pleasance beloved of heaven,
O City, hail! I have sought you in a thousand prayers!
Hail, London! Hail, glorious Troynovant!
Famous for churches, adorned with proud houses,
Haven of justice, home of faith, sanctuary of peace!
Kingdom of learned Mercury, gate of blessed fortune!
Heart, and eye, and theatre of the world,
Hail! Thrice hail, great glory of the earth!
Now, driven from home, I see you for the first time.
You, of Jove's house and royal bed,
For peoples, numbers, courage, power, a city strong,
An opulent world, noble, keen, distinguished,
A city long heard of and revered by me, —
For your excellence and fame were broadcast to the lands, —
You, with God urging me on, drew me willing hither.

18
To London, Eye and Epitome of Britain
(Jan Sictor, 1637)

Nymph of Britain, graced with the seat of kings,
   Head of all the realm in nobility,
What is scattered through the sea-girdled world,
   Thanks to Cynthia,[80] you hold to your breast;
Your bright sun and star-like people make you shine,
   And your clergy raise your face to heaven.
Your highest court of justice, a spacious house,
   Famed theatre of judges, lies open to all;
Like the hinge on a door, your company
   Of magistrates maintains stability.
While every member gives way to the head,
   While the merchant bears his goods to every shore,
While sea and wind bear back wealth-laden ships,
   While concord nurtures and unites you in strength,
And while Pallas[81] summons your strong men to arms,
   Then will you flourish under Britain's king,
And your island world will prosper in good things.

19
[The City Royal]
(Sir William Davenant, 1648)

London, which royal Lud did newly raise,
And newly name, now ought Augusta be. ...
The world too narrow for the fame she bears,
With lofty crest she rolls the heavenly spheres.
   Then, till the Thames shall cease to ebb and flow,
The ground to bear, and skies about to go,
(The heavens and earth to her most friendly both)
Eternal flow'rs the state thereof shall clothe;
For (if God will) beyond the reach of spite,
And never braver, is Augusta right.

20
London's Praise, or, The Glory of the City (1685)[62]
to the tune of 'London is a Brave Town'

Of all the songs that e'er was penned,
   There's none I ever saw,
Old England's glory did commend,
   Which keeps the world in awe;
'Tis London, that renowned place,
   Of which I now shall sing;
All must submit to sword and mace,
   Such terror do they bring;
Then London is a brave town,
   And a fine city:
'Tis governed by a scarlet gown,
   Then mark you well my ditty.

Guildhall a stately structure is,
   Like to a palace brave;
Those that offend and do amiss,
   Their sentence there must have.
Justice with sword and balance stands,
   To weigh aright each case;
The rich with bribes cannot command,
   'Tis equity takes place;
O London is a brave, etc. ...

Unto themselves a charter free,
   This wealthy City holds;
All that have freedom there to be,
   The Chamberlain enrolls.
No foreigner can set up there,
   Their orders are so strong;
In shop they must not sell no ware,
   Lest they the freemen wrong.
Sing London is a brave, etc.

A country boy comes up to town,
   Perhaps no clothes to his back;
Nor to one creature there is known,
   Yet he need never lack.

If that he be but just and true,
　　And have an honest face,
And willing any work to do,
　　He need not want a place.
Sing London is a brave, etc. ....

So every year they change Lord Mayor,
　　To show their mutual love,
And that in power they equal are,
　　And none the other above;
And god preserve our royal Kind,
　　And send the City plenty:
This' the poet's offering,
　　Who hopes it will content ye.
Sing London is a brave town,
　　And a fine city:
'Tis governed by a scarlet gown,
　　Thus I conclude my ditty.

Notes

1. The keeping of custom and ceremony.
2. The obligation of liege man to liege lord, subject to sovereign.
3. Sufficiency, provision, store.
4. What is amiss.
5. Pleasant.
6. Rejoice.
7. Called.
8. Noah.
9. Valiance, strength.
10. Gillyflower, pink.
11. Excelling.
12. Extremely clear.
13. Royal colours flying from the top.
14. Lord.
15. According to popular legend, the Norman Tower was built by Julius Caesar; see, e.g. *Richard III*, III.i.169.
16. Banks.
17. Reputation, renown.
18. Foes.
19. Walls.
20. Cease, fail.
21. Of earth, mortal.
22. Heed, care, provision.
23. Tell.
24. Stow reports that a stone bridge, built next to an older timber structure,

was begun in 1176, in the reign of Henry II, 13 years before the reign of Richard I, and that it was completed in 1209, in the reign of John.

25. Metallic thread.

26. Strongly, well.

27. The arcade in the upper storey of Gresham's Royal Exchange.

28. A market in Walbrook Ward.

29. Wide knee-breeches.

30. Pantoufles, i.e. slipper-like overshoes.

31. In Vintry Ward.

32. St Mary Bow.

33. Ornamental borders.

34. Sweetmeats or confections.

35. Headquarters of the Hanseatic merchants in Dowgate Ward.

36. Referring to strict rules of apprenticeship.

37. Stow notes 'a stew or hothouse' kept in Stew Lane, Queenhithe, not far from the Steelyard.

38. Drudge.

39. Rude, humble.

40. Barren, uninhabited.

41. Have recourse.

42. The London law terms.

43. See Chapter 16.

44. A name given to distinguish Roman provincial towns. London had in fact been called *Augusta Trinovantia*. See no. 19 below.

45. Dignity.

46. Britomart, the heroine of the third book of Spenser's *Faerie Queene*, explains that just as Rome was reared out of Troy's ashes by the heroism of Aeneas, so a third Trojan kingdom has been founded by Aeneas' kinsman Brutus

47. Called.

48. Boundary.

49. In Book IV of *The Faerie Queene*, Spenser recounts the marriage of the rivers Thames and Medway. Attended by his ancient parents, the Rivers Thame and Isis, the vigorous young Thamesis appears in watchet robes and crowned with the city of London.

50. Pale or light blue.

51. Tell, determine.

52. Interlaced ornament.

53. Chariot.

54. The mother-goddess of fertility and of cities.

55. Having battlements.

56. Turban.

57. To perceive.

58. Resident.

59. Johnson's mistake for the Nile.

60. That which.

61. Easter, Trinity, Michaelmas and Hilary, in the order given by Johnson below.

62. William Walworth's killing of Jack Straw; see 10.3, below.

63. Rome.

64. Identified in a marginal note as Joseph of Aremathea, supposed to have brought the Holy Grail to Britain and to have begun Britain's Christianisation.

65. Intently, longingly.

66. The North and South winds.

67. Prevent.

68. To the East and West.

69. On 20 April 1629, Richard Deane, Lord Mayor, issued a drastic order against 'vintners, alehouse keepers, tobacco and strong-water sellers' who 'greatly profane the Sabbath ... contrary to the express commandment of Almighty God, His Majesty's laws in that behalf, and all good government'. Thus began the last major Puritan effort to enforce strict Sabbatarian laws; the Crown reissued the *Book of Sports*, a defence of Sabbath recreations, in 1633.

70. See Jonah 3:4.

71. See 4.11 below; a campaign to restore the badly decayed cathedral was led by Henry Farley, who published pamphlets on the subject in 1616, 1621 and 1622. A 'Proclamation for preventing the decays of churches and chapels for the time to come', supported by Archbishop Laud, was issued in October 1629, and Inigo Jones was commissioned for the repair in 1634.

72. The sides of lanterns were made of horn; an article of the wardmote inquest provided for the hanging and carrying of lanterns at night.

73. Parsimony.

74. Wanton, picking up the allusion to cuckoldry in 'horns' above.

75. Tavern hours were restricted by the City.

76. Proclamations commanding gentlemen to depart from the Court and City and to keep rural hospitality were issued frequently, by James I in 1603, 1622 and 1623 and most recently by Charles I in November 1627. A letter in October 1632, from the Lords of the Council to the Lord Mayor and Aldermen, calls for continued enforcement of the 1627 proclamation.

77. Liable to charge, expense.

78. Bankside and Bloomsbury were frequented by prostitutes.

79. A noted hotbed of Puritanism.

80. Goddess of the moon; referring to the ocean tides, but alluding also to the maritime policies of Elizabeth I.

81. Pallas Athena, goddess of war.

82. An earlier version of this poem, printed in 1660, shows evidence of its being composed before 1648, the date of a ballad that alludes to it.

3

THE ORDER OF SOCIETY:
TESTIMONY OF CHANGE

Just as Tudor–Stuart Englishmen showed a new interest in describing their surroundings, so they made unprecedented attempts to analyse their society. At work here was not simply a new awareness of the social framework, but also a sense that it was changing. And in the anatomy of social change, the role of London bulked large. Early in the Tudor period, Edmund Dudley could still describe English society by invoking the medieval model of the three estates — nobles, clergy and commons, or those who fight, who pray and who work. Following common precedent, he lumped 'merchants, craftsmen, and artificers' in the last category, along with 'franklins, graziers, tillers, and other generally the people of this realm'. By the end of the sixteenth century, however, prosperous urbanites had acquired a status of their own. Both William Harrison and Sir Thomas Smith, the two major anatomists of later Tudor society, proposed a model based on six categories — the monarch, nobles, gentlemen (knights, esquires and 'simple' gentlemen), burgesses, yeomen and the lowest sort of commoners. In the last category they continued the habit of lumping rural occupations together with small urban retailers and craftsmen; but the striking features were the emergence of burgesses in a separate category, the statement that burgesses included wealthy merchants as well as officeholders, and the claim that burgesses might frequently change places with gentlemen. Wealthy merchants had, of course, always posed problems to anatomists of English society; earlier than the fourteenth century a preacher had declared that 'God made the clergy, knights and labourers, but the devil made burghers and usurers.' The traditionally anomalous position of merchants was recognised by Harrison and Smith, however, as a fluid relationship to gentlemen.

What made this relationship a notable hotspot in their social schemes was that it marked the boundary between those who laboured and those who did not, between the mass of Englishmen and the 4 or 5 per cent who belonged to the ruling elite. Though they might lack knighthood or a coat of arms, even simple gentlemen belonged to a single group that included the monarch and the nobility. Thus, while the six categories of Harrison and Smith might appear to represent a smooth continuum of ranks, they did not, individually, represent separate power groups or classes; the only real demarcation of power or class stood at the boundary between those who were gentlemen and those who were not. While they differed from each other in wealth and status, burgesses, yeomen and ordinary commoners were groups based largely on functionally different roles or callings. Status was to be achieved not by moving from one of these callings to another, but by succeeding within them, by earning status in relation to one's peers in family, guild, parish and community. Mobility from one of these lower groups to another was as much horizontal or occupational as vertical, though of course a change of occupation might be related to vertical mobility, as failure forced a change of livelihood or success led to what might now be called diversification. And of course, the possibility of occupational change, like the fluid relationship of gentlemen to burgesses, was a product of changing relations between town and country. No longer enclaves in a wholly agrarian economy, the towns, especially London, were capable of influencing, not just responding to, developments in the countryside. What made the categories of gentleman and burgess so troublesome to Harrison and Smith was that they were not easily accounted for in a status system based on land. Gentlemen might be urban professionals (e.g. lawyers and bureaucrats) and merchants might become landed gentlemen. Much of the hostility directed at merchants was a result of their supposed usurpation of the rural sphere of gentlemen. Merchants 'become landed men and call themselves gentlemen, though they be churls', said Edward VI in a standard complaint. 'The artificer will leave the town, and ... will live in the country.' An important element in the country–city myth at this time (see Chapters 12 and 14) was the belief that the rise of urban interlopers and the flight of ancient families to London had destroyed the tradition of rural hospitality.

It was certainly in the urban sphere that the social categories were most fluid. Though strictly classed among those Harrison called 'the last sort of people ... to be ruled and not to rule', even small retailers and substantial craftsmen were being designated, in the early Stuart period, by the conveniently vague phrase, 'the middling sort'. More substantial citizens were apt to style themselves gentlemen. Yeoman was a title often claimed by journeymen. Civic leaders often demanded to be addressed as gentlemen, while London aldermen styled themselves esquires and the Lord Mayor was knighted. As early as 1508, Thomas Sprig of Lavenham revealed the fluid state of things when he described himself as 'clothmaker alias gentleman, alias yeoman, alias merchant'.

Complaints like those of Philip Stubbes, who claimed that in his day even 'the vilest sort of men must be called by name of masters', are of course grotesque exaggerations, committed in their mythical contrast between the good old days and nowadays to a past that surely never existed. The mobility possible through urban occupations allowed for greater wealth and status, perhaps, but it did not involve any notable acquisition of power, nor did it involve large numbers of people. Indeed, the evidence suggests that while the position of a wealthy minority improved, the prosperity of the great body of artificers, labourers and dependants declined markedly in the sixteenth century. London had its part to play in this development too, as the inflated price of foodstuffs, brought on by rising population, by the need to victual London, and by the impact of the textile trade on food agriculture, showed up in the profits of landowners and made their way to London's luxury purveyors. There is little reason to think that individual cases of social mobility amounted to a major shift in power or class structure. Indeed, the eagerness with which individuals climbed out of their status groups (often taking care to shut the door on those behind them) suggests that the system as a whole remained well entrenched.

This is confirmed by the focus of contemporary writers on the boundary of distinction — the boundary between the lower gentry and the merchant–yeoman class. What tended to soften this boundary was not simply the upward aspirations of the latter, but also the custom of primogeniture, which forced the younger sons of gentlemen — and even nobles — to sustain their status by marriage to an heiress or by entering a profession or business. London abounded in both opportunities. Lord Stafford attempted desperately, in 1591, to marry his son to a wealthy Londoner's daughter,

and in 1592 Lord Howard of Bindon succeeded in making a simi-
lar match. Sir William Hewitt, a Lord Mayor who preferred to
marry his daughter to his apprentice rather than to the Earl of
Shrewsbury, may well have shared with Burghley a conviction that
'a man can buy nothing in the market with gentility'. The London
law courts and bureaucracies provided many younger sons with
means and livelihood, and the fortunes of a minor Northampton-
shire family were made when Euseby Isham apprenticed his three
younger sons to the London Mercers. The sons of gentlemen were
not the most common recruits in the London business world (of
the 881 men admitted to the freedom in 1551–53, 46 were the
sons of gentlemen, 136 the sons of yeomen, and 289 the sons
of husbandmen), but their successes were disproportionately
spectacular.

Those who came to London for marriage, professional training
or apprenticeship were in fact a fortunate elite, a tiny portion of
the migrants who thronged the highways and swelled the popula-
tion of the suburbs. Physical and social mobility, as John Stow's
remark on coaches below suggests (see 3.11), were related pheno-
mena. Pamphlets published in the 1570s listed as many as 17
major routes into London; by the 1630s John Taylor could publish
a list of carrier routes that ran into the hundreds. The anony-
mous author of the *Apology for the City of London* (1580)
argued that the attractions of London were the court and
law bureaucracies and the new business enterprises of gentlemen,
which either brought them to the city or forced their lesser compe-
titors to take to the road. Despite frequent complaints, litigants
often preferred to take their case to London rather than have it
heard in local courts where judges might be biased. Small farmers,
who failed frequently in this period of agricultural change, sought
new occupations in London, and they were followed by the small
retailers and craftsmen from the declining towns that farming once
supported. Luxury goods from London, peddled throughout the
countryside, may well have added to the alluring image of the
urban Eldorado. As always, the destitute and homeless followed
the migration of trade, and they actively sought the organised char-
ity for which London was famous. In the later sixteenth century,
religious wars in France and the Low Countries added a flow
of alien refugees to the many other outgroups — vagabonds,
orphans, criminals and dissenters — whose existence so alarmed the
authorities.

Even before 1500, William Caxton had noted that 'one name and lineage ... in this noble city of London ... rarely continue into the third heir, or scarcely to the second'. An Elizabethan London preacher later remarked that every dozen years or so 'the most part of the parish changeth, as I by experience know, some going and some coming'. An important factor in this rapid turnover was a mortality rate that exceeded the rate of births, so that the city's population had constantly to be replenished by immigration. But a further factor, emigration, resulted in part from the upward mobility of London's most successful business families, who rarely stayed on beyond two or three generations. Of the 48 Elizabethan mayors of London, no two have the same family name, and the aldermanic lists for the same period reveal few family dynasties. According to contemporaries, the pattern of success ended with the purchase of land and with those fortunate marriages which brought gentility to Londoners and money to gentlemen. Harrison attributed the rise of new gentlemen in the countryside to London, 'from which (as it were from a certain rich and wealthy seedplot) courtiers, lawyers, and merchants be continuously transplanted'. William Lambarde noted that in Kent 'the gentlemen be not here (throughout) of so ancient stocks as elsewhere, especially in the parts nearer to London, from which city ... courtiers, lawyers, and merchants be continuously translated, and do become new plants amongst them'. Not all of the new gentry were merchants, but their success was the more spectacular, often being achieved in a single generation, while the rise of yeoman families often took several generations.

The pattern of mercantile success, however, must be hedged about with qualifications. For one thing, as J.H. Hexter has pointed out, it was not entirely new. Geoffrey Chaucer, official and poet, was the son of a London vintner, but his son was, in turn, a man possessed of substantial estates. Many of the fifteenth and sixteenth-century landed families who were seeking lucrative marriages — for example, the Pastons and the Stoners — can be found a few generations earlier purchasing lands on the basis of mercantile success. Furthermore, the number of London families who made it into the gentry was not large. While the average stay of a successful London family was three generations, less successful families often stayed on for many generations. The growth of journeymen's guilds in sixteenth-century London reflects the despair of many lesser craftsmen, who saw little hope of entering their company's livery. Among the emigrants from London, there must have been many failures whose stories were more pleasant to forget.

Furthermore, the retirement of merchant families to the countryside did not signal any shift in power. Having gained power and prestige in the mercantile community, rusticated Londoners often quickly lapsed into provincial obscurity. Only 7 per cent of the early Stuart baronage and 4 per cent of the peerage were drawn from commercial successes. Though more prestigious than commerce, land was a less lucrative investment, returning 5 per cent a year where the money market could return at least twice as much. The primary means of preserving genteel status newly-achieved, land tied up capital at the same time that gentility called for conspicuous consumption. If land investment diminished mercantile resources, the creation of a genteel progeny may have deprived the merchant class of potentially able members. As one London merchant complained around 1630,

> the memory of our richest merchants is suddenly extinguished; the son, being left rich, scorns the profession of his father, conceiving more honour to be a gentleman (although but in name), to consume his estate in dark ignorance and excess, than to follow the steps of his father as an industrious merchant to maintain and advance his fortunes.

It can be argued that, far from signalling the advance of the 'middle class', the rise of London's merchants may actually have retarded it.

Like Harrison and Lambarde before him, Thomas Fuller remarked in 1662 that of the 33 gentry families of Middlesex named in 1433, only three remained in 1593. He concluded that: 'the gentry in Middlesex seem sojourners rather than inhabitants therein'. But unlike Harrison and Lambarde, he stressed the opposite half in the pattern of mobility: 'our English gentry, such as do live southward near London (which from the lustre thereof I may fitly call the sun of our nation) in the warmth of wealth and pleasures, quickly strip and disrobe themselves of their estates and inheritance.' This reciprocal process, centred on London, may account for the frequent mention, in the selections below, of the war between citizens and gentlemen. Drawn along a battle-line dividing country and city, this mythical war is a common subject in literary treatments of the city, from satire and drama (see Chapters 7 and 14) to lyric (see Chapter 12). As myths often do, the country–city myth may simply have imposed a false clarity on a murky and ambiguous situation; the very firmness with which it draws a boundary at London's wall actually conceals a disturbing reciprocity, a point of connection that was unsettling to the social order. In a work as early as Rastell's debate between a knight and merchant, the real issue is not the upstart presumption of the latter but the question of which meaning of nobility and gentleness will fill the definitional vacuum created by the waning of the feudal system. To be sure, the merchant's self-image embodies the aspiring and aggressive tone of an emerging burgher ideology, an ideology delightfully exploited in Gervase Markham's letter (3.13 below) from a scornful apprentice to his scholarly brother. Numerous works, from poems and plays celebrating London worthies to the narratives of Deloney and a variety of manuals on self-advancement, attest to the ambitions of London's merchants and craftsmen. Studies suggest that the literacy rate among urban tradesmen may have been as high as 40 per cent, and even Edmund Dudley had warned that by means of education the lesser sort of men would overtake their betters. But as the passages below by Gainsford and Bolton indicate (3.14 and 3.15), the common claim was not that merchants were better than gentlemen but that they were gentlemen, that trade was no bar to gentility, that 'valiant hearts' and 'noble courages' were 'as well the badge of a merchant as cognizance of a true gentleman'. It is often pointed out that James Whitlocke, a prosperous lawyer who was the fourth son of a London merchant, recalled that his mother 'did bring up all her children in as good sort as any gentleman in England would do'; but it is less often noted that Whitlocke's grandfather had been a country gentleman, or that in buying his way back to the land, the grandson was only reclaiming what he regarded as his true patrimony. However unique the means by which they pursued status — and it can be argued that not even the means were unique — the successful members of London's mercantile world did not so differ in the ends at which they aimed as to be called a 'class'.

1
From *Gentleness and Nobility*
(John Rastell, 1527-30)

The Merchant Oh, what a great wealth and prosperity
   It is to any realm where merchants be,
   Having free liberty and intercourse also,
   All merchandise to convey to and fro;
   Which thing I have used and the very feat found,
   And thereby gotten many a thousand pound.
   Wherefore now, because of my great riches,
   Throughout this land, in every place doubtless,
   I am magnified and greatly regarded,
   And for a wise and noble man esteemed.
The Knight Master merchant, I hear you right well,
   But now in presumption methink ye excel,
   To call yourself noble in presence[1] here.
   I wis[2] men know what your ancestors were,
   And of what great stock descended ye be;
   Your father was but a blacksmith, pardy.[3]
Merchant Why sir, what then? What be you, I pray you?
Knight Marry, I am a gentleman, I would ye know,
   And may dispend yearly five hundred mark land;
   And I am sure all that ye have in hand
   Of yearly rent is not worth five marks.
Merchant But I would thou knewest, for all thy cracks,
   I am able to buy now all the land
   That thou hast, and pay for it out of hand,
   Which I have got by mine own labour and wit.
Knight Yet art thou but a churl, and I have a scorn
   Thou shouldest compare with me, a gentleman born.
Merchant Why, what callest thou a gentleman, tell me?
Knight Marry, I call them gentlemen that be
   Born to great lands by inheritance,
   As mine ancestors, by continuance,
   Have had this five hundred year; of whom now I
   Am descended and comen lineally,
   Bearing the same name and arms also
   That they bare this five hundred year ago.
   Mine ancestors also have ever be
   Lords, knights, and in great authority,

Captains in the war and governors,
And also in time of peace great rulers;
And thine were never but artificers,
As smiths, masons, carpenters or weavers.
Merchant All that is truth, I will not deny now;
Yet I am more gentleman born than thou,
For I call him a gentleman that gently
Doth give unto other men lovingly
Such thing as he hath of his own proper;
But he that taketh aught away from another,
And doth give him nothing again therefore,
Ought to be called a churl evermore.
But mine ancestors have given alway
To thine ancestors such thing as they
By their labours did truly get and win;
For mine ancestors builded houses wherein
Thine ancestors have had their dwelling place;
Also mine ancestors have made tools
To all manner crafty men belonging,
Whereby clothes, and every other thing,
Whereof thine ancestors need have had,
With the same tools have ever be made.
So mine ancestors have given their labours
Ever to comfort and help thine ancestors. ...
Mine ancestors by their wits could work and do;
And as for thine ancestors, I know nothing
They could do by their wits worth of praising,
But use, occupy, and waste evermore
Such things as mine ancestors made before.

2
From *Civil and Uncivil Life*
(Anon., 1579)

It happened, as oft it doth, that divers gentlemen being convited[4]
to dine together, among many other things, they chanced to fall in
speech of the country and courtly lives, reasoning whether it were
better for the gentlemen of England to make most abode in their
country houses, as our English manner is, or else ordinarily to

inhabit the cities and chief towns, as in some foreign nations is the custom. ...

Vincent You know the use and ancient custom of this realm of England was that all noblemen and gentlemen not called to attendance in our prince's service did continually inhabit the countries, continuing there, from age to age and from ancestor to ancestor, a continual house; and hospitality, which got them great love among their neighbours, relieved many poor wretches and wrought also divers other good effects. ... But I see that gentlemen begin to take another course, and falling from the use of their ancestors, do now either altogether or very much leave to dwell in their country houses, inhabiting cities and great towns. ...

Our country lives was more godly than the life of the city. That opinion I conceive because I find there much love and charity, which, as I take it, are two special marks of godliness, and seldom found in cities, where every man, almost, liveth to himself; for whereas neighbours do meet often without ceremony, cheering and conversing one with another, without disdain or envy, as we do in the country, there I judge is love and good neighbourhood. Likewise, where hospitality is liberally kept and many children and servants daily fed, with all other comers, there, as I also think, is much charity. In the town, it seemeth the contrary; there is no meeting of neighbours without special convitation, no salutation without much respect and ceremony, no number of servants but those that for necessary uses are employable. So that, in brief, there seemeth to be little love among equals and less liberality to inferiors. Were it for the worship of a gentleman, having good land and revenues, to keep no more servants than, as they do in cities, those that for their necessary uses they must needs employ? If we gentlemen should so do, how should we furnish our halls? How should we be ready for quarrelers? Or how should our wives be waited on when they ride abroad, as commonly their custom is, chiefly in summer, the fair season and hunting time? ... Then must I speak of the wholesomeness of our dwellings, which without contradiction is much more than your abode in cities, court, or towns, where the air is commonly straight and the concourse of people great, which two things must needs breed contagion and sickness. ...

Let me tell you one touch more of our quiet, which is our authority, for a number of us be justices. ... But if the best of these remained in court, without office there, or in a city or town, the meanest merchant or silliest shoemaker would scantly respect us, and none at all fear us.

Valentine I had rather be worshipped or respected of one civil or wise man ... than of one hundreth country louts.

Vincent I pray you, but not command you, to tell me what is your order of life in the city, and which be your exercises, both of body and mind?

Valentine The manner of most gentlemen, and noblemen also, is to house themselves, if possible they may, in the suburbs of the city, because most commonly the air there being somewhat at large, the place is healthy, and through the distance from the body of the town, the noise not much and so consequently quiet. Also for commodity we find many lodgings, both spacious and roomy, with gardens and orchards very delectable. So as, with good government, we have as little cause to fear infection there as in the very country. Our water is excellent and much better than you have any, our ground and fields most pleasant, our fire equal with yours. ...

Unoccasioned or not contrived, no man will resort unto your town house, except he be your brother, your son, or some dear friend whom you account as yourself; else none without occasion, which happening, they that seek you are so respective as neither at the hour of a dinner or a supper they will look you, if their business doth not very much urge them. ...

When you lust to tarry alone, no man will press you; if you will be accompanied, a small convitation will train friends unto you, and these men of more civility, wisdom, and worth than your rude country gentlemen or rustical neighbours. If you delight in grave men and sober, you shall easily acquaint yourself with such. If you pleasure in mirth and pleasant companions, they are at hand. If you like of learned men, there are they found. ...

In my poor opinion, because ye dwell in remote place, one gentleman far from other, so as the better cannot inform the worse, there is no mean made to instruct the ignorant, but everyone disposeth himself almost as a poor plowman, making profit and riches the marks of all his endeavour. ...

Vincent Then it seemeth that the city, the court, and other places

of assembly (I mean of nobility) doth occasion men to learn the
customs of courtesy and points of honour.

3
[The Urban Population]
(Anon., 1580/1598)

The multitude or whole body of this populous city is two ways to
be considered, generally and specially. Generally, they be natural
subjects, a part of the commons of this realm, and are by birth for
the most part a mixture of all countries of the same, by blood
gentlemen, yeomen, and of the basest sort without distinction, and
by profession busy bees and travellers for their living in the hive of
this commonwealth. But specially considered, they consist of these
three parts, merchants, handicraftsmen, and labourers. Merchan-
dise is also divided into these three sorts, navigation, by which
merchandises are brought and carried in and out over the seas,
invection, by the which commodities are gathered into the city and
dispersed from thence into the country by land, and negotiation,
which I may call the keeping of a retailing or standing shop. In
common speech, they of the first sort are called merchants, and
both the other retailers. Handicraftsmen be those which do exer-
cise such arts as require both labour and cunning, as goldsmiths,
tailors and haberdashers, skinners, etc. Labourers and hirelings I
call those *quorum operae non artes emuntur,*[5] as Tully saith, of
which sort be porters, carmen, watermen, etc. Again these sorts
may be considered either in respect of their wealth or number. In
wealth, merchants and some of the chief retailers have the first
place, the most part of retailers and all artificers the second or
mean place, and hirelings the lowest room; but in number, they of
the middle place be first and do far exceed both the rest; hirelings
be next, and merchants be the last. Now out of this, that the estate
of London, in the persons of the citizens, is so friendly interlaced
and knit in league with the rest of the realm, not only at their
beginning by birth and blood, as I have showed, but also very com-
monly at their ending by life and conversation, for that merchants
and rich men being satisfied with gain do for the most part marry
their children into the country and convey themselves after
Cicero's counsel, *Veluti ex portu in agros et possessiones.*[6] I do
refer[7] that there is not only no danger towards the common quiet

thereby, but also great occasion and cause of good love and amity; out of this — that they be generally bent to travail and do fly poverty, *per marem, per saxa, per ignes,*[8] as the poet saith — I draw hope that they shall escape the note of many vices which idle people do fall into. And out of this, that they be a great multitude, and that yet the greatest part of them be neither too rich nor too poor, but do live in the mediocrity.

4
[City and Country]
(Anon., 1580/1598)

I have shortly to answer the accusation of those men which charge London with the loss and decay of many or most of the ancient cities, corporate towns, and markets within this realm by drawing from them to herself alone, say they, both all trade of traffic by sea and the retailing of wares and exercise of manual arts also. Touching navigation, which (I must confess) is apparently decayed in many port towns and flourisheth only or chiefly at London, I impute that partly to the fall of the Staple.[9] ... As for retailers ... and handicraftsmen, it is no marvel if they abandon the country towns and resort to London; for not only the court (which is nowadays much greater and more gallant than in former times, and which was wont to be contented to remain with a small company sometimes at an abbey or priory, sometimes at a bishop's house, and sometimes at some mean manor of the king's own) is now for the most part either abiding at London, or else so near unto it, that the provision of things most fit for it may easily be fetched from thence; but also by occasion thereof the gentlemen of all shires do fly and flock to this city, the younger sort of them to see and show vanity, and the elder to save the cost and charge of hospitality and housekeeping. For hereby it cometh to pass that the gentlemen being either for a good portion of the year out of the country, or playing the farmers, graziers, brewers or such like more than gentlemen were wont to do within the country, retailers and artificers, at the least of such things as pertain to the back or belly, do leave the country towns where there is no vent and do fly to London, where they be sure to find ready and quick market.

5
From *De Republica Anglorum*
(Sir Thomas Smith, 1583)

The Division of the Parts and Persons of the Commonwealth

We in England divide our men commonly into four sorts: gentlemen, citizens, and yeoman artificers, and labourers. Of gentlemen the first and chief are the king, the prince, dukes, marquises, earls, viscounts, barons; and these are called the nobility, and all these are called lords and noblemen. Next to these be knights, esquiers, and simple gentlemen. ...

Of (Simple) Gentlemen

... Ordinarily the king doth only make knights and create barons or higher degrees; for as for gentlemen, they be made good cheap in England. For whosoever studieth the laws of the realm, who studieth in the universities, who professeth liberal sciences, and, to be short, who can live idly and without manual labour, and will bear the port, charge, and countenance of gentleman, he shall be called Master, for that is the title which men give to esquiers and other gentlemen, and shall be taken for a gentleman.

Of Citizens and Burgesses

Next to gentlemen be appointed citizens and burgesses, such as not only be free and received as officers within the cities, but also be of some substance to bear the charges. But these citizens and burgesses be to serve the commonwealth in their cities and boroughs, or in the corporate towns where they dwell. Generally in the shires they be of none account, save only in the common assembly of the realm to make laws, which is called the Parliament.

6
[Aspirants to Gentility]
(Philip Stubbes, 1583)

Nowadays every butcher, shoemaker, tailor, cobbler, and husbandman, yea, every tinker, peddler, and swineherd, every artificer and other, *gregarii ordinis*,[10] of the vilest sort of men that be, must be called by name of masters at every word. But it is certain that no wise man will entitle them with any of these names, Worshipful and Master, for they are names and titles of dignity, proper to the godly wise.

7
[Gentlemen and Citizens]
(George Whetstone, 1584)

I must here digress from the prodigality of gentlemen unto the covetousness and usury, I cannot properly say of the citizen, although he dwelleth in the city, for the true citizen (whereof London hath plenty) liveth upon his trade, be he an adventurer abroad or a mechanical craftsman at home. But these shames of good citizens tradeth but to a dicing house, or at the farthest travaileth to a bowling alley, and with ease and safety getteth wealth as fast as the other do with great hazard and travail. They come not to play the unthrifts, but to play upon unthrifts; and yet for company, and to avoid suspicion, they will sometime play the good fellows. All the rest are but instruments for these dangerous catchers. These need not too greedily seek for purchases; the necessity of the gentlemen maketh them fair offers, and their spies, the pettifogger and others, giveth them knowledge where there is sound dealing. Among them there is such deceit coloured with such cleanly shifts,[11] as many gentlemen are for a trifle shifted out of their livings without hope of remedy. The extremity of these men's dealings hath been and is so cruel, as there is a natural malice generally impressed in the hearts of the gentlemen of England towards the citizens of London, insomuch as if they odiously name a man, they forthwith call him a trim[12] merchant. In like despite, the citizen calleth every rascal a jolly gentleman.

And truly this mortal envy between these two worthy estates was first engendered of the cruel usage of covetous merchants, in hard bargains gotten of gentlemen, and nourished with malicious words and revenges taken of both parties. ...

I heard a French gentleman resolve a problem very pleasantly and pithily. An Englishman demanded the cause that the young gentlemen of France flourished more than they of England considering that the one were consumed with daily war when the other had continual peace to strengthen them. 'Oh,' quoth the French gentleman, 'the quietness of your peace interrupteth not the deceit of your citizens, who with the feeding of your pride devoureth your livings.'

8
[Gentlemen, Citizens and Merchants]
(William Harrison, 1587)

Citizens and burgesses have next place to gentlemen, who be those
that are free within the cities and are of some likely substance to
bear office in the same. ... In this place also are our merchants to
be installed, as amongst the citizens (although they often change
estate with gentlemen, as gentlemen do with them, by a mutual
conversion of the one into the other) whose number is so increased
in these our days that their only maintenance is the cause of the
exceeding prices of foreign wares, which otherwise when every
nation was permitted to bring in their own commodities were far
better cheap and more plentifully to be had. Of the want of our
commodities here at home, by their great transportation of them
into foreign countries, I speak not, sith the matter will easily be-
wray[13] itself. ... I do not deny but that the navy of the land is in part
maintained by their traffic, and so are the high prices of wares kept
up now they have gotten the only sale of things, upon pretence of
better furtherance of the commonwealth, into their own hands.
Whereas in times past, when strange bottoms[14] were suffered to
come in, we had sugar for four pence the pound, that now at the
writing of this treatise is well worth half a crown. ... And whereas
in times past their chief trade was to Spain, Portugal, France, Flan-
ders, Dansk,[15] Norway, Scotland, and Ireland only, now in these
days, as men not contented with these journeys, they have sought
out the East and West Indies and made now and then suspi-
cious[16] voyages not only unto the Canaries and New Spain, but
likewise unto Cathaia, Muscovia, Tartaria[17] and the regions there-
about, from whence (as they say) they bring home great
commodities. But alas, I see not by all their travel that the prices of
things are any whit abated. ... This only I know, that every func-
tion and several vocation striveth with other which of them should
have all the water of the commodity run into their own cistern. ...

[*Hospitality*]

If the friends also of the wealthier sort come to their houses from
far, they are commonly so welcome till they depart as upon the
first day of their coming, whereas in good towns and cities, as Lon-
don, etc., men oftentimes complain of little room; and in reward of

a fat capon or plenty of beef and mutton largely bestowed upon them in the country, a cup of wine or beer, with a napkin to wipe their lips and an 'You are heartily welcome', is thought to be great entertainment. And therefore the old country clerks have framed this saying in that behalf, I mean upon the entertainment of towns-men and Londoners after their days of abode, in this manner:

> *Primus iucundus, tollerabilis estque secundus,*
> *Tertius est vanus, sed fetet quadriduanus.*[18]

9
[The War of Merchants and Gentlemen]
(Thomas Nashe, 1593)

Let us leave off the proverb which we use to a cruel dealer, saying 'Go thy ways, thou art a Jew,' and say, 'Go thy ways, thou art a Londoner.' For than Londoners are none more hard-hearted and cruel. Is it not a common proverb among us, when any man hath cozened or gone beyond us, to say, 'He hath played the merchant with us'? But merchants they turn it another way and say, 'He hath played the gentleman with them.' The snake eateth the toad, the toad the snake. The merchant eats up the gentleman, the gentleman eats up the yeoman, and all three do nothing but exclaim one upon another.

10
The State of Citizens
(Thomas Wilson, 1600)

These, by reason of the great privileges they enjoy, every city being, as it were, a commonwealth among themselves, no other officer of the queen nor other having authority to intermeddle amongst them, must needs be exceeding well to pass. They are not taxed but by their own officers, every art having one or two of his own which are continually of the council of the city, in all affairs to see that nothing pass contrary to their profit; besides, they are not suffered to be idle in their cities as they be in other parts of Chris-tendom, but every child of six or seven years old is forced by some art to help to enrich his parent or master. .... It is well known that at this time there are in London some merchants worth £100,000 and he is not accounted rich that cannot reach to £50,000 or near it.

11
[A World on Wheels]
(John Stow, 1603)

The number of cars, drays, carts and coaches more than hath been accustomed, the streets and lanes being straitened, must needs be dangerous, as daily experience proveth.

The coachman rides behind the horse tails, lasheth them, and looketh not behind him; the drayman sitteth and sleepeth on his dray and letteth his horse lead him home. I know that by the good laws and customs of this city, shod[19] carts are forbidden to enter the same, except upon reasonable causes, as service of the prince or such like, they be tolerated. Also that the fore-horse of every carriage should be led by hand; but these good orders are not observed. Of old times, coaches were not known in this island, but chariots or whirlicotes, then so called, and they only used of princes or great estates, such as had their footmen about them. ... But now of late years, the use of coaches, brought out of Germany, is taken up and made so common, as there is neither distinction of time nor difference of persons observed; for the world runs on wheels with many whose parents were glad to go on foot.

12
[Merchants and Gentry]
(Fynes Moryson, 1617)

The gentlemen disdain traffic, thinking it to abase gentry; but in Italy, with graver counsel, the very princes disdain not to be merchants by the great, and hardly leave the retailing commodity to men of inferior sort. And by this course they preserve the dignity and patrimony of their progenitors, suffering not the sinew of the commonwealth upon any pretence to be wrested out of their hands. On the contrary, the English and French, perhaps thinking it unjust to leave the common sort no means to be enriched by their industry, and judging it equal that gentlemen should live of their revenues, citizens by traffic, and the common sort by the plough and manual arts, as members of one body, do in this course daily sell their patrimonies; and the buyers (excepting lawyers) are for the most part citizens and vulgar men. And the daily feeling of this mischief makes the error apparent, whether it be the prodigality of the gentry (greater than in any other nation or age), or their too charitable regard to the inferior sort, or rashness or slothfulness which cause them to neglect and despise traffic, which in some commonwealths, and namely in England, passeth all other commodities and is the very sinew of the kingdom.

13
A Letter from a Prentice in London to His Brother, a Scholar at Eton
(Gervase Markham, 1617)

Brother, I thank God I am well and thank you many times for your hearty wishes. If my master's business had given any leisure to my loving thoughts, I should long ere this have wrapped them in a paper and sent them to you, but pardon him that is yours by nature and his own choice, though by duty and law bound to another whose occasions gives me scarce time to think of your happiness; which truly were it so full of glory and splendour as you would make me believe, I envy it not to you, to whom I wish more content than the world can throw upon you. But yet I must ingeniously confess I never thought so, my condition being rather addicted to this kind of life, where a certain and sure course of maintenance is to be expected, than to travail up Parnassus[20] to pick flowers. Surely, brother, your scholars have but a poor crop in it without their mind (which nobody can be witness to) be so well trapped; I am sure their bodies are bare enough and their clothes none of the wholest. It may be the sweetness of the water at Helicon[21] have made them love it ever since, for few of them can attain to beer. And truly I do think we do really and indeed enjoy those fine and flourishing gardens you speak of, and you scholars in conceit and descriptions. However, brother, enjoy your happiness, which with many wishes of much increase I lovingly wish unto you. And I must be contented with my lot, which I will fashion to as near a

degree to goodness and generousness (led by your example) as the
weakness of my mind will give me leave, and cease not to love him
who doth most heartily love you, and pray you live long, to be a
comfort and stay to our family.

Your truly loving brother,
S.H.

14
[Gentle Merchants]
(Thomas Gainsford, 1618)

If you would dispute of valiant hearts, great spirits, ambitious
tumours, noble courages, exalting wisdom, and reposed experi-
ence, it is as well the badge of a merchant as cognizance of a true
gentleman; and again, if you look upon them as the world is now
compacted ... they are commonly of the best reputed families in a
nation or raise up their own houses to make them befitting the
entertainment of the proudest nobles.

15
[A Citizen's Letter on Behalf of his Son]
(Edmund Bolton, 1629)

In the city of London there are at this present many hundreds of
gentlemen's children apprentices; infinite others have been, and
infinite will be; and all the parts of England are full of families,
either originally raised to the dignity of gentlemen out of this one
most famous place, or so restored and enriched as may well seem
to amount to an original raising. And albeit I am very much confi-
dent that by having once been an apprentice in London, I have not
lost to be a gentleman of birth, nor my son, yet shall I ever wish
and pray rather to resemble an heroic Walworth, a noble Philpot,[22]
an happy Capel,[23] that learned Sheriff of London, Mr Fabyan,[24] or
any other famous worthies of this noble city, out of any whatsoever
obscurest patronage, than that being descended out of great
nobles, to fall by vice far beneath the rank of poorest prentices.

Notes

1. In the presence of the King, before whom Rastell's interlude was presumably performed.
2. Know.
3. By God, indeed.
4. Invited.
5. Whose labour, not skills, are bought.
6. As if out of the harbour and into fields and properties.
7. Point out.
8. Through sea, rocks, fire.
9. The export wool trade.
10. Of the common order.
11. Innocent pretences.
12. (Ironic) neat, pretty.
13. Betray, reveal.
14. Foreign ships.
15. Denmark.
16. Exploratory.
17. China, Russia, Asia Minor.
18. The first day is jovial, the second is tolerable. The third is empty and the fourth stinks.
19. With iron wheelrims.
20. Mt Parnassus, near Delphi, sacred to Apollo.
21. A part of Parnassus, the home of the Muses.
22. See 10.2, below.
23. William Capel, Lord Mayor in 1489, was a major benefactor to the Church of St Bartholomew's, a leader in the City's opposition to the unpopular Cardinal Morton and a major contributor to Henry VII's attempt to control vagabonds in London.
24. See 2.4, above.

4

FROM THE PULPIT: SERMONS

Like many other forms of expression, preaching shared in the revival of eloquence during the Tudor–Stuart period. Following the lead of Renaissance humanists, who had returned to the original sources of classical wisdom, religious reformers returned to the source of Christianity in the revealed word of God, the Bible. Based on the essential premise that salvation was to be found in faith rather than in works, the return to Scripture effectively bypassed a centuries-old accumulation of Church ritual and tradition, and substituted for the mediation of the sacraments and church ceremony, the root conviction of salvation available to each believer through the Bible. Along with the publication of vernacular Bibles, the art of preaching became an influential means of spreading the new faith.

Erasmus counselled that in reading Christ's teachings, 'the first step is to know what he taught; the next is to bring it into effect'. These goals were reflected in the basic structure of Tudor–Stuart sermons, which borrowed certain features from classical oratory but which required preachers to perform three essential steps: to read and explain the Scriptures, to gather doctrine from the literal sense (this was sometimes called 'dividing'), and to 'apply the doctrine ... to the life and manners of men in a simple and plain speech'. England's Protestant reformers regarded the Bible not only as a source of faith but also as a guide to righteous action. Henry VIII's Royal Injunction of 1538 required that preachers 'purely and sincerely declare the very Gospel of Christ, and in the same exhort your hearers to the works of charity, mercy, and faith, specially commanded in the Scripture'. In his preface to the 'Great Bible' of 1540, Thomas Cranmer declared that in its pages 'may all manner of persons ... of what estate or condition soever they be ... learn all the things they ought to believe, what they ought to do, and what they should not do, as well concerning Almighty God as also concerning themselves and all other'. To the inhabitants of London, then, the Bible and its preachers had much to say.

Long before the coming of the Reformation — for centuries, in fact — London had been an active centre of outstanding preaching. Thomas Brinton, Bishop of Rochester, felt obliged to preach in London as well as in his own diocese, he said, 'because of the greater devotion and intelligence of the people'. The devotion of Londoners to their preachers was expressed in 1365 when the Lord Mayor wrote to Pope Urban V in an effort to prevent the transfer of one Robert Pynk, Lector at Blackfriars, who had, the Mayor said, 'for twenty years and more preached the word of God in the ... City in the presence of the king, the queen, dukes, earls, and other nobles of the kingdom, as well as ... the common people'. Mendicant and itinerant preachers were of course common in medieval London. But the city's greatest pulpit, at Paul's Cross, was first established when Bishop Gravesend, disturbed by the sloth of the cathedral canons on his visitation in 1280, forced them to fund a lectureship that would include public preaching.

A sermon against covetousness preached in this pulpit by the Master of Wimbledon in 1388 was printed 18 times between 1550 and 1700 (slightly more often than the works of Chaucer). The effort to tailor sermons to the London audience is reflected in the preaching manual of the great Dominican John Bromyard, which included sections on such timely urban subjects as *civitas, labor, mercatio* and *munus*. In practice such topics were fleshed out in dramatic oral fashion, replete with stories and examples, illustrative objects and vivid mimicry, that might include barking like dogs or grunting like pigs.

Nevertheless, this rich medieval background was invigorated by the new religious zeal and controversy of the sixteenth century. The Paul's Cross lectures, which had fallen into disuse during the fifteenth century, were revived by the pre-Reformation Dean of St Paul's, John Colet; from 1534, when registers of sermons were first kept, to the death of Henry VIII in 1547, the pulpit was used to expound the official views on Christian doctrine and the royal supremacy. The views of Londoners were even more overtly policed through the use of the Paul's Cross pulpit for public punishment of religious extremists, now on one side, now another. London had, in fact, become a haven and forum for gospelling zealots of all sorts, from John Harrydance, a Whitechapel brick-

layer who harangued audiences from a tub in his garden, to Robert
Warde, an opinionated rogue who was punished for his 'babble,
talk, and wrangle of the scriptures' in London's alehouses.

Early in the 1540s, before the death of Henry, a Protestant sati-
rist complained that the unpreaching pastors of London were like
'dumb dogs'. But with the accession of the young Edward VI, and
the rise to power of the Protector, Somerset, Londoners were
introduced to a generation of radical reformers whose brilliant
exhortations inaugurated the new tradition of mordant social crit-
icism amply illustrated in the selections below. Nicholas Ridley,
Bishop of London, boasted that his colleagues, Latimer, Lever,
Bradford and Knox, had tongues 'so sharp, they ripped in so deep
in their galled backs to have purged them ... of insatiable cove-
tousness ... that these men, of all other, these magistrates could
never abide'.

In 1571 a country preacher speaking at Paul's Cross declared,
'when I came out of the country hither to the city, methinks I
came into another world, even out of darkness into light; for here
the world of God is plentifully preached'. Tudor–Stuart London
was a city that had, as Francis White declared, 'voices upon voices
sent unto it'; it was 'full of voices ... the Lord's crying voices'.
Blown on the winds of doctrine, these might sometimes be, as they
were for the Marian Catholic preacher, John Feckenham, 'most
monstrous and strange voices', the siren songs and 'strange voices
of deceitful mermaids'. Londoners were forced to steer a course in
conscience amid a stormy sea of threats and exhortations.

For the authorities, it was difficult enough merely to maintain
order. The Paul's Cross pulpit was a frequent scene of confronta-
tion. Gilbert Bourne, Queen Mary's chaplain, was attacked by a
mob when he praised the hated London Bishop, Edmund Bonner,
in August 1553. The following April, when the preacher was Bon-
ner's chaplain, Henry Pendleton, the restive crowd displayed a cat
dressed in a mass priest's regalia; Pendleton's failure to take this
hint was addressed on his next appearance two months later when
he was shot at, the pellet narrowly missing the Lord Mayor. One
divine explained that the sermons at Paul's Cross 'are principally
for the governors of this Honourable City', and this meant in prac-
tice that the City Fathers often found themselves on the defensive.
In 1581, a preacher accused them of Puritanism and usury, and
added if they were allowed to choose the Paul's Cross preachers
'they would appoint such as would defend usury, the Family of

Love, and Puritanism'. In 1586, however, it was a Puritan, George Closse, who accused the Mayor, Wolstan Dixi, of fraud and partiality in justice. Closse's sermon gave such offence that he was ordered to recant in a second appearance, but Closse used this occasion only to continue his attack. Closse was investigated and exonerated by a Clerical Commission, but when he published a smug account of this affair he had gone too far. In his final appearance on the platform he was forced to remain silent while a 'grave or learned person' chastised him.

Paul's Cross was, of course, only one of London's many active and famous pulpits. Another was the cross on the south side of the church of St Mary Spital, where a multi-storeyed pavilion was built to shelter City officials during the Spital sermons, preached annually on Good Friday and Easter Monday, Tuesday and Wednesday. The tight official control maintained over these pulpits demonstrates the inherent conflict between reformist doctrine, which stressed the role of preaching, and Tudor policy, which placed tight restrictions on the content of sermons and on the licensing of preachers. As a result, some parishes went for months or even years without hearing sermons. But the deeper irony was the tendency of official restrictions to encourage more clandestine types of preaching. Rectors deprived for their refusal to conform to the prescriptions of the Book of Common Prayer were frequently provided with lectureships, positions established by the lay members of individual parishes for the sole purpose of preaching. Zealous Puritans like John Field and Robert Crowley preached frequently as lecturers in Puritan hot-beds like Holy Trinity at the Minories and St Antholin, Budge Row. Thomas Sampson, proclaiming that while others might be bishops he would 'undertake the office of a preacher or none at all', took up a lectureship at Whittington College.

Far more marginal were the conventicles that met in secret, such as the one that gathered at Plumbers' Hall to hear the preaching of Miles Coverdale. Finally, however, there were those fortunate parishes whose pulpits owed their fare to their extraordinary rectors, such as St Dunstan in the West, where Donne was a devoted rector from 1624 to 1631, and St Gregory under St Paul's and St Bennet Paul's Wharf, where Thomas Adams preached for years. Long before Launcelot Andrewes became a bishop and a favoured preacher at the Stuart court, he had been preaching from the pulpit at St Giles Cripplegate, once occupied by the zealot, Robert

Crowley; here it was that his eloquence dazzled even the saucy Thomas Nashe, who found him 'the absolutest oracle of all good divinity here among us'. The excerpt from his 1588 Spital sermon, included below (4.4), shows that even the esoterically-inclined Andrewes could appeal in forthright fashion to the basic civic passions. At the same time, the gospeller Robert Crowley was able, in 1574, to endorse the acquisitive instincts he had once condemned. His Guildhall sermon, set beside Andrewes' tribute to the city, suggests that the City's governors could respond to a range of preaching styles and religious convictions. By the early seventeenth century, London's churches, especially those in the suburbs, could no longer accommodate the city's growing population of churchgoers. Something of their zeal may be gathered from a 1641 visit to the city by Johann Comenius, who witnessed half the members of a London congregation taking notes in shorthand.

A number of the preachers represented here, such as Crowley, Donne and Joseph Hall, were outstanding poets, and their potent verse satires (7.3, 7.5 and 7.6) suggest that among the gifts of eloquence that linked their poems and sermons were accurate powers of observation, corrosive irony, and a strong social conscience. Other preachers, like Andrewes and Thomas Adams, secured enduring literary reputations solely on the merits of their sermons, which helped to raise this form of communication to the status of fine art. The excerpts gathered here employ a variety of styles, from the sturdy exhortations of Latimer to the racy colloquialism of John Bridges, from the studied sonorities of Donne to the quirky exegetical probings of Andrewes, and the sometimes macabre brooding of Adams.

But underlying all these styles is a common repertoire of Scriptural schemes and images that helped to organise the experience of London. In the Old Testament prophets, London's preachers found ample precedent for fiery indignation against corruption in high places. They found, too, those legendary cities — Babylon, Nineveh, Nebo, Jerusalem — whose iniquities and sorrows placed their own city in symbolic perspective. The prophetic vision of Jerusalem, especially, enabled them to see beyond the historical moment to its meaning, to see, amid the experience of prosperity, the vision of a city dead; and conversely, to see beyond the experience of ruin and suffering to the vision of a city restored. From the New Testament they gathered the gospel image of a simple countryman and his rural disciples confronting urban hostility —

mighty kings and wicked Pharisees — while making their way to a
meeting with destiny in the capital city. While St Paul reminded
Londoners they had no abiding city on this earth, his numerous
appeals to community and charity inspired countless sermons on
civic spirit and charitable giving. And of course the Book of Reve-
lation closed the New Testament with a vision of the promised
New Jerusalem, a vision which most preachers used cautiously to
distance the present from the end of time, but which none the less
held out the hope and the example of a redeemed order and a city
made glorious beyond all time. In his sermon on the City of Peace
(4.6), Thomas Adams remarks that London 'may not unfitly be
compared to certain pictures, that represent to divers beholders, at
divers stations, divers forms'. For the richness and variety of their
self-images, Londoners owed much to their preachers and the
Book on which they preached.

1
Sermon of the Plow
(Hugh Latimer, 1548)

Now what shall we say of these rich citizens of London? What shall
I say of them? Shall I call them proud men of London, malicious
men of London, merciless men of London? No, no! I may not say
so; they will be offended with me then. Yet must I speak. For is
there not reigning in London as much pride, as much covetous-
ness, as much cruelty, as much oppression, as much superstition, as
was in Nebo?[1] Yes, I think, and much more too. Therefore, I say,
repent, O London; repent, repent! Thou hearest thy faults told
thee. Amend them! Amend them! I think if Nebo had had the
preaching that thou hast, they would have converted. And, you
rulers and officers, be wise and circumspect, look to your charge,
and see you do your duties; and rather be glad to amend your ill
living than to be angry when you are warned or told of your fault.
What ado was there made in London at a certain man because he
said (and indeed at that time on a just cause), 'Burgesses!' quod
he, 'nay, butterflies.' Lord, what ado there was for that word! And
yet would God they were no worse than butterflies! Butterflies do
but their nature: the butterfly is not covetous, is not greedy of
other men's goods, is not full of envy and hatred, is not malicious,
is not cruel, is not merciless. The butterfly glorieth not in her own

deeds, nor preferreth the traditions of men before God's word; it committeth not idolatry, nor worshipeth false gods. But London cannot abide to be rebuked; such is the nature of man. If they be pricked, they will kick; if they be rubbed on the gall, they will wince; but yet they will not amend their faults, they will not be ill spoken of. But how shall I speak well of them? If you could be content to receive and follow the word of God, and favour good preachers, if you could bear to be told of your faults, if you could amend when you hear of them, if you would be glad to reform that is amiss; if I might see any such inclination in you, that leave to be merciless and begin to be charitable, I would then hope well of you, I would then speak well of you. But London was never so ill as it is now. In times past men were full of pity and compassion, but now there is no pity; for in London their brother shall die in the streets for cold; he shall lie sick at their door between stock and stock — I cannot tell what to call it — and perish there for hunger. Was there any more unmercifulness in Nebo? I think not. In times past, when any rich man died in London, they were wont to help the poor scholars at the universities with exhibition. When any man died, they would bequeath great sums of money toward the relief of the poor. When I was a scholar in Cambridge myself, I heard very good report of London, and knew many that had relief of the rich men of London; but now I can hear no such good report, and yet I inquire of it, and harken for it, but now charity is waxed cold: none helpeth the scholar, nor yet the poor. And in those days, what did they when they helped the scholars? Marry, they maintained and gave them livings that were very papists and professed the pope's doctrine; and now that the knowledge of God's word is brought to light, and many earnestly study and labour to set it forth, now almost no man helpeth to maintain them.

O London, London! Repent, repent! For I think God is more displeased with London than ever he was with the city of Nebo. Repent, therefore, repent, London.

2
[A Guildhall Sermon on Electing a Lord Mayor]
(Robert Crowley, 1574/75)

In the second book of Moses called Exodus, and in the 18th chap-

ter of that book, it is written, that such one as shall be chosen to
rule in any degree, must have in him these four qualities: first he
must be wise and active; then he must have in him the fear of God;
thirdly, he must be a true man; and last of all he must hate cove-
tousness. ...

The common sort of men have none other note to know a
covetous man by, but riches. If he be rich, then is he covetous, in
the judgement of most men. But riches is not a note to know a
covetous man by. Riches is the gift of God, and it is not a man's
careful toil that can make him rich, as saith the wise man, much
less is it his covetous dealing, but God giveth riches to whom he
lusteth. He maketh some rich without any great care or toil taken
of them to grow rich; and some other, though they toil never so
sore, and be never so careful, yet can they never be rich. It is there-
fore God's blessing that maketh men rich. Wherefore this reason
holdeth not: he is rich, therefore he is covetous.

3
[Cockering Cockneys]
(John Bridges, 1571)

A great many mothers nowadays cannot abide to have their child-
ren beaten, and a number of fathers as wise as the mothers; the
schoolmaster that should fetch blood of their child, out alas, it
were a pitiful sight. But were it not a more pitiful sight to see how
miserably the one destroyeth the other? They think it love, it is
more than mortal hatred, this foolish cockering[2] of their children.
Which if they feel not in the miseries of this life, whereby repent-
ance may save the soul, howsoever the body aby[3] the folly of this
hateful cockering love: if not, yet after this life, the father and
mother may meet the son in hell, and there repeat those heavy and
horrible curses that Gregory tells of. 'Cursed be the hour,' saith the
father, 'that ever thou wast born.' 'Cursed be the time,' saith the
son, 'that ever thou begottest me.' And thus the one shall curse
and bane the other, and all because of this their cursed cockering.
O ye fathers and mothers, especially you of this noble city of Lon-
don, shame not your city, undo not your children and yourselves
also.

We are throughout all the realm called cockneys that are born
in London, or in the sound of Bow bell. This is your shame;

recover this shame, as God be praised ye do, more than ever was wont to be done. It had wont to be an old saying, that few or none but were unthrifts, and came to nothing, that were cockneys born, for so are we termed abroad. But God be praised, this is now a false rule, and hath been a good while since; chiefly, since the Gospel's light hath shined on this noble city, it hath brought forth many worthy governors, notable preachers, godly pastors, wise counselors, pregnant wits, grave students, wealthy citizens, and is full of marvellous [sic] towards youth, God bless them; and I trust will every day more and more so bless this renowned city, that where before (for wanton bringing up) it hath been, although in other things famous enough, yet in this point of our birthplace, a speck of blushing, a term of cockney, a note of nipping⁴ us — it shall hereafter (by Godly education) be a thing to glory in, that we [sic] born in such a glorious city, as not only God hath made the head of other in wealth and honour, but also a mirror of other in godliness and religion. And that this may be, love your children but hate cockering.

4
[A Spital Sermon]
(Lancelot Andrews, 1588/1629)

O beloved, you that be in wealth and authority, love and reverence the word of God. It is the root that doth bear you, it is the majesty thereof that keepeth you in your thrones, and maketh you be that you are; but for *Ego dixi, Dii estis,*⁵ a parcel-commission out of this commission of ours, the madness of the people would bear no government, but run headlong and overthrow all chairs of estate, and break in pieces all the swords and sceptres in the world, which you of this city had a strange experience of in Jack Straw and his meiny,⁶ and keep a memorial of it in your city scutcheon,⁷ how all had gone down if this word had not held all up. And therefore, honour it I beseech you; I say, honour it. For when the highest of you yourselves, which are but grass, and your lordships' glory and worship, which is the flower of this grass, shall perish and pass away, this word shall continue for ever. And if you receive it now, with due regard and reverence, it will make you also to continue forever.

5
[An Attack on Plays and Players]
(Robert Milles, 1611/1612)

Notwithstanding *Longae sunt Regum manus*, that magistrates have
long arms, and many ears: yet *latet anguis in herba*[8]. When Moses
was on the Mount, Israel played the wanton; and even in this city
(though not in the heart, yet in close back wings and obscure
angles thereof) there be many nests full of idle birds, which the
careful magistrate seldom findeth out. *Ignavum fucos pecus a prae-
sepibus arcent.*[9] There is in the regiment of bees an intrusive and
troublesome drone, which eateth up the sweet honey for which the
poor painful creatures have laboured for long before. And in the
curious beehive of this commonwealth there are four sorts of idle
bees. ...

The fourth idle bee ... I call your mimical comedians and apish
actors, who with Thraso[10] thunder out *sesquipedalia verba*,[11] a
heap of inkhorn terms to the tenor of a poor collier, and with a rid-
iculous *tu quoque*,[12] move many a fool to laugh at their own follies.
And further the licentious poet and player together are grown to
such impudency, as with shameless Shimei,[13] they teach nobility,
knighthood, grave matrons and civil citizens, — and like country
dogs snatch at every passenger's heels. Yea, plays are grown nowa-
days into such high request (*Horresco referens*)[14] as that some
profane persons affirm they can learn as much both for example
and edifying at a play, as at a sermon. *O tempora, O mores*: O
times, O manners.[15] Tremble thou earth, blush ye heavens, and
speak O head, if ever any Sodomite uttered such blasphemy within
thy gates. Did the devil ever speak thus impiously in this conflict
with the archangel? To compare a lascivious stage to this sacred
pulpit and oracle of truth? To compare a silken counterfeit to a
prophet, to God's angel, to his minister, to the distributor of God's
heavenly mysteries. And to compare the idle and scurrile invention
of an illiterate bricklayer,[16] to the holy, pure and powerful word of
God, which is the food of our souls to eternal salvation. Lord for-
give them, they know not what they say.

6
The City of Peace
(Thomas Adams, 1612/1622)

The river that serves this city of peace is prosperity. It is one princ-
ipal happiness of a city to be situated by a river's side, that as it hath
fortified itself by land, so it may have command of the sea. Pros-
perity is the river to this city, that like a loving Meander,[17] winds
itself about, throwing his silver arms upon her sides; ebbing slowly,
but flowing merrily, as if he longed to embrace his love. Peace is
the mother of prosperity, but prosperity is too often the murderer
of peace. For peace breeds wealth, wealth breeds pride, pride
breeds contention, and contention kills peace. Thus she is
often destroyed by her own issue, as Sennacherib[18] was by his own
bowels.

Take this city we live in for an instance. Peace hath brought
God's plenty: the inhabitants neither plough, nor sow, nor reap,
yet are fed like the fowls of heaven. They fare well with less trouble
than if corn grew at their doors, and cattle grazed in their streets.
But as Nilus may rise too high, and water Egypt too much, so the
inundation of opulency may do them hurt. Thus may the influence
of heaven, and the plenty of earth, be a snare unto us, and our
abundance an occasion of our falling. ...

There be (as I heard a worthy divine observe) three main rivers
in the land, whereof this is held the best; and this city is placed in
the best seat of the river, upon the gentle rising of a hill, in the best
air, and richest soil. When a courtier gave it out, that Queen Mary,
being displeased with the city, threatened to divert both Term and
Parliament to Oxford, an alderman asked whether she meant to
turn the channel of the Thames thither or no. If not, saith he, by
God's grace, we shall do well enough. 'The lines are fallen to us in
pleasant places; we have a goodly heritage.'[19] Both the elements
are our friends: the earth sends us in her fruits, the sea her mer-
chandise. We are near enough the benefits, and far enough from
the dangers, of the ocean. Nothing is wanting to the consummation
of our happiness, to keep us in our own country, in our own city,
in our own houses, but that which keeps men in their wits — tem-
perance and thankfulness.

But do we not requite this river of prosperity with ungrateful
impiety, and use the ocean of God's bounty as we do the Thames?
It brings us in all manner of provision, clothes to cover us, fuel to

warm us, food to nourish us, wine to cheer us, gold to enrich us; and we, in recompense, soil it with our rubbish, filth, common sewers, and such excretions. It yields us all manner of good things, and we requite it with all plenty of bad things. It comes flowing in with our commodities, and we send it loaden back with our injuries.

Such toward God is the impious ingratitude of this famous city, which else had no parallel under the sun. She may not unfitly be compared to certain pictures, that represent to divers beholders, at divers stations, divers forms. Looking one way you see a beautiful virgin; another way, some deformed monster. Cast an eye upon her profession, she is a well-graced creature; turn it upon her conversation, she is a misshapen stigmatic. View her peace, she is fairer than the daughters of men; view her pride, the children of the Hittites and Amorites are beauteous to her. Think of her good works; then 'Blessed art thou of the Lord'; number her sins, then 'How is that faithful city become an harlot!'[20] To tell of her charity, and how many hundreds she feeds in a year, you will say with Paul, 'In this I praise her.' To tell of her oppressions and how many thousands she undoes in a year, you will say with him again, 'In this I praise her not.' Behold her like a nurse, drawing her breasts and giving her milk to orphans; you wish her cup to run over with fullness. Behold her like a horse-leech, sucking the blood of the Church, to feed her sacriligious avarice; you will say, her cup is too full. When we think of her prosperity, we wonder at her impiety; when we think of her impiety, we wonder at her prosperity. Oh, that her citizens would learn to manage their liberal fortunes, and to entertain the river of peace 'that makes glad the city of God', with humility and sobriety; that when death shall disenfranchise them here, they may be made free above, in that triumphant city whose glory hath neither measure nor end!

7
The White Devil[21]
(Thomas Adams, 1612/1613)

Shall I speak plainly? You are sick at London of one disease (I speak to you settled citizens, not extravagants) and we in the country of another: a sermon against hypocrisy in most places of the country, is like phlebotomy to a consumption, the spilling of innocent blood. Our sicknesses are cold palsies, and shaking agues; yours in the city are hotter diseases, the burning fevers of fiery zeal, the inflammations and inposthumes of hypocrisy. We have the frosts, and you have the lightnings; most of us profess too little, and some of you profess too much, unless your courses were more answerable: I would willingly be in none of your bosoms. ...

I speak not to discourage your zeal, but to hearten it, but to better it. Your zeal goes through the world, ye worthy citizens: Who builds hospitals? the City. Who is liberal to the distressed gospel? the City. Who is ever faithful to the Crown? the City. Beloved, your works are good; oh, do not lose their reward through hypocrisy. I am not bitter, but charitable; I would fain put you into the chariot of grace with Elias, and only wish you to put off this mantle. Oh, that it lay in my power to prevail with your affections, as well as your judgements; you lose all your goodness, if your hearts be not right: the ostentation of man shall meet with the detestation of God. You lose your attention now, if your zeal be in your eye, more than heart. You lose your prayers, if when the ground hath your knee, the world hath your conscience, as if you had two gods, one for Sundays, another for work days, one for the church, another for the change.[22] You lose your charity, whiles you give glozingly,[23] illiberally, too late; not a window you have erected, but must bear your names. But some of you rob Peter to pay Paul: take tenths from the church, and give not the poor the twentieths of them. It is not seasonable, nor reasonable charity, to undo whole towns by your usuries, enclosings, oppressions, impropriations; and for a kind of expiation, to give three or four the yearly pension of twenty marks:[24] an almshouse is not so big as a village, nor thy superfluity whereout thou givest, like their necessity whereout thou extortest; he is but poorly charitable, that having made a hundred beggars, relieves two.

8
[A Cheapside Maid]
(Joseph Hall, 1618)

Imagine one of our forefathers were alive again, and should see one of these gay daughters walk in Cheapside before him; what do you think he would think it were? Here is nothing to be seen but a vardingale, a yellow ruff, and a periwig, with perhaps some feather waving in the top; three things for which he could not tell how to find a name. Sure, he could not but stand amazed to think what new creature the times had yielded since he was a man; and if then he should run before her, to see if by the foreside he might guess what it were, when his eyes should meet with a powdered frizzle, a painted hide shadowed with a fan not more painted, breasts displayed, and a loose lock erring wantonly over her shoulders, betwixt a painted cloth, and skin, how would he yet more bless himself to think, what mixture in nature could be guilty of such a monster. . . .

There are three things especially wherein ye are beyond others, and must acknowledge yourselves deeper in the books of God than the rest of the world. Let the first be the clear deliverance from that woeful judgement of the pestilence. Oh, remember those sorrowful times, when every month swept away thousands from among you; when a man could not set forth his foot but into the jaws of death; when piles of carcasses were carried to their pits as dung to the fields; when it was cruelty in the sick to admit visitation, and love was little better than murderous; and by how much more sad and horrible the face of those evil times looked, so much greater proclaim you the mercy of God, in this happy freedom which you now enjoy, that you now throng together into God's house without fear, and breathe in one another's face without danger. The second is the wonderful plenty of all provisions both spiritual and bodily. You are the sea, all the rivers of the land run into you. Of the land? yea of the whole world, sea and land conspire to enrich you. The third is the privilege of careful government. Your charters, as they are large and strong, wherein the favour of princes hath made exceptions from the general rules of their municipal laws, so your form of administration is excellent, and the execution of justice exemplary, and such as might become the mother city of the whole earth.

9
[Dead Souls]
(Francis White, 1619)

And as the city Jerusalem was vouchsafed this voice of Mercy, to win her home by repentance to her God, so this our Jerusalem, this city of ours, a city as unkind to God as ever was Jerusalem, yet hath it voices upon voices sent unto it; it is full of voices, and these voices, with that voice of a crier in the third of Matthew, forewarn us to flee from the wrath to come. Some of these voices cry unto the city, to take heed how she harbours drunkards, lest the land spew out her inhabitants, as a loathsome burden to her stomach. Some of these voices cry unto the city to take heed how she deal with pride, less pride, like Samson, carry away the gates of the city upon her back and betray the strength of the city, whilst with her over-curious clothing she leaves the city bare, and like an ague, having fashions for fits, shakes the commonwealth, whilst she makes her wealth too common for other nations, dearly buying at their hands their strange fashions and new devices, till at last pride get a trip and (if prevention step not in) lay the city's honour in the dust. Some again of these voices cry unto the city to take heed she be not too secure, for the devil is like the usurer: all is well with him, so long as he sees security. . . .

Our citizens complain, it is now a dead world, a dead time, and there is little stirring in the world, little trading; but they may more justly complain in another sense, that it is a dead world indeed, men carrying about with them living bodies, but dead souls. And, there is little stirring in the world, for iniquity hath got the upper hand, and jets above honesty everywhere; so that honesty stirs little abroad, for she hath little trading in the world; while wicked men, who make a trade of sinning by their evil customs, make the greater part of the world their customers. And therefore if ever the Lord's crying voices cried to dead men's ears, to hear the word of the Lord, now is the time; for the greater part of men, like the widow which liveth in pleasure, are dead while they live. And could you but every week have bills brought you in, to signify within the city, liberties, and without, how many souls die in a week, some of a surfeit of drunkenness, some of a swelling tympany[25] of pride, some of the burning fever of malice, some of the dropsy of covetousness, some of one or other disease of the soul, you would bless yourselves, to see most men's bodies to be but living sepulchers for dead souls; and you would pity the great task which is imposed upon the Lord's crying voices, . . . Cry then still, ye voices of the Lord, whom God hath made the city's criers, to cry lost children home again to him their heavenly Father, by repentance.

10
[A Plea to Renew St Paul's]
(John King, 1620)

If England be the ring of Europe, your city is the gem. If England
the body, your city the eye; if England the eye, your city the apple
of it. Here is the synopsis, and sum of the whole kingdom. Here
the distillation, and spirits of all the goodness it hath. Here the
chamber of our British Empire. Here the emporium, principal
mart of all foreign commodities, and staple of home-bred. Here
the garrison, and strength of the land, the magazine and storehouse
of the best of God's blessings. Here (if in any place) are the
wooden walls, and gates of iron. With you is the Tagus and
Pactolus, the river that runneth with gold. You have the body of the
king, the morning and midday influence of that glorious sun;
others' parts have but the evening. His houses of mansion and
station are round about you. You, of all others, are nearest the
heart, for care and protection. Here hath the Lord ordained a
lantern for his anointed. Here are the thrones of David, for judge-
ment, and the chair of Moses, for instruction. *O fortunati
nimium,*[26] you have the finest flower of the wheat, and purest
blood of the grape, that is, the choice of his blessed word, hath
God given unto you, and great is the company of the preachers.
And what shall I say more? *Dies deficeret,* the day would forsake
me, to speak of all. Doth any city on the earth bear her head high,
for any one singular felicity? — *Tendimus in Latium,* I am once
more in Italy. *Dites Venetiae* (say they) *ingens Mediolanum,
superba Genoa, nobilis Neapolis,* rich Venice, great Milan, proud
Genoa, noble Naples, and *Roma caput mundi,* Rome the head of
the world. *Contingat mea Roma mihi,* say I, give me London in
England, which is as a lodestar to lead all the rest. ...

Your city hath been anciently styled *Augusta*; Caesar had to
name Augustus (saith the story) *quia natura hominis amplior,*
because he was more than the nature of man. It may be your city
was more than other cities. I am sure it had not that amplitude and
majesty it now hath.

Not to weary mine eyes with wandering and roving after
private, but to fix upon public alone, when I behold that forest of
masts upon your river for traffic, and that more than miraculous
bridge, which is the *communis terminus,* to join the two banks of
that river; your Royal Exchange for merchants, your halls for com-

panies, your gates for defence, your markets for victual, your
aqueducts for water, your granaries for provision, your hospitals
for the poor, your Bridewells for the idle, your chamber for
orphans, and your churches for holy assemblies; I cannot deny
them to be magnificent works, and your city to deserve the name
of an *Augustious* and majestical city. To cast into the reckoning
those of later edition, the beautifying of your fields without,[27] and
pitching your Smithfield[28] within, new gates,[29] new water-works,[30]
and the like, which have been consecrated by you to the days of his
Majesty's happy reign, and I hope the cleansing of the river, which
is the *vena porta*[31] to your city, will follow in good time. But after
all these, as Christ to the young man in the Gospel, which had
done all and more, *Vnum tibi deest, si vis perfectus esse, vade,*
vende,[32] so may I say to you, there is yet one thing wanting unto
you. If you will be perfect, perfect this church; not by parting from
all, but somewhat, not to the poor, but to God himself. This church
is your Sion indeed, other are but synagogues; this your Jerusalem
the mother to them all, other but daughters brought up at her
knees; this the cathedral, other but parochial churches; this the
Bethel[33] for the daily and constant service of God, other have their
intermissions; this the common to you all, and to this do your
tribes ascend in their greatest solemnities, others appropriated to
several congregations; this the standard in the high road of gaze,
others are more retired; this the mirror and mark of strangers,
other have but their side looks; finally, this unto you, as St Peter's
in the Vatican at Rome, St Mark's at Venice, and that of Diana at
Ephesus, and this at Jerusalem of the Jews; or if there be any other
of glory and fame in the Christian world, which they most joy in.

11
The King's Tower and Triumphant Arch of London
(Samuel Purchas, 1622)

That which the face is to the body, the eye to the face, the sight to
the eye, that is London to England; and as the spirits to the eye, so
should this holy place[34] be to London.

Hail, London! Ave! χαιρε! Salve! Peace be within thy walls and
prosperity within thy palaces. ... Great prosperity giveth He to his
king,[35] and where should he bestow it but in the repositorium and

chamber of his kingdom? There hath He set the thrones for judge-
ment, the thrones of the house of David.[36] The Tower of thy king
is in the east for thy safety, the bower and palace of thy king is in
the west for light and majesty; in the middest[37] is thy Guildhall for
justice; besides thee is Westminster Hall that bringeth the whole
kingdom to thee and maketh thy terms and vacations[38] as another
Thames, ebbing and flowing (many people are compared to many
waters).[39] How many gentlemen and noblemen walk with thee into
the fields? How many lawyers sit on thy skirts and suburbs? How
many countrymen, and men of many countries, in thy shops and
markets, quays and custom house? How many companies com-
bined into one company, and now here one congregation? How
many storehouses of provision? How many warehouses of wealth?
How many hospitals for poor? How many halls for rich? How
many temples for devotion? — to omit thy Gresham College
within thee and that Chelsea College in thy borders,[40] a tower of
Sion intended against the tower of Babylon and the quarry of these
our building stones, the very place to our arguments and these
meditations. How hath London enlarged itself beyond the walls,
the butts and bounds of art! beyond the Thames, the bounds of
nature! beyond herself, as it were, sowing Londons in the fields
and villages, beautified by her retiring palaces! *Pars minima est
ipsa puella sui.*[41] Thy bridge is a multitude of towers whose
ambition seemeth to scorn so base a foundation as earth, and, with
a miracle of art (like the Babylonian pensile gardens), not only
joineth City and Borough,[42] but is another city or borough betwixt
both, aspireth into the air, domineereth over the water, and with a
multitude of captived subject fires taketh revenge on that fire
which sometimes destroyed her forest, that is, turned her timber
into stone; which marrieth with a happy conjunction two shires,[43]
and is the semi-circled marriage ring, with twenty semi-circled
arches embossed and with so many piles, as jewels, adorned. How
hath the Water[44] conspired, with art and man's help, to make a
new journey to London, and with a New River sweetened and
cleansed thy streets and houses? How are thy Moorfields nor
moors nor fields any more, but pleasant walks,[45] and, in com-
parison of the former, a petty paradise? Thy Smithfield hath
washed her sooty, mucky filthy face and is made lovely.[46] Thine
Exchange also hath multiplied.[47] What shall I say? *Inopem te* — at
least, *inopem me copia fecit.*[48] When wert thou so long together
delivered from the devouring pestilence? Hast thou not so many

liveries, as the livery of thy freedom? so many scarlets, as banners and ensigns of thy power? the diligence of officers, prudence of counsellors, gravity of aldermen, hospitality of magistrates, magnificence of pomps, sanctity of courts to adorn thee? I could add thy varieties of materials and fashions of attire, if thou didst not hereby mis-fashion and deform thee, thy buildings also now becoming towers indeed.

12
After Our Dispersion, by the Sickness
(John Donne, 1625/1661)

Beloved, as God impaled[49] a Goshen in Egypt, a place for the righteous amongst the wicked, so there is an Egypt in every Goshen, nests of snakes in the fairest gardens, and even in this city (which in the sense of the gospel, we may call, the Holy City, as Christ called Jerusalem, though she had multiplied transgressions, the Holy City, because she had not cast away his law, though she had disobeyed it; so howsoever your sins have provoked God, yet as you retain a zealous profession of the truth of his religion, I may in His name, and do in the bowels of His mercy, call you, the Holy City) even in this city, no doubt but the hand of God fell upon thousands in this deadly infection, who were no more affected with it, than those Egyptians, to cry out, *Omnes moriemur*, we can but die, and we must die: And, *Edamus, et bibamus, cras moriemur*, let us eat and drink, and take our pleasure, and make our profits, for tomorrow we shall die,[50] and so were cut off by the hand of God, some even in their robberies, in half-empty houses, and in their lusts and wantonness in licentious houses; and so took in infection and death, like Judas's sop,[51] death-dipped and soaked in sin. Men whose lust carried them into the jaws of infection in lewd houses, and seeking one sore perished with another; men whose rapine and covetousness broke into houses, and seeking the wardrobes of others, found their own winding-sheet, in the infection of that house where they stole their own death; men who sought no other way to divert sadness, but strong drink in riotous houses, and there drank up David's cup of malediction,[52] the cup of condemned men, of death, in the infection of that place. For these men that died in their sins, that sinned in their dying, that

sought and hunted after death so sinfully, we have little comfort of
such men, in the phrase of this text, They were dead; for they are
dead still: As Moses said of the Egyptians, I am afraid we may say
of these men, we shall see them no more for ever.[53]

Notes

1. See Isaiah 15:2; Jeremiah 48:1.
2. Indulging, pampering.
3. Suffer.
4. Insulting.
5. I say you are gods; see Psalm 82:6–7.
6. Retinue, multitude.
7. According to a myth perpetrated by Holinshed's *Chronicles* (1577), the dagger in the City's arms commemorated the slaying of Jack Straw by William Walworth, Lord Mayor, in 1381 (see 2.13, above; 10.2, below).
8. A snake is concealed in the grass.
9. They keep off the drones, a lazy lot, from the beehives: see Vergil, *Georgics* 4:168.
10. The braggart soldier in Plautus's *Eunuchus*.
11. An excess of (lit. a foot and a half of) words.
12. You too.
13. See 2 Samuel 16:5–8.
14. I shudder to mention it; see Vergil *Aeneid* 2.204.
15. See Cicero's First Oration against Catiline.
16. Ben Jonson.
17. A winding river in Phrygia.
18. See 2 Kings 19:37.
19. Psalms 16:6.
20. Isaiah 1:21.
21. I.e. hypocrisy.
22. The Exchange.
23. Hypocritically.
24. £13.13.4d.
25. Tumour.
26. O fortunate in abundance.
27. Moorfields, laid out with walks in 1605.
28. Smithfield market was paved and railed in the summer of 1615.
29. Aldgate was rebuilt 1607–1609.
30. The New River project, carried out by Hugh Myddleton, was completed in 1613.
31. The main (essential) gate.
32. See Matthew 19:21.
33. See Genesis 12:8.
34. The pulpit at Paul's Cross.
35. See Psalms 122.7.
36. See Psalms 122.5.
37. Midmost.
38. Of the law courts.
39. See Revelation 17:1, 15.

40. Gresham College, founded in 1597, offered public lectures in divinity, civil law, astronomy, music, geometry, rhetoric and physic. Chelsea College, or 'King James's College at Chelsea', was founded in 1610, 'that learned men there might have maintenance to answer all the adversaries of religion'.

41. The smallest part is her very daughter.

42. London and Southwark.

43. Middlesex and Surrey.

44. See n.30 above.

45. See n.27 above.

46. See n.28 above.

47. A second Exchange, called Britain's Borse, opened in the Strand in 1609.

48. Your plenty makes you — makes me, at least — poor; see Ovid, *Metamorphoses*, 3.466.

49. Enclosed, protected.

50. Isaiah 22:13.

51. See John 13:26–7.

52. See Psalms, 11:6, 75:8.

53. Exodus 14:13.

5

LONDON IN JEST: FROM THE JESTBOOKS

Shortly before his death, in *The Dialogue of Comfort*, Thomas More confessed that he was often 'refreshed with a merry foolish tale'. From More's lifetime onward, his countrymen became increasingly avid connoisseurs of facetious stories and apothegms, which were gathered in volumes of 'merry tales', to which Horace Walpole later gave the enduring name of 'jest-books'. From the handful of largely anonymous sixteenth-century collections to the several dozen volumes churned out by popular writers in the earlier seventeenth century, the steady proliferation of the genre was a response to the ever-widening appeal of popular humour in the printed medium. London and Londoners bulk large in this literature, providing a rich, varied and plausible background peopled with prentices, pranksters, Puritans, bumpkins and sharp-tongued wives.

John Taylor, the Water-Poet, who produced several volumes of jests, claimed his materials were 'chargeably collected out of taverns, ordinaries, inns, bowling greens and alleys, alehouses, tobacco shops, highways and water passages'. But in fact, few jokes belong exclusively to Tudor–Stuart London. Frequently repeated, and often plagiarised or translated from earlier collections, Renaissance jests belong rather to a timeless tradition. Diogenes the Cynic was a notably demonstrative jester, as was Socrates, and both Cicero and Quintilian thought it necessary to discuss and demonstrate at length the uses of humour in Roman oratory. Nevertheless, the compilation of jests is largely a post-classical activity, begun in the fifth century by Hierocles of Alexandria and exhaustively pursued by late-medieval preachers, who, like the Roman rhetoricians before them, insisted on the usefulness of a well-placed tale. In these collections of moralised *exempla* and salty *fablieaux*, the Tudor–Stuart humourists found a major source of inspiration. At the same time, however, they were influenced by a second, more recent development — the

119

cultivation of humour among such literary figures as Boccaccio and
Poggio Bracciolini, whose *Facetiae* (1477), a collection of
non-moralising and often scurrilous tales, was translated by
Caxton as *The Fables of Poge the Florentyn* in 1484.

In the new humanistic fashion, which stressed verbal wit in
quick ripostes and clever retorts, lay a vein of humour particularly
well suited to the Renaissance image of urban life. The very titles
of such English collections as *Witty Questions and Quick Answers*
(1567) or *Conceits, Clenches, Flashes and Whimsies* (1639) pay
tribute to the sharp thinking and witty improvisation that
proverbially stamped an urbanite for membership in a competitive
and fast-changing community. Robert Chamberlain noted that
among the varieties of jests 'there be quips, taunts, retorts, flouts,
frumps, mocks, jibes, jests, jeers, etc.', and thereby singled out
precisely those modes of wit by which one man gets the better of
another. Indeed, no less than other forms of urban behaviour, the
well-timed quip was seen as a timely mastery of adverse
circumstance. Machiavelli had concluded that forceful and cunning
improvisation could conquer and shape the vagaries of fortune.
This theory is borne out in countless London jests, in which a last,
unanswerable word, delivered with instinctual savvy and style,
extricates scolds, apprentices, criminals, servants and beggars from
ticklish situations.

A related form of improvisation is the artful, often profitable
stratagem, which enables a rogue like Tarlton to extract a dinner
invitation from my Lord Mayor, or a wily client to turn the tables
on his lawyer by carrying some legal advice to its logical
conclusion. The obverse of such witty triumphs, of course, is the
experience of the victim, and especially the timeless experience of
the homespun rustic, newly-arrived in a bewildering labyrinth
where wallets disappear, stones are tied up and dogs set free, and
where a splendid church can cost 'forty shillings' and more.
Beneath the aggression and adversity, however, lies a deeper sense
of community, and if the Londoners of the jests are at times
divided by their common pursuit of the last word or shilling, they
are just as often reconciled in the equality of laughter. And so,
repeatedly, the narratives explicitly remind us that 'all the audience
made great laughter'.

But if the conclusion of a jest — whether it ends in a victory for
mother wit or in reconciling laughter — is a triumph for coherence
and cohesiveness, the body of a jest is frequently a scene of

confrontation, entanglement or disorientation. The London jests included here turn frequently on awkward, sometimes painful confrontations between the powerful and the impotent, the wealthy and the poor, the established and the marginal. In large measure, the humour of these urban jests arises from the anxious moment when the fissures and divisions in social life are laid bare, when a wastrel stands before the sheriff, or when a group of fastidious gentlemen encounter a particularly unsavoury night-soil crew in the middle of the night. Though safely defused by harmless resolutions, such jests reveal the deeper sources of urban humour in London's own rough and many-threaded social fabric.

One final aspect of London emerges in the titular heroes whose lives and deeds sometimes provide a loose framework around which tales may be gathered. The prototype for this convention is the Til Eulenspiel of popular German tradition, who made his English debut as *Howleglass* no later than 1528, and who was followed by such pranksters and wits as Skelton, Scogin, Tarlton, Armin, George Dobson of Durham, George a Greene the Pinder of Wakefield, and George Peele and his barber associate Anthony Nit. A number of these figures — especially such professional jesters as Skelton and Tarlton — were closely associated with London. Tarlton's feats fall into three parts, one of which comprises 'His Sound City Jests', and the Rabelaisian Mother Bunch of *Pasquil's Jests* (1604) 'dwelled ... in Cornhill (near the Exchange) and sold strong ale'; when she laughed, 'she was heard from Aldgate to the monuments at Westminster, and all Southwark stood in amazement'.

Of such figures, Long Meg of Westminster and Old Hobson the merry Londoner, both given special emphasis in the selection which follows, exhibit in vivid abundance the comic traits associated with Londoners. On the surface, no two characters could be more unlike. The avuncular Hobson, a wealthy haberdasher, wrapped comfortably in his flap-eared cap and ancient slippers, seems never to have known insecurity; he handles Mistress Hobson, his apprentices or his civic superiors with the same jovial ease. The excitable Meg, by contrast, makes her way through London wielding a cudgel. Newly-arrived from Lancashire and taken into service at the Eagle in Westminster, she pays the press-money to release Harry the hosteller from conscription, and goes in his stead to the wars in France, where she leads a successful attack of laundresses on Boulogne. Happily married and awarded a royal pension of 8 pence a year for life, she opens a cheerful establishment in Islington. Though Meg begins her career on the margins of London life, she ends it (in her own way), like Hobson, at its prosperous centre. And though she lacks Hobson's unruffled temperament, she shares with him an enterprising self-confidence, generosity, tolerance and a sense of fair play that transcends the law. In Meg and Hobson, as in the countless cuckolds, dupes and pranksters of their rich jest-book lore, Londoners could thus find a crucial thread of their common life, and could agree with Thomas More that 'a merry tale with a friend refresheth a man much, and without any harm lighteth his mind, and amendeth his courage and his stomach, so that it seemeth but well done to take such recreation'.

1
Of Philip Spencer the Butcher's Man
(from *A Hundred Merry Tales*, 1525)

A certain butcher dwelling in Saint Nicholas Fleshshambles in London, called Paul, had a servant called Peter. This Peter on a Sunday was at the church hearing mass; and one of his fellows, whose name was Philip Spencer, was sent to call him at the commandment of his master. So it happened at the time that the curate preached, and in his sermon touched many authorities of the Holy Scriptures, among all, the words of the Epistle of Saint Paul ad Philippenses: how we be not only bound to believe in Christ but also to suffer for Christ's sake; and he said these words in the pulpit: 'What sayeth Paul ad Philippenses to this?' This young man, that was called Philip Spenser, had went[1] he had spoken of him and answered shortly and said, 'Marry, sir, he bade Peter come home and take his part of a pudding, and he should go for a calf anon.' The curate hearing this, was abashed, and all the audience made great laughter.

2
Of the Friar in the Pulpit that Bade the Woman Leave her Babbling
(from *A Hundred Merry Tales*, 1525)

In a certain parish church in London, after the old laudable and accustomed manner, there was a friar minor; although he were not the best clerk, nor could not make the best sermons, yet by the licence of the curate he there preached to the parishens [parishioners]. Among the which audience there was a wife at that time little disposed to contemplation, who talked with a gossip of hers of other feminine tales so loud that the friar heard and somewhat was perturbed therewith. To whom therefore openly the friar spake and said, 'Thou woman there in the tawny gown, hold thy peace and leave thy babbling; thou troublest the word of God.' This woman therewith suddenly abashed, because the friar spake to her so openly, that all the people her beheld, answered shortly and said, 'I beshrew his heart that babbleth more of us two.' At the which saying the people did laugh, because they felt but little fruit in his sermon.

3
Of Him that Lost His Purse in London
(from *Tales and Quick Answers*, 1535)

A certain man of the country, the which for business came up to London, lost his purse as he went late in the evening; and because the sum therein was great, he set up bills in divers places that, if any man of the city had found the purse and would bring it again to him, he should have well for his labour. A gentleman of the Temple wrote under one of the bills, how the man should come to his chamber, and told him where. So, when he was come, the gentleman asked him first what was in the purse; secondly, what countryman he was; and thirdly, what was his name? 'Sir,' quod he, 'twenty nobles was in the purse; I am half a Welshman; and my name is John up Jankyn.' 'John up Jankyn,' said the gentleman, 'I am glad I know thy name, for so long as I live, thou nor none of thine name shall have my purse to keep; and now farewell, gentle John up Jankyn.' Thus he was mocked to scorn and went his way.

4
[A Country Man in London]
(from *The Sackful of News*, 1557/1673)

There was a man in the country, who had not been any far traveller and dwelt far from any church, except a church that was

seven or eight miles from his house, and there they never sung
mass nor evensong, but did ever say it. And on a time he came to
London, having never been here before, and being in London, he
went to Paul's church, and went into the chapel, where they sung
mass with organs; and when he heard the melody of the organs
and the singing together, that he never heard before, he thought he
should have gone to heaven by and by, and looked and said aloud
that everyone heard: 'O Lord, shall I go to heaven presently? I
would thou wouldst let me alone, till I might go home and fetch my
white stick and black hood, and then I would go gladly with thee.'
Whereat all the people laughed heartily.

5
[An Essex Man in London]
(from *The Sackful of News*, 1557/1673)

There was an Essex man came to London, who had a pair of shoes
full of nails, and as he went along Cheapside he passed by a mer-
chant's house where many young men were at the door, and
among the rest one of them perceived that the man had nails in his
shoes, whereupon he said to him: 'Thou churl, why comest thou
hither with thy nailed shoes, and breakest the stones of our streets?
Indeed I will show my Lord Mayor of it.' When the countryman
heard him, he put off his shoes, and carried them in his hand, and
went in his hose till he came to Paul's; whereat everybody laughed.
And when he perceived that the people laughed at him, he put on
his shoes again.

6
How a Man Told Scogin, that he Thought the Building of Paul's
Cost Forty Shillings
(from *Scogin's Jests*, 1565/1626)

On a time a poor man did come to London to speak with Scogin,
and Scogin had him to Paul's church to talk with him, and both
walked round about the church. The poor man said, 'Here is a
godly church.' 'Yea,' said Scogin, 'what do you think it cost
making?' The poor husbandman said, 'I trow it cost forty shilling.'
'Yea,' said Scogin, 'that it did, and forty shilling thereto.' 'Ho

there,' said the poor man. Here a man may see that a little portion of money is a great sum in a poor man's purse; and he that is ignorant in a matter, should be no judge.

7
Where Meg Was Born, her Coming up to London, and her Usage to the Honest Carrier
(from *Long Meg of Westminster*, 1582)

In the reign of Henry VIII was born in Lancashire a maid called Long Meg. At eighteen years old she came to London to get her a service. Father Willis the carrier, being the wagoner and her neighbour, brought her up with some other lasses. After a tedious journey, being in sight of the desired city she demanded the cause why they looked sad. 'We have no money,' said one, 'to pay our fare.' So Meg replies, 'If that be all, I shall answer your demands,' and this put them in some comfort. But as soon as they came to St John's Street, Willis demanded their money. 'Say what you will have,' quoth she. 'Ten shillings a piece,' said he. 'But we have not so much about us,' said she. 'Nay, then I will have it out of your bones.' 'Marry, content,' replied Meg; and taking a staff in her hand, so belaboured him and his man, that he desired her for God's sake to hold her hand. 'Not I,' said she, 'unless you bestow an angel on us for good luck, and swear ere we depart to get us good mistresses.'

The carrier having felt the strength of her arm, thought it best to give her the money, and promised not to go till he had got them good places.

8
Her Usage of the Bailiff of Westminster, Who Came into her Mistress's and Arrested her Friend

A bailiff, having for the purpose took forty shillings, arrested a gentleman in Meg's mistress's house and desired the company to keep peace. She coming in asked what was the matter? 'O,' said he 'I'm arrested.' 'Arrested! and in our house! why this is an unkind act to arrest one in our house; but however, take an angel and let him go.' 'No,' said the bailiff, 'I cannot, for the creditor is at the door.' 'Bid him come down,' says she, 'and I'll make up the matter.' So the creditor came in; but being found obstinate, she rapped him on the head with a quart pot and bid him go out of doors like a knave. 'He can but go to prison,' quoth she, 'where he shall not stay long, if all the friends I have can fetch him out.'

The creditor went away with a good knock, and the bailiff was going with his prisoner. 'Nay,' said she, 'I'll bring a fresh pot to drink with him.' She came into the parlour with a rope, and knitting her brows, 'Sir knave,' said she, 'I'll learn thee to arrest a man in our house; I'll make thee a spectacle for all catchpoles';[2] and tossing the rope round his middle, said to the gentleman, 'Sir, away, shift for yourself; I'll pay the bailiff his fees before he and I part.' Then she dragged the bailiff into the back side of the house, making him go up to the chin in a pond, and then paid him his fees with a cudgel; after which he went away with the amends in his hands; for she was so well beloved that no person would meddle with her.

9
Of her Keeping House at Islington, and her Laws

After marriage she kept a house at Islington. The constable coming at night, he would needs search Meg's house, whereupon she came down in her shift, with a cudgel, and said, 'Mr Constable, take care you go not beyond your commission, for if you do I'll so cudgel you as never since in Islington has been.' The constable seeing her frown, told her he would take her word, and so departed.

Meg, because in her house there should be a good decorum, hung up a table, containing these principles:

First, if a gentleman or yeoman had a charge[3] about him, and told her of it, she would repay him if he lost it, but if he did not reveal it, and said he was robbed, he should have ten bastinadoes, and afterwards be turned out of doors.

Secondly, whoever called for meat, and had no money to pay, should have a box on the ear and a cross on the back that he might be marked and trusted no more.

Thirdly, if any good fellow came in and said he wanted money, he should have his bellyful of meat and two pots of drink.

Fourthly, if any wrastler came in, and made a quarrel, and would not pay his reckoning, to turn into the fields and try a bout or two with Meg; the maiden of the house should dry beat[4] him, and thrust him out of doors.

These and many such principles, she established in her house, which she kept still and quiet.

10
Master Hobson's Description
(Richard Johnson, 1607)

In the beginning of Queen Elizabeth's most happy reign, our late deceased sovereign, under whose peaceful government long flourished this our country of England, there lived in the city of London a merry citizen, named old Hobson, a haberdasher of small wares, dwelling at the lower end of Cheapside, in the Poultry, as well-known through this part of England as a sergeant knows the Counter[5] gate. He was a homely plain man, most commonly wearing a buttoned cap close to his ears, a short gown girt hard about his middle, and a pair of slippers upon his feet of an ancient fashion; as for his wealth, it was answerable to the better sort of our citizens, but of so merry a disposition that his equal therein is hardly to be found.

11
Of Master Hobson's Proverbs

Not many years since there was Sir John Baines (not by the common voice of the City) chosen Sheriff of London, which man in former times had been Master Hobson's prentice; and riding along the street with the other aldermen about the City business [he] was saluted by Master Hobson in this manner: 'Bones a God man! what a cock-horse knave! and thy master afoot; here's the world turned upside down.' Sir John Baines, hearing this his master's merry salutation, passed along with a pleasant smile, making no answer at all. Upon slight regard, Master Hobson took occasion to say as followeth: 'Here's pride rides on horseback, whilst humility goes afoot.' In speaking these words, came four other aldermen riding after Master Sheriff, whose names were these: Alderman Ramsey, Alderman Bond, Alderman Beecher and Alderman Cooper, at whose passage by he made this pleasant rhyme:

1. Ramsey the rich　　2. Bond the stout
3. Beecher the gentleman　　4. and Cooper the lout.

This pleasant rhyme, so suddenly spoken by Master Hobson, is to this day accounted for his proverb in London.

12
How Master Hobson Allowed his Wife Two Men to Wait on her to the Market

As Master Hobson increased in riches, so increased his wife in pride, in such sort that she would seldom go out of doors without her man before her. Upon a time, having business to Cheapside market amongst many other of her neighbours, the more to show her haughty stomach,[6] [she] desired of her husband that she might have her man to attend her; who, seeing her disposition, willingly consented thereunto, and thereupon called two of his lustiest[7] men, put them in armour with two brown bills[8] on their necks, placing one of them before her, the other after, and so proferred to send her forth to market. She, in a niceness[9], took such displeasure hereat, that for a month after she lay sick in her bed and would eat nothing but caudles[10] made of muscadine.[11]

13
How Master Hobson Found Out the Pie Stealer

In Christmas holidays, when Master Hobson's wife had many pies in the oven, one of his servants had stole one of them out and at the tavern had merrily eaten it. It fortuned that same day some of his friends dined with him, and one of the best pies were missing, the stealer whereof at after dinner he found out in this manner. He called all his servants in friendly sort together into the hall, and caused each of them to drink one to another both wine, ale and beer, till they were all drunk; then caused he a table to be furnished with very good cheer, whereat he likewise pleased them. Being set all together, he said, 'Why sit you not down, fellows?' 'We be set already,' quoth they. 'Nay,' quoth Master Hobson, 'He that stole the pie is not yet set.' 'Yes, that I do,' quoth he that stole it; by which means he knew what was become of the pie; for the poor fellow being drunk could not keep his own secrets.

14
How Tarlton Bade Himself to Dinner to My Lord Mayor's (from *Tarlton's Jests* 1609/1638)

A jest came in Tarlton's head where to dine, and thought he: 'In all that a man does, let him aim at the fairest, for sure, if I bid myself anywhere this day, it shall be to my Lord Mayor's.' And upon this goes to the Counter[12] and entered his action against my Lord Mayor, who was presently told of it and sends for him. Tarlton waits [until] dinner time, and then comes; who was admitted presently. 'Master Tarlton,' says my Lord Mayor, 'Have you entered an action against me in the Poultry Counter?' 'My Lord,' says Tarlton, 'Have you entered an action against me in Wood-street Counter?' 'Not I, in troth,' says my Lord. 'No?' says Tarlton, 'He was a villain that told me so then; but if it be not so, forgive me this fault, my Lord, and I will never offend in the next.' But in the end he begins to swear how he will be revenged on him that mocked him and flings out in a rage. But my Lord said, 'Stay, M. Tarlton, dine with me, and no doubt but after dinner you will be better minded.' 'I will try that, my lord,' says Tarlton, 'and, if it alter mine anger, both mine enemy and I will thank you together for this courtesy.'

15
How Tarlton Jested at His Wife

Tarlton and his wife, keeping an ordinary in Paternoster Row, were bidden out to supper; and because he was a man noted, she would not go with him in the street, but entreats him to keep to one side, and she another, which he consented to. But as he went, he would cry out to her and say, 'Turn that way, wife,' and anon, 'On this side, wife'; so the people flocked the more to laugh at them. But his wife, more than mad angry, goes back again and almost forswore his company.

16
Tarlton's Greeting with Banks His Horse

There was one Banks, in the time of Tarlton, who served the Earl
of Essex, and had a horse of strange qualities, and being at the
Cross Keys in Gracious[13] Street, getting money with him, as he was
mightily resorted to. Tarlton then, with his fellows, playing at the
Bell[14] by, came into the Cross Keys, amongst many people, to see
fashions; which Banks perceiving, to make the people laugh, says,
'Signior,' to his horse, 'Go fetch me the veriest fool in the com-
pany.' The jade comes immediately, and with his mouth draws
Tarlton forth. Tarlton, with merry words, said nothing but 'God a
mercy horse.' In the end, Tarlton, seeing the people laugh so, was
angry inwardly and said, 'Sir, had I power of your horse, as you
have, I would do more than that.' 'Whate'er it be,' said Banks, to
please him, 'I will charge him to do it.' Then says Tarlton, 'Charge
him to bring me the veriest whoremaster in this company.' The
horse leads his master to him. Then 'God a mercy horse, indeed,'
says Tarlton. The people had much ado to keep peace; but Banks
and Tarlton had like to have squared, and the horse to give aim.
But ever after it was a byword through London, 'God a mercy horse',
and is to this day.

17
A Poor Beggar's Answer to a Rich Citizen
(from *Pasquil's Jests*, 1609)

A poor beggar that was foul, black and loathsome to behold came
to a rich citizen and asked his alms. To whom the citizen said, 'I
pray thee get thee hence from me, for thou lookest as though thou
camest out of hell.' The poor man, perceiving he could get
nothing, answered: 'Forsooth, sir, you say troth, I came out of hell
indeed.' 'Why didst thou not tarry there still?' quoth the citizen.
'Marry, sir,' quoth the beggar, 'there is no room for such poor
beggars as I am; all is kept for such gentlemen as you are.'

18
The Subtlety of a Lawyer Repaid with the Like Subtlety
(from *Pasquil's Jests*, 1609)

There was an unthrift in London that had received of a merchant
certain wares which came to fifty pounds, to pay at three months,
but when he had it, he consumed and spent it all; so that at the three
months' end there was not any left to pay the merchant; wherefore
the merchant arrested him. When he saw there was no other
remedy but either to pay the debt or go to prison, he sent to a sub-
tle lawyer, and asked his counsel how he might clear himself of
that debt. 'What wilt thou give me,' quoth he, 'if I do?' 'Five
marks,' quoth the other, 'and here it is; and as soon as you have
done you shall have it.' 'Well,' said the lawyer, 'but thou must be
ruled by my counsel and do thus; when thou comest before the
judge, whatsoever he sayeth unto thee, answer thou nothing, but
cry "Bea" still, and let me alone with the rest.' So when he came
before the judge, he said to the debter: 'Dost thou owe this mer-
chant so much money?' 'Bea,' quoth he. 'What, beast,' quoth he,
'answer to that I ask thee.' 'Bea!' quoth he again. 'Why, how now?'
quoth the Judge, 'I think this fellow hath gotten a sheep's tongue in
his head, for he answers in the sheep's language.' 'Why, sir,' quoth
the lawyer, 'do you think this merchant that is so wise a man would
be so foolish as to trust this idiot with fifty pounds' worth of ware,
that can speak never a word? no, sir, I warrant you'; and so per-
suaded the judge to cast[15] the merchant in his own suit. And so the
judge departed, and the court brake up. Then the lawyer came to
his client and asked him his money, since his promise was per-
formed and his debt discharged.

'Bea,' quoth he. 'Why, thou needst not cry Bea any longer, but
pay me my money.' 'Bea,' quoth he again. 'Why, thou wilt not
serve me so, I hope,' quoth the lawyer, 'now I have used thee so
kindly.' But nothing but 'Bea' could master lawyer get for his
pains, and so was fain to depart.

19
[Courtiers, Citizens and Lawyers]
(attr. to Sir Francis Bacon)

In eighty-eight [1588], when the queen went from Temple Bar

along Fleet Street, the lawyers were ranked on one side, and the companies of the city on the other. Said Master Bacon to a lawyer that stood next to him, 'Do but observe the courtiers; if they bow first to the citizens, they are in debt; if first to us, they are in law.'

20
[Dogs and Stones]
(John Taylor, 1629)

A country fellow that had not walked much in streets that were paved came to London, where a dog came suddenly out of a house and furiously ran at him. The fellow stooped to take up a stone to cast at the dog, and finding them all fast rammed or paved in the ground, quoth he, 'What strange country am I in, where the people tie up the stones, and let the dogs loose.'

21
[Cheaper Without]
(John Taylor, 1629)

A gentlewoman cheapened a close-stool[16] in Paul's churchyard, and the shopkeeper did ask her too much money for it, as she thought. 'Why, mistress,' said he, 'I pray you consider what a good lock and key it hath.' She replied, that she had small use for either lock or key, for she purposed to put nothing into it but what she cared not who stole out.

22
A Welshman's Strange News
(from *A Banquet of Jests*, 1633)

A Welshman having been at London, his friend, according to the common custom, at his return demanded of him what news; who answered that he knew little news, only one strange thing he observed there, that every little boy of five or six years old could speak English perfectly, which he thought very strange, because in his country they learn to speak it as in England they learn to speak French, Italian, and the like.

23
[A Quick Answer]
(from *Conceits, Clinches, Flashes and Whimsies*, 1639)

One passing through Cheapside, a poor woman desired his charity; he, disregarding the woman, kept on walking, and by and by let a ****. The woman, hearing it, said, 'Much good may it do your worship.' He, hearing her say so, turns back and gives her a tester:[17] she thanked him, and told his worship it was a bad wind that did blow nobody good.

24
[Beggars and Brooms]
(from *Conceits, Clinches, Flashes, and Whimsies*, 1639)

One asked why beggars stood in the streets begging with brooms in their hands. It was answered, 'Because they did with them sweep away the dirt out of people's sight, which while they had a mind on they would never part with a penny.'

25
[Ready Reply]
(from *Conceits, Clinches, Flashes and Whimsies*, 1639)

A fellow going down Ludgate Hill, his heels by chance slipping from him, fell upon his breech. One standing by told him London stones were stout and scornful. 'It may be so,' quoth he, 'Yet I made them to kiss my breech, as stout as they were.'

26
Of a Jakes-Farmer Working in the Night
(Robert Chamberlain, 1637)

Certain of those people whom, for modesty's sake, we call gold-finders, being emptying of an house of office,[18] and their carts with their standing tubs blocking the streets, some gentlemen, not able to endure the smell and were to pass that way, flung their cloaks over their faces; which one of them observing, said, 'If you would always keep your tails shut, you should not now have occasion to stop your noses.'

27
Of a Puritan
(Robert Chamberlain, 1637)

One of the tribe coming into Newgate market to buy a cheese of the cheesemonger, and after he had seen two or three several cheeses, the master of the shop desired him to taste of them, to see which he liked best; and putting the taste of the cheese to his mouth, he put off his hat, and began a long grace, which the cheesemonger seeing, snatched up his cheese and said, 'Nay sir, since you, instead of a taste, mean to make a dinner of my cheese, you shall buy none of me, for I did not buy it after that rate.'

Notes

1. Weened, thought.
2. Petty officers, bum bailiffs.
3. A load of money or goods.
4. Beat without drawing blood.
5. The Wood Street Counter and the Poultry Counter were two City gaols in which debtors, especially, were tried and incarcerated.
6. Demeanour.
7. Finest.
8. Pikes.
9. Temper.
10. Hot toddies.
11. Strong, sweet white wine.
12. The City court.
13. Gracechurch Street.
14. Plays were performed in the yard of the Bell Inn, located on the west side of Gracechurch Street, between Lombard Street and Cornhill.
15. Convict, find against.
16. Bargained for a commode.
17. Sixpence.
18. Excrement.

6

SONGS OF THE STREETS:
BROADSIDE BALLADS

In the history of the broadside ballad, the discovery of the urban landscape is bound together with the development of urban literacy and with the printing, folding and cutting of paper. Broadsides — works printed on one side of a single sheet of paper — and broadsheets — printed on both sides — were commonly licensed to the poorest of printers and were the cheapest form of reading available. Folded once, twice or more, such sheets made small pamphlets, called cheap-books or chapbooks, in which were published songs, ballads, sermons, jests and almanacs — a variety of works in prose and verse that shade off, as one historian has noted, toward the ephemeral form of the newspaper and towards the more permanent form of the best-seller. An early means of rapid, cheap and widespread communication, the broadside was perhaps the form of literary reproduction most clearly linked to the explosive, physical and demographic growth of the early modern city.

An essential feature of the protean, prolific nature of the broadside ballad form was its proximity to oral communication. It borrowed, first of all, many of its concerns and formulae from an oral tradition of popular ballads and folk songs; but just as important, even though it was printed, it was printed in such fragile, perishable form that its writers were uninhibited by the possibility of permanence. Continuing to embody the refrains, the seriatim narratives and lists of popular songs, written to be sung to oft-repeated tunes, and dealing with oft-repeated matters, broadsides were printed on a sheet which, turned over, revealed that yet more (usually a 'second part') followed, and which could be mechanically reproduced and imitated *ad infinitum*. These sheets could be posted as decoration, and not uncommonly dozens of them adorned the walls of taverns and alehouses, from ceiling to floor. Occupying a boundary between print and oral culture, they were perhaps more democratic than other literary forms; they were meant to have wide, popular appeal, and they were addressed to familiar and topical matters that did not exclude hearers for social or religious reasons. No doubt a substantial part of their audience was made up of literate urban craftsmen (perhaps 40 per cent of whom could read) as well as illiterate labourers who listened in.

But there is much to suggest that the appeal of ballads transcended boundaries of wealth and status. Snatches of ballads are sung throughout Shakespeare's plays, by characters ranging from Sir Toby Belch and Edgar to Ophelia and Desdemona. The dramatic portraiture of ballad-sellers, like Autolycus in Shakespeare's *The Winter's Tale* or Nightingale in Jonson's *Bartholomew Fair* (see 14.4) implies that they were a common feature of the landscape. The names of more than 200 ballad-writers and sellers survive from the sixteenth century, and for the seventeenth century the number is 250. In all, more than 3,000 ballads were licensed for publication between 1557 and 1709; allowing for unlicensed publication, one scholar estimates that perhaps 15,000 were in circulation.

Given these numbers and the scope of the ballad audience, it is not surprising that the subjects of ballads are nearly infinite. They include topical events, politics, sensational crimes, monstrous births and prodigies, and history (John Aubrey said his nurse could recite English history from the Conquest to Charles I in ballads); popular fiction and domestic matters; Jeremiads, devotional meditations and moralisings on vanities; merry tales and lyrics dealing with love and courtship. Eulogies on virtuous citizens (see 10.1 and 10.2) appealed especially to Londoners, as did praises of the city (see Chapter 2), tributes to heroes like Dick Whittington (see 10.6), and exhortations and warnings to apprentices. The colloquial style of the ballad made it an attractive vehicle for satire and social protest: a major ballad strain, for which the manuscript poem 'London Lickpenny' (6.1 below) is the prototype, recounts the misadventures of simple country-folk in the wicked metropolis. The low style of the ballad could also become the basis for effective parody, as it does in Suckling's famous 'Ballad of a Wedding'.

As a form of street literature, the broadsheet often incorporates elements of London's oral culture. Ballad singers and peddlers belonged to a group that included performers, minstrels (recent work has turned up in parish registers the names of more than 100 Elizabethan Londoners who styled themselves 'minstrel'), and street vendors. One popular ballad-type actually compiled lists or inventories of street cries. 'Turner's Dish of Lenten Stuff' is only one in a series that includes 'A Merry New Catch of All Trades' and 'The Trader's Medley, or The Cries of London'. The music of the streets even found its way into fantasies on sellers' cries by such court musicians as John Dowland and Thomas Ravenscroft, one of whose songs is included at 6.3 below. But with its open-ended, inclusive nature, and its serial structure derived from oral mnemonics, the ballad was used not just to echo street cries but to compile extensive catalogues of taverns, trades and social types. In ballads like 'London's Ordinary' (6.2) or 'Room for Company' (6.5) an overwhelming verbal abundance is used for an all-embracing celebration of the everyday and the mundane.

The quotidian also included crime and vice, and ballads on spectacular crimes abounded. Though based in part on the appeal of the sensational and the ephemeral, such reports as 'The Cries of the Dead' (6.6 below) also share in the element of social protest so congenial to the form. By reporting incidents of brutality, murders, rapes and abductions, ballad-writers held up for contemplation striking examples of the failure of the social order. The treatment of these failures, moreover, was often open-ended and dialectical. In the two-part structure of the ballad form, it has been suggested, no 'third' side or resolution of disaster is proposed. The pat moral pieties interjected seldom explain the monstrosities recorded or offer consolation for the tragic injuries inflicted. Capable of being produced at short notice, furthermore, the ballad was by nature reiterative; each sensational ballad could be quickly answered by another yet more horrific, so that an impression of social chaos might be magnified to near-hysteria.

Because they could respond to the immediate and the topical, and because they could influence so wide an audience, ballad-makers were regarded by the authorities as a threat to the state, and by more established writers as a threat to the republic of letters. A steady flow of laws and proclamations sought to suppress them. A proclamation of 1534 called for an end to 'fond books, ballads, rhymes, and other lewd treatises of the English tongue', and it was followed by half a dozen others in the sixteenth century. An Elizabethan Act classified minstrels with vagabonds, and ordered that if convicted they should be 'grievously whipped and burned through the gristle of the ear with a hot iron of the compass of an inch about'. A third offence was punishable by death.

Only slightly less vehement were the denunciations of writers of pretension against such prolific ballad-writers as Thomas Deloney, 'the balleting silkworm of Norwich', and William Elderton 'of the ale-crammed nose'. Part of the animus was the aversion of serious poets, influenced by the sophistication of classical and continental verse, to the 'rude and beggarly rhyming' of native English tradition. But underlying this was a fundamental insecurity, a fear that popular writers threatened the status of true poets, and that their prolific output threatened to overwhelm the order of language itself. At issue was not simply economic competition or professional jealousy, but a dispute between popular and polite traditions over the proprietorship and destiny of published expression. Despite this conflict, however, the important role of ballad lore and popular motifs in the work of such writers as Jonson and Shakespeare reveals that the literature of the streets was actually a source of inspiration as well as anxiety. By claiming as their province the common, mundane, tawdry life of London's streets, the ballad-writers also claimed for themselves a small but enduring place in the literary system. In the order of words that makes up the literary image of London, their works convey with more success, perhaps, than any other genre the profuse energy of everyday urban life.

1.
London Lickpenny[1]
(Anon., c. 1450–1500)

To London once my steps I bent,
 Where trouth[2] in no wise should be faint;
To Westminster-ward I forthwith went,
 To a man of law to make complaint.
 I said, 'For Mary's love, that holy saint,
  Pity the poor that would proceed.'[3]
  But for lack of money I could not speed.[4]

And as I thrust the press among,
 By froward chance my hood was gone;
Yet for all that I stayed not long,

Till to the King's Bench[5] I was come.
  Before the judge I kneeled anon,
    And prayed him for God's sake to take heed,
    But for lack of money I might not speed.

Beneath them sat clerks, a great rout,
  Which fast did write by one assent;
There stood up one and cried about,
  'Richard, Robert, and John of Kent!'
    I wist not well what this man meant,
      He cried so thick there indeed;
      But he that lacked money might not speed.

Unto the Common Pleas[6] I yode tho,[7]
  Where sat one with a silken hood;
I did him reverence — for I ought to do so —
  And told my case as well as I could,
    How my good were defrauded me by falsehood.
      I gat not a mum of his mouth for my meed,[8]
      And for lack of money I might not speed.

 Unto the Rolls I gat me from thence,
  Before the clerks of Chancery,[9]
Where many I found earning of pence,
  But none at all once regarded me.
    I gave them my plaint upon my knee;
      They liked it well, when they had it read,
      But lacking money I could not be sped.

In Westminster Hall I found out one
  Which went in a long gown of ray;[10]
I crouched and kneeled before him anon,
  'For Mary's love', of help I him pray.
    'I wot not what thou meanest', gan he say;
      To get me thence he did me bid:
      For lack of money I could not speed.

Within this Hall neither rich nor yet poor
  Would do for me ought, although I should die;
Which seeing, I gat me out of the door,
  Where Flemings began on me for to cry:

'Master, what will you copen[11] or buy?
Fine felt hat, or spectacles to read?
Lay down your silver and here you may speed.'

Then to Westminster Gate[12] I presently went,
  When the sun was at high prime.
Cooks to me they took good intent,
    And proffered me bread with ale and wine,
    Ribs of beef both fat and full fine;
      A fair cloth they gan for to spread,
      But wanting money I might not speed.

Then unto London I did me hie,
  Of all the land it beareth the prize.
'Hot peascod!' one began to cry,
    'Strawberry ripe!' and 'Cherries in the rise!'
    One bade me come near and buy some spice,
      Pepper and saffron they gan me bid,
      But for lack of money I might not speed.

Then to the Cheap I gan me draw,
  Where much people I saw for to stand;
One offered me velvet, silk, and lawn,
    Another he taketh me by the hand:
    'Here is Paris thread, the finest in the land.'
      I never was used to such thing indeed,
      And wanting money I might not speed.

Then went I forth by London Stone,
  Throughout all Canwick[13] Street;
Drapers much cloth me offered anon.
    Then comes me one cried, 'Hot sheeps' feet!'
    One cried, 'Mackerel!'; 'Rushes green!' another gan gree
      One bad me buy a hood to cover my head,
      But for want of money I might not be sped.

Then I hied me into Eastcheap.
  One cries, 'Ribs of beef and many a pie!'
Pewter pots they clattered on a heap;
    There was harp, pipe, and minstrelsy.
    'Yea, by cock, nay, by cock!' some began cry.

Some sung of Jenken and Julian for their meed,
But for lack of money I might not speed.

Then into Cornhill anon I yode,
　　Where was much stolen gear there among;
I saw where hung mine own hood
　　That I had lost among the throng.
　　To buy my own hood I thought it wrong
　　　　(I knew it as well as I did my creed);
　　　　But for lack of money I could not speed.

The taverner took me by the sleeve:
　　'Sir,' saith he, 'will you our wine assay?'
I answered, 'That can not much me grieve —
　　A penny can do no more than it may.'
　　I drank a pint and for it did pay,
　　　　Yet sore a-hungered from thence I yede,
　　　　And wanting money I could not speed.

Then hied I me to Billingsgate,
　　And one cried, 'Ho, go we hence!'
I prayed a bargeman for God's sake
　　That he would spare me my expense.
　　'Thou scap'st not here,' quod he, 'under two pence;
　　　　I list not yet bestow my alms-deed.'
　　　　Thus lacking money I could not speed.

Then I conveyed me into Kent,
　　For of the law would I meddle no more;
Because no man to me took intent,
　　I dight[14] me to do as I did before.
　　Now Jesus that in Bethl'em was bore,
　　　　Save London and send true lawyers their meed,
　　　　For whoso wants money with them shall not speed.

2
From *London's Ordinary*
(c. 1605–20)

Through the Royal Exchange as I walked,

Where gallants in satin do shine,
At midst of the day they parted away
To several places to dine.

The gentry went to the King's Head,
The nobles unto the Crown;
The knights went to the Golden Fleece,
And the ploughmen unto the Clown.

The clergy will dine at the Mitre,
The vintners at the Three Tuns;
The usurers to the Devil will go,
And the friars to the Nuns.

The ladies will dine at the Feathers,
The Globe no captain will scorn;
The huntsmen will go to the Greyhound below,
And some townsmen to the Horn.[15]

The plumbers will dine at the Fountain,
The cooks at the Holy Lamb;
The drunkards by noon to the Man in the Moon,
And cuckolds to the Ram.

The roarers[16] will dine at the Lion,
The watermen at the Old Swan;
The bawds will to the Negro go,
And whores to the Naked Man.

The keepers will to the White Hart,
The merchants unto the Ship;
The beggars they must take their way
To the Eggshell and the Whip.

The farriers will to the Horse,
The blacksmiths unto the Lock;
The butchers unto the Bull will go,
And the carmen to Bridewell Dock.

The fishmongers unto the Dolphin,
The bakers to the Cheat Loaf;

The turners unto the Ladle will go,
Where they may merrily quaff.

The tailors will dine at the Shears,
The shoemakers will to the Boot;
The Welshmen they will make their way
And dine at the sign of the Goat....

3
From *City Rounds*
(Thomas Ravenscroft, 1611)

Brooms for old shoes! Pouch rings,[17] boots, and buskings![18]
Will ye buy any new broom? New oysters, new oysters, new!
New cockles! Cockles 'ny? Fresh herrings!
Will ye buy any straw? Ha'y'any kitchen stuff, maids?
Pippins fine, cherry ripe, ripe, ripe! Ha'y'any wood to cleave?
  Give ear to the clock,
  Beware your lock,
  Your fire and your light,
  And God give you good night.
  One o'clock!

4
From *Turner's Dish of Lenten Stuff* (1612)

My masters, all attend you,
  If mirth you love to hear,
And I will tell you what they cry
  In London all the year.
I'll please you if I can,
  I will not be too long;
I pray you all attend awhile,
  And listen to my song.

The fish-wife first begins:
  'Ny mussels lily-white?
Herrings, sprat, or plaice,

Or cockles for delight?
'Ny Wellfleet oysters?'
    Then she doth change her note,
She had need have her tongue be greased,
    For she rattles in the throat. ...

'Old shoes for new brooms!'
    The broom-man he doth sing,
'For hats or caps or buskins,[19]
    Or any old pouch-rings!
Buy a mat, a bed-mat,
    A padlock or a press,
A cover for a close stool,
    A bigger or a less!'

'Ripe cherry, ripe!'
    The costermonger cries,
'Pippins fine or pears!'
    Another after hies,
With basket on his head,
    His living to advance,
And in his purse a pair of dice,
    For to play at mumchance.[20]

'Hot pippin pies,
    To sell unto my friends!
Or pudding pies in pans,
    Well-stuffed with candle-ends!
Will you buy any milk?'
    I hear a wench to cry.
With a pail of fresh cheese and cream,
    Another after hies. ...

'Buy black,' saith the blacking man,
    'The best that e'er was seen!'
'Tis good for poor-men citizens,
    To make their shoes to shine.
Oh, 'tis a rare commodity,
    It must not be forgot;
It will make them glister gallantly,
    And quickly make them rot.

The world is full of threadbare poets
   That live upon their pen,
But they will write too eloquent,
   They are such witty men.
But the tinker with his budget,
   The beggar with his wallet,
And Turner's turned a gallant man,
   At making of a ballet.

5
From *Room for Company* (1614)

Room for company,
   Here comes good fellows,
Room for company
   In Bartholmew Fair.
Cobblers and broom-men,
Jailors and loom-men,
   Room for company,
   In Bartholmew Fair.
Botchers[21] and tailors,
Shipwrights and sailors,
   Room for company,
   At Bartholmew Fair.

Room for company,
   Here comes good fellows, etc.
Tinkers and brasiers,
Glassmen and glaziers,
   Room for company, etc.
Fiddlers and pipers,
Drums, flags, and fifers,
   Room for company, etc.

Room for company,
   Here comes good fellows, etc.
Coopers and cutlers,
Then cooks and butlers,
   Room for company, etc.
Tanners and curriers,

Tawers[22] and furriers,
  Room for company, etc.

Room for company,
  Here comes good fellows, etc.
Paviers, bricklayers,
Potters and brickmakers,
  Room for company, etc.
Pinners and pewterers,
Plumbers and fruiterers,
  Room for company, etc.

Room for company,
  Here comes good fellows, etc.
Pointers[23] and hosiers,
Salesmen and clothiers,
  Room for company, etc.
Horse coursers,[24] carriers,
Blacksmiths and farriers,
  Room for company, etc.

Room for company,
  Here comes good fellows, etc.
Girdlers, embroiderers,
Spurriers and solderers,
  Room for company, etc.
Carmen, caretakers,
And basketmakers.
  Room for company, etc.

Room for company,
  Here comes good fellows, etc.
Turners and draymen,
Horners[25] and laymen,
  Room for company, etc.
Chandlers[26] and salters,
Millers and maltsters,
  Room for company, etc.

Room for company,
  Here comes good fellows, etc.

Bellfounders, clockmakers,
Locksmiths and jackmakers,
   Room for company, etc.
Carpenters and joiners,
Clippers and coiners,
   Room for company, etc. ...

6
From *The Cries of the Dead* (c. 1625)

Methinks I hear a groan
   Of death and deadly dole,
Ascending from the grave
   Of a poor silly soul;
Of a poor silly soul
   Untimely made away.
Come then and sing with me,
   Sobs of sad welladay.

One Price in Southwark dwelt,
   A weaver by his trade,
But a more graceless man
   I think was never made;
All his life wicked was,
   And his mind bent to blood,
Nothing but cruelty did his heart any good.

Many poor prentices
   To himself did he bind,
Sweet gentle children all,
   Of a most willing mind,
Serving him carefully
   In this his weaving art,
Whom he requited still
   With a most cruel heart.

Lawful corrections he
   From his mind cast aside,
Beating them cruelly
   For no cause till they died;

Spurning and kicking them,
   As if dogs they had been,
Careless in cruelty
   Was this wretch ever seen.

Never went they without
   Bruised and broken eyes,
Head and face black and blue,
   Such was their miseries.
What so came next his hand,
   Tongs or fork from the fire,
Would he still lay on them
   In his mad moody ire.

Parents come bend your ears,
   Listen what followed on;
Masters come shed your tears,
   Mothers come make your moan;
Servants with sad laments,
   Rue the calamity
Those gentle children had,
   Living in misery.

The first, a pretty boy,
   Had with a sudden spurn
One of his ears strook off,
   Woefully rent and torn;
Where under surgeons' hands
   He lived long in woe,
By this same grievous wound
   This villain gave him so.....

A poor man's child he had
   Whom he beat back and side,
Continuing it day and hour
   Till this poor prentice died;
For which he was arraigned,
   And by the law had been cast,
But mercy quitted him
   For those offences past.

Yet those fair warnings here
   Wrought in him little good,
But rather drew him on
   For to shed further blood;
And being blinded thus,
With a pursuing ill,
Another poor harmless child
   He did by beating kill.

Harmless indeed was he,
   And a poor neighbour's son,
Whom he did beat and bruise
   Ere since this frost begun,
Only because that he
   Could not work in the cold,
Nor perform such a task
   As he by custom should.

Wherefore this cruel wretch
   Whipped him from top to toe
With a cord full of knots
   Of leather yet to show;
Whereby his tender limbs,
   From his foot to the head,
Are with wounds black and blue,
   Covered o'er all and spread.

Oh cursed cruelties,
   This did not him suffice,
But kept him locked up close
   From sight of neighbours' eyes,
And from his parents dear,
   When they came him to see,
Little misdoubting this
   Their son's extremity.

Thus weary woeful days
   Did this poor child abide,
Where he lay languishing
   Till the hour that he died;
Where his poor mangled corpse

By neighbours there was found,
Bruised and beaten sore
   With many a deadly wound.

His brains nigh broken forth,
   And his neck burst in twain;
On his limbs over all,
   Spots of blood did remain.
And the rim of his womb[27]
   Spurned in pieces is;
Never such martyrdom
   Of a poor child like this.

Oh Price, dear is the price
   For this blood thou must pay;
Life for life, blood for blood,
   On thy doom's dying day.
Pray thou for mercy there
   To save thy sinful soul,
For methinks I do hear
   Thy passing bell doth toll.

Notes

1. Derived either from the verb lick, to drink or lap up, in which case the title describes London, or from lack, in which case it describes the speaker.
2. Combining the sense of truth, correctness, rightness, with the sense of troth, good faith.
3. Plead in law.
4. Prosper, attain success.
5. The chief court of common law, which met in the south-east side of Westminster Hall.
6. A court of common law hearing trials for civil causes.
7. I went then.
8. Reward.
9. After the House of Lords, the highest law court in England, it met in the south-west side of Westminster Hall; also the court of records. The Master of the Rolls was the chief of the 12 assistants to the Lord Chancellor.
10. Striped cloth.
11. Desire.
12. The high gate at the west entrance to the New Palace Yard.
13. Candlewick Street.
14. Proceeded.
15. Citizens were legendary cuckolds.
16. Street rowdies.

17. Rings for closing a pouch or purse.
18. Attire.
19. Half-boots.
20. A game similar to hazard.
21. Menders.
22. Those who prepare white leather.
23. Makers of laces for fastening clothes.
24. Horse dealers.
25. Makers of horn spoons, combs, etc.
26. Candlemakers and sellers, as well as general provisioners, grocers.
27. The peritoneum, the membrane lining the abdomen.

7

NAKED FRAILTIES:
SATIRE AND COMPLAINT

With not a little morbid delight, Richard Brathwaite summed up much of the satiric bias of his age when he chided, 'Oh London, how thy wickedness abounds.' Cities attract satirists much as carrion attracts flies, and the accelerating growth and change of Tudor–Stuart London coincided with the emergence of a remarkable variety of satiric works, from complaints, homilies and ballads, to prose characters, epigrams and formal verse satires. Not so much a distinct genre as a basic impulse, satire transcends individual literary forms even while it plays upon them all. The Latin term *satura*, from which the English word derives, denotes a kind of stew or hash, a miscellany or hodge-podge, and it is through the eclectic use of a variety of literary devices that satire appropriates to itself some of the protean complexity of the city it reviles. Often in loose, episodic, digressive fashion, satirists are apt to deploy the resources of drama, dialogue, debate, fable, portraiture, dream vision, proverb, allegory — all while invoking mighty powers, bringing down maledictions on their victims, and haranguing, cajoling and insulting their audience.

The cornucopian manner of satire is demanded, however, by the extremity and excess of the corrupted world it envisions. From Langland's field full of folk to the nightmare visions of Bosch and Hogarth, the satiric panorama overflows with milling crowds, fools, hucksters, criminals and sybarites, and with the tawdry objects and detritus of their mean pursuits. '*Negotium*,' said Thomas More, is a 'devil that is ever ... tempting folk to much evil business. ... Verily they walk round as it were in a round maze. ... The centre or middle place of this maze is hell.' For the satirist, obsessed with the world's ills, the urban landscape becomes just such a labyrinth; in its centre, the market-place, men are overwhelmed by the *materia mundi*, the matter of the world, a profane and primordial chaos. Its society is broken into atoms, and its ordered space becomes a filthy sprawl. The city is reduced, in Robert Crowley's words (9.3 below), to a pack of people, 'Where every man is for himself,/ And no man is for all.' The extravagant excess of the urban scene amounts, finally, to a terrible deficiency; as John Marston, the *enfant terrible* of Renaissance satirists proclaimed, 'inundation of luxuriousness/ Fats all the world with ... gross beastliness'.

'*Satura ... tota nostra est*' ('Satire ... is wholly our invention'), boasted the Roman rhetorician, Quintilian, and certainly the Roman pedigree of formal verse satire established for all time the metropolitan nature of satire. In praising the now lost works of Lucilius, from whom he drew his inspiration, Horace claimed his predecessor had attacked the town *multa cum libertate* (with great liberty): Persius said more bluntly that Lucilius had simply 'flayed the town'. Horace vowed to sing his own enemies up and down the town, and Persius said that it was in Rome that he would 'dig it in'. Juvenal, who devoted all but one of his satires to the life of Rome, asked, 'What street does not overflow with sad obscenities?' and concluded that Rome was so corrupt it was impossible not to write.

Long before Horace, Persius and Juvenal were little more than impressive names, however, medieval satirists had learned from the Biblical prophets to lash out at cities as among the more corrupt of high places. From Jeremiah and Jonas they had learned to scourge the wickedness of Babylon and Nineveh, but from the psalmist they had learned to see Babylon in Jerusalem: 'Violence and discord fill the city ... tyranny and treachery are never absent from its central square' (Psalms 58:9–11). Much medieval satire was in the nature of general complaint against wickedness, mutability and human vanities. The Biblical resonance of such complaints was rediscovered at the Reformation, when poets and homilists returned to the model of the Jeremiad, reminding London of its likeness to Babylon or Jerusalem, and often predicting vengeance at hand. The sort of Biblical ventriloquism, practised by Henry Brinkelow in his *Lamentation ... Against London* (see 7.1 below), was a vein so familiar that it could be given a parodic twist in Surrey's diatribe against the city.

As the example of Brinkelow suggests, however, even old-fashioned complaint had begun to take on a social and political point. From the mid-fourteenth century onwards, English satirists, following the well-known proverb *vox populi, vox dei*, had frequently identified themselves with the humble, poor and disenfranchised through such simple, rustic personae as Piers Plowman, Long Will, Jack Upland and Colin Clout. Like the medieval homilists, who included themselves in the wretched human state they lamented, these rustic speakers belonged to a common humanity. They spoke no longer, however, against worldliness in general, but against the abuses of the rich and powerful. Even Langland's *Piers Plowman*, which begins in the timeless setting of the Malvern hills, finds its way to contemporary Westminster and Cornhill. By the early Tudor period, responding to new economic hardships and to the crusading impetus of the new religion, writers turned their focus increasingly to specific injustices they believed were emanating from London. Support for this was found in an important traditional ballad-type — extending from 'London Lickpenny' (see 6.1 above) to Munday's 'The Wood-man's Walk' (7.10 below) — in which a simple countryman is disillusioned by the city's vicious maze. The native image of the rustic also combined with the ancient and continental eclogue form to produce a vein of pastoral satire that runs from Barclay to Spenser and beyond.

The detailed satiric anatomy of London life, however, began in the later sixteenth century in such works as Edward Hake's *News out of Paul's Churchyard* (1567), George Whetstone's *Mirror for Magistrates of Cities* (1584) and Thomas Lodge's *Alarum Against Usurers* (1584) — works which inspired the brilliant urban reportage of Thomas Nashe, Robert Greene (see also Chapter 9) and Thomas Dekker. Like their immediate predecessors, these writers continued to work with such medieval schemes as the seven deadly sins, and to attack such traditional scapegoats as usurers, physicians, bawds, lawyers, brokers, prodigals and parasites. They are distinguished, however, by a racy, vivid, colloquial style, a style which owes something to the white-hot sermons of Puritans and which was sharpened by the unbridled excess of a religious pamphlet war known as the Marprelate Controversy. But the style of the new satirists was also a function of their literary self-image, their tendency to implicate themselves in the sordid world they describe. Though every bit as blunt as his plain-speaking forbears, the Piers of Nashe's *Pierce Penniless* is not a simple ploughman but a scholar impoverished by gambling and prodigality, embittered, envious, resentful of success. Nashe wears his urbane, whiplash style as a badge of his toughness, just as Greene backs up his colloquial style with endless professions of personal repentence.

Dekker, who spent much of his life in debtor's prisons, wrote that 'there is a hell named in our creed, and heaven, and the hell comes before: if we look not unto the first, we shall never live in the last'. Even while they continued to invoke traditional morality, these satirists took the essential step of contaminating their own purity. They are less moved by the desire to reform than by the desire to seem authentic, to horrify and to annihilate. Though marked by lavish and precise detail, their writing also has great metaphoric power, which in the selections below accumulates around such motifs as sirens, serpents and shaving.

Like the prose satire with which it is contemporary, the great outpouring of late Elizabethan verse satire exudes a new sense of urbanity, as simple invective of traditional complaint gives way to sophisticated irony, and the persona of the satirist develops an increasingly intimate relation with the urban scene. The publication of the Latin satires of Horace, Persius, Martial and Juvenal, first of all, encouraged late sixteenth-century poets to adapt classical models to the London setting. The fondling motley humourist of Donne's first satire, for example, derives from a bore in one of Horace's satires, and Everard Guilpin's perambulation of London works together bits of Martial with parts of Juvenal's third satire. John Hall's bewigged courtier is in many ways a Horatian portrait type, while Middleton's portrait of Cron the usurer adapts a scapegoat of popular satire to the slick new medium of rhymed couplets.

Perhaps the most influential ancient satirist was the seething, indignant Juvenal. Already accustomed by native tradition to the satiric ideal of plain speaking, the late Elizabethan satirists were taken with the affected insolence and harshness of Juvenalian style. Validating this style was a spurious etymology that derived the term satire from *satyr* and associated the genre both with the flouting of the Greek satyr play and with the rough, uncouth, half-hircine savagery of satyrs themselves. Licensed by the satyr's alien status, and liberated from delusions about reforming a race from which they were disaffected, the satirists were free to rail 'in words compact of fire and rage', as Guilpin put it. Cultivating a style they called 'rough cast', 'shaggy' and 'ugly ill', satirists like Hall and Marston lashed out at vice destructively and with apparent compulsion. Colin Clout and Piers Plowman gave way to such snarling personae as Pasquil and Don Kinsayder, and to such stage satirists as Shakespeare's Thersites and Webster's Bosola.

The annihilating impulse of this type of satire can be summed up in a whole string of titles — *A Whip for Worldlings, The Scourge of Villainy, The Scourge of Folly, Abuses Stripped and Whipped, Superbia Flagellum* (even a satire against satirists was called *The Whipping of the Satire*). In such satires, the affected scorn and isolation of the satirist (one of Marston's contemporaries accused him of 'lifting up your leg and pissing against the world') goes hand in hand with an obsessed self-regard, an almost prideful sense of defilement and contamination. Marston's confession, 'myself am not imaculate', or George Wither's admission to being 'from vice not free', are of course convenient ploys that protect the satirist by undermining his persona. But at the same time, the satirist's corruption lends credence and authority to his claims; it validates such visions as the one in Marston's *Cynic Satire*, where London swarms with swine, where human puppets, painted images and glow worms harbour souls of 'foul filth' and 'slime'.

Next to Marston's nightmare vision, even the scatological fantasy of Jonson's epigram 'On the Famous Voyage' (7.13 below) seems a relief. Jonson — a poet of broader range and sympathies — extracts from this fabulous journey through the underbelly of London's sewers a Rabelaisian exuberance. A disgusting catalogue of stinking 'grease and hair of measled hogs,/ The heads, houghs, entrails, and the hides of dogs' places London's corruption on a massive scale, and the poem's mock-epic underworld motifs evoke the truly hellish foundations on which London is built. But such motifs also pay tribute to the power of the city to magnify human folly to epic proportions.

From the earliest times, satirists were associated with malign powers. According to legend, their invectives had the power of charms and curses, enabling satirists to poison their enemies, to make them hang themselves, to rhyme rats and vermin to death. By raking through the world's corruption, and by exercising their destructive talents, satirists acquired the status of aliens, outcasts, pariahs. Plato observed that 'the satirist makes a wild beast of himself through his rancorous life'; and Swift, comparing the satirist to a broomstick that 'rakes into every slut's corner of nature and raiseth a mighty dust where there was none before', remarked that the satirist shares 'deeply all the while in the very same pollutions he pretends to sweep away'. It is perhaps not surprising that the great satiric outburst of the 1590s culminated in a ban on satires in 1599, when the Bishop of London and Archbishop of Canterbury

called in and burned the satires of Nashe, Marston, Hall and
others. The bishops' ban on published satires may have been as
much responsible as the satiric fashion itself for the emergence of
satiric stage comedy at just this time (see Chapter 14). Satirists
went on to publish subsequently, but with greater circumspection.
Even as mild a figure as George Wither found himself confined in
the Marshalsea in 1613.

The power of satirists to call down blights upon the land, how-
ever, was balanced by their power to bring fertility, to drive away
evil, and to prolong life. The isolation of the satirist could thus be
seen as privilege and licence, as the ritual eminence of the allowed
fool — who by sympathetic magic purges disorder in disordered
speech and thereby stabilises the community's norms. The violent
antipathies of the satirists who lashed out at London bespeak a
sense of isolation, of disaffection with a community crumbling
under the vicious pursuit of money, place, fashion and pleasure.
But these antipathies also reveal a heightened awareness of cor-
porate and communal responsibilities. The very fiction of their
isolation betrays how fundamentally the satirists belonged to the
moral life of London.

1
The Lamentation of a Christian against London
(Henry Brinkelow, 1543)

The great part of these inordinate rich stiffnecked citizens will not
have in their houses that lively word of our souls, nor suffer their
servants to have it; neither yet gladly read it, or hear it read; but
abhorreth and disdaineth all those which would live according to
the gospel. And instead thereof they set up and maintain idolatry
and other innumerable vices and wickednesses of man's invention,
daily committed in the city of London. No reformation or redress
once studied for, whereby to expulse vice and increase virtue, nor
no politic invention for the commonwealth! No, No! Their heads
are so given to seek their own particular wealths only, that they
pass not of no honest provision for the poor, which thing above all
other infidelities shall be your damnation. ...

The greatest part of the seniors or aldermen, with the multitude
of inordinate rich, even as the Jews cried out against Christ, taking
part with the high priests, saying, Matt. 27, 'Crucify him!', even so

doth the rich of the city of London take part, and be fully bent
with the false prophets, the bishops, and other strong, stout and
sturdy priests of Baal, to persecute unto death all and every godly
person, which either preacheth the word or setteth it forth in
writing. ...

Ye abuse your riches, specially you that come to the office of
the City, for ye spend unmeasurably upon whom? Even upon
them that have no need; as upon the nobles and rich gentlemen of
the court, upon the aldermen and other rich commoners, which
have as great need of your feasts as hath the sea at the highest
of a spring tide of the pissing of the wren. [And] the poor forgotten,
except it be with a few scraps and bones, sent to Newgate for a
face!

2
[A Satire on London]
(Henry Howard, Earl of Surrey, c. 1543)

London, hast thou accused me
Of breach of laws, the root of strife,
Within whose breast did boil to see,
So fervent hot, thy dissolute life,
That even the hate of sins that grow
Within thy wicked walls so rife,
For to break forth did convert so
That terror could it not repress?
The which, by words, since preachers know
What hope is left for to redress,
By unknown means, it liked me
My hidden burden to express,
Whereby it might appear to thee
That secret sin hath secret spite;
From justice' rod no fault is free;
But that all such as work unright
In most quiet, are next ill rest.
In secret silence of the night
This made me, with a reckless breast,
To wake thy sluggards with my bow:[1]
A figure of the Lord's behest,
Whose scourge for sin the Scriptures show.

That, as the fearful thunder clap
By sudden flame at hand we know,
By pebble stones the soundless rap,
The dreadful plague might make thee see
Of God's wrath, that doth thee enwrap.
That pride might know, from conscience free,
How lofty works may her defend;
And envy find, as he hath sought,
How other seek him to offend;
And wrath taste of each cruel thought,
The just shape higher in the end;
And idle sloth, that never wrought,
To heaven his spirit lift may begin;
And greedy lucre live in dread
To see what hate ill got goods win;
The lechers, ye that lusts do feed,
Perceive what secrecy is in sin;
And gluttons' hearts for sorrow bleed,
Awaked, when their fault they find;
In loathsome vice, each drunken wight
To stir to God, this was my mind.
Thy windows had done me no spite;
But proud people that dread no fall,
Clothed with falsehood and unright
Bred in the closures of thy wall.
But wrested to wrath in fervent zeal
Thou hast to strife my secret call.
Indured hearts no warning feel.
O shameless whore! Is dread then gone?
Be such thy foes, as mean thy weal?
O member of false Babylon!
The shop of craft! the den of ire!
Thy dreadful doom draws fast upon.
Thy martyrs' blood,[2] by sword and fire,
In heaven and earth for justice call.
The lord shall hear their just desire!
The flame of wrath shall on thee fall!
With famine and pest lamentably
Stricken shall be thy lechers all.
Thy proud towers and turrets high,
Enemies to God, beat stone from stone;

Thine idols burnt that wrought iniquity;
When none thy ruin shall bemoan,
But render unto the righteous Lord
That, so high, judged Babylon,
Immortal praise with one accord.

3
Of Alleys
(Robert Crowley, 1550)

And this is a city
   In name, but in deed
It is a pack of people
   That seek after meed;
For officers and all
   Do seek their own gain,
But for the wealth of the commons
   Not one taketh pain.
An hell without order,
   I may it well call,
Where every man is for himself,
   And no man for all.

4
[Sirens]
(Thomas Nashe, 1593)

Poets talk of enticing sirens in the sea, that on a sunny day lay
forth their golden trammels,[3] their ivory necks, and their silver
breasts, to entice men; sing sweetly, glance piercingly, play on lutes
ravishingly. But I say, there is no such sirens by sea as by land, nor
women as men; those are the sirens that hang out their shining silks
and velvets, and dazzle pride's eyes with their deceitful haber-
dashery. They are like the Serpent that tempted Adam in Paradise,
who whereas God stinted[4] him what trees and fruits he should eat
on, and go no further, he enticed him to break the bonds of that
stint, and put into his head what a number of excellent pleasures
he should reap thereby; so, whereas careful fathers send their

children up to this city, in all gentleman-like qualities to be trained up, and stint them to a moderate allowance, sufficient (indifferently husbanded) to maintain their credit every way and profit them in that they are sent hither for, what do our covetous city bloodsuckers, but hire pandars[5] and professed parasitical epicures to close in with them and (like the serpent) to alienate them from that civil course wherein they were settled? 'Tis riot and misgovernment that must deliver them over into their hands to be devoured.

Those that here place their children to learn wit and see the world are like those that in Africa present their children (when they are first born) before serpents; which if the children (so they present)[6] with their very sight scare away the serpents, then they are legitimate, otherwise they are bastards. A number of poor children and sucklings (in comparison) are, in the Court and Inns of Court, presented to these serpents and stinging extortioners of London, who never fly from them, but, with their tail, wind them in and suck out their souls without scarring their skin. Whether they be legitimate or no that are so exposed to these serpents, I dare not determine, for fear of envy. But sure legitimately (or as they should) they are not brought up, that are manumitted[7] from their parents' awe, as soon as they can go[8] and speak. ...

If one 'tice a prentice to rob his master, it is felony by the law; nay, it is a great penalty if he do but relieve him and encourage him, being fled from his master's obedience and service; and shall we have no law for him that 'ticeth a son to rob his father? nay, that shall rob a father of his son, rob God of a soul?

5

From *Satire I*
'*Away Thou Fondling Motley Humourist*'
(John Donne, *c.* 1593)

... Now we are in the street; he,[9] first of all,
Improvidently proud, creeps to the wall,
And so imprisoned, and hemmed in by me,
Sells for a little state his liberty;
Yet though he cannot skip forth now to greet
Every fine silken painted fool we meet,
He them to him with amorous smiles allures,

And grins, smacks, shrugs, and such an itch endures,
As prentices, or schoolboys which do know
Of some gay sport abroad, yet dare not go.
And as fiddlers stop lowest, at highest sound,[10]
So to the most brave, stoops he nigh'st the ground.
But to a grave man, he doth move no more
Than the wise politic horse[11] would heretofore,
Or thou O elephant or ape[12] wilt do,
When any names the King of Spain to you.[13]
Now leaps he upright, jogs me, and cries, 'Do you see
Yonder well-favoured youth?' 'Which?' 'Oh, 'tis he
That dances so divinely'; 'Oh,' said I,
'Stand still, must you dance here for company?'
He drooped, we went, till one (which did excel
Th'Indians, in drinking[14] his tobacco well)
Met us; they talked; I whispered, 'let us go;
'Tmay be you smell him not, truly I do.'
He hears not me, but, on the other side,
A many-coloured peacock having spied,
Leaves him[15] and me; I for my lost sheep stay;
He follows, overtakes, goes on the way,
Saying, 'Him whom I last left, all repute
For his device, in handsoming[16] a suit,
To judge of lace, pink,[17] panes,[18] print, cut, and pleat,
Of all the Court, to have the best conceit.'
'Our dull comedians want him, let him go;
But Oh, God strengthen thee, why stoop'st thou so?'
'Why? he hath travelled.' 'Long?' 'No, but to me,
Which understand none,[19] he doth seem to be
Perfect French, and Italian'; I replied,
'So is the pox'; he answered not, but spied
More men of sort, of parts, and qualities;
At last his love[20] he in a window spies,
And like light dew exhaled, he flings from me,
Violently ravished to his liberty;
Many[21] were there, he could command no more;[22]
He quarrelled, fought, bled; and, turned out of door,
   Directly came to me hanging the head,
   And constantly a while must keep his bed.

6
[A Courtier]
(Joseph Hall, 1597)

Fie on all court'sy and unruly winds,
Two only foes that fair disguisement finds.[23]
Strange curse! but fit for such a fickle age,
When scalps are subject to such vassalage.
Late travelling along in London way,
Me met, as seemed by his disguised array,
A lusty courtier, whose curled head
With abron[24] locks was fairly furnished;
I him saluted in our lavish wise:
He answers my untimely courtesies.
His bonnet vailed,[25] ere ever he could think,
The unruly wind blows off his periwink.
He lights and runs, and quickly hath him sped,
To overtake his overrunning head.
The sportful wind, to mock the headless man,
Tosses apace his pitched Rogerian,[26]
And straight it to a deeper ditch hath blown;
There must my yonker fetch his waxen crown.
I looked and laughed, whiles in his raging mind,
He cursed all court'sy and unruly wind;
I looked and laughed, and much I marvelled,
To see so large a causeway in his head;
And me bethought, that when it first begun,
'Twas some shrewd autumn[27] that so bared the bone.
Is't not sweet pride, when men their crowns must shade
With that which jerks the hams of every jade,
Or floor-strewed locks from off the barber's shears?
But waxen crowns well 'gree with borrowed hairs.[28]

7
[London]
From *Satire V*, (Everard Guilpin, 1598)

Let me alone I prithee in this cell,
Entice me not into the city's hell,
Tempt me not forth this Eden of content,

To taste of that which I shall soon repent.
Prithee excuse me, I am not alone —
Accompanied with meditation,
And calm content, whose taste more pleaseth me
Than all the City's luscious vanity.
I had rather be encoffined in this chest,
Amongst these books and papers, I protest,
Than free-booting abroad purchase offence,
And scandal my calm thoughts with discontents. ...
    What more variety of pleasures can
An idle City-walk afford a man?
More troublesome and tedious well I know
'Twill be, into the peopled streets to go;
Witness that hotchpotch of so many noises,
Black-saunts[29] of so many several voices,
That chaos of rude sounds, that harmony,
And diapason[30] of harsh Barbary,
Composed of several mouths and several cries,
Which to men's ears turn both their tongues and eyes.
There squeaks a cart-wheel, here a tumbrel[31] rumbles;
Here scolds an old bawd, there a porter grumbles;
Here two tough car-men combat for the way,
There two for looks begin a coward fray;
Two swaggering knaves here brabble for a whore,
There brawls an ale-knight for his fat-grown score.[32]
    But oh purgation! yon rotten-throated slaves,
Engarlanded with cony-catching knaves,[33]
Whores, beadles, bawds, and sergeants filthily
Chant Kempes' jig,[34] or the Burgonians' tragedy,[35]
But in good time, there's one hath nipped a bong,[36]
Farewell my hearts, for he hath marred the song.
    Yet might all this, this too bad be excused,
Were not an ethic soul much more abused,
And her still patience choked by vanity
With unsufferable inhumanity;
For whose gall is't that would not overflow,
To meet in every street where he shall go,
With folly masked in divers semblances?
The city is the map of vanities,
The mart of fools, the magazine of gulls,
The painter's shop of antics;[37] walk in Paul's,[38]

And but observe the sundry kinds of shapes,
Th'wilt swear that London is as rich in apes
As Afric Tabraca.[39] One wries his face:
This fellow's wry neck is his better grace.
He, coined in newer mint of fashion,
With the right Spanish shrug shows passion. . . .
    The further that we walk, more vanity
Presents itself to prospect of mine eye.
Here swears some seller, though a known untruth,
Here his wife's baited by some quick-chapped[40] youth,
There in that window Mistress Minx doth stand,
And to some copemate[41] beck'neth her hand;
In he is gone, Saint Venus be his speed,
For some great thing must be adventured.
There comes a troup of puisnes[42] from the play,
Laughing like wanton schoolboys all the way;
Yon go a knot to Bloome's Ordinary,
Friends and good fellows all now; by and by,
They'll be by the ears, vie stabs, exchange disgraces,
And bandy daggers at each other's faces.
    Enough of these then, and enough of all,
I may thank you for this time spent; but call
Henceforth, I'll keep my study, and eschew
The scandal of my thoughts, my folly's view;
Now let us home, I'm sure 'tis supper time,
The horn hath blown, have done my merry rhyme.

8
A Cynic Satire
(John Marston, 1599)

'A man, a man, a kingdom for a man!'
'Why how now currish mad Athenian?
Thou Cynic dog,[43] see'st not streets do swarm
With troops of men?' 'No, no, for Circe's[44] charm
Hath turned them all to swine; I never shall
Think those same Samian saws[45] authentical,
But rather I dare swear, the souls of swine
Do live in men, for that same radiant shine,
That lustre wherewith nature's nature decked

Our intellectual part, that gloss is soiled
With staining spots of vile impiety
And muddy dirt of sensuality.
These are no men, but apparitions,
Ignes fatui,[46] glowworms, fictions,
Meteors, rats of Nilus, fantasies,
Colosses, pictures, shades, resemblances. ...'
　'Peace, Cynic, see what yonder doth approach.'
'A cart, a tumbrel?' 'No, a badged[47] coach.'
'What's in't? Some man?' 'No, nor yet woman kind,
But a celestial angel, fair refined.'
'The devil as soon. Her mask so hinders me,
I cannot see her beauty's deity.
Now that is off, she is so vizarded,
So steeped in lemon's juice, so surphuled,[48]
I cannot see her face; under one hood,
Two faces,[49] but I never understood,
Or saw, one face under two hoods till now;
'Tis the right semblance of old Janus' brow.
　Her mask, her vizard, her loose-hanging gown
For her loose-lying body, her bright spangled crown,
Her long slit sleeve, stiff, busk,[50] puff verdingale,[51]
Is all that makes her thus angelical.
Alas, her soul struts round about her neck,
Her seat of sense is her rebato[52] set,
Her intellectual is a feigned niceness,
Nothing but clothes, and simpering preciseness.
　Out on these puppets, painted images,
Haberdasher's shops, torch-light maskeries,
Perfuming pans, Dutch ancients,[53] glowworms bright
That soil our souls, and damp our reason's light:
Away, away, hence coachman, go enshrine
Thy new-glazed puppet in Port Esquiline.[54]
Blush Martia, fear not, or look pale, all's one,
Margara keeps thy set complexion.
　Sure I ne'er think those axioms to be true,
That souls of men, from that great soul ensue,
And of His essence do participate
As 'twere by pipes, when so degenerate,
So adverse, is our nature's motion,
To His immaculate condition,

That such foul filth, from such fair purity,
Such sensual acts from such a Deity,
Can ne'er proceed. But if that dream were so,
Then sure the slime that from our souls do flow,
Have stopt those pipes by which it was conveyed,
And now no humane creatures, once disrayed
Of that fair gem.
Beasts' sense, plants' growth, like being as a stone;
But out alas, our cognizance is gone.'

9
Insatiate Cron[55]
(Thomas Middleton, 1599)

... I may find him starting at the Burse,
Where he infecteth other pregnant wits,
Making them co-heirs to his damned fits.
There may you see this writhen-faced mass
Of rotten mouldering clay, that prating ass,
That riddles wonders, mere compact of lies,
Of heaven, of hell, of earth, and of the skies.
Of heaven thus he reasons: heaven there's none,
Unless it be within his mansion;
O, there is heaven! Why? because there's gold,
That from the late to this last age controlled
The massy sceptre of earth's heavenly round,
Exiling forth her silver-paved bound
The leaders, brethren, brazen counterfeits,
That in this golden age contempt begets;
Vaunt then I, mortal, I only king,
And golden god of this eternal being. ...
Th'Exchange for goodly merchants is appointed;
Why not for me, says Cron, and mine annointed?
Can merchants thrive, and not the usurer nigh?
Can merchants live without my company?
No, Cron helps all, and Cron hath help from none;
What others have is Cron's, and Cron's his own;
And Cron will hold his own, or 't shall go hard —
The devil will help him for a small reward.
The devil's help, O 'tis a mighty thing!

If he but say the word, Cron is a king.
O then the devil is greater yet than he!
I thought as much, the devil would master be.
And reason too, saith Cron; for what care I,
So I may live as god, and never die?
Yea, golden Cron, death will make thee away,
And each dog, Cron, must have a dying day;
And with this resolution I bequeath thee
To God or to the devil, and so I leave thee.

10
From *The Wood-man's Walk*
(Anthony Munday, 1600)

Unto the city next I went,
   In hope of better hap,
Where liberally I launched and spent,
   As set on Fortune's lap.
The little stock I had in store,
   Methought would ne'er be done;
Friends flocked about me more and more,
   As quickly lost as won.
For when I spent, they then were kind,
   But when my purse did fail,
The foremost man came last behind:
   Thus love with wealth doth quail.
Once more for footing yet I strove,
   Although the world did frown,
But they before that held me up,
   Together trod me down.
And lest once more I should arise,
   They sought my quite decay;
Then got I into this disguise,
   And thence I stole away.
And in my mind methought I said,
   Lord bless me from the city.

11
Shaving
(Thomas Dekker, 1606)

There is shaving within the walls of this great metropolis, which you never dreamed of, a shaving that takes not only away the rebellious hairs, but brings the flesh with it too; and if that cannot suffice, the very bones must follow. . . .

Shaving is now lodged in the heart of the city, but by whom? and at whose charges? Marry, at a common purse, to which many are tributaries, and therefore no marvel if he be feasted royally. The first that paid their money towards it, are cruel and covetous landlords, who for the building up of a chimney, which stands them not above 30s, and for whiting the walls of a tenement, which is scarce worth the daubing, raise the rent presently (as if it were new put into the subsidy book)[56] assessing it at 3 pounds a year more than ever it went for before. Filthy wide-mouthed bandogs[57] they are, that for a quarter's rent will pull out their minister's throat, if he were their tenant; and (though it turn to the utter undoing of a man) being rubbed with quicksilver, which they love because they have mangy consciences, they will let to a drunken Fleming a house over his own countryman's head, thinking he's safe enough from the thunderbolts of their wives and children, and from curses, and the very vengeance of heaven, if he get by the bargain but so many angels as will cover the crown of his head. . . .

There are likewise other barbers, who are so well customed, that they shave a whole city sometimes in three days, and they do it (as Banks his horse[58] did his tricks) only by the eye and the ear; for if they either see no magistrate coming towards them (as being called back by the commonweal for more serious employments) or do but hear that he lies sick, upon whom the health of a city is put in hazard, they presently (like prentices upon Shrove Tuesday) take the law into their own hands, and do what they list. And this legion consists of market-folks, bakers, brewers, all that weigh their consciences in the scales. And lastly, of the two degrees of colliers, *viz.* those of charcoals, and those of Newcastle. Then have you the shaving of fatherless children, and of widows, and that's done by executors. The shaving of poor clients, especially by the attorney's clerks of your courts, and that's done by writing their bills of costs upon cheverel.[59] The shaving of prisoners by extortion, first taken by their keepers; for a prison is builded on such rank and fertile ground, that if poor wretches sow it with handfulls of small debts when they come in, if they lie there but a while to see the coming up of them, the charges of the house will be treble the demand of the creditor.[60] Then have you brokers; they shave poor men by most Jewish interest; marry, the devils trim them so soon as they have washed others. I will not tell how vintners shave their guests with a little piece of paper not above three fingers broad,[61] for their rooms are like barbers' chairs: men come into them willingly to be shaven. Only (which is worst) be it known to thee (O thou queen of cities) thy inhabitants shave their consciences so close that in the end they grow bald and bring forth no goodness.

12
From *The Scourge of Villainy*
(George Wither, 1613)

Now to thy rest, 'tis night. But here approaches
A troop with torches, hurried in their coaches.
Stay and behold, what are they? I can tell,
Some bound for Shoreditch, or for Clerkenwell;
Oh these are they which think that fornication
Is but a youthful, sportful, recreation;
These, to hold out the game, maintain the back
With marrow pies, potato roots, and sack;[62]
And when that nature hath consumed her part,
Can hold out a luxurious course by art.
Go, stop the horses quickly (lest thou miss)
And tell the coachman's wanton carriage this,
They of their guide must be advised well,
For they are running down the hill to hell.
Their venery will soon consume their stocks,
And bring them to repentance with a pox.

13
From *On the Famous Voyage*[63]
(Ben Jonson, 1616)

... In the first jaws appeared that ugly monster,
Ycleped Mud, which, when their oars did once stir,

Belched forth an air as hot as at the muster
Of all your night-tubs, when the carts do cluster,
Who shall discharge first his merd-urinous load:
Through her womb they make their famous road
Between two walls; where, on one side, to scare me,
Were seen your ugly Centaurs, ye call car-men,[64]
Gorgonian scolds and Harpies; on the other
Hung stench, diseases, and old filth, their mother,
With famine, wants, and sorrows many a dozen,
The least of which was to the plague a cousin.
But they unfrighted pass, though many a privy
Spake to 'em louder, than the ox in Livy;[65]
And many a sink poured out her rage anenst 'em;
But still their valour and their virtue fenced 'em,
And on they went, like Castor brave, and Pollux,
Ploughing the main. When, see, the worst of all lucks,
They met the second prodigy, would fear a
Man that had never heard of a Chimera.
One said it was bold Briareus,[66] or the beadle
(Who hath the hundred hands when he doth meddle);
The other thought it Hydra, or the rock
Made of the trull, that cut her father's lock;[67]
But coming near, they found it but a lighter,[68]
So huge, it seemed, they could by no means quite her.[69]
'Back,' cried their brace of Charons;[70] they cried, 'No,
No going back; on still, you rogues, and row.
How hight the place?' A voice was heard, 'Cocytus.'[71]
'Row close then slaves.' 'Alas, they will beshite us.'
'No matter, stinkards, row. What croaking sound
Is this we hear? Of frogs?' 'No, guts wind-bound,
Over your heads.' 'Well, row.' At this a loud
Crack did report itself, as if a cloud
Had burst with storm, and down fell, *ab excelsis*,
Poor Mercury, crying out on Paracelsùs.[72] ...
            By this, the stem
Of the hulk touched, and, as by Polypheme
The sly Ulysses stole in a sheepskin,[73]
The well-greased wherry[74] now had got between
And bade her farewell sough unto the lurden:[75]
Never did bottom more betray her burden;
The meat-boat of Bears' college, Paris Garden,[76]

Stunk not so ill; nor, when she kissed, Kate Arden.[77]
Yet one day in the year, for sweet 'tis voiced,
And that is when it is the Lord Mayor's foist.[78]
    By this time had they reached the Stygian pool
By which the masters swear, when, on the stool
Of worship, they their nodding chins do hit
Against their breasts. Here, sev'ral ghosts did flit
About the shore, of farts, but late departed,
White, black, blue, green, and in more forms outstarted,
Than all those atomi ridiculous,
Whereof old Democrite,[79] and Hill Nicholas,[80]
One said, the other swore the world consists.
These be the cause of those thick frequent mists
Arising in that place, through which, who goes,
Must try the unused valour of a nose;
And that ours did. For, yet, no nare[81] was tainted,
Nor thumb, nor finger to the stop acquainted,
But open, and unarmed encountered all,
Whether it languishing stuck upon the wall,
Or were precipitated down the jakes,
And, after, swum abroad in ample flakes,
Or that it lay heaped like an userer's mass,
All was to them the same, they were to pass;
And so they did, from Styx to Acheron,[82]
The ever-boiling flood, whose banks upon
Your Fleet-lane furies and hot cooks do dwell,
That, with still-scalding steams, make the place hell.
The sinks ran grease and hair of measled hogs,
The heads, houghs, entrails, and the hides of dogs;
For to say truth, what scullion is so nasty
To put the skins and offal in a pasty?
Cats there lay divers had been flayed and roasted,
And, after moldy grown, again were toasted;
Then, selling not, a dish was ta'en to mince 'em,
But still, it seemed, the rankness did convince 'em.
For, here they were thrown in with the melted pewter,
Yet drowned they not. They had five lives in future.
    But 'mongst these tiberts, who d'you think there was?
Old Banks the juggler, our Pythagoras,
Grave tutor to the learned horse.[83] Both which,
Being beyond sea, burned for one witch,

Their spirits transmigrated to a cat;
And now, above the pool, a face right fat
With great gray eyes, is lifted up, and mewed;
Thrice did it spit, thrice dived. At last, it viewed
Our brave heroes with a milder glare,
And, in a piteous tune, began: 'How dare
Your dainty nostrils (in so hot a season,
When every clerk eats artichokes and peason,
Laxative lettuce, and such windy meat)
Tempt such a passage? when each privy's seat
Is filled with buttock? and the walls do sweat
Urine and plasters? when the noise doth beat
Upon your ears of discords so unsweet?
And outcries of the damned in the Fleet?
Cannot the plague-bill keep you back? nor bells
Of loud sepulchres[84] with their hourly knells,
But you will visit grisly Pluto's hall?
Behold where Cerberus, reared on the wall
Of Holborn (three sergeants' heads) looks o'er,
And stays but till you come unto the door!
Tempt not his fury, Pluto is away;
And Madame Caesar, great Proserpina,
Is now from home. You lose your labours quite,
Were you Jove's sons, or had Alcides'[85] might.'
They cried out 'Puss!' He told them he was Banks,
That had, so often, showed 'em merry pranks.
They laughed at his laugh-worthy fate, and passed
The triple head without a sop.[86] At last,
Calling for Radamanthus, that dwelt by,
A soap-boiler, and Aeacus him nigh,
Who kept an alehouse, with my little Minos,[87]
An ancient purblind fletcher, with a high nose,
They took 'em all to witness of their action;
And so went bravely back, without protraction.
    In memory of which most liquid deed,
The city since hath raised a pyramid.
And I could wish for their eternised sakes,
My Muse had ploughed with his, that sung A-jax.[88]

14
From *A Rhapsody*
(Henry Vaughan, 1646)

Should we go now a wandering, we should meet
With catchpoles, whores, and carts in every street;
Now when each narrow lane, each nook and cave,
Sign-posts, and shop doors, pimp for every knave,
When riotous sinful plush, and tell-tale spurs
Walk Fleet Street and the Strand, when the soft stirs
Of bawdy, ruffled silks, turn night to day;
And the loud whip and coach scolds all the way;
When lust of all sorts, and each itchy blood
From the Tower-wharf to Cymbeline and Lud[89]
Hunts for a mate, and the tired footman reels
'Twixt chair-men, torches, and the hackney wheels.

Notes

1. Surrey was arrested in April 1543, on charges of eating meat in Lent and walking London's streets at night breaking windows with a stone-bow.
2. See Jeremiah 51:47–9.
3. Tresses, but also fish-nets.
4. Restricted.
5. Go-betweens.
6. Claim, believe.
7. Set free.
8. Walk.
9. The poet's companion, the motley humourist; or possibly the poet's active, worldly self, distinguished from the retiring, thoughtful self who is the speaker.
10. Stop the string at the shortest length for the highest note.
11. See 5.16, above.
12. Other popular animal acts; see Jonson's *Bartholomew Fair*, Induction, 11. 15–17.
13. This and the preceding line, which did not appear in the first printed edition of Donne's *Poems by J. D.* (1633), are taken from the second edition, *Poems by J. D.* (1635), Sig. I5V.
14. Inhaling.
15. The smoker.
16. Embellishing, decorating.
17. Scalloped ornamentation.
18. Decorative cloth strips.
19. No French or Italian.
20. A prostitute.
21. Customers, rivals.
22. Intercourse.

23. That expose disguises.
24. Auburn.
25. Lowered, like a flag.
26. Wig.
27. Lit. severe autumn, i.e. venereal disease.
28. With a pun on heirs, to match the pun on 'waxen crowns', or counterfeit money.
29. Burlesque songs.
30. Octave.
31. Dump-cart.
32. Tavern bill.
33. Tricksters, confidence men.
34. Will Kemp, the famous comic actor; a jig is a skit-dance performed to ballad music.
35. A ballad on the Burgundian fencer, John Barrose, hanged in 1598.
36. Cut or snatched a purse (thieves' slang); see 9.4.
37. Grotesques.
38. See, for example, 11.23.
39. Numidia, in North Africa.
40. Thirsty.
41. Companion.
42. Punies, i.e. law students.
43. The Cynic sect of Greek philosophers derived their name from their founder Diogenes, who was nicknamed 'dog' (Gr. Κύων) because of his rigorous self-denial.
44. The sorceress who transforms Odysseus's men into swine.
45. Sayings of Pythagoras of Samos, who believed in the transmigration of the soul.
46. Lit. foolish fires, i.e. will o' the wisps, formed by phosphorescent marsh gas.
47. Liveried, i.e. bearing the coat of arms of nobility.
48. Painted, made up.
49. Proverbial for duplicity.
50. The stiffened panel which ran down the front of the dress from the bust tapering over the stomach.
51. Farthingale, a hooped underskirt.
52. Stiff collar or wire supporting a ruff.
53. Ensigns, banners.
54. In ancient Rome, the gate to the rubbish heap.
55. A usurer.
56. Tax roll.
57. Chained watch-dogs.
58. See 5.16.
59. Pliable kid-leather; like a 'cheverel conscience', a 'cheverel bill' is presumably one that can be stretched.
60. See 15.6, below.
61. A tavern reckoning.
62. All supposed aphrodisiacs.
63. The poem recounts, in mock-epic fashion, a midnight journey (undertaken by Sir Ralph Shelton and a man known only as Heyden) from the Mermaid Tavern to Holborn by way of Fleet Ditch, one of London's largest sewers.
64. Dung-cart drivers, nightsoil men; see 15.13, below.
65. See Livy's history of Rome 25.21.
66. A Titan giant with a hundred hands.

67. Jonson identifies Scylla the sea monster, who dwelt on the rock opposite Charybdis, with Scylla the daughter of Nisus, who cut a lock from her father's hair to win the love of Minos.

68. A barge.

69. Avoid.

70. I.e. their two oarsmen (Charon ferried souls over the river Styx in Hades).

71. The river of lamentation in Hades.

72. Mercury was used in purgative solutions; Paracelsus, the Swiss alchemist and physician, introduced chemistry to medicine.

73. See *Odyssey* 9.431–4.

74. Rowing boat.

75. Gave a parting sigh to the sluggard, i.e. the barge.

76. Animal waste from London's meat markets was ferried across the Thames to the bear-baiting ring, Paris Garden.

77. A famous prostitute.

78. The barge carrying the Lord Mayor in the annual pageant; but to 'foist' or 'fust' also is to smell musty.

79. Democritus, founder of the atomic theory of matter.

80. A Democritan theorist contemporary (c. 1570–1610) with Jonson.

81. Nostril.

82. A river in Hades.

83. For the entertainer Banks and his horse, see 5.16, above; while Jonson claims here that Banks' soul has made a Pythagorean transmigration into the body of a cat, Banks actually lived until 1625.

84. St Sepulchre's.

85. I.e. Hercules'.

86. The honey-cake traditionally thrown to Cerberus as a bribe.

87. Rhadamanthus, Aeacus and Minos are the three judges of Hades.

88. Sir John Harington, the poet credited with the invention of the water-closet, celebrated this achievement in *The Metamorphosis of Ajax* (1596), whose title puns on 'a jakes'.

89. I.e. from east to west in London; statues of Lud, Cymbeline and other legendary kings adorned Ludgate.

8

FOR THE RECORD:
OFFICIAL VOICES

The identity of Tudor–Stuart Londoners was everywhere bound up with words — words hurled from the pulpit and declaimed on the stage, words sung on street corners or in taverns, words chanted in procession or parsed out in Bibles and penny chapbooks, words inscribed on signs, walls, gates and tombs. Yet few of these so explicitly described the city's goals or prescribed the duties of citizens as the words spoken by those in authority. Unlike Florence, which could boast of a Coluccio Salutati or a Leonardo Bruni, or Nuremberg, which could boast of a Willibald Pirckheimer, London could claim no members of its ruling élite who combined leadership and eloquence in such a way as to transform the city's ideals into inspired literary monuments. An image of London's rulers not without a measure of truth is John Earle's satiric portrait of an alderman (see 15.6 below) whose 'head is of no great depth, yet well furnished, and when it is in conjunction with his brethren, may bring forth a city apothegm, or some such matters'.

None the less, while they lacked a great solo voice, the London authorities spoke with choric force and conviction. Their official documents and pronouncements bear the hallmarks of corporate production — a characteristic vagueness, the result not of carelessness but of prudent imprecision; a conservative reliance on well-tried ancestral formulae, the apparently simple surface of which conceals a wealth of assumptions; a tendency to revert, especially in times of crisis, to a few indisputable tenets — loyalty, justice, good order, prudent provision, charity. In the Tudor–Stuart period, the successful government of London did not call for a break with the past but for a reaffirmation of it. And in any case, the purpose of the voice of authority was to be memorable and repeatable, to be ready to hand when needed, to echo clearly

179

in the ears and minds of citizens, or, as in the case of the freeman's oath, to roll forthrightly from the tongue. In short, the institutions of London were enshrined in an order of words.

While the official language of London was fundamentally a product of collective wisdom, compounded of history, experiment and English law, its actual formulae reflect not only the decisions of elected merchant officials but also the acumen of the medieval clerks and legal scholars who compiled the City's customaries and registers. The *Liber Horn,* an early custumal, bears the name of the City chamberlain, Andrew Horn, who compiled it in the early fourteenth century, at a time when the City was winning many important charter concessions from the Crown. Horn incorporated in his work part of a treatise on town government from the *Livres dou Tresor* of Brunetto Latini, a Florentine leader who had tutored Dante Alighieri. Horn thoughtfully inserted the English word *mayor* at the appropriate points in his Latin original. Later, in 1419, John Carpenter, the City's common clerk, gave official sanction to the foundation myth of Troynovant by incorporating it in the custumal known as *Liber Albus.* By seeking to frame the City's constitution in a purposeful vision of community, such writers put into practice the dictum of Thomas Aquinas that the function of law is not simply to enjoin but to educate in virtue.

In the Tudor period as well, the articulation of civic philosophy often fell to men like the lawyer, poet and religious writer, Thomas Norton, who served as the City's first Remembrancer (or Secretary) to the Lord Mayor, or to men like William Fleetwood and Sir Thomas Fleming, who served as Recorder (the City's chief legal officer, charged not only with law enforcement but also with ensuring that London's leaders adhered to the ancient precedents of the City's courts and customs). In their orations instructing London mayors on their office, Remembrancer Norton and Recorder Fleming lay sober stress upon the institutional bases of London's greatness, on the continuities embodied in law, sanctioned by divine and royal decree, and preserved by virtue and obedience.

Officials like these, who belonged to the English legal bureaucracy, who served frequently as MPs, and who were in constant touch with the Crown and Privy Council, were essential links in the chain of authority by which the City was kept obedient to Westminster. A wealth of Royal Proclamations and Privy Council proceedings reveal not only the Crown's stake in London's civic order, but also the patterns of prerogative and deference by which the two were joined. Fleetwood's subservient report to Burleigh on his undercover investigations is an informal instance of a social surveillance that was institutionalised from the highest levels down. The subject of statutes declared or enforced in more than two dozen proclamations between 1487 and 1603, beggars, vagabonds and masterless men were only the most prominent of the many outgroups (including aliens, criminals, prostitutes, players, Anabaptists and recusants) whom the authorities sought to control. By the later sixteenth century the shadowy existence of these groups had become inseparable from the growth of London's population, from the increasing sprawl of its poorly regulated suburbs and from the proliferation of tenements and mean dwellings within the walls. Elizabeth's 1580 proclamation against building and residence in London was the first of many fruitless attempts to restrict London's growth. James I's inspired proclamation of 1615, with its vision of a London changed from straw to brick, was perhaps the product of delusions built up in the half-dozen similar proclamations issued earlier in his reign; it was followed by several more — equally unsuccessful — before the end of his reign.

Nevertheless, if this vast expenditure of official stationery is evidence of persisting ills, it is also evidence of an intricate network of institutions working for stability. The official connections between Westminster and the City are only one instance of a series of overlapping jurisdictions that extended downward and outward to embrace the urban population. And quite apart from explicit statements of principle, the voice of authority is to be heard throughout the extraordinary body of records these jurisdictions produced. By its very nature, record-keeping placed the civic present in the context of memory and foresight; it imposed a systematic order and continuity on the daily conduct of affairs. Valerie Pearl, a leading historian of Stuart London, has noted that 'There are literally hundreds of *series* of manuscript sources in the Guildhall Library and Corporation Record Office nearly all comprising within each series thousands of folios; the single most voluminous record, the repertories of the aldermanic bench, contain about 400 folios for each year.' She also estimates that in sixteenth-century London, each of the 26 wards employed between 100 and 300 elected officers, depending on its size. In so far as it was shared, authority was tempered, transformed from an alien power into an accepted part of the community's identity. Its voice was not foreign but familiar, and it provided — for those more fortunate, at least — a verbal framework for living.

1
[Instructions to the Lord Mayor of London]
(Thomas Norton, 1574)

There be many reasons, which I ought not to doubt, that you do daily call to mind the weight of your charge in the office of the Lord Mayor of London. You are to remember how great a thing is the Lord Mayor, and of London so great a City, the imperial chamber of so great a prince, of our sovereign lady, the immediate lieutenant of the most great and mighty God. You are to think what trust Her Majesty and her progenitors have, and repose, in the corporate and politic body of her City of London, as to commit to ourselves the naming and choice of her deputed chief magistrate here and of our own governor. And how upon Her Highness' pleasure well known, you have been in one and honourable form received and allowed, and your care and fidelity is from and for Her Majesty committed to the keeping of the place, the preservation of the estate, and the government of her people of London, a most dear precious jewel in the crown of England. You are to have in mind what strength of the prince is here kept for her service and for the realm's defence; what polity, what wealth, and what order to be maintained for her use and honour for the common good; what multitudes of subjects, as well inhabiting as repairing, are to be provided for. You are not to forget what care Her Majesty and her council have showed themselves to have, that London be in the charge of a trusty man, and what particular proceedings have brought you and left you in your good acceptation and confidence, for which you are highly to thank God and His ministers. You must thereof gather what necessity is laid unto you to answer good expectation. ...

Yourself is blessed of God with sufficiency for that experience which the honour of the place requireth; by reason whereof you are not subject to such need as might make a man apt to corruption, or to contempt. You bring, I doubt not, an upright mind to serve God and the Queen sincerely; you have been noted a man of good charitable disposition and a tender heart to your poor; you are not young; you have not lived obscurely; you have had long experience and been in place of knowledge, and of both politic and judicial understanding. You are joined with a sufficient number of wise and grave brethren and commons, being companions of a great part of your charge; some of them have passed the way before you, and the rest have 'sayed[1] of others, and all together shall sit with you, shall advise you, shall strengthen you, shall ease your travails, shall supply your lacks, shall defend your doings, shall to you, with you, and for you give, establish, and maintain direction, power, and countenance. ...

You must be careful for provision of victual, fuel, and all things necessary; and that of all things there be true and wholesome stuff, good assize,[2] just weight and measure, and prices reasonable; wherein your best policies shall be by encouragement to permit, and by good foresight not to let slip, the best times of providing or bringing.

Among all your cares do justice with discretion, execute laws uprightly, and keep order. Have ever still a pitiful eye to the poor, and whensoever you see the poor, craving, needing, you aid them in any thing, saving to do wrong. ...

Now, lastly, my Lord, you must not forget that God is the giver of all good things. You must resort to Him daily by prayer, and to pray with heart; not suffered to say over 'Our Father', but to weigh every petition and join thereto a most affectuous[3] desire to obtain it according to his will. In that the Lord's Prayer, so oft as you say it, when you come to this place, 'our daily bread', you must remember that there is not comprised bread only, but therein is meant all things that are necessary for this present life; and among other things His blessing, that you may answer your charge in governing.

2
The Oath of Every Freeman (1580)

Ye shall swear that ye shall be good and true to our sovereign Lady Queen Elizabeth, etc., and to the heirs of our said sovereign Lady the Queen. Obeisant and obedient ye shall be to the Mayor and to the ministers of this City. The franchises and customs thereof ye shall maintain and this City keep harmless in that that in you is.

Ye shall be contributory to all manner of charges within this City, as summons, watches, contributions, tasks, tallages, lot and scot,[4] and all other charges, bearing your part as a freeman ought to do.

Ye shall colour[5] no foreign's goods whereby the Queen might lose her customs or advantages.

Ye shall know no foreign to buy or sell any merchandise within the City or the franchise thereof, but ye shall warn the Chamberlain[6] thereof, or some minister of the chamber.

Ye shall emplead or sue no free man out of this City whiles ye may have right and law within this same City.

Ye shall take none apprentice but if he be free born, that is to say, no bond man's son, and for no less term than for seven years. Within the first year ye shall cause him to be enrolled, and at his term's end ye shall make him free of this City, if he have well and truly served you.

Ye shall also keep the Queen's peace in your person; ye shall know no gatherings, conventicles, nor conspiracies made against the Queen's peace, but ye shall warn the Mayor thereof, or let[7] it to your power.

All these points and articles ye shall well and truly keep, according to the laws and custom of this City to your power. So God you help, and by the holy contents of this Book.

3
From A Royal Proclamation for one Family to a House
(7 July 1580)

The Queen's Majesty, perceiving the state of the City of London (being anciently termed her chamber), and the suburbs and confines thereof, to increase daily by access of people to inhabit in the same in such ample sort as thereby many inconveniences are seen already, but many greater of necessity like to follow, being such as Her Majesty cannot neglect to remedy, having the principal care under almighty God to foresee aforehand, to have her people in such a City and confines not only well governed by ordinary justice to serve God and obey Her Majesty, which by reason of such multitudes lately increased can hardly be done without device of more new jurisdictions and officers for that purpose but also to be provided of sustentation of victual, food, and other like necessaries for man's life upon reasonable prices, without which no city can long continue; and finally to the preservation of her people in health, which may seem impossible to continue, though presently by God's goodness the same is perceived to be in better state universally than hath been in man's memory; yet where there are such great multitudes of people brought to inhabit in small rooms, whereof a great part are seen very poor, yea, such as must live of begging or by worse means, and they heaped up together, and in a sort smothered with many families of children and servants in one house or small tenement, it must needs follow (if any plague or popular sickness should by God's permission enter amongst those multitudes) that the same would not only spread itself and invade the whole city and confines, as great mortality should ensue to the same, where Her Majesty's personal presence is many times required, besides the great confluence of people from all parts of the realm by reason of the ordinary terms for justice there holden, but would be also dispersed through all other parts of the realm to the manifest danger of the whole body thereof, out of the which neither Her Majesty's own person can be (but by God's special ordinance) exempted, nor any other whatsoever they be. For remedy whereof, as time may now serve, until by some further good order to be had in Parliament or otherwise the same may be remedied, Her Majesty by good and deliberate advice of her council, and being also thereto moved by the considerate opinions of the Lord Mayor, Aldermen, and other grave wise men in and about the City, doth charge and straightly command all manner of persons of what quality soever they be, to desist and forbear from any new buildings of any house or tenement within three miles from any of the gates of the said City of London, to serve for habitation or lodging for any person, where no former house hath been known to have been in the memory of such as are now living; and also to forbear from letting, or setting, or suffering any more families than one only to be placed or to inhabit from henceforth in any house that heretofore hath been inhabited.

4
From A Letter of Mr Fleetwood, Recorder of London, to Lord Treasurer Burghley (1583)

Right honourable and my very good Lord ... upon Friday last we sat at the Justice Hall at Newgate from seven in the morning until seven at night, where were condemned certain horsestealers, cut-

purses, and such like, to the number of ten, whereof nine were
executed and the tenth stayed by a means from the court. These
were executed upon Saturday in the morning. There was a shoe-
maker also condemned for wilful murder committed in the
Blackfriars, who was executed upon Monday in the morning. The
same day, my Lord Mayor being absent about the goods of the
Spaniards, and also my Lords the Justices of the Benches being
also away, we few that were there did spend the same day about
the searching out of sundry that were receptors of felons, where we
found a great many as well in London, Westminster, Southwark, as
in all other places about the same. Amongst our travels, this one
matter tumbled out by the way, that one Wotton, a gentleman
born and sometime a merchant man of good credit, who falling by
time into decay kept an alehouse at Smart's Key near Billingsgate,
and after, for some misdemeanour being put down, he reared up a
new trade of life, and in the same house he procured all the cut-
purses about this City to repair to this said house. There was a
schoolhouse set up to learn young boys to cut purses. There were
hung up two devices, the one was a pocket, the other was a purse.
The pocket had in it certain counters and was hung about with
hawk's bells, and over the top did hang a little sacring-bell;[8] and he
that could take out a counter without any noise was allowed to be
a *public foister*. And he that could take a piece of silver out of the
purse without any noise of any of the bells, he was adjudged a
judicial nipper.[9] Nota that a foister is a pickpocket and a nipper is
termed a pickpurse or a cutpurse. And as concerning this matter, I
will set down no more in this place, but refer your Lordship to the
paper herein enclosed.

5
From A Speech of the Recorder of London to the Lord Chief
Baron and Brethren of the Exchequer at the Presentation of Sir
John Spencer as Lord Mayor
(Thomas Fleming, 1594)

The happiness, the continuance, and felicity of this City doth not
consist in our enclosed walls, fair houses, great traffic, rich mer-
chandise, or in multitude of citizens which are great, but in the
wise and moderate government thereof.

A city is a society of men congregated into one place, not only by mutual helps to live together, but to live well and godly together; but can they live well without order and government? And what order or government can there be where there is not one to command, others to obey, one to rule, and others to submit themselves?

6
From A Royal Proclamation for Buildings (16 June 1615)

We do well perceive in our princely wisdom and providence, now, that our City of London is become the greatest, or the next greatest, city of the Christian world; it is more than time that there be an utter cessation of further new buildings, lest the surcharge and overflow of people do bring upon our said City infinite inconveniences, which have been so often mentioned, both in our former proclamations[10] and in the decrees of our High Court of Star Chamber, as it were in vain to repeat them; our purpose and princely resolution being now and hereafter to leave words, and to act and execute our princely ordinances on that behalf, and not to make discourse or recital of them. Therefore, as we do exceedingly approve and commend all edifices, structures, and works which tend to public use and ornament in and about our said City, as the paving of Smithfield, the planting of Moorfields, the bringing of the New Stream into the west parts of the City and suburbs, the Pesthouse, Sutton's Hospital, Britain's Burse, the re-edifying of Aldgate, Hicks Hall,[11] and the like works, which have been erected and performed in greater number in these twelve years of our reign than in whole ages heretofore, so, on the other side, for further addition of private buildings we are fully resolved that this our Royal Proclamation, and final and peremptory commandment, shall be the furthest and utmost period and end of them; only as to private houses, we could desire and wish, according to our former proclamation and ordinances touching brick buildings, that as it was said by the first emperor of Rome, that he had found the city of Rome of brick, and left it of marble, so that we whom God hath honoured to be the first king of Great Britain,[12] mought be able to say in some proportion, that we had found our City and suburbs of London of sticks, and left them of brick, being a material far more durable, safe from fire, beautiful, and magnificent.

7
The Articles of the Wardmote Inquest (1617)

1. *Peace.* Ye shall swear that ye shall truly inquire if the peace of the King our Sovereign Lord be not kept as it ought to be, and in whose default, and by whom it is broken or disturbed.

2. *Frankpledge.* Also if any man be received within this ward but if he be under free pledge, that is to say, be sworn after the alderman at his court, or else afore the said alderman between this and the Monday next after the Feast of Epiphany next coming.

3. *Outlaws, Traitors, Felons, etc.* Also if there dwell any man within the ward that is outlawed, or indicted of treason or felony, or be any receiver of traitors or felons.

4. *Thames.* Also ye shall inquire and truly present all the offences and defaults done by any person or persons within the River of Thames, according to the intent and purport of an act ... for the redress and amendment of the said river, which is now in great decay and ruin, and will be in short time past remedy if high and substantial provision and great help be not had with all speed and diligence possible. ...

5. *Congregations.* Also if any manner of person makes congregation or be receiver or gatherer of evil companies.

6. *Rioter, Barrator*[13]. Also if any man be a common rioter, or a barrator walking by nightertale[14] without light, against the rule and custom of this City.

7. *Peace, Hue and Cry.* Also if there be any man within this ward that will not help, aid, nor succour the constables, beadle, or other minuters[15] of this City in keeping of the peace, and arrest evildoers with rearing of hue and cry.

8. *Hucksters,*[16] *Receivers of Apprentices, Artificers, etc.* Also if there be any huckster of ale and beer that commonly useth to receive any apprentices, servants, artificers, or labourers that commonly use to play at dice, cards, or tables, contrary to the form of the statute in that case ordained and provided.

9. *Innholder, Taverner, Victualler.* Also if there be any innholder, taverner, brewer, huckster, or other victualler that hold open their houses after the hour limited by the Mayor.

10. *Curfew.* Also if any parish clerk do ring the bell called the curfew bell after curfew rungen at the churches of Bow, Barking Church, and St. Giles without Cripplegate.

11. *Bawds, Maintainers of Quarrels.* Also ye shall inquire if any

putour, that is to say, man-bawd or woman-bawd, common hazarders,[17] contectour,[18] maintainer of quarrels, champertors,[19] or embracers of inquests,[20] or other common misdoers be dwelling within this ward, and present their names.

12. *Strumpet, Adulterer, Witch, Scold.* Also if any bawd, common strumpet, common adulterer, witch, or common scold be dwelling within this ward.

13. *Hot-house.* Also if there be any house wherein is kept and holden any hot-house, or sweating-house, for ease and health of men, to which be resorting or conversant any strumpets or women of evil name or fame, or if there be any hot-house or sweating-house ordained for women, to the which is any common recourse of young men, or of other persons of evil fame and suspect conditions.

14. Also if there be any such persons that keeps or hold any such hot-houses, either for men or women, and have found no surety to the Chamberlain[21] for their good and honest behaviour, according to the laws of this City, and lodge any manner person by night contrary to the ordinance thereof made, by the which he or she shall forfeit 20 pounds to the chamber if they do the contrary.

15. *Thames, Ditches, Streets, etc.* Also if any manner of person cast or lay dung, ordure, rubbish, seacoal dust, rushes, or any other thing noyant[22] in the River Thames, Walbrook, Fleet, or other ditches of this City, or in the open streets, ways, or lanes within this City.

16. *Channel.* Also if any person after a great rain falleth, or at any other time, sweep any dung, ordure, rubbish, rushes, seacoal dust, or any other thing noyant, down into the channel of any street or lane, whereby the common course there is let[23] and the same things noyant driven down into the said water of Thames.

17. *Hogs, Kine,[24] Oxen, Ducks.* Also if any manner person nourish hogs, oxen, kine, ducks, or any beasts within this ward to the grievance and disease of their neighbours.

18. *Usurer.* Also if any usurers or false chevisancers[25] be dwelling within this ward.

20. *Colouring Foreign Goods.* Also if any free man against his oath make, conceal, cover, or colour the goods of foreigns, by the which the king may in any wise lose, or the franchises of this City be imblemished.

21. *Foreign Buying and Selling.* Also if any foreign buy and sell with any other foreign within this City or the suburbs thereof any

goods or merchandises, the same goods or merchandises be forth-
with forfeit to the use of the commonalty of this City.

22. Also if any freeman, which receiveth or taketh the benefit
and enjoyeth the franchises of this City, be continually dwelling
out of the City, and hath not ne will not, after his oath made, be at
scot and lot, nor partner to the charges of this City, for the worship
of this same City, when he is duly required. ...

26. *Purprestures.* Also if any make purprestures, that is to say,
encroach or take of the common ground of this City by land or
water, as in walls, pales,[26] stoops,[27] greces[28] or doors, or cellars, or
in any other like within the ward, or if any porch, penthouse, or
jetty[29] be too low in letting of men that ride beside or carts that go
thereforth. ...

30. *Regraters, Forestallers.* Also if any regrater or forestaller of
victual, or of any other merchandise which should come to this City
to be sold, be dwelling in this ward. A regrater is as much as to say
as he that buyeth up all the victual or merchandises, or the most
part thereof, when it is come to the City or the suburbs of the same
at a low price, and then afterwards selleth it at his own pleasure at
a high and excessive price. A forestaller is he that goeth out of the
city and meeteth with the victual or merchandise by the way,
coming unto the city to be sold, and there buyeth it. ...

37. *House, Tile.* Also ye shall inquire if any house be covered
otherwise than with tile, stone, lead, for peril of fire.

38. *Leper, Beggar.* Also if any leper, faitour,[30] or mighty beggar
be dwelling within this ward. ...

40. *Painted Visage.* Also if any man go with painted visage. ...

46. *Freemen to Show Their Copies.* Also, forasmuch as it is
thought that divers and many persons dwelling within the liberties
of this City daily occupy as freemen, whereas indeed they be none
nor never were admitted into the liberties of this City, ye shall
therefore require every such person dwelling within this ward,
whom ye shall suspect of the same, to show you the copy of his
freedom under the seal of office of the Chamberlain of the said
City; and such as ye shall find without their copies, or to deny to
show their copies, ye shall write and present their names in your
indentures. ...

54. *Buildings, Divided Houses, Inmates.* Also if any make or
cause to be made any new building or buildings, or divide or cause
to be divided any house or houses, or receive any inmate or
inmates, contrary to the King's Majesty's Proclamation, or con-

trary to law or any statute of this realm.

55. *Hawkers.* Also if any be dwelling in this ward which do offer or put to sale any wares or merchandises in the open streets or lanes of this City, or go from house to house to sell the same, commonly called hawkers, contrary to an act made in that behalf. ...

58. *Women Receivers of Servants.* Ye shall also inquire if there be dwelling within your ward any woman broker, such as resort unto men's houses, demanding of their maid servants if they do like of their services; if not, then they will tell them they will help them to a better service, and so allure them to come from their masters to their houses, where they abide as boarders until provided for. In which time, it falleth out that by lewd young men that resort to those houses, they be oftentimes made harlots to their utter undoing and the great hurt of the commonwealth. Wherefore, if any such be, you shall present them, that order may be taken for reformation.

59. *Privies.* Also if any have or use any common privy having issue into any common sewer of the City. ...

61. *Poor.* Also if any to whom the execution of the statute made for relief of the poor appertain be remiss in discharging his duty touching the execution of the same statute, and wherein the default is. ...

63. *Drunkard, Whoremonger, Sabbath, Jesuit, Seminary Priest, Secular Priest, Popish Recusant, Cozeners, etc.* Ye shall inquire whether there be within your ward any common drunkard, whoremonger, blasphemer of God's holy name, profaner of the sabbath, Jesuit, seminary priest, or secular priest, or any receiver, reliever, or maintainer of any of them, or any popish recusant, cozener, or swaggering idle companion, such as cannot give account how they live; if there be any such, you shall present them and the names of those that lodge or aid them. ...

67. *Assembly Monthly.* You shall assemble yourselves once every month, or oftener if need require, so long as you shall continue your inquest, and present the defaults which you shall find to be committed concerning any of the articles of your charge to the end due remedy may be speedily supplied and the offenders punished as occasion shall require.

Notes

1. Assayed, observed, tested.
2. Regulation of price and quality.
3. Earnest, ardent.
4. Local taxes.
5. Enter a foreigner's goods at the customs under a freeman's name.
6. The City's chief financial officer.
7. Prevent, hinder.
8. The bell rung at the consecration of the host or, after the Reformation, to summon the congregation forward for communion.
9. See 9.2 below.
10. Issued in 1603, 1605, 1607, 1608, and twice in 1611.
11. Smithfield market was paved and railed in the summer of 1615. A public park was laid out in Moorfields in 1605. The New River project, bringing a new water supply to London, was completed in 1613. The Pesthouse, in Old Street, Clerkenwell, was built from a tax, levied after the plague of 1593, on companies profiting from Sir Walter Raleigh's seizure of a Portuguese carrack. Thomas Sutton, merchant, purchased the former Carthusian monastery of the Charterhouse, and founded the Charterhouse School and a Hospital for the Poor Brethren in 1611. Britain's Burse, or the New Exchange, opened in the Strand in 1609. Aldgate was rebuilt 1607–1609. Hicks Hall was a new sessions house for Clerkenwell, built in 1612.
12. As James VI of Scotland, James I united the kingdoms of England and Scotland.
13. A rowdy.
14. By night.
15. Note-takers.
16. Petty retailer.
17. Dice players.
18. Quarrellers.
19. Persons helping plaintiffs or defendants win their case in exchange for money.
20. Jury corrupters.
21. Are not bonded with the Chamberlain, the City's chief financial officer.
22. Noxious.
23. Stopped up.
24. Cows.
25. Unlicensed money-lenders.
26. Fences.
27. Posts, pillars.
28. Steps, stairways.
29. Overhang.
30. Imposter.

9

GUIDES FOR THE PERPLEXED:
VARIETIES OF ADVICE

There is very little in the literature of Tudor–Stuart London that could not be construed as advice. Literary commonplace held that it was the function of literature to teach as well as delight, and in virtually every word they heard or read, Londoners could find counsel. Exhorted to Christian living by sermons, tutored in wisdom and good order by the stage, and enjoined to obedience by the voice of authority, they inhabited what was, to a large degree, a prescriptive verbal order. But a special strain of practical advice was concerned with negotiating the urban labyrinth. Balancing the aspirations and choices of the individual against the opportunities and perils of urban living, the literature of advice shows how much the ideas of freedom and self-cultivation owed to the world of the city.

The literature of practical advice grew out of an ancient tradition, represented by works like Plato's *Republic* or Xenephon's *Cyropaideia*, in which the person was conceived as an artefact that might be shaped like any other. As later Roman and Hellenistic writers understood it, the moral shaping of the individual was not just a matter of principle, but was also geared pragmatically to social situation and environment; an essential component of ethos or character was that adaptable and suave regard for the mores of the community that Roman writers called *urbanitas*. Reaching back to this tradition, Renaissance moralists and pedagogues tended to assume, as Erasmus put it, 'Men are made, not born.' In assembling practical advice on the shaping of character, the humanists displayed not only confidence in human potential for development, but also an awareness of the social context in which development takes place. In practical terms, successful negotiation amidst the shared values of large communities required a charm and persuasiveness that extended beyond mere wisdom and eloquence to demeanour and bearing. As early as 1290, a Milanese

193

grammarian paused in his treatise to remind his charges of dining etiquette: they must not criticise the food, they must not put their hands in their hair or on foul parts of the body, they must not stroke pets while eating or clean their fingers by licking. The mid-fifteenth-century English poem 'Urbanitas' advises household pages to remove their hats before their lords and to break wind silently. The more sublime culmination of such advice, of course, was Baldassare Castiglione's *Book of the Courtier*, where *sprezzatura* (an affected nonchalance) is only the most impressive in a complex repertoire of skills that exploit the inherent theatricality of social situations.

Castiglione's *Courtier*, and its many Italian imitations, met with almost immediate and widespread success among England's courtly and gentle élite, where a tradition of education in demeanour had long existed. But by the late sixteenth century, the ideal of self-cultivation extended far downwards and outwards, to embrace large portions of London's aspiring urban population. The author of the *Apology of the City of London* (*c.* 1584) could boast of the good manners of Londoners, explaining that 'good behaviour is yet called *urbanitas* because it is rather found in cities than elsewhere'.

At the most basic level, the proliferation of grammars and handbooks, together with the rise of such innovative London schools as St Paul's and the Merchants Taylors' School, testify to the progressive ambitions of Londoners, a large portion of whom were literate. Just as important as literacy was numeracy, and in addition to frequently published arithmetics there were literally dozens of manuals, listing weights, measures and trade routes, and tabulating percentages and interest rates. There were other types of mercantile advice, however, in which such economic virtues as thrift and diligence were soberly exalted side by side with godliness and cleanliness. An important offshoot of the abundant advice to apprentices, represented by the selection from Anthony Nixon (9.7 below), was the creation of a gallery of London worthies who rose to spectacular success from humble apprenticeship (see Chapter 10). Just as important were practical discussions of the varieties of trades and their techniques. To fathers and sons facing the question of career choice, Thomas Powell makes the unusual and progressive recommendation (9.8 below) of manufacture, at a time when conventional wisdom exalted trade above production. And William Scott's *Essay of Drapery* addresses itself to precisely those questions of rhetoric and demeanour that occupied courtiers and concludes that fundamental honesty must needs be hedged about with ceremony and dissemblance.

Thomas Dekker's *Gull's Handbook*, a parody of advice on demeanour that ridicules the calculated ostentation of would-be urban gentlemen, suggests that the issue of personal bearing — of recognisable urbane style — went far beyond the counter in the merchant's shop. The glittering allure of London's urban fashion, the subject of Northumberland's admonition to his son, is an important element of anti-urban ideology that can be traced as far back in England as the twelfth-century chronicle of Richard of Desvizes, in which a French–Jewish cobbler advises his apprentice, 'If you come to London, pass through it quickly for ... every corner of it abounds in grave obscenities. ... Whatever evil or malicious thing can be found in any part of the world, you will find it in that one city.' The gamblers, parasites, actors and prodigals the cobbler mentions are the stock-in-trade of much advice on bad companions. What Northumberland presents as a hideous defilement, however, George Whetstone approaches as a necessary evil in his advice to gentlemen students at the Inns of Court; and his very exploitation of the sense of alienation and anxiety with which provincial sojourners might regard the capital is itself an expression of London's growing domination of the country. By the mid-seventeenth century, Henry Peacham shrewdly blends fearmongering and reassurance in an effort clearly meant to capitalise on the tides of seasonal migration.

The quickening pace of interchange between country and city is reflected, too, in the emergence of such practical pamphlets as John Taylor's lists of taverns and carriage depots. A medieval tradition of guides to pilgrim sites, which contributed much to the genre of urban description, had long existed, but comprehensive handbooks like Taylor's represent an early emergence of the commercial side of travel guides. In an age still poised between oral and written culture, the compiling of information was apparently regarded with a certain defensive suspicion. Recounting the difficulties he met in compiling his list of carriers and inns, Taylor reports ruefully that:

in some places I was suspected for a projector, or one that had devised some new trick to bring the carriers under some new taxation; and sometimes I was held to have been a man-taker, a

sergeant or bailiff, to arrest or attach men's goods or beasts. ...
In some inns or hostelries, I could get no certain intelligence, so
that I did take instructions at the next inn unto it.

The hostellers and restaurateurs of today would presumably be
less reluctant to have their name in travel guides.

By far the most outrageous exploitation of the advice tradition is
the great body of cony-catching literature that emerged in the later
sixteenth century. Though it originated in accounts of provincial
rogues and vagabonds, it quickly found its way to its natural sub-
ject and audience in London. In large part, the ostensible purpose
of counselling unsuspecting citizens and visitors is a convenient
fiction, a literary strategy providing the occasion for colourful and
often lurid portraiture of stereotypical urban criminals. The under-
world accounts of Greene, Dekker and others achieve much of
their descriptive force by pitting the personal fears and perplexities
of Englishmen against London's size and complexity. They
attempt to mystify London, to present it as an alien realm honey-
combed with shadowy sub-communities. In their frequently
reprinted phrasebooks of underworld jargon, the pamphleteers
were not only making an alien tongue intelligible; they were, in a
larger sense, providing their readers with a map to the labyrinth, a
key that would unlock London's perplexing secrets. And by
affecting an intimate and thorough knowledge of the urban scene,
they helped to valorise the toughness, the know-how, and survival-
istic mother wit that had long been implicit parts of the ideal of
urbanity.

Survival is quite literally the issue in practical advice on dealing
with the epidemic diseases that so frequently made London a
death-trap. Printed with enterprising dispatch at each major onset
of the disease, the plague pamphlets were often well-intended and
timely — at least, in their advice to flee the city; but just as often
they advertised the very sorts of quack remedies that at times of
health were warned against in advice on crime. Londoners them-
selves, however, were perhaps less concerned with the potential
cacophony of information than with seeking advice wherever it
was available. The notorious Simon Forman, who prepared a
thousand horoscopes a year and received enquiries for many more,
was one of the many professional astrologers and forecasters for
which London was famous. (A London Society of Astrologers
held annual dinners between 1649 and 1658.) The number of title-

pages identifying almanacs, calculated 'especially for the Meridian of this honourable City of London', suggests that in London publishers found not only their largest but their most receptive audience for universal horoscopes. Less important, perhaps, than the almanacs' nondescript advice on health and crops was their implicit potential for more creative interpretation. It was not uncommon, for example, for pamphlets to print one table describing the effects of planetary movements on individuals' temperaments or astrological types and another table giving dates of planetary movements; the frequent addition of a third table, giving the dates of the London law terms suggests that, without explicitly saying so, Londoners were keeping all bets covered. Quite apart, then, from the attitudes revealed in individual works, the varieties of urban advice contribute to a portrait of urbanity in which enterprise and caution, openmindedness and fear, civility and raw aggression are mixed in equal parts.

1
From *Fifty Apples of Admonition, Bestowed on ... Gentlemen of Furnivall's Inn*
(George Whetstone, 1576)

Beware of tailors' curious cuts for they will shake your bags;
The merry mean I hold for best 'tween roist'ring silks and rags.
The tippling tavern, and such like, to haunt have small desire;
Of all reports it is the worst to be a drunken squire. ...
Out of the merchants' journals keep, buy seldom ware on trust;
Such usury bites above the rest, do try whoso lust. ...
When wedlock life doth like your mind, match with a virtuous
       maid;
The mischief of the contrary a plague next hell is said.
And married well, the city leave, sing then Piers Plowman's song;
For women used to London once will ever thither long.

2
From *The Second Part of Cony-Catching: Nip and Foist*
(Robert Greene, 1591)

Now, gentlemen, merchants, farmers, and termers,[1] yea, whoso-

ever he be that useth to carry money about him, let him attentively
hear what a piece of new-found philosophy I will lay open to you,
whose opinions, principles, aphorisms, if you carefully note and
retain in memory, [may] perhaps save some crowns in your purse
ere the year pass; and therefore thus: The nip and foist, although
their subject is one, which they work — that is, a well-lined purse
— yet their manner is different, for the nip useth his knife and the
foist his hand, the one cutting the purse, the other drawing the
pocket. But of these two scurvy trades, the foist holdeth himself of
the highest degree, and therefore they term themselves gentlemen
foists and so much disdain to be called cutpurses as the honest man
that lives by his hand or occupation; insomuch that the foist
refuseth even to wear a knife about him to cut his meat withal, lest
he might be suspected to grow into the nature of the nip. Yet, as I
said before, is their subject and haunt both alike, for their gains lies
by all places of resort and assemblies; therefore their chief walks is
Paul's, Westminster, the Exchange, Plays, Bear Garden,[2] running
at tilt,[3] the Lord Mayor's day, any festival meetings, frays, shoot-
ings, or great fairs. To be short, wheresoever there is any
extraordinary resort of people, there the nip and the foist have
fittest opportunity to show their juggling agility. Commonly, when
they spy a farmer or merchant whom they suspect to be well-
moneyed, they follow him hard until they see him draw his purse;
then, spying in what place he puts it up, the stall or the shadow
being with the foist or nip, meets the man at some straight turn
and jostles him so hard that, the man marvelling and perhaps
quarelling with him, the whiles the foist hath his purse and bids
him farewell.

3
From *A Treatise of the Plague*
A Rule and Instruction to Preserve such as be in Health from the Infection
(Thomas Lodge the Physician, 1603)

Whenas, by the will of God, the contagion of the plague is gotten
into any place, city or country, we ought to have an especial regard
of the general good, and by all means to study for their preser-
vation who are in health, lest they fall into such inconveniency.

First of all, therefore, it behoveth every man to have especial care
that he frequent not any places or persons infected, neither that he
suffer such to breathe upon him, but ... estrange himself, as far as
[in] him lieth, from their society. The first and chiefest remedy,
then, is to fly far and return late. .... And if necessity constraineth
us to frequent the infected, either to be assistant to our friends or
otherwise, every man ought to demean[4] himself in such sort that
the sick man's breath do not attaint him; which may very easily be
done, if a man have the skill to choose and take the wind that
properly bloweth towards the sick and infected, and not from the
infected to the healthful; and therefore in that case the healthful
ought to keep themselves under, not over, the wind. The first part
of preservation is to purify and purge the air from all evil vapours,
scents, stench, corruption, putrefaction, and evil quality. For which
cause it is necessary to make good fumes in our houses of sweet
and wholesome wood, as rosemary, juniper, and laurel or bays,
and to perfume the whole house and chambers with the fume of
rosemary, juniper, the parings of apples, storax,[5] benjamin,[6]
incense, dried roses, lavender, and such like, both evening and
morning. It is not amiss likewise at every corner of the street, at
least twice in the week, to make clear and quick bonfires to con-
sume the malignant vapours of the air. ... It is good also to wear
sweet savours and perfumes about us, such as in winter time are
majoram, rosemary, storax, benjamin; or to make a pomander,
after this sort that ensueth, and to wear it about us to smell, too,
upon all opportunities. ... It shall not be amiss, likewise, to carry
an angelica root in your mouth, or a gentian or zedoary root,[7] or
else the rind of an orange, lemon, or pomecitron.[8]

4
[A Phrasebook for the Underworld]
(Thomas Dekker, 1609)

It was necessary that a people so fast increasing and so daily
practising new and strange villainies, should borrow to themselves
a speech which, so near as they could, none but themselves should
understand; and for that cause was this language, which some call
peddler's French, invented, to the intent that, albeit any spies
should secretly steal into their companies to discover them, they
might freely utter their minds one to another, yet avoid any

danger. The language thereof of canting they study even from their infancy. . . .

A Canter in Prose

Stow you, bene cose; and cut benar whids and bing we to Romeville to nip a bong. So shall we have lowre for the bowsing ken, and when we bing back to the Dewsaville, we will filch some duds off the ruffmans, or mill the ken for a lag of duds.

Thus in English

Stow you, bene cose: hold your peace, good fellow.
And cut benar whids: and speak better words.
And bing we to Romeville: and go we to London.
To nip a bong: to cut a purse.
So shall we have lowre: so shall we have money.
For the bowsing ken: for the alehouse.
And when we bing back: And when we come back.
To the Dewsaville: into the country.
We will filch some duds: we will filch some clothes.
Off the ruffmans: from the hedges.
Or mill the ken: or rob the house.
For a lag of duds: for a buck[9] of clothes.

5

From *The Gull's Hornbook*
How a Young Gallant Should Behave Himself in an Ordinary
(Thomas Dekker, 1609)

First, having diligently enquired out an ordinary of the largest reckoning, whither most of your courtly gallants do resort, let it be your use to repair thither some half hour after eleven, for then you shall find most of your fashion-mongers planted in the room, waiting for meat. Ride thither upon your Galloway nag or your Spanish jennet,[10] a swift ambling pace, in your hose and doublet (gilt rapier and poniard bestowed in their places), and your French lackey carrying your cloak and running before you; or rather in a coach, for that will both hide you from the basilisk-like eyes of your creditors and outrun a whole kennel of bitter-mouthed sergeants.

Being arrived in the room, salute not any but those of your acquaintance; walk up and down by the rest as scornfully and as carelessly as a gentleman usher. Select some friend (having first thrown off your cloak) to walk up and down the room with you; let him be suited, if you can, worse by far than yourself. He will be a foil to you, and this will be a means to publish your clothes better than Paul's, a tennis court, or a playhouse. Discourse as loud as you can, no matter to what purpose; if you but make a noise, and laugh in fashion, and have a good sour face to promise quarrelling, you shall be much observed. ...

Before the meat come smoking to the board, our gallant must draw out his tobacco-box, the ladle for the cold snuff into the nostril, the tongs and prining-iron[11] — all which artillery may be of gold or silver. If he can reach to the price of it, it will be a reasonable useful pawn at all times when the current of his money falls out to run low. And here you must observe to know in what state tobacco is in town better than the merchants, and to discourse of the pothecaries where it is to be sold, and to be able to speak of their [leaves] as readily as the pothecary himself reading the barbarous hand of a doctor. Then let him show his several tricks in taking of it, as the whiff, the ring, etc.; for these are complements that gain gentlemen no mean respect, and for which indeed they are more worthily noted, I assure you, than for any skill that they have in learning.

6
[A Nobleman's Advice to his Son]
(Henry Percy, 9th Earl of Northumberland, 1609)

The next endeavour[12] will be to steer another of your actions, as where to bestow your residence fittest for their ends; for if they be gallants that are delighted with the pretty contentments of this town, as with love of pleasures, I will not say whorings; or gay clothes, I dare not say wastings of their estates; or merry society, I dare not say bitterness and jests to get the name of a wit; or feastings, to bestow whole days' thoughts after a morsel of meat, which for a world I will not call gluttony; or for good fellowship, to which I will not give the attribute of drinking drunk; or to see plays, which must not be named idleness in them whose hours seem wearisome and heavy because they know not what to do with themselves; or to see and be seen, which comprehends in itself love of novelties or self-conceit. These kind of men will tell you that a country life is tedious, where your conversation will be but among peasants; that your hopes that are in a good way will run a hazard; and to bury yourself alive were pity, since all men's eyes are upon you; all men honour you; all men prizes you; ladies look after you; all men will follow you; when their ends is but to pass their times here by the helps of your expense, or by the grace of your favours, which beginning to ebb in either of those powers, then farewell to those followers; and soon will they find occasions to sever that society, that friendship, that acquaintance. It will not be preposterous to warn you that gamesters may be remembered in this train, as dicers, carders, bowlers, cockers, horserunners, etc., that will lay you aboard with their persuasions, and that will be for one of these two ends, either to cheat you themselves, or to use you as an instrument to cover their packs; because men of your place will be less suspected than those whose necessities enforces to such a trade of life.

7
[Advice to Apprentices]
(Anthony Nixon, 1613)

Live carefully, young prentice, be no waster
Of others' goods, abandon filthy whores
And dissolute assemblies; please thy master,
And all the night keep close within his doors.
   Rove not about the suburbs and the streets
   When he doth think you wrapped between his sheets.

Too many take such courses vile and base,
To their own miseries and masters' fall;
But if thou do thy duty in thy place,
And providently keep within thy stall,
   When they ride bound or lurk in some by-lane,
   Thou mayest ride with thy footcloth and gold chain.

8
From *The Art of Thriving*
(Thomas Powell, 1631)

The first question is to what trade you will put your son and which is most worthiest of choice. For the merchant it requireth great stock, great experience in foreign estates, and great hazard and adventure at the best. ... For the shopkeeper, his welfare, for the most part, depends upon the prosperity of the merchant, for if the merchant sit still, the most of them may shut up their shop windows. Little skill, art, or mystery shall a man learn in shopkeeping. ... The most use or advantage he can make of it is to benefit between the mart and the market,[13] than which nothing is more uncertain, seeing there is not true judicial of the falling and rising of commodities. ... Take this for a general note, that those trades which ask most with an apprentice are incertainest of thriving and require the greatest stocks of setting up. Amongst trades, give me those that have in them some art, craft, or science by which a man may live. ...

I would have you know that the maker was before the retailer, and most shopkeepers are but of a sublimated trade and retail — but as attorney to the maker. But if the maker, without dispute of freedom in any corporation, might set up shop and sell his commodity immediately, it would be a great deal better for the commonwealth than now it is. Besides, it is no matter of difficulty, burden, or disgrace for a shopkeeper, yea, a merchant or a gentleman, to have the skill of some one of these manufactures, besides his revenue or profession, to accompany him, what fortune soever may carry him into countries unknown. The shopkeeper is a cleanly trade, especially your linen draper, which company hath the greatest commonalty and the largest privileges of all other; and yet they maintain nothing by charter, for indeed they have none. But a manufacture for my money, especially if he sell to the wearer immediately.

9

From *An Essay of Drapery, or The Complete Citizen*
(William Scott, 1635)

He shall live pleasingly to others. Which that he may perform, he

must be assisted by behaviour; without this, his other qualities will
not help him. It cannot but be distasteful to any man coming into a
shop, when he sees a man stand as if he were drowned in phlegm
and puddle, having no other testimony of his being awake than
that his eyes are open. It is expected that the outward carriage
should promise what's within a man. ... Small ceremonies win
great commendations, because they are continually in use and
note, whereas the occasion of a great virtue cometh but seldom. ...
In some cases my citizen may mingle profit with honesty and enter
into a composition[14] with both. He must never turn his back to
honesty, yet sometimes go about and coast[15] it, using an extra-
ordinary skill, which may be better practiced than expressed. Some
things, which may be done openly, must be done secretly, because
of the misconstruing world; but this is a good rule: avoid unjust
ways, and of just ways, take those that are most plausible.[16]

It is necessary my citizen defend himself by this buckler, dis-
trust, which is a great part of prudence; it is even the very sinew of
wisdom for a man's self to take heed of all men. The nature of the
world induceth a man to this, which is wholly composed of lies,
fraud, and counterfeit dealing.

10
From *The Worth of a Penny*
(Henry Peacham, 1641/1677)

For a penny you may hear a most eloquent oration upon our
English kings and queens, if, keeping your hands off, you seriously
listen to him[17] who keeps the monuments at Westminster.

Some, for want of a penny, have been constrained to go from
Westminster about by London Bridge to Lambeth, and might say
truly *Defessi sumus ambulando.*[18]

You may have in Cheapside your penny tripled in the same
kind, for you shall have pennygrass, pennywort and pennyroyal for
your penny.

For a penny you may see any monsters, jackanapes,[19] or those
roaring boys, the lions.[20]

For a penny you may have all the news in England and other
countries, of murders, floods, witches, fires, tempests, and what
not in one of Martin Parker's[21] ballads. ...

For a penny you may be advanced to that height that you shall be above the best in the city, yea the Lord Mayor himself; that is, to the top of Paul's. ...

For a penny you may walk within one of the fairest gardens in the city[22] and have a nosegay or two made you of what sweet flowers you please.

11
From *The Art of Living in London*
(Henry Peacham, 1642)

Now the city being like a vast sea, full of gusts, fearful-dangerous shelves and rocks, ready at every storm to sink and cast away the weak and unexperienced bark with her fresh-water soldiers, as wanting her compass and skilful pilot, myself, like another Columbus or Drake, acquainted with her rough entertainment and storms, have drawn you this chart or map for your guide, as well out of mine own as my many friends' experience.

Who therefore soever shall have occasion to come to the city ... the first thing he is to do is to arm himself with patience and to think he is entered into a wood where there is as many briars as people, everyone as ready to catch hold of your fleece as yourself. For we see that sheep, when they pass through a thorny or a bushy place, they leave locks of wool behind them; so imagine a populous city could not live nor subsist (like the stomach) except it have help and nourishment from the other parts and members. Therefore the first rule I give you, next to the due observation of God on the Sabbath and at other times, is the choice of your company and acquaintance. ...

Let him also in the city have a special care whom he entertains into his service. Let him or they have friends of his acquaintance who may undertake for them, but not at all adventure every straggler. ... And if you bring one with you out of the country, except you have a great eye over him he will quickly be corrupted in the city with much acquaintance. Then you shall help yourself to bed, see your horse starved in the stable and never rubbed, your linen lost at the laundresses; in a word, yourself everywhere neglected. Think it therefore no disgrace in a city inn to see your horse every day yourself, and to see him well meated [fed], rubbed, and watered. ...

Next after the setting-up of their horses and seeing them well

used, which should be your chiefest care at your first alighting in
the city, with all diligence follow your business. Let not vain and
by-occasions take you off from it, as going to taverns, seeing plays,
and now and then to worse places — so you lose your time, spend
your money, and sometimes you leave your business uneffected.
To avoid these, take a private chamber, wherein you may pass
your spare time in doing some thing or other; and what you call
for, pay for, without going upon the score, especially in city ale-
houses, where in many places you shall be torn out of your skin, if
it were possible, even for a debt of twopence. And though you
have spent twenty or forty pounds in one of their houses, your
host, especially your hostess, will hardly bid you drink in a
twelvemonth; but if they be at dinner or supper, never to eat a bit
with them, for that were an undoing to them in their opinion.

Again, walking abroad, take heed with what company you sort
yourself withal. If you are a countryman and but newly come to
town, you will be smelt out by some cheaters or other, who will
salute, call you by your name — which perhaps one of their com-
pany meeting you in another street hath learned by way of
mistaking you for another man, which is an old trick — carry you
into a tavern, saying they are akin to someone dwelling near you,
etc. . . .

You shall not do amiss if you send for your diet to your own
chamber a hot joint of meat, of mutton, veal, or the like; what you
leave covered with a fair napkin will serve you to breakfast the
next morning, or when you please. Keep out of throngs and public
places where multitudes of people are — for saving your purse.
The fingers of a number go beyond your sense of feeling. . . .

Now for such as are of the poorest condition, and come to the
city compelled by necessity to try their fortunes, to seek services or
other means to live: let them presently provide for themselves if
they can — for here is employment for all hands that will work —
or return home again before they find or feel the extremity of
want. . . . Here are more occasions to draw them into ill courses than
there, as being constrained to steal and to shorten their days; to
seek death in the error of their lives, as Solomon saith; young
maids, who never knew ill in their lives, to be enticed by impudent
bawds to turn common whores; and the like. But if they can pro-
vide themselves and take honest courses, by the blessing of God
they may come to as great preferment as aldermen and aldermen's
wives. For poverty of itself is no vice, but by accident. Whom hath

the City more advanced than poor men's children? the City itself being the most charitable place of the whole, and having done more good deeds than half the land beside. In a word, for a conclusion, let me give all comers, not only to London but all other populous places, this only rule never to be forgotten, which is, to serve God, avoid idleness, to keep your money, and to beware of ill company.

Notes

1. People associated with the London law terms.
2. The bear-baiting ring in Southwark.
3. Tilts were held annually in Westminster on the anniversary of Elizabeth I's accession.
4. Bear.
5. Balsam.
6. Spicebush, from which benzoin is extracted.
7. Spice similar to ginger.
8. Lime.
9. A washtub.
10. Pony.
11. Used in gunnery for cleaning touchholes and vents.
12. Of the young nobleman's feckless companions, about whom his father is offering advice.
13. Between wholesale and retail.
14. Compromise.
15. Skirt.
16. Pleasing.
17. At the time of the first edition of this work, the tour of Westminster Abbey was given by a man named David Owen.
18. 'We are tired out from walking'; a boat could be taken directly across the river for as little as a penny.
19. Monkeys.
20. Kept at the Tower.
21. A prolific printer of ballads in the 1630s.
22. Moorfields.

10

WORTHIES REMEMBERED: CIVIC MYTHS AND HEROES

An important element in the ideology of civic pride was the creation of a gallery of famous Londoners to whom citizens could turn as examples of public virtue and personal achievement. Along with buildings, institutions, bequests, tombs and inscriptions, a growing body of legend and literature helped to preserve their memory and spread their fame. Underlying the literary portraiture of London's heroes was the new pragmatism of humanistic education, a sense that more could be learned from example than from abstract doctrine. Man, said Aristotle, 'is the most imitative creature in the world and learns at first by imitation'; to this the Roman rhetorician, Quintilian, added: 'We should wish to copy what we approve in others.' In Renaissance ethics, as in literature, emulation was based upon the power of great examples to inspire the mind, to elicit wonder and admiration, to rouse the soul's highest instincts. There could be no worthier examples than heroes. As Sir Philip Sidney said, 'The lofty image of such worthies most inflameth the mind with desire to be worthy and informs with counsel how to be worthy.'

Where heroic inspiration was concerned, literature and history were elastic, overlapping categories. In fact, many of the concepts and techniques of heroic portraiture were derived from history, which was widely regarded as an ancillary to the study of ethics, a storehouse of 'the examples of virtue and vice'. A favourite technique of Renaissance historians was the portraiture of great and famous persons, a procedure modelled on the eulogies of ancient historians and guided by long-established rhetorical rules on the praise of character through ancestry, education and *res gestae* (great feats). A poetic tradition of exemplary portraiture extended from Petrarch's *De Viris Illustribus* and Boccaccio's *De Casibus Virorum Illustrium* to Lydgate's *Fall of Princes* (*c.* 1435) and the highly influential *Mirror for Magistrates* (1559 ff.). In England, the emergence of a work like the *Mirror for Magistrates* went hand in hand with the developing national pride and historic consciousness represented by the chronicles of Edward Hall, John Foxe and Raphael Holinshed and by a series of verse chronicles based upon them. The negative, monitory examples — of which England had its fair share — were balanced by a positive sense that there was, as one rhetorician said, 'no one thing in the world with more delectation reviving our spirits than to behold as it were in a glass the lively image of our forefathers'. By the later sixteenth century, the interest in history and historic portraiture had combined with the dramatic precedent of Biblical chronicles to produce the heroic chronicle play, 'wherein,' said Thomas Nashe, 'our forefathers' valiant acts ... are revived and they themselves raised from the grave of oblivion'.

Like the chronicles on which they were based, these plays concerned themselves not only with England's history and heroes, but also with the official Tudor doctrines of service and obedience. Almost from the beginning, Londoners figured in heroic history as loyal and obedient subjects; in Shakespeare's 2 *Henry VI* (1590–91) they fight for king, for country and for their lives against Jack Cade's rebellion; and in Heywood's *Edward IV* (1600), 'the prentices do great service' along with other Londoners in repulsing Fauconbridge's siege of London. In the dramatic depiction of Thomas More's suppression of the Evil May Day riot of 1517, a scene probably written by Shakespeare, Londoners were regaled with a native son's triumphant exhortation on obedience. As important as More's lecture on obedience, however, is his compassionate appeal to the values of *communitas*, and it seems unlikely that this rather dubious exemplar of Tudor obedience could have been presented in this play as 'the best friend the city ever had' were it not for a deep civic pride, a parochialism that, from the fifteenth century on, had led London chroniclers to date each year of English history from 29 October, and to begin the year's events with the election of London's Lord Mayor and sheriffs. The rapid appropriation of patriotic heroic drama for local purposes is reflected in the fact that, by 1606, in *The Knight of the Burning Pestle*, Francis Beaumont could parody an already well-established popular fashion for 'something notable in honour of the commons of the city' (see 14.2).

Part of the appeal of such plays was the simple glorification of

London through heroic lore, adventure and pageantry. Heywood's *Edward IV*, for example, calls for a scene in which 'the whole companies of Mercers, Grocers, Drapers and the rest' come on stage in full livery and regalia. The aim was sometimes to lend prestige to individual trades and guilds. Deloney's prose narrative on the famous clothier, *Jack of Newbury* (1597), was meant, he said, to show 'the great worship and credit which men in this trade have in former times come into'; and Deloney's similar treatment of shoemakers, in *The Gentle Craft* (1597), inspired Thomas Dekker's ebullient stage biography of the legendary Simon Eyre. As the spectacular rise of Eyre in Dekker's play suggests, however, an essential feature of citizen heroics was the economic romance of individual acquisitive success. Heywood's *Edward IV*, for example, depicts the career of Sir John Crosby, from his early days as a castaway and a shoemaker's apprentice to his entry into the Company of Grocers and his triumph as Lord Mayor. Dekker's Simon Eyre and Heywood's Thomas Gresham, exuberant and self-confident, hobnob with kings and princes, though they rarely share their doubts and burdens. Cheerful tolerance and imperturbability govern their every act, making burdens light and charity a welcome pleasure. They hold out to aspiring apprentices not only the promise of ultimate success but also the guarantee that every step along the way will be attended by benign paternalism and solidarity. In their heroic proportions — as witness the colossal arrogance with which Gresham drinks down pearls and dances at the loss of £60,000 — they exalt the power and glory of London's merchant community.

Less spectacular but far more common than such heroic plays were the dozens of broadside elegies or verse remembrances in which a variety of contemporary Londoners — preachers, merchants, benefactors, officials and their wives — were held up for emulation. Often commissioned by the families of the deceased, and usually written by hack poets, these works are a blend of sycophancy, *memento mori* themes, and civic pieties, but their widespread circulation in the streets provided Londoners with yet another mirror in which to see their best potential. The portrait of Francis Benison, for example, might well be taken for a portrait of the ideal businessman.

As Heywood's staging of a scene in Alexander Nowell's portrait gallery suggests, the heroic self-image of London was based not simply on individual myths but also on the multiplication of such myths into a potent body of mythology. Richard Johnson's *Nine Worthies of London* assembles from the lives of heroic Londoners an imposing roll of fame. It was to celebrate this rich background of achievement that Richard Niccols devoted a separate canto in his praise of London to 'those sons of fame/ Whose deeds do now nobilitate her name' (see 2.13 above). In London's mayoral pageants, the City's leading companies similarly commissioned bowers and houses of fame, in which they enshrined their worthy forbears in the manner of patron saints.

From the many legends current in Tudor–Stuart London, two stand out. The first is the legendary foundation of London by Trojan Brute, a descendant of Aeneas. Derived from the twelfth-century chronicle of Geoffrey of Monmouth, the myth had an obvious appeal to the classicising temperaments in Tudor–Stuart London — few capitals of Renaissance Europe lacked Trojan foundations. But, in fact, the myth ran deeper than literary fashion. It had been inseparably wedded to English history in the Brute chronicles of the fifteenth century; works written in London, by Londoners, these were developed side by side with the first vernacular city chronicles. Later, the Welsh Tudors seized upon the myth as a means of justifying their shaky dynastic claims. A commemoration of Henry VII's victory at Bosworth praises the King as 'the tall pillar from Brutus', descended from 'the line of Dardan, the line of Troy'. A Commission appointed to report upon the Tudor genealogy confirmed that 'King Henry the Seventh is lineally descended by issue-male ... in five score degrees' from 'Brutus which first inherited this land'. The genealogy proved useful in justifying Henry VIII's break with Rome on the grounds that England was an *imperium* as old as Rome itself; but just as important was its appeal to Londoners themselves. For John Carpenter, for example, the compiler of the city's *Liber Albus*, Brute's foundation of London was a symbol of the city's 'classical' civic liberties and privileges (see 1.1 above), and the name Troynovant embodied a prestige that could be traced to the most fundamental of all of Europe's heroic legends. Historians and scholars were sceptical, but Camden thought that antiquity might 'be pardoned, if by intermingling falsities and truths ... it make the first beginnings of nations and cities more noble, sacred, and of greater majesty'. Ben Jonson only half-apologised for including mention of Brute in his *Londinium* arch for the 1604 coronation pageant (see 16.3 below). 'Rather than the city should want a founder,' he explained, 'we choose to follow the received story whether fabulous or true, — and not altogether unwarranted in poetry, since it is a favour of antiquity to few cities to let them know their first authors.' The real dissenters were hard-nosed and alien humanists, like the Italian Polydore Vergil and the Scottish George Buchanan. The latter provoked the most extensive defence of the myth from Gabriel Harvey's brother Richard, who claimed in *Philadelphus* (1593), that 'puissant Brute is no fabulous prince but a true example, no counterfeit man but a corporal possessor of this land — let them say what they will!' Brute was subsequently defended several times — in 1607 and 1615, for example — and made his last serious stand in the early eighteenth century.

But if Shakespeare's London found new meanings for the myth of Brute, it may be said to have invented the myth of Dick Whittington, a myth that for centuries epitomised the spirit of enterprise. A fifteenth-century London chronicle pays brief tribute to 'that most famous merchant and mercer Richard Whittington', and the memory of Whittington's financial and administrative achievements had been kept alive through his buildings and endowed institutions. After listing Whittington's benefactions, Stow remarked in 1598 that 'he hath well deserved to be registered in the book of fame. ... Look upon this, ye aldermen, for it is a glorious glass.' But it was at just this point in time, when the commercial expansion of London was well under way, and the literature of heroic citizens had begun to emerge, that Dick Whittington was transformed almost overnight from a pious benefactor to the archetypal self-made man. Both a play entitled 'Richard Whittington', registered in February 1605 and mentioned in the Induction to *The Knight of the Burning Pestle*, and a ballad, registered in July 1605, are now lost. But from Richard Johnson's 1612 ballad on the same subject (see 10.6 below), it may be gathered that these lost works first laid down the essential elements of the story. The appeal of the story perhaps resulted from its peculiar combination of magical romance and realism. On the one hand, the tale bears all the marks of a certain kind of economic romance: the cat that brings unexplained good fortune (an element that has been traced, variously, to medieval Persian tales and Bhuddist religious motifs), the sea-venture, the performing of labours for an eastern king — these are elements that effectively mystify the economic process, concealing the actual processes by which wealth is accumulated. On the other hand, the story also embodies the experience of failure, the mean hardship of a scullion boy thrust down amidst the pots and spits, the desolation of taking to the road in despair. The two parts of the story hinge on the music of Bow bells, a siren-song through which the city exerts its economic magnetism. Like later ones in 1641 and 1656, Johnson's ballad (and the form itself is important) makes mention of Whittington's charity and benefactions, but there is no mistaking where its focus lies. Early in the seventeenth century, Renold Estracke attempted to capitalise on Whittington's new fame by issuing an engraved portrait in which the hero's right hand rests on a *memento mori*, a skull. As a response, no doubt, to popular opinion, the skull was quickly re-engraved, in later editions, to represent the now famous cat. Like the many ballad elegies on prosperous Londoners, the visual and verbal portraits of Whittington were less concerned with how to leave the world than with how to live in it.

1
From *An Epitaph of Master Francis Benison, Citizen and Merchant of London*
(John Awdeley, 1570)

Of merchants all he was the flower for wisdom and good skill,
    And right expert in every trade, delighting therein still.
This three and twenty years or more, in traffic he did toil;
    His will and skill was always such he thought it no turmoil.
With forecast he and diligence did comprehend, no doubt,
    The understanding of all trades, near Christendom throughout.
And having opportunity, no time he would omit
    His full pretence to bring to pass and purpose for to hit.
When wind and tide did speed require, all one was night or noon,
    His watchings he did nothing weigh till his attempts were done.
He oft would say that Diligence good Fortune's mother was,
    Which brought his enterprises all more luckily to pass.
Full quick and ready with his pen, and cunning too likewise,
    Of right good skill for to indite,[1] to serve each enterprise.
As well for friend as for himself when need the same did crave,
    Whether it were in merchant's trade or other matters grave.

Besides his native English tongue, the French and Dutch he spake;
  With pen and speech in pleasant style he arguments could
     make.
And for his time his trade hath been as ample, I am sure,
  As any merchant of this land whilst here he did endure.
The Queen's revenues of her crown he thereby did enlarge,
  With great preferment[2] of all youth committed to his charge.
Beneficial eke he was to each sort and degree;
  He traded so by land and sea it could none other be.
[Thus passed] he with good name and fame, to each man's
     contentation
  That with him dealt in any trade, to his great commendation.
And though besides his proper stock he used credit large,
  Yet each contract in traffic done right well he did discharge.
And his courageous attempts by forecast[3] so did frame,
  That divers men did muse thereat, and some maligned the same.
Which to him known, full wisely he could temper nature so,
  That he unquiet would not be, but let all malice go,
And leave to God the whole revenge, still seeking quietness;
  So his affairs they framed well and better had success.
To taste the sour with the sweet himself so did prepare,
  When any loss he did sustain, that patience conquered care.
Citizen-like in every point himself he did behave,
  With comely gesture and attire, right decent, sad, and grave,
With cheerful salutations, right courteous to all men,
  And how to use audacity he knew place, time, and when.
To noble and to worshipful sure known he was as well
  As unto the inferior sort, this just report can tell.
Also known in prince's court by his solicitation,
  As well for causes of his own as others of his nation.
He left behind him worldly goods all men to satisfy,
  And for to comfort wife and friends also abundantly.
And where he was a governor for the impotents' defense,
  He charitably unto them gave his benevolence.
His will long time lay by him made, which he from year to year
  Did oversee and order so as Death were ever near.

2
From *The Nine Worthies of London*
[Dedication to Sir William Webbe, Lord Mayor]
(Richard Johnson, 1592)

Being not altogether, right honourable, unacquainted with the
fame of this well-governed city, the head of our English flourishing
commonwealth, I thought nothing (considering it somewhat
touched my duty) could be more acceptable to your honour than
such principles as first grounded the same, as well by domestical
policy of peace as foreign excellence in resolution of war. This
caused me to collect from our London gardens such especial
flowers that savoured as well in the wrath of winter as in the pride
of summer, keeping one equivalence at all kind of seasons. Flowers
of chivalry, right honourable, I mean, some that have sucked
honey from the bee, sweetness from war, and were possessed in
that high place of prudence whereof your lordship now partaketh;
other some that have been inferior members and yet have given
especial aid to the head, been buckler to the best, and thereby
reached to the aspiring top of arms. If your lordship shall but like
of it, proceeding from the barren brain of a poor apprentice that
dare not promise molehills, much less mountains, I shall think this
by-exercise, which I undertook to expel idleness, a work of worth,
whatsoever the gentle-called kind, that are ungently enkindled,
shall with ostentation inveigh. ...

A Catalogue or Brief Table, Declaring the Names Of These
Worthy Men and When They Lived

Sir William Walworth, Fishmonger, in the time of Richard the
    Second.
Sir Henry Picard, Vintner, in the time of Edward the Third.
Sir William Sevenoke, Grocer, in the time of Henry the Fifth.
Sir Thomas White, Merchant Tailor, in the time of Queen Mary.
Sir John Bonham, Mercer, in the time of Edward the First.
Sir Christopher Croker, Vintner, in the time of Edward the Third.
Sir John Hawkwood, Merchant Tailor, in the time of Edward the
    Third.
Sir Hugh Caverly, Silk-weaver, in the time of Edward the Third.
Sir Henry Malveret, Grocer, in the time of Henry the Fourth.

From *Sir William Walworth, Fishmonger*

'In Richard's reign, the Second of that name,

Of London's weal Lieutenant to his grace,
Walworth was chose, unworthy of the same,
Within his hand to bear the City's mace;
　　To Fishmongers the honour did redound,
　　Whose brotherhood was my[4] preferment's ground.

'These were not days of peace, but broiling war;
Dissension spread her venom through the land,
And stirred the prince and subject to a jar
Hated love; rigour duty did withstand
　　In such a tempest of unbridled force,
　　As many lost their lives without remorse.

'For by a tax the king required to have,
The men of Kent and Essex did rebel;
Their first decree concluded none to save,
But havoc all, a heavy tale to tell;
　　And so when they were gathered to a head,
　　Towards London were these graceless rebels led....

'In these extremes it was no boot to fight;
The rebels marched with so huge an host,
The king craved parley, by a noble knight,
Of stern Wat Tyler, ruler of the roost,
　　A country boor, a goodly proper swain
　　To put his country to such wretched pain....

'The place appointed where to meet these mates
(That like audacious peasants did prepare,
As if their calling did concern high states,
With brazen looks devoid of awful care)
　　Was Smithfield, where his majesty did stay
　　An hour ere these rebels found the way.

'At last the leaders of that brutish rout,
Jack Straw, Wat Tyler, and a number more,
Approached the place with such a yelling shout
As seldom had the like been heard before;
　　The king spake fair and bade them lay down arms,
　　And he would pardon all their former harms....

'Their loathsome talk enkindles anger's fire,
And fretting passions made my sinews shake;
'Twas death to me to see the base aspire:
Such wounds would men in deadly slumber wake.
    Yet I refrained, my betters were in place;
    It were no manners nobles to disgrace.

'But when I saw the rebels' pride increase,
And none control and countercheck their rage,
'Twere service good, thought I, to purchase peace,
And malice of contentious brags assuage;
    With this conceit all fear had taken flight,
    And I alone pressed to the traitors' sight.

'Their multitude could not amaze my mind,
Their bloody weapons did not make me shrink;
True valour hath his constancy assigned:
The eagle at the sun will never wink.
    Amongst their troops, incensed with mortal hate,
    I did arrest[5] Wat Tyler on the pate.

'The stroke was given with so good a will,
It made the rebel couch unto the earth;
His fellows that beheld, 'tis strange, were still —
It marred the manner of their former mirth.
    I left him not, but ere I did depart,
    I stabbed my dagger to his damned heart.

'The rest perceiving of their captain slain,
Soon terrified did cast their weapons down,
And like to sheep began to fly amain;
They durst not look on Justice' dreadful frown.
    The king pursued, and we were not the last,
    Till fury of the fight were overpast.

'Thus were the mangled parts of peace recured,
The prince's falling state by right defended;
From commonweal all mischief quite abjured,
With love and duty virtue was attended.
    And for that deed that day, before 'twas night,
    My king in guerdon[6] dubbed me a knight.

'Nor ceased he so to honour that degree:
A costly hat his highness likewise gave,
That London's maintenance might ever be;
A sword also did ordain to have,
  That should be carried still before the mayor,
  Whose worth deserved succession to that chair.'

This much in age, when strength of youth was spent,
Hath Walworth by unwonted valour gained;
'Twas all he sought, his country to content.
Success hath Fortune for the just ordained,
  And when he died, this order he began,
  Lord Mayors are knights their office being done.

3
From *The Book of Sir Thomas More*
(William Shakespeare, Anthony Munday, Thomas Dekker,
Henry Chettle, *et al.*, 1590–95)

[The Book of Sir Thomas More *is the manuscript of a play
written in the hands of several collaborating dramatists and
showing evidence of revision in response to official censor-
ship. The main author was almost certainly Anthony
Munday, but other hands have been tentatively identified as
those of Henry Chettle, Thomas Heywood, Thomas Dekker,
and William Shakespeare. The play depicts the rise of Thomas
More from his early days as sub-sheriff to his elevation to the
Lord Chancellorship; the play ends with More's fall and
execution. The selection below, most of which (up to More's
exhortation 'submit you to these gentlemen') was probably
written by Shakespeare, depicts the riot against foreigners in
London on Evil May Day in 1517. The selection begins mid-
way through a scene of confrontation between the leaders of
the riot (John Lincoln, Williamson and his wife, Doll,
Sherwin, and George and Ralph Betts, the last of whom is
also referred to as the 'Clown') and a group of officials (a
sergeant-at-arms, the Earls of Surrey and Shrewsbury, and
Thomas More, the under-sheriff of London). Surrey and
Shrewsbury are shouted down, but when More speaks, the
leaders of the mob call for silence. More's brilliant oration*

restores order, and he is rewarded by being knighted at the end of the scene.]

Lincoln, Betts Peace, peace, silence, peace!

More You that have voice and credit with the number,
    Command them to a stillness.

Lincoln A plague on them! they will not hold their peace; the
    devil cannot rule them.

More Then what a rough and riotous charge have you,
    To lead those that the devil cannot rule!
    Good masters, hear me speak.

Doll Ay, by the mass, will we, More; thou art a good house-
    keeper, and I thank thy good worship for my brother, Arthur
    Watchins.

All Peace, peace!

More Look, what you do offend you cry upon,
    That is, the peace; not one of you here present,
    Had there such fellows lived when you were babes,
    That could have topped the peace, as now you would,
    The peace wherein you have till now grown up
    Had been ta'en from you, and the bloody times
    Could not have brought you to the state of men.
    Alas, poor things! what is it you have got,
    Although we grant you get the things you seek?

Betts Marry, the removing of the strangers, which cannot choose
    but much advantage the poor handicrafts of the city.

More Grant them removed, and grant that this your noise
    Hath chid down all the majesty of England;
    Imagine that you see the wretched strangers,
    Their babies at their backs and their poor luggage,
    Plodding to the ports and coasts for transportation,
    And that you sit as kings in your desires,
    Authority quite silent by your brawl,
    And you in ruff of your opinions clothed;
    What had you got? I'll tell you: you had taught
    How insolence and strong hand should prevail,
    How order should be quelled; and by this pattern
    Not one of you should live an aged man,
    For other ruffians, as their fancies wrought,
    With self same hand, self reasons, and self right,

Would shark on you; and men, like ravenous fishes,
Would feed on one another.
Doll Before God, that's as true as the gospel.
Lincoln Nay, this' a sound fellow, I tell you; let's mark him.
More Let me set up before your thoughts, good friends,
One supposition, which, if you will mark,
You shall perceive how horrible a shape
Your innovation bears: first, 'tis a sin
Which oft th'apostle did forewarn us of,[7]
Urging obedience to authority;
And 'twere no error, if I told you all,
You were in arms 'gainst God.
All Marry, God forbid that!
More Nay, certainly you are;
For to the King God hath His office lent
Of dread, of justice, power and command,
Hath bid him rule, and willed you to obey;
And, to add ampler majesty to this,
He hath not only lent the King His figure,
His throne and sword, but given him His own name,
Calls him a god on earth. What do you then,
Rising 'gainst him that God Himself installs,
But rise 'gainst God? What do you to your souls
In doing this, O desperate as you are?
Wash your foul minds with tears, and those same hands
That you, like rebels, lift against the peace,
Lift up for peace, and your unreverent knees,
Make them your feet. To kneel to be forgiven
Is safer wars than ever you can make,
Whose discipline is riot. In, in, to your
Obedience! Why, even your hurly[8]
Cannot proceed but by obedience.
Tell me but this: what rebel captain,
As mutinies are incident, by his name
Can still the rout? Who will obey a traitor?
Or how can well that proclamation sound
When there is no addition but a rebel
To qualify a rebel? You'll put down strangers,
Kill them, cut their throats, possess their houses,
And lead the majesty of law in lyam[9]
To slip him like a hound. Alas, alas, say now the King,

As he is clement, if th'offender mourn,
Should so much come too short of your great trespass
As but to banish you, whither would you go?
What country, by the nature of your error,
Should give you harbour? Go you to France or Flanders,
To any German province, to Spain or Portugal,
Nay, anywhere that not adheres to England,
Why you must needs be strangers; would you be pleased
To find a nation of such barbarous temper
That, breaking out in hideous violence,
Would not afford you an abode on earth,
Whet their detested knives against your throats,
Spurn you like dogs, and like as if that God
Owed not nor made not you, nor that the elements
Were not all appropriate to your comforts,
But chartered unto them? What would you think
To be thus used? This is the strangers' case,
And this your momtanish[10] inhumanity.

All Faith, 'a says true; let's do as we may be done by.

Lincoln We'll be ruled by you, Master More, if you'll stand our
friend to procure our pardon.

More Submit you to these noble gentlemen,
Entreat their mediation to the King,
Give up yourselves to form, obey the magistrate,
And there's no doubt but mercy may be found,
If you so seek. To persist in it
Is present death; but if you yield yourselves,
No doubt what punishment you in simplicity
Have incurred, his Highness in mercy
Will most graciously pardon.

All We yield, and desire his Highness' mercy.

                              [*They lay by their weapons.*]

More No doubt his Majesty will grant it you;
But you must yield to go to several prisons,
Till that his Highness' will be further known.

All Most willingly, whither you will have us. ...

Mayor Lincoln and Sherwin, you shall both to Newgate;
The rest unto the Counters.

Palmer Go guard them hence; a little breath well spent
Cheats expectation[11] in his fair'st event.

Doll Well, Sheriff More, thou hast done more with thy good

words than all they could with their weapons. Give me thy
hand; keep thy promise now for the King's pardon, or, by the
Lord, I'll call thee a plain conycatcher.

Lincoln Farewell, Sheriff More, and as we yield by thee,
So make our peace; then thou deal'st honestly.

Clown Ay, and save us from the gallows, else the devils dibble[12]
honestly.   (*They are led away.*)

Mayor Master Sheriff More, you have preserved the city
From a most dangerous fierce commotion;
For if this limb of riot, here in St Martin's,[13]
Had joined with other branches of the city
That did begin to kindle, 'twould have bred
Great rage; that rage much murder would have fed.
Not steel but eloquence hath wrought this good:
You have redeemed us from much threatened blood.

More My lord and brethren, what I have here spoke,
My country's love, and next the city's care,
Enjoined me to; which, since it thus prevails,
Think God hath made weak More His instrument
To thwart sedition's violent intent.
I think 'twere best, my lord, some two hours hence,
We meet at the Guildhall, and there determine
That through every ward the watch be clad,
In armour; but especially provide
That at the city gates selected men,
Substantial citizens, do ward[14] tonight,
For fear of further mischief.

Mayor It shall be so.
But yond methinks' my lord of Shrewsbury.

Enter Shrewsbury

Shrewsbury My lord, his majesty sends loving thanks
To you, your brethren, and his faithful subjects,
Your careful citizens. But Master More, to you
A rougher yet as kind a salutation:
Your name is yet too short — nay, you must kneel —
A knight's creation is this knightly steel.
Rise up, Sir Thomas More.

4
From *The Shoemaker's Holiday*
(Thomas Dekker, 1600)

[*In this scene, Firk the journeyman returns from the
Guildhall to Simon Eyre's shop in Tower Street, where he
announces his master's election as Sheriff to Hodge, Eyre's
foreman, and to Mistress Margery, Eyre's wife. He is accom-
panied by Hans Meulter, really Rowland Lacy, nephew of the
Earl of Lincoln, who has disguised himself as a Flemish
shoemaker and entered Eyre's service in order to win the hand
of Rose, daughter of Sir Roger Oteley, Lord Mayor of
London and one of Eyre's business partners. Mistress Eyre,
carried away with the news, begins to put on airs, only to be
corrected by the shoemakers. Arriving home in his scarlet
robes and chain of office, Eyre bestows a French hood on his
wife, and promises to make his shop over to Hodge, to make
Firk foreman, and to repay Hans fivefold for the loan on
which he has built his success.*]

Act III, scene iv

Enter Hans and Firk, running.

Firk Run, good Hans. O Hodge, O mistress! Hodge, heave up
thine ears! Mistress, smug[15] up your looks, on with your best
apparel. My master is called, nay condemned, by the cry of the
country, to be Sheriff of the City for this famous year now to
come and time now being. A great many men in black gowns
were asked for their voices and their hands, and my master had
all their fists about his ears presently, and they cried 'ay, ay, ay,
ay'; and so I came away.
Whereof without other grieve,
I do salute you mistress shrieve.

Hans Yaw, my mester is de groot man, de shrieve.

Hodge Did not I tell you mistress? Now I may boldly say 'Good
morrow to your worship'.

Wife Good morrow, good Roger. I thank you my good people
all. Firk, hold up thy hand; here's a threepenny piece for thy
tidings.

Firk 'Tis but three halfpence, I think. Yes, 'tis threepence; I smell
the rose.[16]

Hodge But, mistress, be ruled by me, and do not speak so pulingly.[17]

Firk 'Tis her worship speaks so, and not she. No, faith, mistress, speak me in the old key: 'To it, Firk. There, good Firk', 'Ply your business, Hodge' — 'Hodge', with a full mouth — 'I'll fill your bellies with good cheer till they cry twang.'

Enter Simon Eyre wearing a gold chain.

Hans See, myn liever broder, heer compt my meester.

Wife Welcome home, Master Shrieve. I pray God continue you in health and wealth.

Eyre See here, my Maggy, a chain, a gold chain for Simon Eyre. I shall make thee a lady. Here's a French hood for thee; on with it, on with it! Dress thy brows with this flap of a shoulder of mutton[18] to make thee look lovely. Where be my fine men? Roger, I'll make over my shop and tools to thee. Firk, thou shalt be foreman. Hans, thou shalt have an hundred for twenty.[19] Be as mad knaves as your master Sim Eyre hath been and you shall live to be shrieves of London. How dost thou like me, Margery? Prince am I none, yet am I princely born. Firk, Hodge, and Hans!

All three Ay, forsooth, what says your worship, Mistress Shrieve?

Eyre Worship and honour, you Babylonian knaves, for the Gentle Craft![20] But I forgot myself; I am bidden by my Lord Mayor to dinner to Old Ford.[21] He's gone before; I must after. Come, Madge, on with your trinkets! Now, my true Trojans, my fine Firk, my dapper Hodge, my honest Hans, some device, some odd crotchets,[22] some morris[23] or suchlike, for the honour of the gentle shoemakers. Meet me at Old Ford — you know my mind. Come, Madge, away;
Shut up the shop, knaves, and make holiday!

[*Near the end of the play, as he is about to be sworn in as London's new Lord Mayor, Eyre reflects in soliloquy on his success, and he recalls a promise he made in youth to his fellow apprentices: when he became Lord Mayor he would feast them all and close the shops of shoemakers for holiday on every Shrove Tuesday.*]

From *Act V, scene i*

Eyre By the Lord of Ludgate, it's a mad life to be a Lord Mayor;

it's a stirring life, a fine life, a velvet life, a careful life. Well, Simon Eyre, yet set a good face on it, in the honour of St Hugh! Soft, the King this day comes to dine with me, to see my new buildings. His Majesty is welcome; he shall have good cheer, delicate cheer, princely cheer. This day my fellow prentices of London come to dine with me, too; they shall have fine cheer, gentlemanlike cheer. I promised the mad Cappadocians,[24] when we all served at the Conduit[25] together, that if ever I came to be Mayor of London, I would feast them all; and I'll do't, I'll do't, by the life of Pharaoh, by this beard, Sim Eyre will be no flincher. Besides, I have procured that upon every Shrove Tuesday, at the sound of the pancake bell,[26] my fine dapper Assyrian lads[27] shall clap up their shop windows and away. This is the day, and this day they shall do't.

Boys, that day are you free. Let masters care,
And prentices shall pray for Simon Eyre.

[*Exit.*]

5
From *If You Know Not Me, You Know Nobody* (Thomas Heywood, 1606)

Part 2, scene vi

[*This scene transpires in the portrait gallery of the house of Dr Alexander Nowell, Dean of St Paul's. At the request of Lady Ramsey, Nowell has made peace between Sir Thomas Gresham and Sir Thomas Ramsey, who had been feuding over Gresham's purchase of the estate at Osterley. Driven indoors by the same rainstorm that inspires Gresham's eventual building of the Royal Exchange, these several London worthies, together with the legendary laughing haberdasher, Hobson, reflect on the London heroes enshrined in Nowell's portrait gallery.*]

Enter D. Nowell, Gresham, Sir Thomas Ramsey, Hobson, Lady Ramsey.

Gresham Come, Master Dean Nowell, now we have done
Our worst to your good cheer, we'd fain be gone.
Only we stay my kinsman's[28] long return,

To pay this hundred pound to Sir Thomas Ramsey.
Nowell Then assure you, he will be here presently.
    In the meantime, I have drawn you to this walk,
    A gallery wherein I keep the pictures
    Of many charitable citizens,
    That having fully satisfied your bodies,
    You may by them learn to refresh your souls.
Gresham Are all these pictures of good citizens?
Nowell They are, and I'll describe to you some of their births,
    How they bestowed their lives and did so live
    The fruits of this life might a better give.
Gresham You shall gain more in showing this to us
    Than you have shown.
Lady Ramsey Good Master Dean, I pray you show it us.
Nowell This was the picture of Sir John Philpot, sometimes
        mayor.
    This man at one time, at his own charge,
    Levied ten thousand soldiers, guarded the realm
    From the incursions of our enemies.
    And in the year a thousand three hundred and eighty,
    When Thomas of Woodstock, Thomas Percy, with other noble
        men,
    Were sent to aid the Duke of Brittany,
    This said John Philpot furnished out four ships
    At his own charges and did release the armour
    That the poor soldiers had for victuals pawned.
    This man did live when Walworth was Lord Mayor,
    That provident, valiant, and learned citizen
    That both attached and killed the traitor Tyler;
    For which good service Walworth the Lord Mayor,
    This Philpot, and four other aldermen
    Were knighted in the field.
    Thus did he live, and yet before he died,
    Assured relief for thirteen poor for ever.
Gresham By the merry God, a worthy citizen.
    Oh, good my Dean.
Nowell This' Sir Richard Whittington, three times mayor,
    Son to a knight and prentice to a mercer,
    Began the library of Greyfriars in London;
    And his executors after him did build
    Whittington College, thirteen almshouses for poor men,

Repaired St Bartholomew's in Smithfield,
Glazed the Guildhall, and built Newgate.
Hobson Bones o' me, then, I have heard lies,
For I have heard he was a scullion
And raised himself by venture of a cat.
Nowell They did the more wrong to the gentleman.
This' Sir John Allen, Mercer and Mayor of London,
A man so grave of life that he was made
A privy councillor of King Henry the Eight.
He gave this City a rich collar of gold,
That by the succeeding mayor should be worn;
Of which Sir William Laxton was the first,
And is continued even unto this year.
A number more there are, of whose good deeds
This city flourished.
Gresham And we may be ashamed,
For in their deeds we see our own disgrace.
We that are citizens as rich as they were
Behold their charity in every street,
Churches for prayer, almshouses for the poor,
Conduits which bring us water; all which good
We do see and are relieved withal,
And yet we live like beasts, spend time and die,
Leaving no good to be remembered by.
Lady Ramsey Among the stories of these blessed men,
So many that enrich your gallery,
There are two women's pictures: what were they?
Nowell They are two that have deserved a memory
Worthy the note of our posterity.
This' Agnes Foster, wife to Sir A. Foster,
That freed a beggar at the grate of Ludgate,
Was after mayor of this most famous City,
And builded the south side of Ludgate up,
Upon which wall these verses I have read:
Devout souls that pass this way,
For M. Foster late Mayor honestly pray,
And Agnes his wife to God consecrate
That of pity this house made for Londoners in Ludgate,
So that for lodging and water here nothing they pay,
As their keepers shall answer at dreadful doomsday.
Lady Ramsey Oh, what a charitable deed was this!

Nowell This' Ann Gibson, who in her husband's life,
   Being a grocer and a Sheriff of London,
   Founded a free school at Ratcliffe,
   There to instruct three score poor children,
   Built fourteen almshouses for fourteen poor,
   Leaving for tutors fifty pounds a year,
   And quarterly for every one a noble.
Lady Ramsey Why should not I live so, that being dead,
   My name might register with theirs?
Gresham Why should not all of us, being wealthy men,
   Cast in our minds how we might them exceed
   In goodly works, helping of them that need?
Hobson Bones o' me, 'tis true. Why should we live
   To have the poor to curse us being dead?
   Heaven grant that I may live that when I die,
   Although my children laugh, the poor may cry.
Nowell If you will follow the religious path
   That these have beat before you, you shall win heaven.
   Even in the midday walks you shall not walk the street,
   But widows' orisons, lazars' prayers, orphans' thanks
   Will fly into your ears, and with a joyful blush,
   Make you thank God that you have done for them;
   When otherwise they'll fill your ears with curses,
   Crying, 'We feed on woe, you are our nurses.'
   Oh, is't not better that young couples say,
   'You raised us up', than 'You were our decay'?
   And mothers' tongues teach their first-born to sing
   Of your good deeds than by the bad to wring?
Hobson No more, Master Dean Nowell, no more;
   I think these words should make a man of flint
   To mend his life. How say you Master Gresham?
Gresham 'Fore God, they have started tears into my eyes.
   And Master Dean Nowell, you shall see
   The words that you have spoke have wrought effect in me.
Nowell Begin, then, whilst you live, lest being dead,
   The good you give in charge be never done.
   Make your own hands your executors, your eyes overseers,
   And have this saying ever in your mind:
      Women be forgetful, children be unkind.
      Executors be covetous and take what they find.
Hobson In my time I have seen many of them.

Gresham I'll learn, then, to prevent them whilst I live;
The good I mean to do, these hands shall give.

From *scene x*

[*Following the completion of the Royal Exchange, Sir Thomas Gresham entertains the Russian ambassador at his home. Also present are Sir Thomas Ramsey, now Lord Mayor, Lady Ramsey, Master Hobson and an entourage of gentlemen. A merchant arrives and attempts to sell a pearl so costly that kings and dukes have declined to buy it. Then, as the selection here begins, Gresham is greeted with two bits of bad news. First, a ship bearing the portraits of English monarchs, with which Gresham had intended to adorn his new Exchange, has sunk. Second, the £60,000 he has laid out for the right to trade in sugar during the lifetime of the King of Barbary is lost with the King's sudden death. His successor refuses to respect the agreement or to return the money, sending only a dagger and pair of slippers instead. Gresham is galvanised to a splendid display of equanimity. He purchases the priceless pearl, grinds it to a powder, and drinks it off in his wine while dancing in his slippers.*]

Enter a Mariner.

Gresham ... What news from sea?
How stands my ships?
Mariner Your ships in which all the kings' pictures were,
From Brute unto our Queen Elizabeth,
Drawn in white marble, by a storm at sea
Is wracked and lost.
Gresham The loss, I weigh not this;
Only it grieves me that my famous building
Shall want so rich and fair an ornament.
Lady Ramsey It touches all the City, for those pictures
Had doubly graced this royal edifice.
Ramsey Methinks the ship's loss most should trouble you.
Gresham My ship's but wealth: why, we have wealth;
The pictures were the grace of my new Burse:
So I might them in their true form behold,
I cared not to have lost their weights in gold.
First Lord (aside) A noble citizen!

Enter a Factor.

Gresham Our factor, what good news from Barbary?
  What says the king? Speak, didst thou summon him?
  Or hast thou brought my threescore thousand pound?
  Or shall I have the sugars at that rate?
  If so, new marble pictures we'll have wrought,
  And in a new ship from beyond sea brought.
Factor The king that in the regal chair succeeds
  The king late dead I summoned, and demanded
  Either your money tendered or the sugars,
  After the rate proposed; he denied both,
  Alleging though he was successive heir,
  He was not therefore either tied to pay
  The late king's debts, nor yet to stand unto
  Unnecessary bargains. Notwithstanding,
  To gratify your love, the king hath sent you
  As presents, not as satisfaction,
  A costly dagger and a pair of slippers,
  And there's all for your threescore thousand pound.
Gresham By'r Lady, a dear bargain.
First Lord (aside) I fear me this will plague him, a strange cross.
  How will he take this news, loss upon loss?
Second Lord (aside) Nay, will it not undo him?
  Doth he not wish his buildings in his purse?
Gresham A dagger, that's well;
  A pair of slippers — Come, undo my shoes.
  What, thirty thousand pound in sterling money,
  And paid me all in slips? Then, hautboys, play!
  On slippers I'll dance all my care away.
  Fit, fit, he had just the length of my foot.
  You may report, lords, when you come to court,
  You Gresham saw a pair of slippers wear
  Cost thirty thousand pound.
First Lord (aside) Somewhat too dear.
Gresham Nor yet, for all this treasure we have lost,
  Repents it us one penny of our cost.
Second Lord (aside) As royal in his virtues as his buildings.
Ramsey These losses would have killed me.
Gresham   Jeweller,
  Let's see thy pearl. Go pound it in a mortar,
  Beat it to powder, then return it to me.

(Exit Jeweller.)

What dukes, and lords, and these ambassadors
Have even before our face refused to purchase,
As of too high a price to venture on,
Gresham, a London merchant, will here buy.

(Enter Jeweller.)

What, is it broken small? Fill us some wine,
Fuller, yet fuller, till the brim o'erflows.
Here sixteen thousand pound at one clap goes;
Instead of sugar, Gresham drinks this pearl
Unto his queen and mistress — Pledge it, lords!
Who ever saw a merchant bravelier fraught
In dearer slippers, or a richer draught?
Ramsey You are an honour to all English merchants,
    As bountiful as rich, as charitable
    As rich, as renowned as any of all.
Gresham I do not this as prodigal of my wealth;
    Rather, to show how I esteem that loss
    Which cannot be regained. A London merchant
    Thus treads on a king's present.

6

A Song of Richard Whittington
(Richard Johnson, 1612)

To the tune of 'Dainty, Come thou to Me'

Here must I tell the praise
    Of worthy Whittington,
Known to be in his days
    Thrice Lord Mayor of London.
But of poor parentage
    Born he was, as we hear,
And in his tender age
    Bred up in Lancashire.

Poorly to London, then,
    Came up this simple lad,
Where with a merchant man,

Soon he a dwelling had,
And in a kitchen placed,
   A scullion for to be,
Whereas long time he passed,
   In labour drudgingly.

His daily service was
   Turning spits at the fire,
And to scour pots of brass
   For a poor scullion's hire.
Meat and drink all his pay,
   Of coin he had no store;
Therefore, to run away,
   In secret thought he bore.

So from this merchant man,
   Whittington secretly
Towards his country ran,
   To purchase liberty;
But as he went along,
   In a fair summer's morn,
London bells sweetly rung,
   'Whittington, back return.'

Ever more sounding so,
   'Turn again, Whittington,
For thou in time shalt grow
   Lord Mayor of London' —
Whereupon back again
   Whittington came with speed,
A prentice to remain,
   As the Lord had decreed.

'Still blessed be the bells',
   This was his daily song;
'They my good fortune tells,
   most sweetly have they rung.
If God so favour me,
   I will not prove unkind;
London my love shall see,
   And my great bounties find.'

But see his happy chance:
    This scullion had a cat,
Which did his state advance,
    And by it wealth he gat.
His master ventured forth,
    To a land far unknown,
With merchandise of worth,
    As is in stories shown.

Whittington had no more
    But his poor cat as than,[29]
Which to the ship he bore,
    Like a brave merchant man.
'Venturing the same,' quoth he,
    'I may get store of gold,
And Mayor of London will be,
    As the bells have me told.'

Whittington's merchandise
    Carried was to a land
Troubled with rats and mice,
    As they did understand;
The king of that country there,
    As he at dinner sat,
Daily remained in fear
    Of many a mouse and rat.

Meat that on the trenchers lay,
    No way they could keep safe,
But by rats born away,
    Fearing no wand nor staff;
Whereupon, soon they brought
    Whittington's nimble cat,
Which by the king was bought,
    Heaps of gold given for that.

Home again came these men,
    With their ship loaden so;
Whittington's wealth began
    By this cat thus to grow.
Scullion's life he forsook

To be a merchant good,
And soon began to look
    How well his credit stood.

After this he was chose
    Shrieve of this City here,
And then full quickly rose
    Higher, as did appear;
For to this City's praise,
    Sir Richard Whittington
Came to be in his days,
    Thrice Mayor of London.

More his fame to advance,
    Thousands he lent his king
To maintain wars in France,
    Glory from thence to bring.
And after, at a feast
    That he the king did make,
Burned all the bonds in jest,
    And would no money take.

Ten thousand pound he gave
    To his prince willingly,
And would not one penny have;
    Thus in kind courtesy,
God did thus make him great;
    So would he daily see
Poor people fed with meat,
    (To show his charity).

Prisoners, poor, cherished were,
    Widows sweet comfort found;
Good deeds, both far and near,
    Of him do still resound.
Whittington College is
    One of his charities;
Records reporteth this
    To lasting memories.

Newgate he builded fair
   For prisoners to live in,
Christ Church[30] he did repair,
   Christian love for to win.
Many more such like deeds
   Was done by Whittington,
Which joy and comfort breeds
   To such as looks thereon.

Lancashire, thou hast bred
   This flower of charity;
Though he be gone and dead,
   Yet lives he lastingly.
Those bells that called him so,
   'Turn again, Whittington',
Call you back many mo,
   To live so in London.

Notes

1. To write, compose.
2. Advancement.
3. Foresight.
4. Walworth himself narrates the story.
5. Strike.
6. Recompense.
7. See Romans 13.
8. Rebellion.
9. Leash.
10. Mountainish; perhaps also 'Mohammetanist' (Evans).
11. Ambition, presumption.
12. Dig.
13. The district around the former collegiate church of St Martin-le-Grand, located on the east side of St Martin's Lane. Hall's *Chronicle* reports that the riot began in Cheapside and 'ran a plump through St Nicholas Shambles and at St Martin's Gate there met with them Sir Thomas More'.
14. Watch.
15. Brighten up.
16. The Tudor rose appeared on the threepenny piece from 1551.
17. Querulously.
18. The hood is trimmed with sheep's wool.
19. Disguised as Hans, Rowland Lacy has previously loaned to Eyre 20 Portuguese gold coins, two-thirds of a gift from his uncle, thereby enabling Eyre to speculate successfully on the cargo of a Dutch freighter.
20. Proverbial for the trade of shoemaking, derived, alternatively, from the Legend of St Hugh, patron saint of shoemakers, or as a title bestowed by King

Edward; in frequent use in the 1590s by writers like Robert Wilson, Robert Greene and Thomas Deloney.

21. The home of Sir Roger Oteley, located in the village of Old Ford.

22. Fancies.

23. Dance.

24. Rascals.

25. Probably the Great Conduit in Cheapside; apprentices gathered at the conduits to fetch water for their masters.

26. Church bells ringing on Shrove Tuesday.

27. Pearls, good fellows.

28. Gresham has sent his nephew, mad Jack Gresham, for the £100 settlement that ends his quarrel with Ramsey.

29. At that time.

30. I.e. Christchurch, Farringdon, constituted from the old church of the Greyfriars after the Dissolution.

11

THE CITY IN A NUTSHELL: EPIGRAMS

Though it enjoyed a special vogue from 1590 to 1620, the epigram was a form widely practised throughout the English Renaissance, from Thomas More and the jester John Heywood, to Donne, Jonson and Herrick. One Latin humanist declared that 'there are as many kinds of epigrams as of things', and indeed, the English epigramatists, typically gentlemen of a wide swallow, wrote in a variety of epigramatic forms on a variety of subjects. But a large and distinctive portion of their work was devoted to the life of London. A few of these poems, like the ones which begin the selections here, praise London or pay tribute to such prominent officials as Alexander Nowell, a sixteenth-century Dean of St Paul's. Most London epigrams, however, are not the poised and polished sort that Ben Jonson called his 'riper studies', but a comparatively raw variety, satiric and sometimes scurrilous, composed by young wits at the Inns of Court, and by popular and professional satirists. They are coloured by the facetious spirit invoked by Sir John Davies when he sends his 'merry Muse unto that merry town,/ ... where all good spirits love to be'. Their aim, in the words of one contemporary, is to be 'pithy and pleasant ... pretty, short, witty, quick, and quipping'.

The epigram was imitated from classical models, especially from the Roman poet, Martial, whose satiric epigrams provided perhaps the nearest classical equivalent to what English poets regarded as their own urbanity. The use of Latin names in the epigrams below, whether to conceal the identity of a specific victim or to invoke a broad Latin stereotype, is but one means by which English epigramatists acknowledged the Roman pedigree of the form. But it would be as mistaken to equate English with Roman urbanity as to trace the London of the English epigram exclusively to Rome. The merchants, apprentices, aldermen and decayed gentlemen of the

239

London epigram belong just as surely to the mobile urban culture of the Renaissance as do the native forms of raillery and jest, which, along with Martial, helped to shape the genre. Indeed, like the jests represented in Chapter 5, the epigram emphasises the sort of witty improvisation by which an urbanite achieves a timely mastery over his environment. Through their love of vigorous, aggressive, urbane wit, Londoners learned to identify the epigram as a form of street wisdom as well as a Roman importation. From John Stow's translation of Fitzstephen's twelfth-century *Descriptio Londinae* they could discover that for centuries London schoolboys had been 'nipping and quipping their fellows' in epigrams and rhymes. In his *Survay of London* (1598), Stow pauses to record several epigrams in which clever language compensates for the social and economic disequilibrium of city life; the overweening goldsmith, Jasper Fisher, for example, found his ostentatious house immortalised with those of other parvenus in 'Kirby's castle, and Fisher's folly,/ Spinola's pleasure, and Meggs's glory'. Old Hobson, the merry Londoner, forever linked four aldermen in the epigram, 'Ramsey the rich, Bond the stout,/ Beecher the gentleman and Cooper the lout'. No wonder, then, that Shakespeare defined the epigram as a paper bullet.

The lapidary neatness of such formulaic barbs in fact exploits by parody the memorial inscriptions from which the ancient epigram evolved and which Londoners found everywhere in their environment, on walls, gates, tombs and monuments. Through these inscriptions, wealthy citizens and officials sought to make the urban space an articulate order. Over the portal to the Leadenhall, for example, the irrepressible Simon Eyre summarised his remarkable career in the candid admission, *dextra Domini exaltavit me*, the right hand of God has raised me up.

But the impulse to immortalise by inscription could easily become the satiric impulse to fix a neat, indelible image in a last, unanswerable word. Sir Thomas Gresham, who built the Royal Exchange but prudently left his sedate tomb uninscribed, failed to escape the facetious epitaph of John Hoskyns (see 11.6 below). The parody of inscriptions was carried to its logical conclusion when the epigram was actually posted as a sign or memento. George Puttenham traced the life of the epigram to 'our tavern and common tabling houses, where many merry heads meet, and scribble with ink, with chalk, or with a coal such matters as they would every man should know, and descant upon'. The epigram could thus become a sophisticated form of graffiti. Stow records that in St Paul's, under the 'most sumptuous monument' of Sir Christopher Hatton, which overshadowed those of the popular Sir Philip Sidney and Sir Francis Walsingham, 'a merry poet writ thus: "Philip and Francis have no tomb,/ For great Christopher takes all the room".' The jest-book hero Tarlton scrawled his salty epigrams on the wainscoting, and in the series of incidents that led to his expulsion from the Middle Temple for brawling, young John Davies found himself libelled in epigrams 'set up against him in all the famous places of the city'.

These physical manifestations underline the extent to which the epigram was a means for labelling or anatomising the urban landscape. A number of the examples included here satirise merchants, merchants' wives, aspiring apprentices and parvenus, whose ambitions and mobility challenged the stability of the social order. In these epigrams, the writer holds out the hope that his world may still, in Hamlet's phrase, be bounded in a nutshell. The main poetic resources of the epigram, which are not elaborate conceits and metaphors but clever schemes of balance and antithesis, enable the epigramatist to schematise his city or the social order, to organise names, places and social types in revealing counterpoint. This is perhaps most strikingly apparent in those epigrams which build themselves specifically around place names.

A further feature of the epigram, its concluding witty turn or exclamation, helped to reinforce the hope of binding the city in a nutshell, but as Thomas Freeeman's epigram on the growth of London indicates, this could sometimes be a futile enterprise. Indeed, several of the longer epigrams included here (and their length is itself revealing) are teeming with a wealth and variety of lively detail that defies containment in such narrow room as the epigram affords. The epigramatists themselves frequently admitted to the strains that London could place on their enterprise, as if it refused to be encapsulated. Despite the lapidary origins of the epigram, despite its traditional aim of rendering things permanently memorable, the London epigram sometimes led its practitioners into an obsession with their own ephemerality. The earliest manuscript title of Sir John Davies' epigrams was 'English Epigrams much like Buckminster's Almanac, serving for all England, but especially for the meridian of the honourable city of London calculated by John Davies ... Anno 1594 in November'. John Weever similarly complained that 'Epigrams are much like

unto almanacs, serving especially for the year in which they are
made; ... being one year penned, and in another printed: are past
due before they come from the press.' Beyond the calculated
sprezzatura of such remarks lies a deeper ambivalence about the
form, an awareness that the epigram sometimes perishes in the task
it performs, confounded not by ineffable beauty, love, or the might
of the divine, but by a concrete mystery antithetical to the sublime,
the mystery of a city vibrantly alive.

1
London, Anciently Called Troynovant
(John Owen, 1628)

As from the old Phoenix' ashes a new springs,
So from Troy's ashes, London her birth brings.

2
London Like a Laurel Leaf
(James Howell, 1657)

London is like a laurel leaf; may she
Be verdant still, and flourish like the tree.

3
London's Loadstone
(John Owen, 1628)

As Thames devours many small brooks and rills,
So smaller towns with their wealth London fills;
But though that Thames empt's itself in the sea,
Wealth once at London never runs away.

4
London Like a Spleen
(James Howell, 1660)

London to the rest of England is like the spleen,

Whose swelling makes the rest of the body lean,
And lank.

5
To Alexander Nowell
(John Parkhurst, 1577)

Great Alexander all the world did in subjection bring:
Rude barbarous people thou dost tame; thou dost a greater thing.

6
Of Sir Thomas Gresham
(John Hoskyns)

Here lies Gresham under the ground,
   As wise as fifty thousand pound.
   He never refused the drink of his friend;
Drink was his life and drunk was his end.

7
[Four Famous Aldermen]
(Richard Johnson, 1607)

Ramsey the rich, Bond the Stout,
Beecher the gentleman, and Cooper the lout.

8
[The Houses of Four Parvenus]
(John Stow, 1598)

Kirby's castle, and Fisher's folly,
Spinola's pleasure, and Meggs's glory.

9
An Enigma
(John Cooke, 1604)

The Court hath got the City with child,
Which well hath cost their purse;
The Country with it is beguiled,
With whom it is at nurse. ·

10
To Hornet
(Ben Jonson, 1616)

Hornet, thou hast thy wife dressed, for the stall,
To draw thee custom: but her self gets all.

11
[A Painted Lady]
(Richard Niccols, 1614)

A friend and I consorting on our way,
In midst of Cheap upon a working day,
Spied a fair painted picture, as we thought,
Upon a stall, set to be sold and bought.
But mark our gross mistake, when we drew near
To view the same, it plainly did appear
    By knocking those light heels against the bench,
    'Twas no dead picture, but a lively wench.

12
***Ostendis haedera vinum*[1]**
(Henry Parrot, 1608)

A scoffing mate, passing along Cheapside,
Incontinent[2] a gallant lass espied;
Whose tempting breasts (as to the sale laid out)
Incites this youngster thus to 'gin to flout[3].
'Lady,' quoth he, 'is this flesh to be sold?'

'No Lord,' quoth she, 'for silver nor for gold;
But wherefore ask you?' (and there made a stop).
'To buy,' quoth he, 'if not, shut up your shop.'

13
In Quandam [On a Certain Woman]
(Richard West, 1608)

Is she that merchant's wife? I know that face,
And sure have seen it, in some other place.
Let's see, did not I meet her on the way?
Or see her at a sermon, or a play,
Or where was it? I'faith t'would please me well,
If I for certainty the place could tell;
   Oh now I have't, but 'tis not worth a louse:
   'Twas but her picture, at a bawdy house.

14
Against the Nobly-Descended Museus
(John Davies of Hereford, 1611)

The well-born Museus wedded hath of late
A butcher's daughter fat, for pounds and plate:
Which match is like a pudding, sith in that
He puts the blood, her father all the fat.

15
[A City Wife]
(Richard Niccols, 1614)

What have we here? a city dame? sure no,
'Tis Jove's own Iris,[4] or she should be so.
How daintily the rainbow round dispred
Under her light-scotch[5] hat becomes her head;
It is a sign the weather will be fair.
To the new walks[6] she is gone to take the air,
But at that little gate how gets she out,
Her head with such a compass arched about?

With much ado; therefore these dames desire
Great London will build little Moregate[7] higher.

16
Upon Rusco
(Henry Peacham, 1620)

Rusco to London having brought his son,
To bind him prentice, asked of the lad,
What trade best liked him, for he must take one,
And only stick to that he chosen had.
'Then father, if unto an Alderman
For seven years I were bound, I did not care,
    So after I my time had served,' quoth John,
    'I might be sure for to be Lord Mayor.'

17
Hinc illae lacrimae[8]
(Thomas Freeman, 1614)

Alas the while, poor kitchen boys may curse
That whirling lacks, and dogs in wheels turn broaches,[9]
And serving men, poor souls, have fared the worse,
Since great men got the trick to ride in coaches.
These first of these for food may now go starve,
Nor needs th'attendance of a servingman,
A horse-paced footman and a coach will serve;
For certainly since first the world began,
    And great men, with the world, to run on wheels,
    They have got but few or no men at their heels.

18
In Rusticum, A Charitable Clown
(Roger Sharpe, 1610)

Rusticus an honest country swain,
Whose education simple was, and plain,
Having surveyed the City round about,

Emptied his purse, and so went trudging out.
But by the way he saw, and much respected,
A door belonging to a house infected;
Whereon was placed (as 'tis the custom still)
LORD HAVE MERCY UPON US; this sad bill
The sot perused, and having read, he swore
All London was ungodly, but that door.
'Here dwells some virtue yet,' says he, 'for this
A most devout religious saying is.'
And thus he wished (with putting off his hat)
That every door had such a bill as that.

19
In Priscum
(Richard Niccols, 1614)

'Mongst the monopolists on London's Burse,
Priscus was ta'en for cutting of a purse,
And being reviled, made this bold question, 'Why
Are these monopolists excused, since I
Did cut but one man's purse, while they cut all?'
But thus we see, the weakest goes to th' wall.

20
Partiality
(John Taylor, 1614/1630)

Strato the gallant reels alongst the street,
His addle head's too heavy for his feet;
What though he swear and swagger, spurn and kick,
Yet men will say the gentleman is sick,
And that 'twere good to learn where he doth dwell,
And help him home, because he is not well.
Straight staggers by a porter, or a carman,
As bumsy[10] as a foxed flapdragon[11] German:
And though the gentleman's disease and theirs,
Are parted only with a pair of shears,
Yet they are drunken knaves, and must to th'stocks,
And there endure a world of flouts and mocks.

Thus when brave Strato's wits with wine are shrunk,
The same disease will make a begger drunk.

21
Upon Rosimus
(Henry Peacham, 1620)

Mishaps as well by water as by land,
Our human frailty every hour attend,
With all his wit which man cannot withstand;
As may appear by Rosimus my friend,
    Who going to Duke Humphrey's[12] to sup,
    Was on the Thames by baillies snapped up.

22
***Semel insanivimus*[13]**
(Sir John Mennes and James Smith, 1640)

Bedlam, fate bless thee, thou want'st nought but wit,
And having gotten that, we're free from it;
Bridwell, I cannot any way dispraise thee,
For thou dost feed the poor, and jerk the lazy.
Newgate, of thee I cannot much complain;
For once a month, thou freest men out of pain;
But from the Counters, gracious Lord defend us!
To Bedlam, Bridewell, or to Newgate send us,
For there in time wit, work, or law sets free;
But here wit, work, nor law gets liberty.

23
***Quisquis sibi quaerit egenus*[14]**
(Henry Parrot, 1608)

'This observation seems', quoth Fisco, 'strange,
Why merchants walk in Paul's[15] and knights the Exchange:
Belike the one seeks those their debts should pay,
Whiles th'other goes to crave a longer day.'

24
[The Old and New Exchanges]
(John Heywood, 1562)

Few gallants lately will, nor is it strange,
Bargain for needments in the New Exchange;[16]
For on the Strand, the New stands bleak and cold,
And they are hot in credit with the Old.[17]

25
Of Naevia
(Everard Guilpin, 1598)

Naevia is one while of the Inns of Court,
Toiling in Brooke, Fitzherbert, and in Dyer;[18]
Another while th'Exchange he doth resort,
Moiling as fast, a seller, and a buyer.
    Will not he thrive (think ye) who can devise,
    Thus to unite the law and merchandise?
    Doubtless he will, or cozen[19] out of doubt;
    What matters that? his law will bear him out.

26
Seeking for a Dwelling Place
(John Heywood, 1562)

Still thou seekest for a quiet dwelling-place:
What place for quietness hast though now in chase?
London Bridge? That's ill for thee, for the water.
Queenhithe? That's more ill for another matter.
Smart's Key? That's most ill for fear of smarting smart.
Carter Lane? Nay, nay! that soundeth all on the cart.
Paul's Chain? Nay, in no wise dwell not near the chain.
Wood Street? Why wilt thou be wood[20] once again?
Bread Street? That's too dry, by drought thou shalt be dead.
Philpot Lane? That breedeth moist humours in thy head.
Silver Street? Coppersmiths[21] in Silver Street; fie!
Newgate Street? 'Ware that, man! Newgate is hard by.
Foster Lane? Thou wilt as soon be tied fast, as fast.
Crooked Lane? Nay, crook no more, be straight at last.

Creed Lane? They fall out there, brother against brother.[22]
Ave Mary Lane? That's as ill as t'other.[23]
Paternoster Row? Paternoster Row?
Agreed! That's the quietest place I know.

27
[The Seven Sights of London]
(Richard Brathwaite, 1638)

Seven hills there were in Rome, and so there be
Seven sights in New Troy crave our memory:
Tombs,[24] Guildhall giants, stage-plays, Bedlam poor,
Ostrich,[25] Bear Garden, lions in the Tower.

28
London's Progress
(Thomas Freeman, 1614)

Why how now, Babel, whither wilt thou build? —
The old Holborn, Charing Cross, the Strand,
Are going to St Giles' in the Fields,
Saint Katherine she takes Wapping by the hand,
And Hogsdon will to Highgate ere't be long.
London has got a great way from the stream.
I think she means to go to Islington,
To eat a dish of strawberries and cream.
The City's sure in progress, I surmise,
Or going to revel it in some disorder,
Without the walls, without the liberties,
Where she need fear nor Mayor nor Recorder.
Well, say she do, 'twere pretty, yet 'tis pity,
A Middlesex bailiff should arrest the City.

29
Of a Gull
(Sir John Davies, 1590)

Oft in my laughing rhymes, I name a gull,
But this new term will many questions breed;
Therefore at first I will express at full,
Who is a true and perfect gull indeed.

A gull is he, who fears a velvet gown,
And when a wench is brave, dares not speak to her;
A gull is he which traverseth the town,
And is for marriage known a common wooer.

A gull is he, which while he proudly wears
A silver-hilted rapier by his side,
Endures the lies and knocks about his ears,
Whilst in his sheath, his sleeping sword doth bide.

A gull is he which wears good handsome clothes,
And stands in presence stroking up his hair,
And fills up his unperfect speech with oaths,
But speaks not one wise word throughout the year.

But to define a gull in terms precise,
A gull is he which seems, but is not wise.

30
[A Gull]
(Everard Guilpin, 1598)

He is a gull, whose indiscretion
Cracks his purse strings to be in fashion;
He is a gull, who is long in taking root
In barren soil, where can be but small fruit;
He is a gull, who runs himself in debt
For twelve days' wonder, hoping so to get;
He is a gull, whose conscience is a block,
Not to take interest, but to waste his stock;
He is a gull, who cannot have a whore,

But brags how much he spends upon her score;
He is a gull, that for commodity
Pays ten times ten, and sells the same for three;
He is a gull, who passing finical,
Peiseth[26] each word to be rhetorical;
And to conclude, who self-contentedly
Thinks all men gulls, there's none more gull than he.

31
In Philonem
(Sir John Davies, 1590)

Philo the gentleman, the fortune teller,
The schoolmaster, the midwife, and the bawd,
The conjurer, the buyer and the seller
Of painting[27] which with breathing will be thawed,
   Doth practise physic, and his credit grows
    As doth the ballad-singer's auditory,
    Which hath at Temple Bar his standing chose,
    And to the vulgar sings an ale-house story.
First stands a porter, then an oyster-wife
Doth stint her cry and stay her steps to hear him,
Then comes a cutpurse ready with his knife,
And then a country client presseth near him;
   There stands the constable, there stands the whore,
    And hark'ning to the song mark not each other.
   There by the sergeant stands the debtor poor,
    And doth no more mistrust him than his brother:
Thus Orpheus to such hearers giveth music,
And Philo to such patients giveth physic.

32
In Publium
(Sir John Davies, 1590)

Publius, student at the common law,
Oft leaves his books, and for his recreation,
To Paris Garden doth himself withdraw;
Where he is ravished with such delectation,

As down amongst the dogs and bears he goes,
Where whilst he skipping cries, 'To head, to head,'
His satin doublet and his velvet hose
Are all with spittle from above bespread.
Then is he like his father's country hall,
Stinking with dogs, and muted all with hawks.
And rightly too on him this filth doth fall,
Which for such filthy sports his books forsakes,
Leaving old Plowden, Dyer and Brooke[28] alone,
To see old Harry Hunkes[29] and Sacarson.[30]

33
[Sir Revel]
(Samuel Rowlands, 1604)

'Speak gentlemen, what shall we do today?
Drink some brave health upon the Dutch[31] carouse,
Or shall we to the Globe to see a play,
Or visit Shoreditch for a bawdy-house?
Let's call for cards or dice, and have a game;
To sit thus idle, is both sin and shame.'
Thus speaks Sir Revel, furnished out with fashion,
From dish-crowned hat unto the shoe's square toe,
That haunts at whore-house but for recreation,
Plays but a dice to cony-catch, or so;
Drinks drunk in kindness, for good fellowship,
Or to the play goes but some purse to nip.

34
A Strange Sighted Traveller
(Samuel Rowlands, 1608)

An honest country fool, being gentle bred,
Was by an odd conceited humour led
To travel, and some English fashions see,
With such strange sights as here at London be.
Stuffing his purse with a good golden sum,
This wand'ring knight did to the City come,
And there a servingman he entertains,

An honester in Newgate not remains.
He showed his master sights to him most strange,
Great tall Paul's steeple and the Royal Exchange,
The Boss at Billingsgate[32] and London Stone,[33]
And at Whitehall the monstrous great whale's bone;
Brought him to the Bankside where bears do dwell,
And unto Shoreditch where the whores keep hell;
Showed him the lions, giants in Guildhall,
King Lud at Ludgate, the baboons and all;
At length his man, on all he had did prey,
Showed him a thievish trick and ran away.
The traveller turned home exceeding civil,
And swore in London he had seen the Devil.

35
Of Caius
(Everard Guilpin, 1598)

As Caius walks the streets, if he but hear
A blackman[34] grunt his note, he cries, 'oh rare!'
He cries, 'oh rare,' to hear the Irishmen
Cry 'Pip, fine pip' with a shrill accent when
He comes at Mercer's Chapel; and, 'oh rare,'
At Ludgate at the prisoner's plain-song there;
'Oh rare,' sings he, to hear a cobbler sing,
Or a wassail on twelfth night, or the ring
At cold St Pancras church,[35] or any thing;
He'll cry, 'oh rare,' and scratch the elbow too,
To see two butcher's curs fight; the cuckoo
Will cry, 'oh rare,' to see the champion bull,
Or the victorious mastiff with crowned scull;
And garlanded with flowers, passing along
From Paris Garden he renews his song,
To see my L. Mayor's henchmen; or to see
(At an old Alderman's blessed obsequy)
The Hospital boys[36] in their blue equipage.
Or at a carted bawd, or whore in cage;
He'll cry, 'oh rare,' at a gong-farmer's[37] cart,
'Oh rare,' to hear a ballad or a fart.
Briefly, so long he hath used to cry, 'oh rare,'

That now that phrase is grown thin and threadbare;
But sure his wit will be more rare and thin,
If he continue as he doth begin.

Notes

1. 'You advertise wine by means of ivy'; the ivy bush was commonly displayed on the signs of wine shops.
2. Immediately.
3. Mock.
4. Goddess of the rainbow.
5. Cheap lawn.
6. In Moorfields, a fen drained in 1527 and laid out with walks in 1606.
7. I.e. Moorgate, the City gate leading to Moorfields.
8. Hence those tears (Terence).
9. That dogs on treadmills replace kitchen boys in turning spits (broaches).
10. Tipsy.
11. A raisin floated and sipped off flaming brandy; used in contempt of Germans, who were proverbial drunkards.
12. On the south side of the nave of St Paul's, the tomb of John Beauchamp, mistakenly identified as that of Humphrey, Duke of Gloucester, was a common meeting-place of penniless gentlemen in search of dinner invitations.
13. We go mad once for all.
14. Whoever is poor seeks for himself.
15. A common haunt of idle, debt-ridden gentlemen.
16. Opened in the Strand by James I in 1609.
17. I.e., Sir Thomas Gresham's Royal Exchange, finished in 1567.
18. Sir Robert Brooke, Sir Anthony Fitzherbert, and Sir James Dyer were judges who published major legal compilations during the sixteenth century.
19. Cheat.
20. Mad.
21. Jewellers who falsely sold as silver, rings made principally of copper.
22. Alluding to the Reformation conflicts over religious doctrines.
23. Because it suggests the Catholic veneration of the Virgin Mary.
24. In Westminster Abbey.
25. Unidentified.
26. Weighs.
27. Cosmetics.
28. Like Brooke, Fitzherbert and Dyer, Edmund Plowden was a sixteenth-century legal scholar.
29. A famous bear.
30. A famous bear-baiting dog.
31. I.e.Germans, who were known as proverbial drinkers.
32. A drinking fountain.
33. A milestone, of unknown date, located in Candlewick or Cannon Street.
34. A seller of boot-blacking, see 6.4.
35. Stow notes that St Pancras has such stinting benefactors as 'the least bell in their church being broken, have rather sold the same for half the value, than put the parish to charge with new casting'.
36. The orphan boys of Christ's Hospital.
37. Privy-farmer, scavenger.

12

COMING AND GOING:
POEMS OF TRANSIT

Lyric poetry frequently concerns itself with those gaps of space and time that lie between here and there, between what is and what might be. On occasion, lyric poets span these gaps in the celebration of paradise found. But a more common mood in the poetry of place is the longing for a realm elsewhere, a longing that may be fed by revulsion toward familiar ground or by hope in what lies over the horizon. Given the spatial dynamics of lyric desire, it is not surprising to find cities often prominently featured in the lyric landscape.

Whether pastoral or Horatian, the ancient contrast between country and city provided Englishmen with a mythical language in which to register their responses to London and to its impact on traditional English society. The alleged decline in rural hospitality and the growing challenge to traditional social structures encouraged poets to set the busy and unstable life of London against the ostensibly abiding virtues of the countryside. Even the extreme versions of this strategy — in primitivistic pastorals which present the country as both historically and ideally prior to urban life — have their ultimate relation to the image of London. But the poems below take the city, rather than the country, as their focus, and they register the poet's relation to the city as he anticipates his departure or arrival. Thomas Randolph's ode to Anthony Stafford, for example, captures much of the prophetic force of Horace's sixteenth epode, which summons better Romans to abandon their city and seek the Islands of the Blessed; but his ridicule of London betrays an intimate acquaintance with the urban environment, and the alternative rural conviviality it proposes is both Horatian and fundamentally urbane. The contrast between country and city, *otium* and *negotium*, leisure and business, seems, in fact, to have had its greatest appeal at precisely that point where the actual

257

boundaries between the two were breaking down, as physical and economic mobility, the London law terms, its marriage market, and the business transactions of rural gentlefolk were establishing the migratory rhythms of the London season. Several of the poems here, such as Donne's epistle to his fellow satirist, Everard Guilpin, a bureaucrat who resided in suburban Highgate, or William Habington's defence of the Long Vacation, approach these rhythms as matters of civilised conoisseurship rather than moral crisis.

However, the city may also be the object of poignant nostalgia. The origin of the English word 'nostalgia' in the Greek word *nostos* helps to explain the peculiar resonance in this form of coming and going. Homer's *Odyssey* records the stories of the *nostoi*, or homecomings, of the Greek heroes from Troy, and in the homecoming of his greatest hero, Odysseus, Homer established the pattern of departure and return that is the basis of all later romance. As they anticipate their returns to London, Sir Thomas Wyatt and Robert Herrick draw considerable force from the narrative roots of romance, even while Wyatt's chivalric *élan* contrasts strongly with Herrick's modest, autobiographical and Horatian assertion of his free-born, burgherly status. At the opposite pole of this rhythm, leavetaking may be as plangent as in Herrick's 'Tears to Thamesis', as joyous as in Thomas Tomkins' pert lyric, or as affectedly contemptuous as is Thomas Randolph's ode. Occasionally, the perils of the journey to London merge with the narrative roots of romance to produce comic incident, as when Francis Thynne's traveller encounters a disillusioned visitor in headlong flight from the city.

Because movement in space is frequently a metaphor for change in time, several of the poems below enact crucial transitions or transformations, as the traveller, caught in mid-journey, ponders his goal. Perhaps the most famous English poem in this genre is Donne's 'Good Friday 1613, Riding Westward', but the wider use and popularity of the genre is reflected in Thomas Freeman's ridicule of a poem written on horseback. In the poems by Thomas Howell and George Gascoigne, London seems on the one hand to provide only the thinnest excuse for conventional meditations on fortune, worldliness and the vanity of human wishes. But on the other hand, the opening allusions to London in these poems, however lightly touched, establish an essential premise; London is a consummate symbol of the pursuit of worldly goods and the unreliability of shifting fortune. Perhaps the prototype in these cases is not Odysseus but — especially for Gascoigne — St Paul, who experienced his conversion in transit to the city. Another prototype, ironically, may be the legendary Dick Whittington, hero of a new type of economic romance, who renounced and returned to London on the single day that was to make his fortune. It is as such a symbol of earthly fortune that London becomes, in the lamenting song of a play by Nashe, performed in Croydon during an exodus from the plague-ridden city, the focus of the ultimate leavetaking.

1
Of his Return from Spain[1]
(Sir Thomas Wyatt, 1539/1557)

Tagus, farewell, that westward with thy streams
Turns up the grains of gold already tried,[2]
For I with spur and sail go seek the Thames,
Gainward the sun that showeth her wealthy pride,
And to the town that Brutus sought by dreams,
Like bended moon that leans her lusty side.
My King, my country, I seek for whom I live,
O mighty Jove! the winds for this me give.

2
To His Friend, Riding to London-Ward[3]
(George Turberville, 1567)

... O London loathsome lodge,
    why dost thou so procure
My love to leave this pleasant soil
    that hath my heart in cure?
Since needs it must be so,
    gainsend her home in haste:
Let her retire with harmless health
    that sickless hence is past.
Yield me a good accompt
    of her that is my joy,
And send her to her Troilus
    that longs for her in Troy.

3
Gascoigne's *De Profundis* (1573)

The skies gan scowl, o'ercast with misty clouds,
When (as I rode alone by London way,
Cloakless, unclad) thus did I sing and say:
'Behold,' quoth I, 'bright Titan how he shrouds
His head aback, and yields the rain his reach,
Till in his wrath, Dan Jove have soused the soil,
And washed me, wretch, which in his travail toil.
But holla, here, doth rudeness me apeach,
Since Jove is lord and king of mighty power,
Which can command the sun to show his face,
And, when him list, to give the rain his place,
Why do not I my weary muses frame
(Although I be well soused in this shower),
To write some verse in honour of his name?'

4
A Winter's Morning Muse
(Thomas Howell, 1581)

As by occasion late, towards Brutus' city old,
With quiet pace alone I rode, in winter sharp and cold,
In my dilating brains, a thousand thoughts were fed,
And battle-wise a war they made in my perplexed head.
I thought on timely change, and mused on yearly waste,
How winter aye devours the wealth that pleasant summer placed.
I saw the naked fields unclothed on every side,
The beaten bushes stand all bare, that late were decked with
    pride. ...
For as I musing rode, I plainly might perceive,
That like both change and chance there was, man's state that did
    bereave.
I saw the mounting mind, that climbed to reach the skies,
Advanced up by fortune's wheel, on tickle stay that lies,
Fall soon to flat decay, and headlong down doth reel,
As fickle Fortune list to whirl her round unstable wheel. ...
When thus along my way I diversely had mused,
I found whom fortune high did heave, on sudden he refused.

Than he by virtue stayed, me thought the rest did pass,
So far as doth the purest gold, the vile and basest brass.
Even he I deemed blest, that wearing virtue's crown,
Doth live content, not caring ought, how fortune smile or frown.

5
Galloping
(Francis Thynne, 1600)

From Windsor riding, to the stately town,
The seat of famous kings and England's pride,
In haste, I met, in midst of Hounslow down,
A gentle youth which postingly did ride,
A friend of mine, whom I forced there to stay,
To know the cause he rid so fast away.

Who said, 'Muse not, I friendly thee require,
To see me gallop with so light a head,
Since I far lighter am in this retire,
Than when to London I my journey sped.
For when I went, my creed twelve parts did hold,
But one is lost (so I more light and bold):
The twelfth; eleven I keep in store;
Christ went not unto hell:[4] what would you more?'

6
[Autumn][5]
(Thomas Nashe, 1592/1600)

Autumn hath all the summer's fruitful treasure,
Gone is our sport, fled is poor Croydon's pleasure;
Short days, sharp days, long nights come on apace,
Ah, who shall hide us from the winter's face?
Cold doth increase, the sickness will not cease,
And here we lie God knows with little ease.
   From winter, plague, and pestilence, good Lord deliver us.

London doth mourn, Lambeth[6] is quite forlorn,
Trades cry woe worth that ever they were born;

The want of term[7] is town and city's harm,
Close chambers we do want to keep us warm.
Long banished must we live from our friends;
This low-built house will bring us to our ends.
    From winter, plague, and pestilence, good Lord deliver us.

7
To Mr E. G.[8]
(John Donne, *c.* 1593)

Even as lame things thirst their perfection, so
The slimy[9] rhymes bred in our vale below,
Bearing with them much of my love and heart,
Fly unto that Parnassus[10] where thou art.
There thou o'erseest London; here I have been
By staying in London too much overseen.
Now pleasure's dearth our city doth possess;
Our theatres are filled with emptiness;
As lank and thin is every street and way
As a woman delivered yesterday.
Nothing whereat to laugh my spleen essays[11]
But bear-baitings or law exercise.
Therefore I'll leave it, and in the country strive
Pleasure, now fled from London, to retrieve.
Do thou so too; and fill not, like a bee,
Thy thighs with honey, but as plenteously
As Russian merchants, thyself's whole vessel load,
And then at winter retail it here abroad.
Bless us with Suffolk's[12] sweets; and, if it is
Thy garden, make thy hive and warehouse this.

8
In Iactantem Poetastrum[13]
(Thomas Freeman, 1614)

One told me once of verses that he made
    Riding to London on a trotting jade;
I should have known, had he concealed the case,
    Even by his verses, of his horse's pace.

9
[A Farewell]
(Thomas Tomkins, 1622)

Adieu, ye city-prisoning towers;
Better are the country bowers.
Winter is gone, the trees are springing;
Birds on every hedge sit singing.
Hark, how they chirp, come love, delay not,
Come, sweet love, O come and stay not.

10
From *Elegy I: To Charles Diodati*[14]
(John Milton, 1626/1645; William Cowper 1792/1808)

I well content, where Thames with refluent tide
My native city laves, meantime reside,
Nor zeal nor duty, now, my steps impell
To reedy Cam and my forbidden cell.
Nor aught of pleasure in those fields have I,
That, to the musing bard, all shade deny.
'Tis time that I a pedant's threats disdain,
And fly from wrongs my soul will ne'er sustain.
If peaceful days, in lettered leisure spent
Beneath my father's roof, be banishment,
Then call me banished; I will ne'er refuse
A name expressive of the lot I choose.
I would that, exiled to the Pontic shore,
Rome's hapless bard[15] had suffered nothing more.
He then had equalled even Homer's lays,
And Virgil! thou hadst won but second praise:
For here I woo the muse with no control,
And here my books — my life — absorb me whole.
Here too I visit, or to smile or weep,
The winding theatre's majestic sweep;
The grave or gay colloquial scene recruits[16]
My spirits, spent in learning's long pursuits. ...
Nor always city-pent, or pent at home,
I dwell; but, when spring calls me forth to roam,
Expatiate in our proud suburban shades

Of branching elm that never sun pervades.
Here many a virgin troop I may descry,
Like stars of mildest influence gliding by.
Oh forms divine! Oh looks that might inspire
E'en Jove himself, grown old, with young desire! ...
Oh city, founded by Dardanian[17] hands,
Whose towering front the circling realm commands,
Too blest abode! no loveliness we see
In all the earth, but it abounds in thee.
The virgin multitude that daily meets,
Radiant with gold and beauty, in thy streets,
Outnumbers all her train of fiery stars,
With which Diana[18] gilds thy lofty spires.
Fame says that, wafted hither by her doves,
With all her host of quiver-bearing loves,
Venus, preferring Paphian[19] scenes no more,
Has fixed her empire on thy nobler shore.
But lest the sightless boy enforce my stay,
I leave these happy walls while yet I may.
Immortal moly[20] shall secure my heart
From all the sorc'ry of Circaean art,
And I will e'en repass Cam's reedy pools
To face once more the warfare of the schools.

11
To My Worthy Cousin Mr E.C.[21]
In Praise of the City Life, in the Long Vacation[22]
(William Habington, 1634)

I like the green plush which your meadows wear,
I praise your pregnant fields, which duly bear
Their wealthy burden to th' industrious boor.
Nor do I disallow that who are poor
In mind and fortune thither should retire;
But hate that he who's warm with holy fire
Of any knowledge, and 'mong us may feast
On nectared wit, should turn himself t'a beast,
And graze ith' country. Why did nature wrong
So much her pains, as to give you a tongue
And fluent language, if converse you hold

With oxen in the stall, and sheep ith' fold?
But now it's Long Vacation you will say,
The town is empty, and who ever may
To th' pleasure of his country home repair,
Flies from th' infection of our London air.
In this' your errour. Now's the time alone
To live here, when the city dame is gone
T' her house at Brentford; for beyond that she
Imagines there's no land but Barbary,
Where lies her husband's factor.[23] When from hence
Rid is the country justice whose nonsense
Corrupted had the language of the Inn;
Where he and his horse littered, we begin
To live in silence; when the noise o' th' Bench
Not deafens Westminster, nor corrupt French[24]
Walks Fleet Street in her gown. Ruffs of the Bar
By the Vacation's power translated are,
To cut-work bands.[25] And who were busy here
Are gone to sow sedition in the shire.
The air by this is purged, and the term's strife
Thus fled the city: we the civil life
Lead happily. When, in the gentle way
Of noble mirth, I have the long-lived day
Contracted to a moment, I retire
To my Castara,[26] and meet such a fire
Of mutual love, that if the city were
Infected, it would purify the air.

12
An Ode to Mr Anthony Stafford, to Hasten him away into the Country
(Sir Thomas Randolph, 1638)

Come spur away,
I have no patience for a longer stay,
But must go down,
And leave the chargeable[27] noise of this great town.
I will the country see,
Where old simplicity,
Though hid in grey,

Doth look more gay
Than foppery in plush and scarlet clad.
  Farewell you city wits that are
    Almost at civil war;
'Tis time that I grow wise, when all the world grows mad.

          More of my days
I will not spend to gain an idiot's praise,
          Or to make sport
For some slight puny[28] of the Inns of Court.
      Then worthy Stafford say,
      How shall we spend the day,
        With what delights
        Shorten the nights?
When from this tumult we are got secure,
    Where mirth with all her freedom goes,
      Yet shall no finger lose;[29]
Where every word is thought, and every thought is pure.

          There from the tree
We'll cherries pluck, and pick the strawberry,
          And every day
Go see the wholesome country girls make hay;
      Whose brown hath lovelier grace,
      Than any painted face
        That I do know
        Hyde Park can show;
Where I had rather gain a kiss than meet
    (Though some of them in greater state
      Might court my love with plate[30])
The beauties of the Cheap, and wives of Lombard
      Street. ...

          And when we mean
To taste of Bacchus' blessings now and then,
          And drink by stealth
A cup or two to noble Berkeley's health,
      I'll take my pipe and try
      The Phrygian[31] melody;
        Which he that hears
        Lets through his ears

A madness to distemper all the brain.
  Then I another pipe will take,
    And Doric[32] music make,
To civilise with graver notes our wits again.

13
His Tears to Thamesis[33]
(Robert Herrick, 1648)

I send, I send here my supremest kiss
To thee my silver-footed Thamesis.
No more shall I reiterate thy Strand,
Whereon so many stately structures stand;
Nor in the summer's sweeter evenings go
To bathe in thee, as thousand others do.
No more shall I along thy crystal glide
In barge (with boughs and rushes beautified)
With smooth-soft virgins (for our chaste disport)
To Richmond, Kingston, and to Hampton Court;
Never again shall I with finny oar
Put from, or draw unto thy faithful shore;
And landing here, or safely landing there,
Make way to my beloved Westminster,
Or to the golden Cheapside, where the earth
Of Julia Herrick gave to me my birth.
May all clean nymphs and curious water dames,
With swan-like state, float up and down thy streams;
No drought upon thy wanton waters fall
To make them lean and languishing at all;
No ruffling winds come hither to disease
Thy pure and silver-wristed Naiades.
Keep up your state ye streams; and as ye spring,
Never make sick your banks by surfeiting.
Grow young with tides, and though I see ye never,
Receive this vow, so fare ye well forever.

14
His Return to London
(Robert Herrick, 1648)

From the dull confines of the drooping West,
To see the day spring from the pregnant East,
Ravished in spirit, I come, nay more, I fly
To thee, blest place of my nativity!
Thus, thus with hallowed foot I touch the ground
With thousand blessings by thy fortune crowned.
O fruitful genius! that bestowest here
An everlasting plenty, year by year.
O place! O people! Manners! framed to please
All nations, customs, kindreds, languages!
I am a free-born Roman;[34] suffer then,
That I amongst you live a citizen.
London my home is, though by hard fate sent
Into a long and irksome banishment;
Yet since called back, henceforward let me be,
O native country, repossessed by thee!
For, rather than I'll to the West return,
I'll beg of thee first here to have mine urn.
Weak I am grown, and must in short time fall;
Give thou my sacred relics burial.

15
Of Solitude
(Abraham Cowley, 1668)

Thou the faint beams of Reason's scattered light
    Dost like a burning-glass unite,
    Dost multiply the feeble heat,
And fortify the strength, till thou dost bright
    And noble fires beget.

Whilst this hard truth I teach, methinks I see
    The monster London laugh at me;
    I should at thee too, foolish city
(If it were fit to laugh at misery),
    But thy estate I pity.

Let but thy wicked men from out thee go,
    And all the fools that crowd thee so,
    And even thou, who dost thy millions boast,
A village less than Islington wilt grow,
    A solitude almost.

Notes

1. Wyatt was sent as an ambassador to Spain in 1537 and returned to England for the final time in June 1539.

2. The River Tagus in Spain and Portugal was proverbially supposed to turn up sands of sifted gold.

3. In several of his poems, Turberville adopts the persona of Tymetes, the unrequited lover of Pyndara (Anne Russell, Countess of Warwick), who has left him in the countryside and gone to London (see 13.3, below). Tymetes frequently compares himself to Troilus and his Pyndara to Cressida, thereby reversing the common association of London (Troynovant) with Troy.

4. The youth has lost his faith in that part of the Apostles' Creed which says that Christ descended into hell, because Christ has not been in London.

5. This song ends Thomas Nashe's *Summer's Last Will and Testament,* a play performed in 1592 at the Croydon palace of the Archbishop of Canterbury, while the plague was ravaging London.

6. The Archbishop's London place was in Lambeth, on the south bank of the Thames opposite Westminster.

7. The plague had caused the removal of the law term from London, but the phrase may also mean that the plague is without term or end.

8. Everard Guilpin (see, e.g., 7.7, above).

9. The sun was said to breed crocodiles from the silt of the River Nile.

10. Guilpin resided in Highgate, from whence he could look down on London; Parnassus, near Delphi, was sacred to Apollo and the Muses.

11. Tests, tastes.

12. Guilpin was descended from a Suffolk family.

13. On a vainglorious poetaster.

14. At the end of his first year at Cambridge in 1626, Milton was apparently rusticated as the result of friction with his tutor, William Chapell. He returned to his father's London home, where he wrote a Latin elegy on the subject of his exile to his closest friend and classmate both at St Paul's School and Cambridge, Charles Diodati. The translation of the elegy printed here was done by William Cowper and first published in 1808.

15. Ovid, whose spirit pervades Milton's elegy, was exiled from Rome to Tomis.

16. Replenishes.

17. Trojan; see I.1, above.

18. The moon.

19. Paphos, in Cyprus, was famed for its temple of Venus.

20. The magical herb which protected Odysseus from Circe's charms; a symbol of temperance.

21. Not identified.

22. The season when the London law courts are closed, between the end of Trinity Term, in late July, and the beginning of Michaelmas Term, in early October.

23. A merchant's overseas agent.
24. The Norman French of the law courts.
25. Short collars.
26. Castara, the poetic name given by Habington to Lucy Herbert, daughter of the first Baron Powis, whom he married in 1633, provides the title for Habington's 1634 collection of verse.
27. Burdensome.
28. Puisne — junior, inferior, puny.
29. Randolph lost a finger in a drunken brawl.
30. With a merchant's dowry of silver plate.
31. War-like.
32. Simple and solemn.
33. Herrick, the son of a London goldsmith, was in 1630 installed as vicar of Dean Prior, a parish in a desolate part of Devonshire; he did not return permanently to London until 1647.
34. See Acts 22:27–8.

13

LONDON IN LOVE: EROTICA

In the poetry of love, time and space typically form a background for the erotic, lyric present. Dante could trace to the 1st of May 1274, his first meeting with Beatrice in the house of her wealthy Florentine father, Folco Potinari, and it was just nine years later, at 3 p.m., that Beatrice first saluted him while 'passing along a certain street' in Florence. Petrarch, too, could claim he first laid eyes on Madonna Laura, the daughter of an Avignon burgher, on 6 April 1327, during matins in the Avignon church of St Clare. Few English poets fixed their erotic focus with quite this degree of precision, yet there are times when the London landscape emerges from their poems to clarify or complicate the experience of love. As in other kinds of writing, the evocation of place in time seems to have helped to bring the individual subject into being.

It has even been suggested, perhaps a little naively, that the rise of capitalistic urban commerce lies behind the rich decor of the late Elizabethan sonnet, with its galleys laden with emotion, its merchants longing for the return of their ships, its ungenerous ladies bedecked with jewels and gold. The popular ballad 'Fain Would I Have a Pretty Thing', which facetiously conceals an off-colour joke beneath an erstwhile lover's shopping trip for baubles, may actually lend support to the idea that love and wealth owe some of their associations to mercantile life. At the very least, the city does sometimes serve as an appropriately dismal setting for poems based on the conventional theme of the beloved's absence. The 'people-pestered' streets of London in Nicholas Grimald's lyric, like the city's gaudy life and rumbling coaches in Drayton's sonnet, are part of a strategy by which the object of desire is purified and exalted above the commonplace. In the poems of George Turberville and Sir Philip Sidney, by contrast, the London setting, especially the majestic Thames, becomes the scene for a triumphal conquest over time and mutability.

271

Just as neo-Platonists linked erotic to divine love, so civic humanists held that *amor* and *caritas* were near kin, and that love and marriage were the origin of communal life. A Florentine preacher had remarked that 'the word "city" (*civitas*) sounds amost like the word "love" (*caritas*), and through love are cities built, since men delight to live together'. So common was the notion that even the pamphleteer, Robert Greene, could invoke the Italian proverb, *Amor è la madre del buon città* (Love is the mother of the good city). From their books and pulpits Londoners heard frequently that marriage is 'the seminary of the commonwealth ... the foundation of ... cities'. Spenser's magnificent marriage hymn, the 'Prothalamion', is quite significantly set in London, and the civic implications of marriage are the basis, too, for Donne's 'Epithalamion Made at Lincoln's Inn', which bears a striking resemblance to a passage in which Stow records the marriage of the three daughters of Mr Atkinson, a London scrivener, at St Mary Woolnoth in 1560:

> They were in their hair and goodly apparel set out with chains, pearls, and stones. Thus they went to church, all three one after the other with three goodly caps garnished with laces, gilt, and fine flowers and rosemary strewed for their homecoming, and so to their father's house, where a great dinner was prepared.

Arranged marriages and dowries were in fact a principal means by which London's patrician families consolidated their wealth and power. By the end of the sixteenth century, the rising status of the merchants combined with the declining fortunes of many aristocrats to make the London 'season' a marriage market for titled heirs or younger sons in search of wealthy brides. In a society where arranged marriages were the norm, choice, affection and erotic freedom were perhaps most available to the well-born youth who served in large courtly households. London was legendary among travellers, however, for the respect and freedom generally extended to women. The tendency of wealthy merchants to marry much younger women created a large number of widows, who came into their own upon their husbands' death and were ardently pursued. Their relative youth may account for the contemporary claim that they commonly married their husbands' apprentices. Clandestine marriages could be accommodated in a number of places, including the Tower chapel, the chapel of the old Savoy hospital, and several taverns around the Fleet prison. Alarmed by the poverty created by 'over-hasty marriages and soon setting up of households by the youth', London's Common Council in 1556 effectively barred early marriage by restricting the freedom of the city to those 24 years of age or older. A large youth population, made up of apprentices and serving-girls, contributed to the number of foundlings and dead infants that turn up in the parish registers. Pregnant women were often rusticated, though London's newly-arrived immigrants must have included many women like Jane Crooke of Oxford, whose lover sent her to London 'until that she had been delivered' of his child.

Inseparable from London's erotic life and its literary image were the prostitutes who plied their trade throughout the city. The Bankside 'stews' (so named from their association with hot baths), once controlled by the Bishop of Winchester, had been in existence for centuries, as had those in Smithfield. They amounted to an erotic sub-culture, and had, as Stow reports, many long-established legal customs. Provided they did not keep women with venereal disease, did not do business on the sabbath or holy days, and submitted to regular inspections, the brothels were allowed to remain open. Any woman not kept against her will could receive a customer, provided she remained with him all night. A 'single women's' burial ground was kept for prostitutes who died without repenting. The rationale for the official toleration of prostitution was that it provided an essential outlet for male concupiscence. Brothels, Aquinas had said, are like 'the sewer in a palace. Take away the sewer and you will fill the place with pollution.' The coming of the Reformation, together with an outbreak of syphilis that ravaged Europe a quarter-century after the return of Columbus from America, led to several attempts to close the brothels down, but three years after the most stringent enactments of 1546, Hugh Latimer the preacher was complaining: 'Ye have put down the stews, but, I pray you, what is the matter amended? ... I say there is now more whoredom than ever there was on the Bank.' Indeed, by the later sixteenth century, prostitutes could be found outside the eastern walls in Petticoat Lane, Hog Lane and St Katherine's, in Westminster, Smithfield, Shoreditch, Turnbull Street in Clerkenwell, and on the Bankside, where the brothels' large, colourful signs faced directly on to the river, greeting clients borne by water. Prostitutes worked the liberties of Whitefriars, St Martin-le-Grand and Coldharbour, and they had even moved into such City jurisdictions as Billingsgate, Queenhithe and Ave Maria Abbey near St Paul's: 'Into the heart of the City' as Nashe puts it in a selection below, 'is uncleannesss crept.'

For writers like Nashe, the sale of love for money and the use of flesh as a commodity were deeply revealing metaphors for London's underlying sickness. Middleton's *A Chaste Maid in Cheapside* (see Chapter 14) presents the sale of human flesh as the logical culmination of Londoners' commercial zeal, and the final syphilitic sneer of the Trojan go-between Pandarus in Shakespeare's *Troilus and Cressida* (1601–2) would not have been lost on those Londoners who knew their city as Troynovant. Drawing on a native tradition of ribald jest and *fabliau* at least as old as Chaucer, the satirists and playwrights produced a rogues' gallery of London whores and bawds — among them Tickleman, Mistress Splay, Doll Tearsheet, Shave 'em and Ursula — without whom the literary image of London would be poorer.

Finally, just as revealing as the prostitute in the image of London is the senescent merchant-cuckold, the feeble, impotent hoarder. The cuckolding of the *senex* is, of course, almost as old as comedy itself, but the Harebrains and Fitzdottrels of Tudor–Stuart literature owe their life as well to a deep-seated resentment of the rich and to a fondness among courtiers and urbane gentlemen for baiting and ridiculing London's seemingly conservative merchant class. Aristotle held that it was unnatural for money to beget money, and a long tradition of anti-usury literature based on this idea had depicted the usurer who multiplies his wealth by taking interest as sexually impotent or sterile. The accumulation of capital, moreover, was commonly regarded as unproductive hoarding, so that the merchant's wealth was thought to stem from a life-denying asceticism. (It has more recently been argued that the tendency of men to delay marriage beyond the time of optimum sexual drive may have channelled sexual energies towards economic enterprise.) The merchant's fumbling, puling, lecherous sexual manner can be traced to the same timeless association of money with filth and defilement that earned London's sewage-men the name of 'goldfinders' (see 15.13). With peculiarly trenchant justice, literary convention rewarded grasping merchants not only with young, unfaithful wives, but also with hopelessly prodigal heirs, or worse, with puritanical sons who mounted the pulpit to cry out against their fathers. The frequency with which the wives of London merchants are cuckolded by courtiers and aspiring

gallants, however, reflects as much upon the parasites who preyed
upon London's wealth as upon the merchants who heaped it up.
Thus, in the poems by Donne and Cleveland (13.8 and 13.10
below), the flippant ridicule of burghers incapable of love is itself
revealing of a social antagonism between those who amassed
London's wealth and those who lived on it.

1
From *The Lover to his Dear, of his Exceeding Love*
(Nicholas Grimald, 1557)

In all the town, what street have I not seen?
In all the town, yet hath not Carie[1] been.
Either thy sire restrains thy free outgate,
O woman, worthy of far better state;
Or people-pestered London likes[2] thee not,
But pleasant air, in quiet country sought.
Perchance in olds[3] our love thou dost repeat,
And in sure place wouldst every thing retreat.
Forth shall I go, ne will I stay for none,
Until I may somewhere find thee alone.

2
Fain Would I have a Pretty Thing
(Clement Robinson, 1565/1584)

Fain would I have a pretty thing
    To give unto my lady.
I mean no hurt, I mean no harm,
    But as pretty a thing as may be ...

I walk the town and tread the street,
    In every corner seeking;
The pretty thing I cannot meet,
    That's for my lady's liking.

The mercers pull me going by,
    The silk wives say, 'What lack ye?'

'A thing that you have not', say I,
    'You foolish fools, go pack ye.'

It is not all the silk in Cheap,
    Nor all the golden treasure,
Nor twenty bushels in a heap,
    Can do my lady's pleasure.

The gravers of golden shows
    With jewels do beset me.
The shemsters[4] in the shops that sews,
    They do nothing but let[5] me.

For were it in the wit of man
    By any means to make it,
I would for money buy it then,
    And say, 'Fair lady, take it.'

But, lady, what a luck is this,
    That my good willing misseth,
To find what pretty thing it is
    That my good lady wisheth.

3

**The Lover to the Thames of London
To Favour his Lady Passing Thereon
(George Turberville, 1567)**

Thou stately stream that, with the swelling tide,
'Gainst London walls incessantly dost beat,
Thou Thames, I say, where barge and boat doth ride
And snow-white swans do fish for needful meat,
    Whenso my love of force or pleasure shall
Flit on thy flood as custom is to do,
Seek not with dread her courage to appall,
But calm thy tide and smoothly let it go:
As she may joy, arrived to siker[6] shore,
To pass the pleasant stream she did before.
    To welter up and surge in wrathful wise
(As did the flood where Helle[7] drenched was)

Would but procure defame of thee to rise;
Wherefore let all such ruthless rigour pass,
So wish I that thou mayst with bending side
Have power for ay in wonted gulf to glide.

4
From *Astrophel and Stella*
(Sir Philip Sidney, 1582/1591)

O happy Thames that didst my Stella bear,
I saw thee with full many a smiling line
Upon thy cheerful face joy's livery wear,
While those fair planets[8] on thy streams did shine.
The boat for joy could not to dance forbear,
While wanton winds, with beauties so divine
Ravished, stayed not, till in her golden hair
They did themselves (o sweetest prison) twine.
And fain those Aeol's youth[9] there would their stay
Have made, but forced by nature still to fly,
First did with puffing kiss those locks display.
She, so dishevelled, blushed; from window[10] I
With sight thereof cried out, 'O fair disgrace,
Let honour's self to thee grant highest place.'

5
[Madame Troynovant]
(Thomas Nashe, 1592)

What drugs, what sorceries, what oils, what waters, what ointments
do our curious dames use to enlarge their withered beauties? Their
lips are as lavishly red as if they used to kiss an ochreman every
morning, and their cheeks sugar-candied and cherry-blushed so
sweetly, after the colour of a new Lord Mayor's posts,[11] as if the
pageant of their wedlock holiday were hard at the door; so that if a
painter were to draw any of their counterfeits on table, he needs no
more but wet his pencil and dab it on their cheeks and he shall
have vermilion and white enough to furnish out his work, though
he leave his tar-box[12] at home behind him. ...
    I warrant we have old hacksters in this great Grandmother of

Corporations, Madame Troynovant, that have not backbited any of their neighbours with the tooth of envy this twenty year, in the wrinkles of whose face ye may hide false dice, and play at cherry-pit[13] in the dint of their cheeks; yet these aged mothers of iniquity will have their deformities new plastered over, and wear nosegays of yellow hair on their foreheads, when age hath written 'No God be here' on their bald burnt parchment pates. Pish, pish, what talk you of old age or bald pates? Men and women that have gone under the South Pole[14] must lay off their furred nightcaps in spight of their teeth and become yeomen of the vinegar bottle;[15] a close periwig hides all the sins of an old whore-master, but *Cucullus non facit monachum*:[16] 'tis not their new bonnets will keep them from the old bone-ache. 'Ware when a man's sins are written on his eyebrows, and that there is not a hair-breadth betwixt them and the falling sickness.

6
[Love on the River]
(Robert Greene, 1592)

Now Master Waterman you will say there is no subtlety in you, for there is none so simple but that knows your fares and what is due between Greenwich and London, and how you earn your money painfully with the sweat of your brows. All this is true, but let me whisper one thing in your ear, you will play the good fellow too much if you be well greased in the fist,[17] for if a young gentleman and a pretty wench come to you and say, 'Waterman, my friend and I mean to go by water and to be merry a night or two; I care not which way nor wither we go, and therefore where thou thinkest we may have best lodging, thither carry us', then off goes your cap and away they go, to Brentford or some other place. And then you say, 'Hostess, I pray you use this gentleman and his wife well, they are come out of London to take the air and mean to be merry here a night or two, and to spend their money frankly' — when God wot they are neither man nor wife, nor perhaps of any acquaintance before their match made in some bawdy tavern. But you know no such matter, and therefore Waterman I pardon you.

7
[Lust]
(Thomas Nashe, 1592)

To my journey's end I haste, and descend to the second continent
of Delicacy, which is Lust or Luxury. In complaining of it, I am
afraid I shall defile good words and too long detain my readers. It
is a sin that now serveth in London instead of an afternoon's
recreation. It is a trade that heretofore thrived in hugger-mugger,[18]
but of late days walketh openly by daylight, like a substantial grave
merchant. Of his name or profession he is not ashamed; at the first
being asked of it, he will confess it. Into the heart of the City is
uncleanness crept. Great patrons it hath got: almost none are
punished for it that have a good purse. Every quean[19] vaunts her-
self of some or other man of nobility.

London, what are thy suburbs but licensed stews? Can it be so
many brothel houses of salary[20] sensuality and sixpenny whoredom
(the next door to the magistrate's) should be set up and main-
tained, if bribes did not bestir them? I accuse none, but certainly
justice somewhere is corrupted. Whole hospitals of ten-times-a-
day dishonested strumpets have we cloistered together. Night and
day the entrance unto them is as free as to a tavern. Not one of
them but hath a hundred retainers. Prentices and poor servants
they encourage to rob their masters. Gentlemen's purses and
pockets they will dive into and pick, even whiles they are dallying
with them. . . .

Every one of them is a gentlewoman, and either the wife of
two husbands or a bed-wedded bride before she was ten years old.
The speech-shunning sores and sight-irking botches of their
insatiate intemperance they will unblushingly lay forth and jestingly
brag of wherever they haunt. . . .

Ere they come to forty you shall see them worn to the bare
bone. At twenty their lively colour is lost, their faces are sodden
and parboiled with French surfeits.[21] That colour you behold on
their cheeks superficialized is but Sir John White's or Sir John
Red-cap's livery. The alchemist of quicksilver[22] makes gold. These
(our openers to all comers) with quickening and conceiving get
gold. The souls they bring forth, at the latter day, shall stand up
and give evidence against them. The devil, to enfranchise them of
hell, shall do no more but produce the misbegotten of their loins.
Those that have been daily fornicatresses and yet are unfruitful he

shall accuse of ten thousand murders, by confusion of seeds and barrening their wombs by drugs. There is no such murderer on the face of the earch as a whore. Not only shall she be arraigned and impeached of defeating an infinite number of God's images, but of defacing and destroying the mold wherein he hath appointed them to be cast. . . .

Great cunning do they ascribe to their art, as the discerning by the very countenance a man that hath crowns in his purse; the fine closing in with the next justice or alderman's deputy of the ward; the winning love of neighbours round about, to repel violence, if haply their houses should be environed or any in them prove unruly (being pilled and polled too unconscionably). They forecast for back doors to come in and out by undiscovered. Sliding windows also, and trap-boards in floors, to hide whores behind and under, with false counterfeit panes in walls, to be opened and shut like a wicket. . . .

Monstrous creatures are they, marvel it is fire from heaven consumes not London, as long as they are in it. A thousand parts better it were to have public stews than to let them keep private stews as they do. The world would count me the most licentiate loose strayer under heaven, if I should unrip but half so much of their venerial machiavellianism as I have looked into. We have not English words enough to unfold it. Positions and instructions have they to make their whores a hundred times more whorish and treacherous than their own wicked affects (resigned to the devil's disposing) can make them. Waters and receipts have they to enable a man to the act after he is spent, dormative potions to procure deadly sleep, that when the hackney he hath paid for lies by him, he may have no power to deal with her, but she may steal from him, whiles he is in his deep memento, and make her gain of three or four other.

8
From an *Epithalamion Made at Lincoln's Inn*
(John Donne, *c.* 1594/1633)

Daughters of London, you which be
Our golden mines and furnished treasury,
    You which are angels, yet still bring with you
Thousand of angels[23] on your marriage days,

Help with your presence and devise to praise
   These rites, which also unto you grow due.
   Conceitedly dress her,[24] and be assigned,
By you, fit place for every flower and jewel;
   Make her for love fit fuel,
      As gay as Flora,[25] and as rich as Inde;
So may she, fair and rich, in nothing lame,
Today put on perfection, and a woman's name.

And you frolic patricians,
Sons of these Senators' wealth's deep oceans,[26]
   Ye painted courtiers, barrels of others' wits,
Ye country men, who but your beasts love none,
Ye of those fellowships[27] whereof he's[28] one,
   Of study and play made strange Hermaphrodites,
   Here shine; this bridgegroom to the temple bring.
Lo, in yon path which store of strewed flowers graceth,
   The sober virgin paceth;
      Except my sight fail, 'tis no other thing;
Weep not nor blush, here is no grief nor shame,
Today put on perfection, and a woman's name.

9
From *Idea*
(Michael Drayton, 1619)

How many paltry, foolish, painted things,
That now in coaches trouble every street,
Shall be forgotten, whom no poet sings,
Ere they be wrapped in their winding sheet?
Where I to thee eternity shall give,
When nothing else remaineth of these days,
And queens hereafter shall be glad to live
Upon the alms of thy superfluous praise;
Virgins and matrons reading these my rhymes
Shall be so much delighted with thy story,
That they shall grieve, they lived not in these times,
To have seen thee, their sex's only glory:
   So shalt thou fly above the vulgar throng,
   Still to survive in my immortal song.

10
On an Alderman who Married a Very Young Wife
(John Cleveland, *c.* 1645)

Let's charm some poet from his grave
   That many ages hath been dead:
A nuptial ode this night must have
To bring the bridegroom to his bed.
   So old, so wondrous old,
   That his chin felt the weight
   Of an Alderman's beard
   Before eighty-eight.[29]

His thin mustachio still decays,
   Like winter's snow chilled into cares.
But 'cause he's rich we'll change our phrase,
   And call his grayness silver hairs.
      So old, etc.

A hair or two is all the tithe
   That from his bald pate you can gather;
Give him an hourglass or a scythe,
   You'll style him Time or else Time's father.
      So old, etc.

His brinish spittle from his jaws
   Hangs dingle-dangle to his coat,
Like hocus-pocus[30] when he draws
   Some yards of ribbon through his throat.
      So old, etc.

In summer time, to cause a sweat,
   He lays on thirty folds of clothes;
Yet all this will not get him heat,
   But pus a dropping at the nose.
      So old, etc.

And when he coughs to hold his back,
   A man would think that he was gone;
His guts within him they do crack

Like eel-skins dried in the sun.
    So old, etc.

But let not this his bride offend,
    Old men are twice children rightly styled;
If he be able to ascend,
      'Tis ten to one she bears a child.
        So old, etc.

Notes

1. From the use of her first name here and the use of her surname in another love poem, it may be gathered that Grimald addresses a woman named Carie Day.

2. Pleases.

3. I.e. wolds, woods.

4. Seamstresses.

5. Stop, hinder.

6. Sure, certain, safe.

7. Helle fell from the flying ram of the Golden Fleece and drowned in the strait between Europe and Asia, which became known as the Hellespont.

8. Stella's eyes.

9. Children of Aeolus, god of the wind.

10. Leicester House, the London home of Sidney's uncle, Robert Dudley, was located in the Strand next to the Temple and overlooked the Thames. Sidney resided there frequently.

11. Each year, posts at the Lord Mayor's house were painted (McKerrow).

12. A paint-box.

13. A children's game.

14. Fornicated; the phrase can also refer to the female genitals.

15. Vinegar was a supposed cure for venereal disease.

16. Proverbial: the hood does not make the monk.

17. Well paid.

18. In secret.

19. Prostitute.

20. Saleable.

21. Sores, perhaps with a pun on surfles (cosmetics).

22. A supposed cure for syphilis was 'taking the tub', a fumigation treatment in which cinnabar (mercuric sulphide) was volatised from a chafing dish and allowed to condense on the skin.

23. Gold coins stamped with angels, worth 8s 6d.

24. The bride.

25. Roman goddess of flowers, associated with sexual licence.

26. Sons of the wealth of these senators (i.e. aldermen or wealthy London merchants).

27. The Inns of Court.

28. The groom.

29. I.e. before 1588, a year that stood for an almost mythical age by the mid-seventeenth century.

30. A street magician.

14

THEATRUM MUNDI:
THE CITY IN STAGE COMEDY

The writer who described Queen Elizabeth's 1559 coronation pageant said that 'a man ... could not better term the City of London that time than a stage'. For Renaissance writers, the ancient proverbial analogy betwen life and stage was epitomised by the urban environment. Providing numerous possibilities for social interchange, a variety of histrionic styles to be played, and a protean potential for conflict, betrayal and extravagant display, the city abounded in the drama of community and human relationship. It has been suggested that in the ideal city views of the Italian Renaissance, with their perspectival streets and squares, the urban space is deliberately conceived as a theatrical setting for significant human action; by the sixteenth century, certainly, the major architectural treatises included plans for stage sets based on urban perspective scenes appropriate to individual dramatic genres. In England, the records of the Office of Revels reveal that cities are among the earliest and most common sets required for professional performances at court.

It was, in fact, in the cities themselves, with their vast resources and cultural sophistication, that Renaissance theatres found their permanent home. The first permanent theatre was erected in the London suburbs in 1576, and in the next half-century nearly a dozen more followed. From the founding of the first theatre in 1576 to Shakespeare's retirement from the theatre around 1613, at least 800 plays were performed on London' stages.

All through this period, except for periods when the theatres were closed by the plague, people of all classes and persuasions flocked daily to witness the pageants of history, the triumphs and tragic falls of kings, the antics of knaves and clowns and the follies of young lovers. Although preachers inveighed against them (see 4.5), and the authorities half-heartedly attempted to suppress them, the theatres were an essential institution in the life of London. The

lasting impression they left in the minds of foreign visitors amply
justifies Thomas Heywood's claim, in his *Apology for Actors*
(1612), that 'playing is an ornament to the city'.

In the large and varied repertory of the period, plays devoted to
the life of London occupied a substantial place. Unified by their
concern with the urban setting and milieu rather than by their
treatment of single issues, classes or social types, plays on London
fall into many genres, from the farcical and the heroic to the homi-
letic and the romantic, the domestic and the melodramatic. The
most striking plays about London, however, are the many satiric
works that emerged in the first decade of the seventeenth century,
works in which the city was a setting for elaborate webs of financial
intrigue, deception, folly and vice. Interweaving the fortunes of
citizens, grasping magnates and decayed gentlemen with the
schemes of prodigals, gallants, hucksters and bawds, these so-
called city comedies were both a culmination of earlier dramatic
traditions and a pointed response to the social and economic
changes wrought by the growth of London.

The preoccupation of these plays with familiar social types and
scenes of common life reflects the ancient roots of comic tradition.
In the definition known to every Tudor schoolboy, the ancient
grammarian, Donatus, had said that comedy is 'an imitation of life,
the mirror of custom'; Sir Philip Sidney had laid similar stress on
the everyday when he declared that comedy is an 'imitation of the
common errors of our life'. Even before the classical revival,
medieval miracle plays were punctuated with comic scenes drawn
from low life, and morality plays called for vices and henchmen
who were, increasingly, often recognisable, contemporary urban
types. With the moral interludes of the early Tudor period, overt
reference to the London underworld had begun to lend realistic
point to moral lessons, and with the coming of the Reformation,
plays on social duties and the proper use of wealth transformed the
traditional moral abstractions into greedy merchants, misers,
wastrels and rapacious landlords. A major development of the
later sixteenth century was the importation of prodigal son plays
from the Lowlands, a burgherly genre in which the waywardness of
youth allowed for the introduction of urban bawds, parasites and
dissolutes from the New Comedy of Plautus and Terence. In
England, both the well-established model of the jest-books and the
newer genres of the cony-catching pamphlet and character study
provided native counterparts for the classical comic types. In a

related development, a sense of civic pride and responsibility, together with the example of heroic chronicle plays, had combined with these traditions to produce such homiletic plays as *The Three Lords and Three Ladies of London* (1590) and *The Four Prentices of London* (1592) and such celebrations of virtuous citizenship as Dekker's *Shoemaker's Holiday* (see Chapter 10).

A definitive trait of the new city comedy is its incorporation of these earlier developments in a self-conscious, critical and parodic way. The opening scene of *Eastward Ho* (1606), for example, with its contrast between good and bad apprentices, ridicules the traditional morality pattern on which it is so clearly built; the virtuous apprentice Golding is not so much a diligent youth as a self-righteous prig, and the master Touchstone's pious invocation of citizen morality verges on the purely fatuous. In the same way, the induction to Beaumont's *The Knight of the Burning Pestle* (1607/1613) cleverly ridicules the taste of London citizens as the expression of a narrow and socially inept mentality. The often harsh and intellectually cruel tone of city comedy can be traced in part to the contemporary emergence of private indoor theatres, whose clientele was perhaps at first more elite and educated than that of the older public playhouses. Many of the city comedians associated with these new theatres — Marston, Middleton and Jonson, for example — were also experienced in writing the new verse satire, and possibly the 1599 ban on the publication of satire (see Chapter 8) encouraged them to use the stage as another outlet for attacks on London's vices.

But in more general terms, the tilt of dramatic tradition toward realism and satire also expressed a sense of moral, social and economic crisis. In one of his prologues, Ben Johnson noted that his was a 'money-get, mechanic age', and that the aim of his plays was to present 'the times' deformity/Anatomised in every nerve and sinew'. Most frequently set in London, and written as the rise of monopolies, syndicates and credit systems was allowing fortunes to be made overnight and lands held for generations to change hands with the stroke of a pen, the Jacobean city comedies explore the distortion of human values and relationships by the power of money. While Johnson, Middleton and others imitated the intrigues of Plautus and Terence, they transformed the traditional comic strife between rebellious youth and stinting elders into pointed economic conflicts between such recognisable social types as upstart gallants and grasping citizens, aspiring London hucksters and obtuse gentry. In rich and vivid detail, the plays dramatise the contemporary dictum of Sir Francis Bacon: 'the ways to enrich are many, and most of them foul'.

Perhaps the most common situation in these plays is the defrauding of unsuspecting gentry by sharp-witted and malicious Londoners. The situation turns on the mythical contrast between country and city and borrows from that myth the supposition that the forces destroying traditional life throughout the country emanate from London. In Middleton's *Michaelmas Term*, as in a tradition running from 'London Lickpenny' to the cony-catching pamphlets, London is a 'man-devouring city'; the comic villain of Middleton's play, the linen-draper, Quomodo, speaks for a progeny of similar characters when he gloats that 'gentry is the chief fish we tradesmen catch'. Quicksilver, too, the evil apprentice in *Eastward Ho*, specialises in cheating gentlemen of their wealth. Middleton, whose hallmark was plots of this kind, returns to it in *A Chaste Maid in Cheapside*, where a number of Londoners, including the willing cuckold Allwit, attempt to capitalise on the greed and stupidity of the country gentleman, Sir Walter Whorehound. Like the house in Jonson's *The Alchemist*, Ursula's booth in *Bartholomew Fair*, a lair infested by denizens of the London underworld, epitomises the urban concentration of folly and vice; it entangles in mayhem every countryman, sturdy citizen and upstart who dares approach it.

Built on stereotypes, and exploiting the inherently dramatic power of intrigue, city comedies are, of course, a problematic guide to actual historical developments. An important part of their continuing appeal (the part perhaps most evident in short excerpts of the kind included here), is their delightfully detailed portraiture of contemporary characters and manners. But this portraiture is firmly circumscribed by fixed dramatic types. The very names of these types reveal that the dramatists were drawing on a common fund made up of avaricious merchants and usurers (Hoard, Lucre, Quomodo, Pennyboy Sr, Yellowhammer, Falso), foolish and grasping magnates (Sir Giles Overreach, Sir Walter Whorehound, Sir Epicure Mammon, Sir Bounteous Progress), dim-witted country gulls (Smallshanks, Easy, Rearage, Salewood, Gullman, Frippey), city wits, rakes and gallants (Cocledemoy, Witgood, Follywit, Wittipol), whores both good (Doll, Moll) and bad (Franceschina, Tickleman, Mistress Splay), pompous and short-sighted citizens (Harebrain, Mulligrub, Adam Overdo, Sir John Frugal,

Fitzdottrel) and hypocritical Puritans (Penitent Brothel, Tribula-
tion Wholesome, Zeal-of-the-Land Busy, Dryfat).

Like these stereotypes, the country–city oppositions around
which these plays were so frequently built were not so much con-
cerned with social class and economics as with moral values,
especially with a mythical contrast between a virtuous agrarian past
and the contemporary vicious urban world of nowadays. Most fre-
quently, the dramatists direct their satire at traditional scapegoats
and stock villains like usurers rather than at the credit system, or at
the newly rich rather than at established wealth. Then too, as
Raymond Williams has argued, the fiction of country–city conflict
may actually have concealed an underlying economic symbiosis by
confining greed to the urban sphere while presenting country
gentlemen as guileless victims. The tendency of traditional
morality to override secular analysis often emerges most clearly in
the endings of city comedy, where the comic exaltation of hoary
moral pieties fails to address the deeper challenges the intrigue of
the plot has actually laid against the economic system.

In the greatest of city comedies, however, the very roots of the
country–city conflict — and thus, in a sense, of capitalism — are
exposed. Characters like Sir Walter Whorehound are shown to be
at least as vicious as such urbanites as Allwit, while such pursuits as
fortune-hunting on the marriage market, usury and the seduction
of citizens' wives unite rural gentlemen with Londoners in a single
circle of vice. Ursula's booth in *Bartholomew Fair* is not so much a
source of evil as a convenience, a clearing-house for the mad, sor-
did pursuits of every social class. If Ursula embodies all the city's
stench and filth, she none the less possesses a vitality and resilience
lacking in her hypocritical social betters.

It is in their zestful, lavish and sometimes loving treatment of
urban vice that the dramatists rise beyond the narrower range of
conventional morality. The city comedies, as Alexander Legatt has
said, concern themselves with the material side of social relations,
with sex, marriage, money and property; and their 'social morality
is finally a morality of property and possession. Each man should
keep what is rightfully his, whether his land or his wife.' But this
conservative morality is often balanced by the more anarchic and
rebellious qualities of comedy, by an antipathy to the stiff and
sober pretensions of ownership, by an aversion to moderation and
stability, and by a not so secret identification (for the plotting
dramatist, a complicity) with the exuberant wiles of shifty

merchants, cons and prodigals.

In its extreme form, the lively anarchy of city comedy verges on the absurd, the strange, the unreal. The intricate elaboration of mistaken identity, for example, sometimes reduces sober financial transactions to complete absurdity. In *Volpone* and *The Alchemist*, Jonson specialised in the comic use of exotic and absurd crimes, and in the lyrical, rhapsodical outbursts of such villains as Hoard, Lucre and Quomodo, Middleton seems to have followed Jonson into the realm of mad obsession. In this respect, the writers of city comedy may have recovered some of the original anxieties of New Comedy, whose concern with deception and mistaken identity originated during the mass displacements of the Hellenistic period, and whose deeper meaning was perhaps lost on the more secure Romans, Plautus and Terence, who imitated it. A world inhabited by protean tricksters who have the power to make and unmake men, the London of the city comedies — despite, or perhaps because of its 'realism' — is not unlike the realms of romance. In *The Alchemist*, Jonson's Subtle doubles as a wizard, and Doll as the Queen of Fairy; and in Middleton's *Michaelmas Term* Quomodo's assistants, Shortyard and Falselight, are known as his 'spirits'. Middleton's *A Mad World My Masters* includes a succubus; and both Dekker and Jonson wrote plays in which the devil is sent to do his work in London.

Thus, as they verge on the grotesque, the phantasmal and the absurd, the city comedies transcend their conventional characters and plots and metaphorically expose as insane the acquisitive and materialist values of contemporary society. The scene below from Middleton's *A Chaste Maid in Cheapside* depicts the ugly situation of a grasping citizen fawning on the gentleman to whom he pimps his own wife; later in the play, when Allwit presents his wife's latest infant to the embarrassed Sir Walter, Middleton carries this image of monstrosity to its limit with perfect insouciance. Allwit declares that he thrives 'As other trades thrive, butchers by selling flesh,/ Poulters by vending conies, or the like'. His declaration echoes metaphorically through all the play's undercover transactions, in each of which human flesh is put up for sale. Middleton drives the metaphor home when a country wench disposes of her unwanted infant by passing it off as a piece of meat. Such grotesque images suggest that the comic dramatists were indeed responding to a contemporary London scene which they regarded as truly threatening.

1
From *Eastward Ho*
(George Chapman, Ben Jonson and John Marston, 1605)
Act 1, scene i

*Enter Master Touchstone and Quicksilver at several doors,
Quicksilver with his hat, pumps, short sword, and dagger, and
a racket trussed up under his cloak. At the middle door, enter
Golding discovering a Goldsmith's shop and walking short
turns before it.*

Touchstone And whither with you now? What loose action are you
bound for? Come, what comrades are you to meet withal?
Where's the supper? Where's the rendezvous?

Quicksilver Indeed, and in very good sober truth, sir —

Touchstone 'Indeed, and in very good sober truth, sir?' Behind
my back thou wilt swear faster than a French footboy and talk
more bawdily than a common midwife, and now 'Indeed, in
very good sober truth, sir.' But if a privy search[1] should be
made, with what furniture are you rigged now? Sirrah, I tell
thee, I am thy master William Touchstone, Goldsmith, and thou
my prentice Francis Quicksilver, and I will see whither you are
running. Work upon that now!

Quicksilver Why, sir, I hope a man may vie his recreation with his
master's profit.

Touchstone Prentices' recreations are seldom with their masters'
profit. Work upon that now. You shall give up your cloak,
though you be no alderman.[2] (*Touchstone uncloaks
Quicksilver.*) Heyday, Ruffians' Hall![3] Sword, pumps! Here's a
racket indeed!

Quicksilver Work upon that now!

Touchstone Thou shameless varlet, dost thou jest at thy lawful
master contrary to thy indentures?

Quicksilver Why, 'sblood, sir, my mother's a gentlewoman and
my father a justice of the peace and of quorum,[4] and though I
am a younger brother and a prentice, I hope I am my father's
son; and by God's lid 'tis for your worship and for your com-
modity that I keep company. I am entertained among gallants,
true; they call me cousin Frank, right; I lend them monies,
good; they spend it, well. But when they are spent, must not

they strive to get more? Must not their land fly? And to whom? Shall not your worship ha' the refusal? Well, I am a good member of the City if I were well considered. How would merchants thrive, if gentlemen would not be unthrifts? How could gentlemen be unthrifts, if their humours were not fed? How should their humours be fed, but by whitemeat[5] and cunning secondings?[6] Well, the City might consider us. I am going to an ordinary now; the gallants fall to play; I carry light gold with me; the gallants call, 'Cousin Frank, some gold for silver'; I change, gain by it; the gallants lose the gold, and then call, 'Cousin Frank, lend me some silver.' Why —

Touchstone Why? I cannot tell, seven score pound art thou out in the cash, but look to it, I will not be gallanted out of my monies. As for my rising by other men's fall, God shield me. Did I gain my wealth by ordinaries? No! By exchanging of gold? No! By keeping of gallants' company? No! I hired me a little shop, bought low, took small gain, kept no debt book, garnished my shop, for want of plate, with good wholesome thrifty sentences, as, 'Touchstone, keep thy shop, and they shop will keep thee.' 'Light gains makes heavy purses.' ''Tis good to be merry and wise.' And when I was wived, having something to stick to, I had the horn of suretyship[7] ever before my eyes. (*To the audience.*) You all know the device of the horn, where the young fellow slips in at the butt end and comes squeezed out at the buccal?[8] (*To Quicksilver.*) And I grew up, and, I praise providence, I bear my brows now as high as the best of my neighbours. But thou, — well, look to the accounts, your father's bond[9] lies for you; seven score pound is yet in the rear.

Quicksilver Why, 'slid, sir, I have as good, as proper, gallants' word for it as any are in London, gentlemen of good phrase, perfect language, passingly behaved, gallants that wear socks and clean linen and call me 'kind cousin Frank', 'good cousin Frank', for they know my father; and by God's lid shall not I trust them? Not trust?

Enter a Page, as inquiring for Touchstone's shop.

Golding What do ye lack, sir? What is't you'll buy, sir?

Touchstone Ay, marry, sir, there's a youth of another piece. There's thy fellow-prentice, as good a gentleman born as thou art — nay, and better meaned.[10] But does he pump it, or racket it? Well, if he thrive not, if he outlast not a hundred such crackling bavins[11] as thou art, God and men neglect industry.

Golding (To the Page) It is his shop, and here my master walks.

Touchstone With me, boy?

Page My master, Sir Petronel Flash,[12] recommends his love to you, and will instantly visit you.

Touchstone To make up the match with my eldest daughter, my wife's dilling,[13] whom she longs to call madam. He shall find me unwillingly ready, boy. (*Exit Page.*) (*Aside*) That's another affliction, too. As I have two prentices, the one of a boundless prodigality, the other of a most hopeful industry, so have I only two daughters, the eldest of a proud ambition and nice wantonness, the other of a modest humility and comely soberness. The one must be ladyfied, forsooth, and be attired to the court cut and long tail. So far is she ill-natured to the place and means of my preferment and fortune that she throws all the contempt and despite hatred itself can cast upon it. Well, a piece of land she has, 'twas her grandmother's gift; let her and her Sir Petronel flash that out. But as for my substance, she that scorns me, as I am a citizen and tradesman, shall never pamper her pride with my industry, shall never use me as men do foxes — keep themselves warm in the skin and throw the body that bare it to the dunghill. I must go entertain this Sir Petronel. [*To Golding*] Golding, my utmost care's for thee, and only trust in thee — look to the shop. [*To Quicksilver*] As for you, Master Quicksilver, think of husks, for thy course is running directly to the prodigal's hogs' trough. Husks, Sirrah! Work upon that now!   (*Exit.*)

Quicksilver Marry, faugh, goodman flat-cap. 'Sfoot, though I am a prentice I can give arms,[14] and my father's a justice a' peace by descent, and 'sblood —

Golding Fie, how you swear!

Quicksilver 'Sfoot, man, I am a gentleman and may swear by my pedigree, God's my life. Sirrah, Golding, wilt be ruled by a fool? Turn good fellow, turn swaggering gallant and let the welkin roar, and Erebus also;[15] look not westward to the fall of Dan Phoebus but to east — eastward ho!

> Where radiant beams of lofty Sol appear,
> And bright Eous[16] makes the welkin clear.

We are both gentlemen and therefore should be no coxcombs; let's be no longer fools to this flat-cap Touchstone — eastward, bully — this satin belly and canvas-backed[17] Touchstone. 'Slife,

man, his father was a malt-man, and his mother sold ginger-
bread in Christ Church.

Golding What would ye ha' me do?

Quicksilver Why, do nothing, be like a gentleman; be idle, the
curse of man is labour. Wipe thy bum with testons[18] and make
ducks and drakes with shillings! What, eastward ho! Wilt thou
cry, 'What is't ye lack?' Stand with a bare pate and a dropping
nose under a wooden penthouse, and art a gentleman? Wilt
thou bear tankards,[19] and may'st bear arms? Be ruled, turn
gallant, eastward ho! Ta ly re, ly re ro. 'Who calls Jeronimo?
Speak, here I am.'[20] Godso, how like a sheep thou look'st, a' my
conscience, some cowherd begot thee, thou Golding of Golding
Hall. Ha, boy?

Golding Go, ye are a prodigal coxcomb! I a cowherd's son,
because I turn not a drunken whore-hunting rakehell[21] like
thyself?

Quicksilver Rakehell? Rakehell? (*Offers to draw, and Golding
trips up his heels and holds him.*)

Golding Pish, in soft terms ye are a cowardly bragging boy. I'll ha'
you whipped.

Quicksilver Whipped? That's good, i' faith. Untruss me!

Golding No, thou wilt undo thyself. Alas, I behold thee with pity,
not with anger. Thou common shot-clog,[22] gull of all com-
panies, methinks I see thee already, walking in Moorfields
without a cloak, with half a hat, without a band,[23] a doublet with
three buttons, without a girdle, a hose with one point[24] and no
garter, with a cudgel under thine arm, borrowing and begging
threepence.

Quicksilver Nay, 'slife, take this and take all. As I am a gentleman
born, I'll be drunk and grow valiant and beat thee.   (*Exit.*)

Golding Go, thou most madly vain, whom nothing can recover
but that which reclaims atheists and makes great persons some-
times religious: calamity. As for my place and life, thus have I
read:

> Whate'er some vainer youth may term disgrace,
> The gain of honest pains is never base;
> From trades, from arts, from valor honour springs,
> These three are fonts of gentry, yea, of kings.

(*Exit.*)

2
From *The Knight of the Burning Pestle*
(Francis Beaumont 1607/1613)

[*Each of the two plots of* The Knight of the Burning Pestle *parodies a contemporary literary taste. In one of these, the apprentice of a London grocer becomes a Grocer Errant and pursues a variety of absurd adventures that burlesque chivalric romance. In the other, an apprentice falls in love with his master's daughter and marries her in a parody of romantic love. The second plot, which is presented as a play performed by a London acting company and called* The London Merchant, *is repeatedly interrupted by scenes from the first, which are acted by Ralph, an apprentice present in the audience of* The London Merchant. *Ralph is assigned his role in the play's clever Induction, when his master and mistress disrupt the Prologue to* The London Merchant *by declaring their preference for an old-fashioned exaltation of citizen heroism.*]

[*The Induction*]
Enter Prologue.

From all that's near the court, from all that's great,
Within the compass of the City walls
We now have brought our scene —

Enter Citizen [from the audience].

Citizen Hold your peace, goodman boy!
Prologue What do you mean, sir?
Citizen That you have no good meaning. This seven years there hath been plays at this house, I have observed it, you have still girds[25] at citizens; and now you call your play *The London Merchant.* Down with your title,[26] boy, down with your title!
Prologue Are you a member of the noble City?
Citizen I am.
Prologue And a freeman?
Citizen Yea, and a grocer.
Prologue So, grocer, then by your sweet favour, we intend no abuse to the City.
Citizen No sir? Yes sir! If you were not resolved to play the

jacks,[27] what need you study for new subjects purposely to abuse your betters? Why could you not be contented, as well as others, with *The Legend of Whittington,*[28] or *The Life and Death of Sir Thomas Gresham, with the Building of the Royal Exchange?*[29] Or *The Story of Queen Eleanor, with the Rearing of London Bridge upon Woolpacks?*[30]

Prologue You seem to be an understanding man; what would you have us do, sir?

Citizen Why, present something notably in honour of the commons of the City.

Prologue Why, what do you say to *The Life and Death of Fat Drake, or The Repairing of Fleet Privies?*[31]

Citizen I do not like that; but I will have a citizen, and he shall be of my own trade.

Prologue Oh, you should have told us your mind a month since; our play is ready to begin now.

Citizen 'Tis all one for that; I will have a grocer, and he shall do admirable[32] things.

Prologue What will you have him do?

Citizen Marry, I will have him —

Wife [*below*] Husband, husband! —

Rafe [*below*] Peace, mistress!

Wife Hold thy peace, Rafe; I know what, I do warrant'ee. Husband, husband!

Citizen What say'st thou, cunny?[33]

Wife Let him kill a lion with a pestle, husband, let him kill a lion with a pestle!

Citizen So he shall. I'll have him kill a lion with a pestle.

Wife Husband, shall I come up, husband?

Citizen Ay, cunny. Rafe, help your mistress this way. [*To gentlemen seated on the stage.*] Pray, gentlemen, make her a little room. I pray you, sir, lend me your hand to help up my wife. I thank you, sir, So.

(*Wife climbs onto the stage.*)

Wife By your leave, gentlemen all, I'm something troublesome. I'm a stranger here. I was ne'er at one of these plays, as they say, before; but I should have seen *Jane Shore*[34] once, and my husband hath promised me any time this twelvemonth to carry me to *The Bold Beauchamps,*[35] but in truth he did not. I pray you, bear with me.

Citizen Boy, let my wife and I have a couple stools, and then begin; and let the grocer do rare things.

Prologue But sir, we have never a boy to play him; everyone hath a part already.

Wife Husband, husband, for God's sake, let Rafe play him. Beshrew me if I do think he will go beyond them all.

Citizen Well remembered, wife. Come up, Rafe. I'll tell you, gentlemen, let them but lend him a suit of repparel[36] and necessaries, and by gad, if any of them blow wind in the tail[37] on him, I'll be hanged.

[*Rafe climbs onto the stage.*]

Wife I pray you, youth, let him have a suit of repparel. I'll be sworn, gentlemen, my husband tells you true; he will act you sometimes at our house, that all the neighbours cry out on him. He will fetch you up a couraging part so in the garret, that we are all as 'feard, I warrant you, that we quake again. We'll fear our children with him; if they be never so unruly, do but cry, 'Rafe comes, Rafe comes', to them, and they'll be quiet as lambs. Hold up thy head, Rafe. Show the gentlemen what thou canst do; speak a huffing[38] part. I warrant you, the gentlemen will accept of it.

Citizen Do, Rafe, do.

Rafe 'By heaven, methinks it were an easy leap
    To pluck bright honour from the pale-faced moon,
    Or dive into the bottom of the sea,
    Where never fathom line touched any ground,
    And pluck up drowned honour from the lake of hell.'[39]

Citizen How say you, gentlemen, is it not as I told you?

Wife Nay, gentlemen, he hath played before, my husband says, *Mucedorus* before the wardens of our company.

Citizen Ay, and he should have played *Jeronimo*[40] with a shoemaker, for a wager.

Prologue He shall have a suit of apparel, if he will go in.

Citizen In, Rafe, in, Rafe, and set out the grocery in their kind,[41] if thou lov'st me.   [*Exit Rafe.*]

Wife I warrant, our Rafe will look finely when he's dressed.

Prologue But what will you have it called?

Citizen *The Grocer's Honour.*

Prologue Methinks *The Knight of the Burning Pestle*[42] were better.

Wife I'll be sworn, husband, that's as good a name as can be.

Citizen Let it be so. Begin, begin; my wife and I will sit down.

Prologue I pray you, do.

Citizen What stately music have you? You have shawms?

Prologue Shawms? No.

Citizen No? I'm a thief if my mind did not give me so. Rafe plays a stately part, and he must needs have shawms. I'll be at the charge of them myself, rather than we'll be without them.

Prologue So you are like to be.

Citizen Why, and so I will be. There's two shillings. Let's have the waits[43] of Southwark; they are as rare fellows as any are in England. And that will fetch them all o'er the water with a vengeance, as if they were mad.

Prologue You shall have them. Will you sit down, then?

Citizen Ay, come wife.

Wife Sit you merry all, gentlemen; I'm bold to sit amongst you for my ease.

Prologue From all that's near the court, from all that's great,
Within the compass of the City walls
We now have brought our scene; fly far from hence
All private taxes,[44] immodest phrases,
Whate'er may but show like vicious;
For wicked mirth never true pleasure brings,
But honest minds are pleased with honest things.
Thus much for what we do; but for Rafe's part,
You must answer for yourself.

Citizen Take you no care of Rafe, he'll discharge himself,[45] I warrant you.

Wife I' faith, gentlemen, I'll give my word for Rafe.

3
From *A Chaste Maid in Cheapside*
(Thomas Middleton, 1613/1631)

[*In each of its several plots,* A Chaste Maid in Cheapside *explores the sale of love for money. In one plot, the grasping and lascivious Sir Walter Whorehound pursues the daughter of a wealthy London goldsmith while attempting to pass his mistress off as his niece in order to marry her to the gold-smith's son. In another, a man driven to poverty and forced to*

*separate from his family because of his wife's repeated
pregnancies, makes money by impregnating the wife of an
impotent and dim-witted knight in need of an heir. In what is
perhaps the most excruciating plot of all, Allwit, a Londoner,
allows his wife to be kept as one of Whorehound's mistresses
— and to bear his children — in exchange for the comfortable
household maintenance Whorehound supplies. In the first of
the scenes below, Allwit greets the news of Whorehound's
arrival in London by gloating over his scheme, and he greets
Sir Walter himself by presenting him with his bastard
children. In a second scene, Middleton gives a further twist to
the knife, as Allwit coolly presents Whorehound with his
wife's newborn child.]*

Act I, scene ii

Enter Davy[46] and Allwit severally.

Davy [*aside*] Honesty wash my eyes, I have spied a wittol.[47]

Allwit What, Davy Dahanna, welcome from North Wales, i' faith;
and is Sir Walter come?

Davy New come to town, sir.

Allwit In to the maids, sweet Davy, and give order his chamber be
made ready instantly. My wife's as great as she can wallow,
Davy, and longs for nothing but pickled cucumbers and his
coming. And now she shall ha't, boy.

Davy She's sure of them, sir.

Allwit Thy very sight will hold my wife in pleasure till the knight
come himself. Go in, in, in Davy.   [*Exit Davy.*]
The founder's come to town; I'm like a man
Finding a table furnished to his hand,
As mine is still to me, prays for the founder,
'Bless the right worshipful, the good founder's life!'
I thank him, h'as maintained my house this ten years,
Not only keeps my wife, but a' keeps me
And all my family; I am at his table,
He gets me all my children, and pays the nurse
Monthly or weekly; puts me to nothing,
Rent, nor church duties, not so much as the scavenger,
The happiest state that ever man was born to.
I walk out in a morning, come to breakfast,

Find excellent cheer, a good fire in winter,
Look in my coal-house about midsummer e'en;
That's full — five or six chaldron[48] new laid up.
Look in my back yard, I shall find a steeple
Made up with Kentish faggots, which o'erlooks
My water-house and the windmills. I say nothing,
But smile and pin[49] the door. When she lies in —
As now she's even upon the point of grunting —
A lady lies not in like her; there's her embossings,
Embroiderings, spanglings, and I know not what,
As if she lay with all the gaudy shops
In Gresham's Burse about her; then her restoratives,
Able to set up a young pothecary
And richly stock the foreman of a drug shop;
Her sugar by whole loaves, her wines by rundlets.[50]
I see these things, but like a happy man,
I pay for none at all, yet fools think's mine;
I have the name, and in his gold I shine.
And where some merchants would in soul kiss Hell
To buy a paradise for their wives, and dye
Their conscience in the blood of prodigal heirs
To deck their night-piece,[51] yet all this being done,
Eaten with jealousy to the inmost bone —
As what affliction nature more constrains,
Than feed the wife plump for another's veins?
These torments stand I freed of; I am as clear
From jealousy of a wife as from the charge.
O, two miraculous blessings! 'Tis the knight
Hath took that labour all out of my hands;
I may sit still and play, he's jealous for me,
Watches her steps, sets spies; I live at ease.
He has both the cost and torment; when the strings
Of his heart frets, I feed, laugh, or sing,
La dildo, dildo la dildo, la dildo dildo de dildo!

Enter two Servants.

First Servant What, has he got a singing in his head now?
Second Servant Now's out of work, he falls to making dildoes.[52]
Allwit Now, sirs, Sir Walter's come.
First Servant Is our master come?
Allwit Your master! What am I?

First Servant Do not you know, sir?

Allwit Pray, am not I your master?

First Servant Oh, you are but our mistress's husband.

Allwit Ergo, knave, your master.

Enter Sir Walter and Davy.

First Servant Negatur argumentum.[53] Here comes Sir Walter.
   [*Aside.*] Now a' stands bare as well as we; make the most of
   him, he's but one peep above a serving-man, and so much his
   horns make him.

Sir Walter How dost, Jack?

Allwit Proud of your worship's health, sir.

Sir Walter How does your wife?

Allwit E'en after your own making, sir, she's a tumbler,[54] a' faith,
   the nose and belly meets.

Sir Walter They'll part in time again.

Allwit At the good hour they will, and please your worship.

Sir Walter [*to Servant*] Here, sirrah, pull off my boots. [*Servant
   pulls off boots.*] Put on, put on,[55] Jack.

Allwit I thank your kind worship, sir.

Sir Walter [*to Servant*] Slippers! Heart, you are sleepy!

Allwit [*aside*] The game begins already.

Sir Walter Pish, put on, Jack.

Allwit [*aside*] Now I must do it, or he'll be as angry now as if I had
   put it on at first bidding. 'Tis but observing, 'tis but observing of a
   man's humour once, and he may ha' him by the nose all his life.

Sir Walter What entertainment has lain open here? No strangers
   in my absence?

First Servant Sure, sir, not any.

Allwit [*aside*] His jealousy begins; am not I happy now,
   That can laugh inward whilst his marrow melts!

Sir Walter How do you satisfy me?

First Servant Good sir, be patient.

Sir Walter For two months' absence I'll be satisfied.

First Servant No living creature entered.

Sir Walter Entered? Come, swear.

First Servant You will not hear me out, sir.

Sir Walter Yes, I'll hear't out, sir.

First Servant Sir, he can tell himself.

Sir Walter Heart, he can tell!
   Do you think I'll trust him? As a usurer

With forfeited lordships![56] Him? O monstrous injury!
Believe him? Can the devil speak ill of darkness?
What can you say, sir?

Allwit Of my soul and conscience, sir, she's a wife as honest of her
body to me as any lord's proud lady can be.

Sir Walter Yet, by your leave, I heard you were once offering to
go to bed with her.

Allwit No, I protest, sir.

Sir Walter Heart, if you do, you shall take all; I'll marry.

Allwit Oh, I beseech you, sir —

Sir Walter [*aside*] That wakes the slave and keeps his flesh in awe.

Allwit [*aside*] I'll stop that gap
  Where'er I find it open; I have poisoned
  His hopes in marriage already [with]
  Some old rich widows and some landed virgins,[57]
  And I'll fall to work still before I'll lose him;
  He's yet too sweet to part from.

Enter two Children.

First Boy [*to Sir Walter*] God-den, father.

Allwit Ha, villain, peace!

Second Boy God-den, father.

Allwit Peace, bastard! [*Aside*] Should he hear 'em! these are two
foolish children;
They do not know the gentleman that sits there.

Sir Walter Oh, Wat! How dost, Nick? Go to school, ply your
books, boys, ha?

Allwit Where's your legs, whoresons? They should kneel indeed,
If they could say their prayers.

Sir Walter [*aside*] Let me see — stay,
  How shall I dispose of these two brats now,
  When I am married; for they must not mingle
  Amongst my children that I get in wedlock;
  'Twill make foul work, that, and raise many storms.
  I'll bind Wat prentice to a goldsmith,
  My father Yellowhammer,[58] as fit as can be;
  Nick with some vintner; good, goldsmith and vintner;
  There will be wine in bowls, i'faith. ...

4
From *Bartholomew Fair*
(Ben Jonson, 1614/1631/1640)

[*With this scene Jonson introduces his audience to
Bartholomew Fair, in Smithfield, and to the booth of the pig-
woman, Ursula. Around this seedy establishment — 'the very
womb and bed of enormity' — the action of the next three acts
revolves, as a variety of low-life types (brawlers, cutpurses,
and bawds) become involved in a series of steadily deepening
imbroglios with the supercilious gallants, foolish gentlefolk
and pretentious citizens who are drawn to the Fair by their
various obsessions. Already on stage at the beginning of the
scene is Adam Overdo, citizen, scrivener and justice of the
peace, who has come to the Fair disguised as a madman in
order to spy out enormities. He soon enough becomes
enbroiled himself, as he is joined by several of the Fair's
veteran hawkers and then by the prodigious Ursula, 'the sow
of Smithfield', 'the fatness of the Fair', a 'bawd in grease'.
Presiding over her booth — an emporium for the body that
offers roast pork and bottle ale up front, a fencing operation,
makeshift whorehouse, and semi-public privy in the rear —
and incarnating the fleshly spirit of the Fair, Ursula is at once
a magical Circe, a smoky-faced and limping Ate, and a figure
of the original mother Eve, sweating away 'to the first
woman, a rib again'.*]

Act II, scene ii

[*Leatherhead, a seller of dolls and hobby-horses and Trash, a
seller of gingerbread men, set up their booths: Adam Overdo,
disguised, apart.*]

Leatherhead The Fair's pestilent dead, methinks; people come
  not abroad today, whatever the matter is. Do you hear, Sister
  Trash, Lady o' the Basket? Sit farther with your gingerbread
  progeny there, and hinder not the prospect of my shop, or I'll
  ha' it proclaimed i' the Fair what stuff they are made on.
Trash Why, what stuff are they made on, Brother Leatherhead?
  Nothing but what's wholesome, I assure you.
Leatherhead Yes, stale bread, rotten eggs, musty ginger, and dead
  honey, you know.

Overdo [*aside*] Ay, have I met with enormity so soon?

Leatherhead I shall mar your market, old Joan.

Trash Mar my market, thou too-proud peddler? Do thy worst, I
defy thee, ay, and thy stable of hobby-horses. I pay for my
ground as well as thou dost; an' thou wrong'st me, for all thou
art parcel-poet[59] and an inginer,[60] I'll find a friend shall right
me, and make a ballad of thee and thy cattel[61] all over. Are you
puffed up with the pride of your wares? Your arsedine?[62]

Leatherhead Go to, old Joan, I'll talk with you anon, and take you
down, too, afore Justice Overdo. He is the man must charge
you. I'll ha' you to the Pie Powders.[63]

Trash Charge me? I'll meet thee face to face, afore his worship,
when thou dar'st; and though I be a little crooked o' my body,
I'll be found as upright in my dealing as any woman in
Smithfield, I. Charge me?

Overdo [*aside*] I am glad to hear my name is their terror yet; this
is doing of justice.

[*Enter Passengers.*]

Leatherhead What do you lack? What is't you buy? What do you
lack? Rattles, drums, halberts,[64] horses, babies o' the best!
Fiddles o' the finest!

[*Enter Costermonger.*]

Costermonger Buy any pears! Pears, fine, very fine pears!

Trash Buy any gingerbread, gilt gingerbread!

[*Enter Nightingale, a ballad-seller.*]

Nightingale [*sings*] Hey, now the Fair's a-filling!
 O, for a tune to startle
The birds o' the booths here billing
Yearly with old Saint Bartle!
The drunkards they are wading,
The punks[65] and chapmen[66] trading,
Who'ld see the Fair without his lading.[67]

Buy any ballads? New ballads!

[*Enter Ursula, the pig woman, from her booth.*]

Ursula Fie upon't! Who would wear out their youth and prime
thus, in roasting of pigs, that had any cooler vocation? Hell's a

kind of cold cellar to't, a very fine vault, o' my conscience! [*To Mooncalf, her tapster.*] What, Mooncalf!

Mooncalf [*within*] Here, mistress.

Nightingale How now, Ursula? In a heat? In a heat?

Ursula [*to Mooncalf*] My chair, you false faucet, you, and my morning's draught, quickly, a bottle of ale to quench me, rascal. I am all fire and fat, Nightingale; I shall e'en melt away to the first woman, a rib again, I am afraid. I do water the ground in knots[68] as I go, like a great garden-pot:[69] you may follow me by the S's I make.

Nightingale Alas, good Urs; was 'Zekiel here this morning?

Ursula 'Zekiel? What 'Zekiel?

Nightingale 'Zekiel Edgeworth, the civil cutpurse; you know him well enough. He that talks bawdy to you still. I call him my secretary.

Ursula He promised to be here this morning, I remember.

Nightingale When he comes, bid him stay. I'll be back again presently.

Ursula Best take your morning's dew in your belly, Nightingale. (*Mooncalf brings in the chair.*) Come, sir, set it here. Did not I bid you should get this chair let out o' the sides for me, that my hips might play? You'll never think of anything, till your dame be rump-galled. 'Tis well, changeling;[70] because it can take in your grasshopper's thighs, you care for no more. Now you look as you had been i' the corner o' the booth, fleaing your breech with a candle's end,[71] and set fire o' the Fair. Fill, stote,[72] fill.

Overdo [*aside*] This pig-woman do I know, and I will put her in for my second enormity; she hath been before me, punk, pinnace,[73] and bawd, any time these two and twenty years, upon record in the Pie-powders.

Ursula Fill again, you unlucky vermin.

Mooncalf Pray you, be not angry mistress; I'll ha' it widened anon.

Ursula No, no, I shall e'en dwindle away to't ere the Fair be done, you think, now you ha' heated me! A poor vexed thing I am; I feel myself dropping already, as fast as I can. Two stone o' suet a day is my proportion. I can but hold life and soul together with this (here's to you, Nightingale) and a whiff of tobacco, at most. Where's my pipe now? Not filled? Thou errant incubee![74]

Nightingale Nay, Urs'la, thou'lt gall between the tongue and the teeth with fretting, now.

Ursula How can I hope that ever he'll discharge his place of trust
— tapster, a man of reckoning under me — that remembers
nothing I say to him? But look to't, sirrah, you were best.
Threepence a pipeful I will ha' made of my whole half pound of
tobacco, and a quarter of a pound of coltsfoot mixed with it too,
to itch[75] it out. I that have dealt so long in the fire will not be to
seek in the smoke now. Then six and twenty shillings a barrel I
will advance o' my beer, and fifty shillings a hundred o' my
bottle ale; I ha' told you the ways how to raise it. Froth your
cans well i' the filling, at length, rogue, and jog your bottles o'
the buttock, sirrah. Then skink[76] out the first glass ever, and
drink with all companies, though you be sure to be drunk; you'll
misreckon the better and be less ashamed on't. But your true
trick, rascal, must be to be ever busy, and mistake away the
bottles and cans in haste, before they be half drunk off, and
never hear anybody call (if they should chance to mark you) till
you ha' brought fresh, and be able to forswear 'em. Give me a
drink of ale.
Overdo [*aside*] This is the very womb and bed of enormity, gross
as herself! This must all down for enormity, all, every whit on't.
(One knocks.)
Ursula Look who's there, sirrah! Five shillings a pig is my price, at
least; if it be a sow-pig, sixpence more. If she be a great bellied
wife and long for't, sixpence more for that.
Overdo [aside] *O tempora! O mores!*[77] I would not ha' lost my
discovery of this one grievance for my place and worship o' the
bench. How is the poor subject abused here! Well, I will fall in
with her, and with her Mooncalf, and win out wonders of
enormity. [*To Ursula.*] By thy leave, goodly woman, and the
fatness of the Fair, oily as the King's constable's lamp, and
shining as his shoeing horn! Hath thy ale virtue or thy beer
strength, that the tongue of man may be tickled and his palate
pleased in the morning? Let the pretty nephew here go search
and see.
Ursula What new roarer[78] is this?
Mooncalf Oh, Lord, do you not know him, mistress? 'Tis mad
Arthur of Bradley[79] that makes brave orations. Brave master,
old Arthur of Bradley, how do you? Welcome to the Fair.
When shall we hear you again, to handle your matters? With
your back again a booth, ha? I ha' been one o' your little
disciples i' my days!

Overdo Let me drink, boy, with my love, thy aunt here, that I may be eloquent; but of thy best, lest it be bitter in my mouth and my words fall foul on the Fair.

Ursula Why dost thou not fetch him drink and offer him to sit?

Mooncalf It's ale, or beer, Master Arthur?

Overdo Thy best, pretty stripling, thy best; the same thy dove drinketh and thou drawest on holy days.

Ursula Bring him a sixpenny bottle of ale; they say a fool's handsel[80] is lucky.

Overdo Bring both, child; ale for Arthur and beer for Bradley. Ale for thine aunt, boy. [*Aside.*] My disguise takes to the very wish and reach of it. I shall, by the benefit of this, discover enough and more, and yet get off with the reputation of what I would be, a certain middling thing between a fool and a madman.

[*The scene continues at Ursula's booth. In the intervening scenes, Ursula and Overdo (still disguised as mad Arthur of Bradley) have been joined by Jordan Knockem, a pugnacious horse-dealer, and by the cutpurse, Ezekiel Edgeworth. Scene v begins with the arrival of Winwife, a gentleman, and his companion Quarlous, a gamester. Winwife and Quarlous have come to the Fair to observe the follies of Bartholomew Cokes, the dim-witted squire of Harrow, and his entourage.*]

Act II, scene v

Enter Winwife and Quarlous.

Winwife We are here before 'em, methinks.

Quarlous All the better; we shall see 'em come in now.

Leatherhead What do you lack, gentlemen? What is't you lack? A fine horse? A lion? A bull? A bear? A dog or a cat? An excellent fine Barthol'mew-bird? Or an instrument? What is't you lack?

Quarlous 'Slid! Here's Orpheus[81] amongst the beasts, with his fiddle and all!

Trash Will you buy any gingerbread, gentlemen?

Quarlous And Ceres selling her daughter's picture in gingerwork!

Winwife That these people should be so ignorant to think us chapmen[82] for 'em! Do we look as if we would buy gingerbread or hobbyhorses?

Quarlous Why, they know no better ware than they have, nor

better customers than come. And our very being here makes us
fit to be demanded as well as others. Would Cokes would come;
there were a true customer for 'em.

Knockem *(to Edgeworth)* How much is't?[83] Thirty shillings?
Who's yonder? Ned Winwife and Tom Quarlous, I think! Yes.
(Gi' me it all, gi' me it all.) Master Winwife! Master Quarlous!
Will you take a pipe of tobacco with us? (Do not discredit me
now, 'Zekiel.)

Winwife [*to Quarlous*] Do not see him! He is the roaring horse-
courser. Pray thee, let's avoid him; turn down this way.

Quarlous 'Slood, I'll see him, and roar with him, too, an' he
roared as loud as Neptune; pray thee, go with me.

Winwife You may draw me to as likely an inconvenience, when
you please, as this.

Quarlous Go to, then; come along, we ha' nothing to do, man, but
to see sights now.

Knockem Welcome, Master Quarlous and Master Winwife! Will
you take any froth[84] and smoke with us?

Quarlous Yes, sir; but you'll pardon us if we knew not of so much
familiarity between us afore.

Knockem As what, sir?

Quarlous To be so lightly invited to smoke and froth.

Knockem A good vapour![85] Will you sit down, sir? This is old
Urs'la's mansion; how like you her bower? Here you may ha'
your punk and your pig in state, sir, both piping hot.

Quarlous I had rather ha' my punk cold, sir.

Overdo [*aside*] There's for me. Punk and pig!

Ursula What, Mooncalf, you rogue!

Mooncalf By and by; the bottle is almost off[86], mistress. Here,
Master Arthur.

Ursula [*going within*] I'll part you and your playfellow there 'i the
guarded[87] coat, an' you sunder not the sooner.

Knockem Master Winwife, you are proud, methinks. You do not
talk nor drink; are you proud?

Winwife Not of the company I am in, sir, nor the place, I assure
you.

Knockem You do not except at the company, do you? Are you in
vapours, sir?

Mooncalf Nay, good Master Dan Knockem, respect my mistress'
bower, as you call it. For the honour of our booth, none o' your
vapours here.

Ursula (She comes out with a firebrand.) Why, you thin lean pole-
cat, you, an' they have a mind to be in their vapours, must you
hinder 'em? What did you know, vermin, if they would ha' lost
a cloak or such a trifle? Must you be drawing the air of pacifi-
cation here, while I am tormented within i' the fire, you weasel?

Mooncalf Good mistress, 'twas in the behalf of your booth's credit
that I spoke.

Ursula Why? Would my booth ha' broke if they had fall'n out in
it, sir? Or would their heat ha' fired it? In, you rogue, and wipe
the pigs and mend the fire, that they fall not, or I'll baste you
and roast you till your eyes drop out like 'em. Leave the bottle
behind you and be cursed a while.   [*Exit Mooncalf.*]

Quarlous Body o' the Fair! What's this? Mother o' the bawds?

Knockem No, she's mother o' the pigs, sir, mother o' the pigs!

Winwife Mother o' the Furies, I think, by her firebrand.

Quarlous Nay, she is too fat to be a Fury; sure, some walking sow
of tallow!

Winwife An inspired[88] vessel of kitchen-stuff! *(She drinks this
while.)*

Quarlous She'll make excellent gear for the coachmakers here in
Smithfield to anoint wheels and axle-trees with.

Ursula Ay, ay, gamesters, mock a plain plump soft wench o' the
suburbs, do, because she's juicy and wholesome. You must ha'
your thin-pinched ware, pent up i' the compass of a dog-collar
(or 'twill not do), that looks like a long laced conger set upright,
and a green feather, like fennel i' the jowl on't.

Knockem Well said, Urs, my good Urs; to 'em, Urs.

Quarlous Is she your quagmire, Dan Knockem? Is this your bog?

Nightingale We shall have a quarrel presently.

Knockem How? Bog? Quagmire? Foul vapours! Hum'h!

Quarlous Yes, he that would venture for't, I assure him, might
sink into her and be drowned a week ere any friend he had
could find where he were.

Winwife And then he would be a fortnight weighing up[89] again.

Quarlous 'Twere like falling into a whole shire of butter; they had
need be a team of Dutchmen[90] should draw him out.

Knockem Answer 'em, Urs; where's thy Bartholomew wit now,
Urs, thy Bartholomew wit?

Ursula Hang 'em, rotten, roguy cheaters, I hope to see 'em
plagued one day (poxed they are already, I am sure) with lean
playhouse poultry[91] that has the bony rump sticking out like the

ace of spades or the point of a partizan,[92] that every rib of 'em is like the tooth of a saw, and will so grate 'em with their hips and shoulders as, take 'em all together, they were as good lie with a hurdle.[93]

Quarlous Out upon her, how she drips! She's able to give a man the sweating sickness with looking on her.

Ursula Marry, look off, with a patch[94] o' your face and a dozen i' your breech, though they be o' scarlet, sir. I ha' seen as fine outsides as either o' yours bring lousy linens to the brokers, ere now, twice a week!

Quarlous Do you think there may be a fine new cucking-stool[95] i' the Fair to be purchased? One large enough, I mean? I know there is a pond of capacity for her.

Ursula For your mother, you rascal! Out, you rogue, you hedge-bird, you pimp, you pannier-man's[96] bastard, you!

Quarlous Ha, ha, ha.

Ursula Do you sneer, you dog's head, you trendle-tail![97] You look as you were begotten atop of a cart in harvest time, when the whelp was hot and eager. Go, snuff your brother's bitch, Mistress Commodity; that's the livery you wear; 'twill be out at the elbows shortly. It's time you went to't, for the tother remnant.

Knockem Peace, Urs, peace, Urs. [*Aside.*] They'll kill the poor whale and make oil of her. Pray thee go in.

Ursula I'll see 'em poxed, and piled[98] — and double piled.

Winwife Let's away; her language grows greasier than her pigs.

Ursula Does't so, snotty nose? Good lord, are you snivelling? You were engendered on a she-beggar in a barn, when the bald thrasher, your sire, was scarce warm.

Winwife Pray thee, let's go.

Quarlous No, faith, I'll stay the end of her now. I know she cannot last long; I find by her similes she wanes apace.

Ursula Does she so? I'll set you gone. Gi' me my pig-pan hither a little. I'll scald you hence, an' you will not go.   [*Exit.*]

Knockem Gentlemen, these are very strange vapours! And very idle vapours, I assure you!

Quarlous You are a very serious ass, we assure you.

Knockem Humh! Ass, and serious? Nay, then, pardon me my vapour. I have a foolish vapour, gentlemen; any man that does vapour me the ass, Master Quarlous —

Quarlous What then, Master Jordan?

Knockem I do vapour him the lie.

Quarlous Faith, and to any man that vapours me the lie, I do
vapour that.   [*Strikes him.*]

Knockem Nay, then, vapours upon vapours.

Edgeworth, Nightingale 'Ware the pan, the pan, the pan! She
comes with the pan, gentlemen! *(Ursula comes in with the
scalding-pan. They fight. She falls with it.)* God bless the
woman!

Ursula Oh!   [*Exeunt Winwife and Quarlous.*]

Trash What's the matter?

Overdo Goodly woman!

Mooncalf Mistress!

Ursula Curse of hell, that ever I saw these fiends! Oh! I ha'
scalded my leg, my leg, my leg, my leg! I ha' lost a limb in the
service! Run for some cream and salad oil,[99] quickly. [*To
Mooncalf.*] Are you under-peering, you baboon? Rip off my
hose, an you be men, men, men!

Mooncalf Run you for some cream, good mother Joan. I'll look to
your basket.   [*Exit Trash.*]

Leatherhead Best sit up i' your chair, Urs'la. Help, gentlemen.

Knockem Be of good cheer, Urs, thou hast hindered me the
currying of a couple of stallions, here, that abused the good
race-bawd[100] o' Smithfield. 'Twas time for 'em to go.

Nightingale I' faith, when the pan came, they had made you run
else. [*To Edgeworth.*] This had been a fine time for purchase,[101]
if you had ventured.

Edgeworth Not a whit; these fellows were too fine to carry money.

Knockem Nightingale, get some help to carry her leg out o' the
air. Take off her shoes. Body o' me! she has the mallanders, the
scratches, the crown scab, and the quitter bone[102] i' the tother
leg.

Ursula Oh, the pox! Why do you put me in mind o' my leg thus,
to make it prick and shoot? Would you ha' me i' the hospital
afore my time?

Knockem Patience, Urs, take a good heart; 'tis but a blister, as big
as a windgall;[103] I'll take it away with the white of an egg, a little
honey, and hog's grease; ha' thy pasterns well rolled and thou
shalt pace again by tomorrow. I'll tend thy booth and look to
thy affairs the while; thou shalt sit i' thy chair and give
directions and shine *Ursa major*. [*They carry Ursula into the
back of her booth.*]

Notes

1. A close search.
2. Quicksilver apparently wears a cloak above his station.
3. West Smithfield was known as Ruffian's Hall for the swaggering brawlers alleged to frequent it.
4. An eminent justice whose presence was required to constitute a bench.
5. Food prepared from milk.
6. Food of next best quality.
7. Because suretyship involved entering a bond for another man's debt, it might be regarded as a form of cuckoldry, traditionally associated with horns.
8. The narrow end of a horn; just such an image appears in a sixteenth century emblem for the evils of suretyship.
9. Promising payment for his son's indenture.
10. Having better means.
11. Bundles of kindling; highly flammable and short-lived.
12. A new-made knight and penniless scoundrel who is angling for the land which is the inheritance of Touchstone's 'proud' and 'ladified' elder daughter, Gertrude.
13. Darling.
14. Bear an armorial device.
15. See Shakespeare, *2 Henry IV*, II. iv. 170, 181.
16. Goddess of dawn.
17. Like other tradesmen, Touchstone wears clothes with a satin front and canvas back.
18. Sixpences.
19. Large containers in which apprentices drew water from the public conduits.
20. See Kyd, *The Spanish Tragedy*, II.v.4.
21. A dissolute.
22. An unwelcome companion tolerated because he pays for the rest.
23. Collar.
24. Lace.
25. Gibes.
26. Hung on the stage to announce the play.
27. Act like rogues.
28. Such a play was registered in 1605 but never printed; see 10.6, above.
29. The second part of Heywood's *If You Know Not Me*; see 10.5, above.
30. George Peele's *Edward I* (1593).
31. Probably the Prologue's contemptuous invention.
32. Wonderful, amazing.
33. Lit. cony, i.e. term of endearment, pet.
34. A favourite literary subject; treated in Heywood's *Edward IV* (1600).
35. A lost play, possibly by Heywood.
36. The grocer's slip for 'apparel'.
37. Insult, ridicule.
38. Bombastic, ranting.
39. See Shakespeare, *1 Henry IV*, I.iii.201-5.
40. The hero of Kyd's *The Spanish Tragedy* (c. 1589).
41. In their true nature; perhaps also in their proper livery.
42. As importers and dealers in spices, grocers commonly made use of mortars and pestles. The suggestive shape of the pestle is here reinforced not only by the adjective but also by an off-colour pun on 'pizzle' [penis].

43. City trumpeters, derived from watchmen equipped with horns to sound alarm.

44. Attacks on individuals.

45. Picking up on the off-colour title of the play.

46. Servant of Sir Walter Whorehound.

47. Contented cuckold; also the two syllables of Allwit's name reversed.

48. 1 chaldron = 32 bushels; 1 bushel = 8 gallons

49. Bolt.

50. Barrels holding 18 ½ gallons.

51. Mistress.

52. A crude pun in this context.

53. Therefore your proof is denied.

54. Acrobat.

55. Allwit has removed his hat in deference.

56. Mortgaged estates subject to forfeit.

57. Perennially desirable as marriage partners.

58. Sir Walter seeks to marry Yellowhammer's daughter.

59. Part-time poet.

60. Inventor, deviser of puppet shows.

61. I.e. chattels; goods, gear.

62. A gold-coloured alloy leaf used to ornament toys.

63. From Fr. *pied poudreux* (dusty foot); temporary courts set up to deal with itinerants and fairs.

64. Halberds, or battle-axes; all of these are, of course, toys.

65. Whores.

66. Stall-keepers.

67. Purchases.

68. Intricate patterns.

69. Watering can.

70. A child left by fairies in exchange for one stolen.

71. Removing fleas from trousers with a candle flame.

72. Weasel, referring to Mooncalf's small stature.

73. Prostitute.

74. Incubus, demon.

75. Eke.

76. Pour.

77. See Cicero's First Oration against Catiline.

78. Brawler.

79. A madman of ballad and legend.

80. The first money taken by a trader in the morning, thought to be lucky.

81. Orpheus charmed beasts with his music.

82. Customers.

83. Knockem and Edgeworth have been counting out money in the preceding scene.

84. Bottled ale.

85. A word used obsessively by Knockem to mean nearly anything; but used especially for the game of senseless quarreling in which each speaker deliberately contradicts the one preceding him.

86. Empty.

87. Ornamented.

88. Divinely influenced, but also puffed up.

89. Being dredged up, salvaged.

90. Proverbially known as butter-boxes.

91. Prostitutes who worked the theatres.

92. A long spear.
93. An instrument of torture.
94. Used for treating the pox.
95. A chair for ducking scolds.
96. Peddler's.
97. Mongrel.
98. Denuded of hair; Ursula's trading involved singeing the bristles from the pig's carcase.
99. Used as a dressing for pork.
100. A bawd of breeding stock.
101. For cutting a purse.
102. All horse diseases.
103. Tumour on a horse's leg.

15

FISHWIVES AND OTHERS: VARIETIES OF CHARACTER-WRITING

Strictly speaking, the 'character' is a short, witty prose portrait of distinctive moral and social types, a literary fashion that suddenly sprang up and then faded during the early Stuart period. The paradox is that this specific genre, which can be assigned a precise pedigree and be neatly defined, seems to overlap with so many other literary developments and, through them, to shade off into the life of London itself. As a distinctive genre, character-writing can be traced in England to a 1592 Latin translation of the *Ethical Characters* of the Greek writer, Theophrastus (372–287 BC). A student of Aristotle, and writing in the same sophisticated Athens that produced Menander's New Comedy of social manners, Theophrastus had reinforced both his master's ideal of the golden mean and the conformist outlook of Athens by composing portraits of some 30 unpleasant Athenian types who lapsed in some way from the accepted civilised norms. Beginning with a short definition, each of his portraits of flatterers, bores, braggarts, misers and cowards was illustrated by examples and anecdotes. Among the first to imitate Theophrastrus in England was the satirist and preacher, Joseph Hall (see 4.8 and 7.6 above), who composed, in his *Characters of Virtues and Vices* (1608), a portrait-gallery of good and bad moral types designed to illustrate the Christian–Stoic values of aloofness, self-mastery and denial. It was the emphasis of Theophrastus on social manners, rather than Hall's moralism, however, that prevailed in the first truly successful character-book, the 22 prose characters composed by Sir Thomas Overbury 'and other learned gentlemen his friends', which were appended to the second edition of Overbury's poem, *A Wife* (1614). No doubt aided by Overbury's sensational murder in 1613, these portraits, some of which were written by John Donne and the dramatists Thomas Dekker and John Webster, became an overnight best-seller. They received four editions in the three months that followed the first publication, and were joined by a further 60 characters by the time of the 11th edition in 1622. Numerous imitators quickly followed, the most successful of whom was the Oxford divine, John Earle, whose collection received five editions between 1628 and 1629.

To trace this vogue solely to Theophrastus, however, is to overlook a rich body of related developments. While providing a specific form and style of description, the Theophrastan example also gave classical sanction to several long-established traditions of portraiture. Tudor schoolboys, for example, cut their teeth on that branch of rhetorical description known as *prosopographia*, or the verbal portraiture of persons, while preachers and their congregations had long before discovered common ground in the vivid sermon *exemplum*. Medieval allegory had established an elaborate and precise language for portraying moral types, and in the General Prologue of *The Canterbury Tales*, Chaucer had negotiated skilfully between allegorical tradition and the subtle portrayal of realistic detail. Writers of advice, moreover, had acquainted readers with the perils of their environment through the lucid delineation of underworld denizens (see Chapter 9); the thieves and hucksters in the cony-catching pamphlets of Greene and others take their place in a body of urban reportage beside the subjects of Thomas Lodge's *Alarum Against Usurers* (1584), the whores and upstarts of Nashe's prose satires, and the sextons, graverobbers and 'charewomen' (the last included in 15.1 below) of Dekker's macabre plague pamphlets. Citizen mythology, moreover, had long encouraged the portraiture of worthies to be imitated (see Chapter 10). Horace and Juvenal had provided models for the derisory portraiture of types and individuals in the formal verse satire of the 1590s (see Chapter 7). In the satiric epigram (a form closely related to the prose character), the effort to fix character in neat lapidary schemes had carried verbal portraiture toward one sort of artistic perfection (see Chapter 11). Many of these genres, together with the example of Terence and Plautus, helped to shape the detailed portraiture of contemporary Londoners in city comedy. Ben Jonson drew on contemporary medicine and psychology in order to develop a brand of character portrayal based on the theory of humours. Jonson's *Every Man Out of His Humour* (1599) begins with a series of prose portraits

of the eccentric *dramatis personae,* and the even more elaborate
sketches of courtly types in *Cynthia's Revels* (1600) suggests that
Jonson was intimately acquainted with Theophrastus long before
the appearance of Hall's volume. There were already, then, many
traditions of character-writing, including several varieties well con-
nected with the literary image of London, and it is not surprising to
find that Londoners figure prominently among the types examined
in the formal character-books.

Even more, perhaps, than other kinds of portraiture, the formal
character lays a heavy stress on the verbal medium through which
the world is seen. When Overbury defined the character as 'a
picture (real or personal) quaintly drawn in various colours' he
meant by 'colours' the ostentatious devices of rhetoric; and this
rhetorical bias is confirmed by Overbury's further use of musical
tropes describing the genre as 'a quick and soft touch of many
strings ... wit's descant on any plain song'. As the last phrase
suggests, the aim of character-writing was to combine the light
treatment of everyday matters with the charm of form, to use the
everyday as an occasion for the display of ingenuity and conceited
wit in the making of fine phrases. 'More Seneca than Cicero',
speaking 'rather the language of oracles than orators', the
character was not so much an expansive medium for detailed
reportage as an imagistic and allusive prose lyric. In the puns and
double entendres by which they associated the appearance and
activities of persons with moral and social values, the character-
writers engaged in the sort of verbal game that extends from the
Anglo-Saxon riddle to the facetious epitaph of the Tudor–Stuart
period.

Yet precisely this verbal sophistication identifies the character
with the literary life of London. Most of its early practitioners, like
Hall and Overbury, were associated with the court and affected the
cult of civilised modernity, the calculated insincerities that were
fashionable with what H.V. Routh has called the 'gilded vaga-
bonds', the new gentleman urbanites of the Stuart age. In its
offhand, conversational idiom, and in its clipped, circumscribed
form, the character, like the verse epigram, attempts to establish
the writer's urbane mastery over his environment. Not all
characters, of course, are drawn from London life (they may, in
fact, be slightly outnumbered by those which are not), and not all
characters are facetious. Overbury's volume consisted of eulogistic
and humorous characters as well as satirical, while Breton's eulogy

of a merchant (see 15.4 below), shows that the form could express popular ideals as well as aggressive elitism. But the element of fashionable sophistication actually contributed to the increasing prominence of London as a source of characters. Because it was, like the sonnet, a highly conventionalised and frequently imitated form, the character challenged its writer to display his originality either through conceited and burlesque imitation of his pre-decessors or through expansion of the repertoire, which forced him to seek out increasingly rare, topical, idiosyncratic and local subjects. In the selections below, Henry Parrot's Ballad-Maker and John Earle's Player (based on an earlier eulogy by Webster in the Overbury volume) exemplify the former tendency, while John Earle's Mere Alderman and Lupton's Goldfinders exemplify the latter.

In their reductive treatment of citizens and obscure urban types, the writers often display a satiric condescension that is perhaps revealing of real social tensions. The salacious, sneering style of the courtier Francis Lenton is perhaps predictable; but even in the putatively gentle and contemplative John Earle there is at times the rancid flavour of condescension and contempt. The compen-sation, however, is the elaborate and detailed exploration of the hidden corners of London life. From Dekker's prison characters in the Overbury volume, for example, there quickly developed a sub-genre of characters drawn from London's prison life, represented by such works as William Fennor's *The Compters' Commonwealth* (1617) and Geoffrey Minshull's *Essays and Characters of a Prison and Prisoners* (1618). Both Earle and Donald Lupton developed characters on London locales as well as people (see 1.21 above), and with Lupton's sketches of fishwives and night-soil men, the genre had begun to verge on genuine reportage.

The character was a genre both too limited and too good to last in isolation. In the short term, it was quickly absorbed into the essay, into the polemical characters of the Civil War, and into the partisan biographies of the Civil War's historians. In the longer run, it re-emerged in branches of the short story and the novel, and even in sociology. It would be going a bit far to see in Lupton's fishwives and scavengers the Londoners who tell their wretched stories in the pages of Mayhew and Booth. But in the first person narrative (too lengthy for inclusion here) of a London whore in Greene's *Disputation Between a He-Cony Catcher and a She-Cony Catcher* (1592), it is possible to see a glimmer of the impulse underlying Mayhew, or, for that matter, Defoe. And in the singing chimneysweep of the otherwise flinty William Strode it is possible to hear — 150 years before he sang his song of innocence — the urchin sweep of William Blake. Even in their broad, typical outlines, the seventeenth century characters show that the city could disclose important sides of human nature; in their moments of acute focus, they show the exploration of the city giving birth to the individual.

1
The Abuses of Keepers, Nurses, or Charewomen[1]
(Thomas Dekker, 1608/1632)

Their tongues are lickerish[2] as flies', eyes are quick-sighted as cats' at midnight, hands as catching as birdlime, hearts as false as dice, yet running smoothly.

They are called keepers, because whatsoever they get but hold of, they keep it with griping paws never to let it go. They are dry nurses and starve, so far as they dare, all that come under their fingers.

They are called charewomen, because when Death sits all night by the sick man's bedside, they by their good wills sit till morning by a good fire in easy chairs and are therefore christened by the names of charewomen.

Or, if you will, that word chare comes from the Latin word *chara*, which signifies dear. And they that hire these night-crows into their houses shall find them dearer ware than bullocks in Smithfield. Thousands, in and about London and Westminster, have bought their attendance so dear that their lives have gone for it. The watchmen of the City get not so much amongst all their chalky bills[3] in a month as one of these scrapes to herself in one night, when she plucks but a shirt over a dead man's head and ears. Those shirts are their fees; so are waistcoats, nightcaps, sheets, pillow-beres,[4] bands, handkerchers, anything. Rats are not such gnawers of linen, nor moths of woollen, as these are of both.

If a rich bachelor sicken, it is an East Indian voyage when she hoists up sail from her own house unto his; and when he dies, then she and her lading comes home: Breda is then taken, and she alone has the spoil.

The sight of a doctor strikes her into a paleness, an apothecary's man with his urine eyes[5] gives her a purge; for anyone that brings health in his hand puts sickness into her.

The tolling of bells[6] is music to her. She cares not how few live, over whom she is matron, nor how many die, though in her arms. The more water she fishes in, her fare is the better.

Art thou sick and trusteth one of these to make thy broth? Some of them are such cooks that what good thing soever is prescribed for thy recovery shall be sure to be left out.

If hot drinks would save thy life, she will persuade thee to poor, thin cold beer. Hast thou any infected part of thy body, take heed to her plasters and her surgery, for she cares not how soon a cold strikes to thy heart, if thou art to leave anything behind thee to warm her.

One charitable quality she has, for at midnight if she be alone with thee and perceives any signs of death in thy speech, thy pillow will she pull away to hasten thee on thy journey.

2
A Fantastic Inns of Court Man
(Sir Thomas Overbury, 1615)

He is distinguished from a scholar by a pair of silk stockings and a beaver hat, which makes him contemn[7] a scholar as much as a scholar doth a schoolmaster. By that[8] he hath heard one mooting[9] and seen two plays, he thinks as basely of the university as a young sophister[10] doth of a grammar school. He talks of the university with that state as if he were her chancellor; finds fault with alterations and the fall of discipline with an 'It was not so when I was a student', although that was within this half-year. He will talk ends of Latin, though it be false, with as great confidence as ever Cicero could pronounce an oration, though his best authors for't be taverns and ordinaries. He is as far behind a courtier in his fashion as a scholar is behind him, and the best grace in his behaviour is to forget his acquaintance.

He laughs at every man whose band fits not well or that hath not a fair shoe-tie, and he is ashamed to be seen in any man's company that wears not his clothes well. His very essence he placeth in his outside, and his chief prayer is that his revenues may hold out for taffeta cloaks in the summer and velvet in the winter. For his recreation, he had rather go to a citizen's wife than a bawdy-house, only to save charges, and he holds fee-tail[11] to be absolutely the best tenure. To his acquaintance he offers two quarts of wine for one he gives. You shall never see him melancholy but when he wants a new suit or fears a sergeant,[12] at which times only he betakes himself to Ploydon. By that he hath read Littleton, he can call Solon, Lycurgus, and Justinian[13] fools, and dares compare his law to a Lord Chief Justice's.

3

A Drunken Dutchman Resident in England (Sir Thomas Overbury, 1615)

Is but a quarter master with his wife. He stinks of butter, as if he were anointed all over for the itch. Let him come over never so lean, and plant him but one month near the brew-houses in St Katherine's, and he'll be puffed up to your hand like a bloat herring. Of all places of pleasure he loves a common garden; and, with the swine of the parish, had need be ringed for rooting. Next to these he affects lotteries naturally, and bequeaths the best prize in his will aforehand; when his hopes fall, he's blank. They swarm in great tenements like flies; six households will live in a garret. He was wont, only to make us fools, to buy the foxskin for threepence and sell the tail for a shilling. Now his new trade of brewing strong waters[14] makes a number of mad men. He loves a Welshman extremely for his diet and his orthography, that is, for a plurality of consonants and cheese. Like a horse, he's only guided by the mouth. When he's drunk, you may thrust your hand into him like an eelskin and strip him his inside outwards. He hoards up fair gold and pretends 'tis to seethe in his wife's broth for a consumption, and loves the memory of King Henry the Eight most especially for his old sovereigns. He says we are unwise to lament the decay of timber in England, for all manner of buildings or fortification whatsoever, he desires no other thing in the world than barrels and hop-poles. To conclude, the only two plagues he trembles at is small beer and the Spanish Inquisition.[15]

4
A Worthy Merchant
(Nicholas Breton, 1616)

A worthy merchant is the heir of adventure, whose hopes hang much upon wind. Upon a wooden horse he rides through the world, and in a merry gale makes a path through the seas. He is a discoverer of countries and a finder-out of commodities, resolute in his attempts and royal in his expenses. He is the life of traffic and the maintainer of trade, the sailor's master and the soldier's friend. He is the exercise of the exchange, the honour of credit, the observation of time, and the understanding of thrift. His study is number, his care his accounts, his comfort his conscience, and his wealth his good name. He fears not Scylla and sails close by Charybdis, and having beaten out a storm, rides at rest in a harbour. By his sea-gain he makes his land-purchase, and by the knowledge of trade finds the key of treasure. Out of his travails[16] he makes his discourses, and from his eye-observations brings the models of architectures. He plants the earth with foreign fruits and knows at home what is good abroad. He is neat in apparel, modest in demeanour, dainty in diet, and civil in his carriage. In sum, he is the pillar of a city, the enricher of a country, the furnisher of a court, and the worthy servant of a king.

5
A Ballad Maker
(Henry Parrot, 1626)

Is a kind of owl or bat that flieth in the night and dares not his deformities should appear by day. He's one that (from first shameless, desperate become of late) to be more impudent sets this last rest up for his latest refuge. His *primum mobile*[17] of ragged ancestry sprang from the patchings of some paltry poet; whence learning how to rhyme unreasonably makes this the mainmast of his occupation. His choicest plots or grounds to work upon are drawn most commonly from thieves and murderers, or such notorious malefactors as puts him in great hope to purchase forty pence. His highest ambition he aims at is to be entitled *The Times' Intelligencer* or *Nuncius of News at the Second Hand.* 'The Punk's Late Ballad of the New Bridewell' was his chief masterpiece, that purchased him perhaps a pair of boots over and above his usual bargaining. He spends most part of his time in's bed, partly for saving charge of botching,[18] but chiefly devising what were best to write on, when no one calls on him for what's to pay. *Omnia mea mecum, etc.*[19] may very rightly be verified in him that hath no riches more than what he wears and comes to him commonly by deed of gift. The alewife is enforced to trust him weekly, and that without all hope of having aught, unless some ballad chance to be composed upon some dismal or doleful accident as may be sung to the tune of 'Welladay'. If anything happen to help besides, it must accrue from the next sessions,[20] provided there be some to travel westward,[21] on whom he is to make that recantation as if himself were the theme he writes on. No massacre or murder comes to him amiss, but brings sufficient matter for invention; wherein he shows himself so nimble that if any witch be by chance condemned, he'll have a ballad out in print before such time as she goes to Tyburn, wherein all her confession and the manner of her death shall be described by way of prophesy — witness the famous Witch of Edmonton, condemned at Newgate these four years past.[22] No printer deals with him that loves his credit, but must be induced thereunto for want of work, and then the press begins to sweat when monstrous news comes trundling in the way. His greatest volume, done in folio, is to be purchased but for two brass tokens, which either you may please to light tobacco with or sacrifice to A-jax[23] for purgation. In brief, the sum of all his practices is but to shift him sometime in clean linen, that he appear not lousy to posterity; and so I leave him.

6
A Mere Alderman
(John Earle, 1629)

He is venerable in his gown, more in his beard, wherein he sets not forth so much his own as the face of a city. You must look on him as one of the town gates and consider him not as a body, but a corporation. His eminency above others hath made him a man of worship, for he had never been preferred but that he was worth thousands. He oversees the commonwealth as his shop, and it is an argument of his policy that he has thriven by his craft. He is a rigorous magistrate in his ward, yet his scale of justice is suspected, lest it be like the balances in his warehouse. A ponderous man he is, and substantial, for his weight is commonly extraordinary, and in his preferment nothing rises so much as his belly. His head is of no great depth, yet well furnished, and when it is in conjunction with his brethren, may bring forth a city apothegm, or some such matter. He is one that will not hastily run into error, for he treads with great deliberation, and his judgement consists much in his place. His discourse is commonly the annals of his mayoralty and what good government there was in the days of his gold chain, though his door-posts[24] were the only things that suffered reformation. He seems not sincerely religious, especially on solemn days, for he comes to church to make a show and is a part of the choir-hangings. He is the highest stair of his profession and an example to his trade of what in time they may come to. He makes very much of his authority, but more of his satin doublet, which, though of good years, bears its age very well and looks fresh every Sunday; but his scarlet gown is a monument and lasts from generation to generation.

7
A Mere Gull Citizen
(John Earle, 1629)

Is one much about the same model and pitch of brain that the clown is, only of somewhat a more polite and finical[25] ignorance, and as sillily scorns him as he is sillily admired by him. The quality of the city hath afforded him some better dresses of clothes and language, which he uses to best advantage, and is so much the more ridiculous. His chief education is the visits of his shop, where if courtiers and fine ladies resort, he is infected with so much more eloquence, and if he catch one word extraordinary, wears it forever. You shall hear him mince a compliment sometimes that was never made for him; and no man pays dearer for good words, for he is oft paid with them. He is suited rather fine than in the fashion, and still has something to distinguish him from the gentleman, though his doublet cost more — especially on Sundays, bridegroom-like, where he carries the state of a very solemn man and keeps his pew as his shop. And it is a great part of his devotion to feast the minister. But his chiefest guest is a customer, which is the greatest relation he acknowledges, especially if you be an honest gentleman, that is, trust him to cozen you enough. His friendships are a kind of gossiping friendships, and those commonly within the circle of his trade, wherein he is careful principally to avoid two things, that is, poor men and suretyships. A man that will spend his sixpence with a great deal of imputation, and no man makes more of a pint of wine than he. He is one bears a pretty kind of foolish love to scholars, and to Cambridge especially, for Sturbridge Fair's sake, and of these all are truants to him that are not preachers, and of these the loudest be the best; and he is much ravished with the noise of a rolling tongue. ... One that does nothing without his chuck, that is, his wife, with whom he is billing still in conspiracy, and the wantoner she is, the more power she has over him. And she never stoops so low after him, but is the only woman goes better off a widow than a maid. In the education of his child, no man fearfuller, and the danger he fears is a harsh schoolmaster, to whom he is alleging still the weakness of the body, and pays a fine extraordinary for his mercy. ... He is one loves to hear the famous acts of citizens, whereof the gilding of the Cross he counts the glory of his age, and the Four Prentices of London[26] above all the Nine Worthies. He entitles himself to all the merits of his company — whether schools, hospital, or exhibitions — in which he is a joint benefactor (though four hundred years ago) and upbraids them far more than those that gave them. Yet with all this folly he has wit enough to get wealth, and in that a sufficienter man than he that is wiser.

8
A Player
(John Earle, 1629)

He knows the right use of the world, wherein he comes to play a part, and so away. His life is not idle, for it is all action, and no man need be more wary in his doings, for the eyes of all men are upon him. His profession has in it a kind of contradiction, for none is more disliked and yet none is more applauded. And he has this misfortune of some scholars: too much wit makes him a fool. He is like our painting gentlewomen, seldom in his own face, seldomer in his clothes, and he pleases the better he counterfeits, except only when he is disguised with straw for gold lace. He does not only personate on the stage, but sometime in the street, for he is masked still in the habit of a gentleman. His parts find him oaths and good words, which he keeps for his use and discourse and makes show with them of a fashionable companion. He is tragical on the stage, but rampant in the tiring house,[27] and swears oaths there which he never conned. The waiting-women spectators are over ears in love with him, and ladies send for him to act in their chambers. Your Inns of Court men were undone but for him; he is their chief guest and employment, and the sole business that makes them afternoon's men.[28] The poet only is his tyrant, and he is bound to make his friend's friend drunk at his charges. Shrove Tuesday he fears as much as the bawds, and Lent is more damage to him than to the butcher[29]. . . . But to give him his due, one well-furnished actor has enough in him for five common gentlemen, and if he have a good body for six, and for resolution, he shall challenge any Cato,[30] for it has been his practice to die bravely.

9
A Shopkeeper
(John Earle, 1629)

His shop is his well-stuffed book, and himself the title-page of it, or index. He utters much to all men, though he sells but to a few, and entreats for his own necessities by asking others what they lack. No man speaks more[31] and no more, for his words are like his wares, twenty of one sort; and he goes over them alike to all comers. He is an arrogant commender of his own things, for whatever he shows you is the best in the town, though the worst in his shop. His conscience was a thing that would have laid upon his hands, and he was forced to put it off, and makes great use of honesty to profess upon. He tells you lies by rote, and not minding, as the phrase to sell in and the language he spent most of his years to learn. He never speaks so truly as when he says he would use you as his brother, for he would abuse his brother, and in his shop thinks it lawful. His religion is much in the nature of his customers' and indeed the pander to it, and by a misinterpreted sense of Scripture makes a gain of his godliness. He is your slave while you pay him ready money, but if he once befriend you, your tyrant, and you had better deserve his hate than his trust.

10
A Waterman
(Wye Saltonstall, 1631)

Is like a piece of Hebrew, spelled backward, or the emblem of
deceit, for he rows one way and looks another. When you come
within ken of them, you shall hear a noise worse than the con-
fusion of Bedlam, and if you go with a sculler, the oars think you
are no gentleman. He carries many a bankrout[32] over the water,
and yet, when he sets them ashore, makes them landed men. If you
dislike the roughness of the water, he warrants you a safe passage
and, on that condition, gives you his hand to help you into the
boat, and his first question is where you'll be. Though he be ne'er
sober, yet he's ne'er drunk, for he lives by water, and is not
covetous to get any great estate, for he's best contented when he
goes most down the wind. A fresh water soldier he is, and there-
fore gets to wear some nobleman's badge to secure him from
pressing.[33] He knows all the news and informs men of the names of
noblemen's houses toward the Thames. A man would take him for
a very busy fellow, for he has an oar in every boat, which though it
leak not, yet 'tis ever ready to take water. He's so seldom drunk
that 'tis chalked up for a miracle, for he goes commonly on the
score.[34] Thus he lives, and when he dies, he's sure his soul shall
pass to the Elysian Fields, for if Charon[35] should deny him
passage, he means to steal his boat and so ferry himself over.

11
A Sempster[36] *Shopkeeper*
(Francis Lenton, 1631)

Is a feminine creature furnished with the finest ware, making her
greatest gain of sindon, or fine linen, transforming it into several
shapes for that purpose, and may be called the needle-work pearl
of prettiness. She is very neatly spruced up and placed in the
frontispiece of her shop, of purpose (by her curious habit) to allure
some custom, which still increaseth and decreaseth as her beauty is
in the full, or the wane. She hath a pretty faculty in presenting her-
self to the view of passengers by her rolling eyes, glancing through
the hangings of tiffany and cobweb-lawn,[37] that the travellers are
suddenly surprised and cannot but look back, though but to view

babies in her face, and, in affection to her comeliness, must needs cheapen her commodity, where they are rapt into a bargain by her beauty, and do kiss the nurse for the child's sake, which she kindly accepts, and desires them, as they like that, she may have more of their custom. In her trade, she is much troubled with stitches, amongst which, back-stitch is the most ordinary, easy, and pleasant to her; and if you cannot bargain for her ruffs in her shop, she will fit you with choice at your chamber, so you will pay her well for her pains. ...

12
Fisherwomen
(Donald Lupton, 1632)

These crying, wandering, and travailing creatures carry their shops on their heads, and their storehouse is ordinarily Billingsgate or Bridge-Foot, and their habitation Turnagain Lane.[38] They set up every morning their trade afresh. They are easily set up and furnished, get something and spend it jovially and merrily; five shillings a basket and a good cry is a large stock for one of them. They are merriest when all their ware is gone. In the morning they delight to have their shop full, and at even they desire to have it empty. Their shop's but little — some two yards' compass — yet it holds all sorts of fish, or herbs, or roots, strawberries, apples or plums, cucumbers, and such like ware; nay, it is not destitute sometimes of nuts, and oranges, and lemons. They are free in all places and pay nothing for shop-rent, but only find repairs to it. If they drink out their whole stock, it's but pawning a petticoat in Long Lane,[39] or themselves in Turnbull Street,[40] for to set up again. They change every day almost, for she that was this day for fish may be tomorrow for fruit, next day for herbs, another for roots; so that you must hear them cry before you know what they are furnished withal. When they have done their fair, they meet in mirth, singing, dancing, and, in the middle (as a parenthesis), they use scolding; but they do use to take and put up words, and end not till either their money or wit or credit be clean spent out. Well, when in an evening they are not merry in a drinking-house, it is suspected they have had bad return, or else have paid some old score, or else they are bankrupts. They are creatures soon up and soon down.

13
Scavengers and Goldfinders [41]
(Donald Lupton, 1632)

These two keep all clean, the one the streets, the other the back-sides, but they are seldom clean themselves; the one, like the hangman, doth his work all by day; the other, like a thief, doth all theirs in the night. The goldfinders hold the sense of smelling the least of use and do not much care for touching the business they have in hand. They both carry their burdens out into the fields, yet sometimes the Thames carries away their loads. They are something like the trade of the barbers, for both do rid away superfluous excrements. The barber's profession is held chief, because that deals with the head and face, but these with the excrements of the posteriorums. The barber's trade and these have both very strong smells, but the goldfinder's is the greatest for strength, the other's is safest and sweetest. The barber useth washing, when he hath done, to cleanse all, and so do these; the barber useth a looking-glass, that men may see how he hath done his work, and these use a candle. They are all necessary in the city; as our faces would be foul without the barber, so our streets without the scavenger and our backsides without the goldfinder. The scavenger seems not to be so great an officer as the goldfinder, for he deals with the excrements chiefly of beasts, but this latter of his own species. Well, had they been sweeter fellows I would have stood longer on them, but they may answer, they keep all clean and do that work which scarce anyone but themselves would meddle withal.

14
Chimney-Sweeper's Song
(William Strode, c. 1635)

Hath Christmas furred your chimneys,
  Or have the maids neglected,
Do fireballs drop from your chimney's top?
  The pigeon is respected; [42]
Look up with fear and horror,
  O how my mistress wonders!

The street doth cry, the news doth fly,
   The boys they think it thunders.
Then up I rush with my pole and brush,
   I scour the chimney's jacket;
I make it shine as bright as mine,
   When I have rubbed and raked it.

Take heed, ten groats you'll forfeit,
   The mayor will not have under.
In vain is dung, so is your gun,
   When bricks do fly asunder.
Let not each faggot fright ye,
   When threepence will call me in;
The bishop's foot is not worse than soot,[43]
   If ever it should fall in.
Up will I rush, etc.

The scent, the smoke, ne'er hurts me,
   The dust is never minded;
Mine eyes are glass, men swear as I pass,
   Or else I had been blinded.
For in the midst of chimneys,
   I laugh, I sing, I hollow,
I chant my lays in Vulcan's praise,
   As merry as the swallow.
Still up I rush, etc.

With engines and devices,
   I scale the proudest chimney;
The prince's throne to mine alone
   Gives place, the stars I climb nigh.
I scorn all men beneath me,
   While there I stand a-scouring;
All they below look like a crow,
   Or men on Paul's a-tow'ring.
Then down I rush, etc.

And as I downward rumble,
   What think you is my lot then?
A good neat's[44] tongue, in the inside hung,
   The maid hath it forgotten.

If e'er the wanton mingled
    My ink with soot, I wist not;
Howe'er, the neat and harmless cheat
    Is worth a penny, is't not?
Still do I rush, etc.

Then clothed in soot and ashes,
    I catch the maids that haste out:
Whosoe'er I meet with smut I greet,
    And pounce their lips and waistcoat.
But on the Sunday morning,
    I look not like a widgin,[45]
So brave I stand with a point in my band,
    Men ask if I be Pidgin.
Yet will I rush, etc.

Mulsack[46] I dare encounter,
    For all his horn and feather;
I'll lay him a crown I'll roar him down,
    I think he'll ne'er come hither.
The boys that climb like crickets
    And steal my trade, I'll strip them;
By privilege I, grown chimney high,
    Soon out of town will whip them.
Then will I rush, etc.

Notes

1. Apparently Dekker's conflation of *charewoman* with *chair*.
2. Greedy, lustful.
3. The mortality bills keeping a tally of the plague fatalities.
4. Pillowcases.
5. I.e. urinalysis.
6. See 1.16, above.
7. Despise.
8. Because.
9. Debate.
10. Undergraduate.
11. An inheritance.
12. Pursuing him for debt.
13. Ploydon and Littleton compiled English legal handbooks; Solon, Lycurgus and Justinian were famous lawgivers of antiquity.
14. *Aqua fortis*, spirits.
15. Established in the Low Countries in 1522 by Charles V and harshly

reimposed by Philip II during the unsuccessful Protestant revolt of the later sixteenth century.

16. Travels, as well as labours.

17. The first moving thing, the ninth (or tenth) sphere of Ptolemaic astronomy.

18. Mending.

19. All I own is on my person.

20. The criminal sessions of Oyez and Terminez associated with Newgate Prison.

21. I.e. from Newgate up Holborn to the Tyburn gallows.

22. Elizabeth Sawyer of Edmonton was executed for witchcraft on 19 April 1621; by the end of the same year, John Ford, William Rowley and Thomas Dekker had written a play called *The Witch of Edmonton.*

23. See Ch 7, note 88.

24. See 13.5, above

25. Simpering.

26. The Cross in Cheapside was regilded or burnished by the London authorities several times in the sixteenth century, — 1522, 1533, 1554, 1595–96, and 1599–1600. Thomas Heywood was the author of *The Four Prentices of London* (*c.* 1592–1600).

27. The dressing room at the rear of the Elizabethan outdoor stage.

28. Plays were performed at 2 p.m.

29. Theatres were closed during Lent.

30. Marcus Porcius Cato made his last stand for liberty in 46 BC, providing for the escape of his friends and preferring to die rather than surrender to Julius Caesar.

31. I.e. no man speaks so few words so many times over.

32. Bankrupt.

33. Conscription into military service.

34. On the slate; i.e. is given credit for drink.

35. Charon ferried souls across the River Styx in Hades to Elysium.

36. Seamstress.

37. A very fine transparent lawn or linen.

38. London's most famous cul-de-sac, ending, according to Stow, at Fleet Dike, 'from whence men must turn again the same way they came, for there it stopped'.

39. Famous for pawn-shops and old-clothes dealers.

40. The most disreputable street in London, a haunt of thieves and loose women.

41. Street cleaners and night-soil men, respectively.

42. Respited, out off, neglected.

43. To 'put the bishop's foot' in something was, proverbially, to burn it. The chimneysweep's flaming faggots are not as bad as the soot they burn away.

44. Ox-tongue.

45. Widgeon, a wild duck.

46. A famous chimneysweep; a highwayman named Cottington, alias 'Mulled Sack', was sometimes confused with him.

16

THEATRE IN THE STREETS:
OFFICIAL PAGEANTRY

Dramatists would not so readily have adapted the city to the stage had not London so frequently seemed to be a theatre. The ancient *topos* that equated life with the stage made Londoners acutely conscious of the inherent theatricality of urban life. The greatest expressions of this theatricality were the Royal Entries and annual mayoral pageants of the period, in which officials, dramatists, artisans, wealthy citizens and thronging spectators united in celebration of the order and power of London. The communal achievements of the form were inseparable, however, from a general publicity in human relationships and from a habit of celebrating such relationships formally through festivity. Coronation pageants, for example, were rare, but the presence of the royal seat at Westminster provided numerous opportunities for public celebration in London. Marriages and births in the royal family were occasions for prodigious bonfires, and royal progresses by water to Greenwich were attended by fireworks and festive barges. Monarchs, furthermore, were eager to impress visiting ambassadors and dignitaries by lavish receptions into London. In November, during the reign of Elizabeth, elaborate Accession Day tilts were held at Whitehall, and Elizabeth's visits to London were routinely surrounded with ceremony and acclamation.

Civic life, too, abounded in ceremony. Though mayoral pageants were held annually, a pamphlet published by City officials specified processional order and attire for literally dozens of occasions, from the presentation of churchwardens to the election of parliamentary burgesses and bridgemasters, from the burial of aldermen to the series of public sermons in Easter week. The annual musters of the watches and militias and the drills of artillery companies and archery societies provided yet more spectacle, as did the public execution of criminals, the carting of

333

whores, and the ducking of scolds. Never quite separate from official life were the rituals associated with the Church year and the seasonal rhythms. A social historian has written that in traditional societies 'man lives in remembrance of one festival and in expectation of the next'. In Tudor–Stuart London such intervals were never long. The festivities associated with such religious holidays as Shrove Tuesday or such pagan holidays as May Day are too well known to need comment, but their occasional eruption into political riot demonstrates how thin could be the line between licensed misrule and open rebellion. By the mid-Tudor period such Christmas festivities as the boy bishop had been suppressed, but Stow reports that Londoners remained firmly attached to Christmas celebrations. Prolonged from Christmas day to Epiphany, the twelve days of Christmas also marked the beginning of the festive season at court, which extended until Lent. Further occasions for ceremony were such saints' feasts as Michaelmas, Martinmas, and St Bartholomew's Day, the occasion of London's great fair at Smithfield. Together with such rites of passage as betrothals, weddings and funerals, the festive year solidified the life of family, parish, guild, ward, City and nation.

Nevertheless, for Londoners in the age of Shakespeare, the greatest of communal occasions was the annual mayor's pageant, held on 29 October, 'on the morrow of the feast of St Simon and Jude'. Unlike the coronation processions of Elizabeth (1559) and James I (1604), which can be linked to a medieval tradition of royal triumphs and entries (see e.g. 2.1–2), the mayoral pageant appears to have been a special creation of Tudor–Stuart London. The first recorded mention of a mayoral pageant, in 1535, indicates that the form perhaps emerged as a replacement for the midsummer show and watches suppressed at about that time. Henry Machyn's diary mentions eight pageants staged between 1550 and 1563, but the first mention of the content of a pageant appears in 1561 in the records of the Company of Drapers. The Company's expense of £151 also provides the first sign of the spirit of rivalry that characterised these shows, as each guild supplying the mayor for a given year strove to surpass the others in lavish showmanship. The first record of the expense for printing a show, in 1566, is a further sign of the companies' investment in their prestige, and with George Peele's pageant of 1585 (see 16.2 below), the earliest published show to survive and the first known to have been written by an established dramatist, the pageant form entered its maturity as a collaborative art-work, involving the wealth of London's leading citizens, the talents of some of its most popular dramatists, and the pervasive ideology of its citizen class.

Of the 39 recorded pageants prior to the Civil War, 25 were written by professional dramatists experienced in pageantry, myth and rhetoric, in the manipulation of mass emotion, and in the entrepreneurial skills of organising complex performances. Dekker, Middleton and Thomas Heywood were frequent contributors, but the recognised leader in the medium was the prolific Anthony Munday, who had a hand in at least 15 pageants. Satirised by Ben Jonson as Antonio Balladino, pageant-poet to the city of Milan, Munday was labelled by his rival Middleton 'an impudent common writer'. John Chapman, however, called Middleton himself 'a poor chronicler of a Lord Mayor's truth (that peradventure will last his year)', and such labels indicate the low esteem in which the form was held by writers of any pretension. The Haberdashers' records of 1604 show that even Ben Jonson was persuaded to write a pageant, though his feelings may be best reflected in his failure to include it in his published works.

The alliance between City capitalists — who frequently harassed the theatres — and dramatists — who frequently satirised the citizen class — was in certain respects an unlikely and perhaps uneasy one. But if the enterprising capitalism of the dramatists is reflected in this alliance, so too is the theatrical self-consciousness of the merchant class. The records show that company members exercised vigilant oversight and often contributed creatively to their pageants. They were prepared to spend lavishly to enhance their prestige and outshine their rivals — the most expensive pageant of the period, the Grocers' of 1613, cost over £1,300. It must be noted, however, that in 1612 Dekker referred discreetly to the 'sumptuous thriftiness in these civil ceremonies', and that while company records register lavish expense, they also take careful account of each penny. On occasion, pageant writers were reprimanded or refused payment for failure to perform according to contract, and once their pageants were over, the companies disassembled them and sold them piece by piece. The spirit of competition, in other words, was always balanced by prudent thrift: Thomas Heywood garnered the 1635 pageant from the Ironmongers by underbidding John Taylor by £10.

By far the largest portion of the costs was laid out for building the tableaux and spectacles themselves. The increasing disparity between the portion of the poet and the portion of the artificer demonstrates that the verbal and visual collaboration — as essential to this form as to the indoor court masque — was undergoing essential change. Peele's 1585 pageant, for example, consists almost entirely of verse, and offers little description of the spectacle itself. By contrast, the water pageant of Webster's 1624 show calls for an elaborate spectacle. By the end of the first decade of the seventeenth century, major artificers like John Grinkin and Gerard Christmas and his sons — normally carvers for the navy — were receiving lavish compliments from their poet collaborators. By 1634, John Taylor could write that Robert Norman, the artificer, 'was indeed the prime inventor, prosecutor, and furnisher of these shows'.

The domination of speeches by spectacle — or of soul by body, to use Dekker's terms — was, of course, inevitable in such a public, outdoor form. Dekker complained, in his version of the 1604 coronation pageant, that the heads of the multitude 'will miserably run a-woolgathering if we do but offer to break them with hard words'; and Jonson scoffed in his version of the same that 'their grounded judgements did gaze, said it was fine, and were satisfied'. In all fairness, however, even the recorded responses of educated spectators indicate a high level of bewilderment, despite Munday's recommendation that 'the personages [should] have all emblems and properties in their hands, and so bear them that the weakest capacity may take knowledge of them'. In addition to the pageants themselves, a variety of peripheral activities added further colour, excitement and confusion. The Venetian ambassador reported in 1617, for example, that a pageant wagon was 'laden with bales from which the lads took sundry confections, sugar, nutmeg, dates, and ginger, throwing them among the crowd'; the crowd, he added, was kept back by men 'masked as wild giants, who by means of fireballs and wheels hurled sparks in the faces of the mob and over their persons'. Company records, in fact, often show substantial expenses for green men, whifflers, fencers and fiends. By the 1630s Thomas Heywood had hit on the expedient of inserting a purely antic presentation, or anti-masque, among the more allegorical pageants, explaining that 'without some such intruded anti-masque, many who carry their ears in their eyes will not stick to say "I will not give a pin for the show".'

Nevertheless, the elaborate arbors, mountains, thrones, monuments and chariots of the artificers remained firmly grounded in the allegorical soul worked out by the company and its writer. Unlike the stationary arches and scaffolds of the coronation entries, the pageants of the Lord Mayor's shows were portable and joined the procession at various points along the route. Ordinarily, the Mayor and his entourage took a barge from the Three Cranes in Vintry Ward to Westminster, where he was sworn in before the Lord Chief Justice; when he returned to the city by barge, he was greeted at Baynard's Castle by the first of the pageants, the water show. He then processed uphill to Paul's Chain and the church-yard, and from there along Cheapside from the Little Conduit to the Standard. The pageants performed at each of these points were inserted into the procession just before the Lord Mayor, in the tra-ditional position of conquered victims in Roman triumphs. After the Mayor's feast at the Guildhall, the procession accompanied him back to St Paul's, and after prayers the Mayor received a final exhortation before retiring for the night and beginning his year of office. The individual shows were thus yoked together by a cumu-lative significance, as the procession moved temporally from the mythological fantasies of the water pageants, through the political and historical allegories of the land pageants, to a final, timely exhortation on the duties of the coming year. In the most success-ful pageants, the entire procession enacted a kind of allegorical quest. In Dekker's 1612 pageant, for example, the Mayor's pro-cession, having witnessed and gathered up the Throne of Virtue in Paul's churchyard, was able to pass safely by the Castle of Envy at the Little Conduit on its way to the House of Fame at the Standard in Cheap; but only on its return from the Guildhall, having achieved Fame, was the procession, in a passage reproduced below, able to lay Envy to rest.

The pageant writers drew on a variety of materials for their alle-gories. Most frequently personified are the *desiderata* of communal life (Peace, Felicity, Plenty, Prosperity) and the virtues of governors (Justice, Wisdom, Religion, Nobility, Vigilance, Liberal-ity) and citizens (Obedience, Loyalty, Unity, Charity). The political ideals celebrated in such abstractions were supplemented by tributes to learning, industry and philanthropy, and by mytho-logical figures who exemplified virtue and glorified the city. An important feature were such resurrected London worthies (see Chapter 10) as Farringdon, Walworth and Fitz-Alwin, historical figures who were offered not simply as models but as embodiments of the prestige of the venerable companies with which they were associated. Webster's celebration of the royal connections of the Merchant Taylors, included here, simplifies considerably an earlier celebration by Dekker, who mentions a total of 171 worthies connected with the same company. The glorification of particular trades is carried to an extreme in such devices as Dekker's celebration of 'The Glory of Furs' for the Skinners. Even the overt commercialism of such presentations, however, is inseparable from a broader spirit of mercantile ethos, a spirit which led Webster to glorify England's navigators in his pageant, and which led many writers to represent London's far-flung commercial network in such exotic figures as Moors and Indians.

Beneath the exoticism, however, is an underlying sobriety, embodied in both the grander heroes — Ulysses, Orpheus, Jason, Brute — and the humbler analogies — gardeners, seamen, shepherds, and bridegrooms — held up for the Lord Mayor's emulation. In the evening's final exhortation, delivered directly to the Mayor by such stark figures as Justice, Government and Truth, the day's glorious visions faded into confrontation with the realities of rule. It has been speculated that this final speaker may have descended from the 'Ribald', a figure in medieval pageants whose function was to ride uppermost in the chariot, smiting the triumphator on the head in order to bring home the lesson of humility. In any case, the farewell ceremonies clarify an assumption implicit throughout the pageant: if others were merely to gaze, the Mayor was to hear, and in a certain sense to participate in, the dramatic celebration of his rule.

The participatory nature of the pageants was after all the heart of the form. It accounts for the peculiar success of the form at this period and offers an interesting point of comparison with the coronation ceremonies. The glowing report of Elizabeth's procession attributes to the Queen a subtle and profound grasp of civic theatricality, by which she turned the City's unsubtly simultaneous presentation of an English Bible and 1,000 marks into a personal triumph. By contrast with the focus on the Queen's own role in 1559, the accounts of James's entry in 1604 lay almost exclusive stress on the static and imposing arches erected by the City against the King's arrival. James's own role is registered not through the improvisations by which he enhanced his image but by his failure to turn up at the appropriate time and by his refusal to hear all the prepared speeches. 'He endured the day's brunt with patience,' one chronicler later wrote, 'but afterwards in his public appearances the access of the people made him so impatient that he often dispersed them with frowns.' Even James's grudging patience, however, was preferable to the supercilious response of his son, Charles. Like his father's, Charles's coronation entry was initially postponed by a visitation of the plague, but when, months later, the City fathers went forward with plans to 'show and perform their loyalties' by erecting pageants, Charles sent a tart command to dismantle them: 'which besides the particular charge they cause the City, do choke and hinder the passage of such as in coaches or with their carriages, have occasion to pass up and down'.

The increasingly lavish mayoral pageants of the Stuart period clearly invite comparison with the court masques held at Westminster; at least one historian suggests that the mayors' shows were intended to rival the court masques in an increasingly 'dangerous and aggressive spirit'. With all its splendour, the Londinium arch of 1603 is a forceful declaration of the City's power, but it lacks any of the warmth of the 1559 pageants. And the harmonious subordination of Mayor to Queen and Queen to God in Peele's pageant of 1585 becomes in Heywood's 1631 pageant merely a stark command ('serve and obey') that is unsupported by any glorious image of power. The image of the withered branch in this work, or the figure of storm-tossed Ulysses who presides throughout, typify the beleaguered and twilight spirit of Heywood's pageants, written during the 1630s, on the eve of a civil war that brought the pageants to a halt for more than 20 years. The festive symbolism of London's power was most exuberant, clearly, not when raised in defiance but when offered in celebration of unity, however illusory.

1
[The Coronation Procession of Elizabeth I]
(Anon., 1559)

... If a man should say well, he could not better term the City of London that time than a stage, wherein was shown the wonderful spectacle of a noble-hearted princess toward her most loving people and the people's exceeding comfort in beholding so worthy a sovereign and hearing so prince-like a voice, which could not but have set the enemy on fire. ...

At the Standard in Cheap, which was dressed fair against the time, was placed a noise of trumpets, with banners and other furniture. The Cross likewise was also made fair and well trimmed. And near unto the same, upon the porch of St Peter's church door, stood the waits[1] of the City, which did give a pleasant noise with their instruments as the Queen's Majesty did pass by; which on every side cast her countenance and wished well to all her most loving people. Soon after Her Grace passed the Cross, she had espied the pageant erected at the Little Conduit in Cheap and incontinent required to know what it might signify. And it was told Her Grace that there was Time. 'Time,' said she, 'and Time hath brought me hither.' And so, forth the whole matter was opened to Her Grace as hereafter shall be declared in the description of the pageant. But in the opening, when Her Grace understood that the Bible in English should be delivered unto her by Truth, which was therein represented by a child, she thanked the City for that gift and said that she would oftentimes read over that book, commanding Sir John Perrot, one of the knights which held up her canopy, to go before and to receive the book. But learning that it should be delivered unto Her Grace down by a silken lace, she caused him to stay, and so passed forward till she came against the aldermen in the high end of Cheap tofore the Little Conduit, where the companies of the City ended, which began at Fenchurch, and stood along the streets one by another enclosed with rails hanged with cloths, and themselves well appareled with many rich furs and their livery hoods upon their shoulders in comely and seemly manner, having before them sundry persons well appareled in silks and chains of gold, as whifflers[2] and guarders of the said companies, besides a number of rich hangings, as well of tapestry, arras, cloths of gold, silver, velvet, damask, satin and other silks plentifully hung all the way as the Queen's Majesty passed from the Tower through the City. Out at the windows and penthouses of every house did hang a number of rich and costly banners and streamers, till Her Grace came to the upper end of Cheap. And there, by appointment, the right worshipful Master Ranulph Cholmley, Recorder of the City, presented to the Queen's Majesty a purse of crimson satin richly wrought with gold, wherein the City gave unto the Queen's Majesty a thousand marks in gold, as Master Recorder did declare briefly unto the Queen's Majesty, whose words tended to this end: that the Lord Mayor, his brethren, and the commonalty of the City, to declare their gladness and goodwill towards the Queen's Majesty, did present Her Grace with that gold, desiring Her Grace to continue their good and gracious Queen, and not to esteem the value of the gift but the mind of the givers. The Queen's Majesty with both her hands took the purse and answered him again marvellous pithily, and so pithily that the standers by, as they embraced entirely her gracious answer, so they marvelled at the couching thereof, which was in words truly reported these: 'I thank my Lord Mayor, his brethren, and you all. And whereas your request is that I should continue your good lady and queen, be ye assured that I will be as good unto you as ever queen was to her people. No will in me can lack; neither, do I trust, shall there lack any power. And persuade yourselves that for the safety and quietness of you all I will not spare, if need be, to spend my blood. God thank you all.' Which answer of so noble an hearted princess, if it moved a marvellous shout and rejoicing, it is nothing to be marvelled at, since both the heartiness thereof was so wonderful and the words so jointly knit.

2
From *The Device of the Pageant Borne Before Wolston Dixi*[3] —
(George Peele, 1585)

A speech spoken by him that rid on a lucern[4] before the pageant apparelled like a Moor

From where the sun doth settle in his wain[5]
And yokes his horses to his fiery cart,
And in his way gives life to Ceres' corn,
Even from the parching zone, behold I come,
A stranger strangely mounted as you see,
Seated upon a lusty lucern's back,
And offer, to Your Honour (good my Lord)
This emblem[6] thus in show significant.
Lo, lovely London, rich and fortunate,
Famed throughout the world for peace and happiness,
Is here advanced and set in highest seat,
Beautified throughly, as her state requires.
First, over her a princely trophy stands
Of beaten gold, a rich and royal arms,
Whereto this London evermore bequeaths

Service of honour and of loyalty.
Her props are well-advised magistrates,
That carefully tend her person still.
The honest franklin and the husbandman
Lays down his sacks of corn at London's feet,
And brings such presents as the country yields.
The pleasant Thames, a sweet and dainty nymph,
For London's good, conveys with gentle stream
And safe and easy passage what she can,
And keeps her leaping fishes in her lap.
The soldier and the sailor, frankly both,
For London's aid are all in readiness
To venture and fight by land and sea.
And this thrice-reverend honourable dame,
Science, the sap of every commonwealth,
Surnamed Mechanical or Liberal,
Is vowed to honour London with her skill.
And London, by these friends so happy made,
First thanks her God, the author of her peace,
And next, with humble gesture as becomes,
In meek and lowly manner doth she yield
Herself her wealth, with heart and willingness,
Unto the person of her gracious Queen,
Elizabeth, renowned through the world,
'Stalled and anointed by the highest power,
The God of kings, that with His holy hand
Hath long defended her and her England.
This now remains, right honourable Lord,
That carefully you do attend and keep
This lovely lady rich and beautiful,
The jewel wherewithal your sovereign Queen
Hath put Your Honour lovingly in trust;
That you may add to London's dignity,
And London's dignity may add to yours;
That worthily you may be counted one
Among the number of many more,
Careful lieutenants, careful magistrates,
For London's welfare and her worthiness.

3
[The Coronation Procession of James I]
(Thomas Dekker, 1604)

... All that was spoken sounded to this purpose, that still his Majesty was coming. They have their longings, and behold, afar off they spy him, richly mounted on a white jennet[7], under a rich canopy sustained by eight Barons of the Cinque Ports;[8] the Tower serving that morning but for his withdrawing chamber wherein he made him ready, and from thence stepped presently into his City of London, which for the time might worthily borrow the name of his Court Royal; his passage alongst that court (offering itself for more state) through seven gates, of which the first was erected at Fenchurch.[9]

Thus presenting itself.

It was an upright flat square (for it contained fifty foot in the perpendicular and fifty foot in the ground line); the upper roof thereof (one distinct [gate]) bore up the true models of all the notable houses, turrets, and steeples within the City. The gate under which His Majesty did pass was twelve foot wide and eighteen foot high, a postern[10] likewise (at one side of it) being four foot wide and eight foot in height. On either side of the gate stood a great French term[11] of stone, advanced upon wooden pedestals; two half pilasters of rustic standing over their heads. ...

The personages, as well mutes as speakers, in this pageant were these, *viz*.:

1. The highest person was the Britain Monarchy.
2. At her feet sat Divine Wisdom.
3. Beneath her stood the Genius of the City, a man.
4. At his right hand was placed a personage figuring the Counsel of the City.
5. Under all these lay a person representing Thamesis the River.

Six other persons, being daughters to Genius, were advanced upon him, on a spreading ascent, of which the first was

1. Gladness.
2. The second, Veneration.
3. The third, Promptitude.

4. The fourth, Vigilance.
5. The fifth, Loving Affection.
6. The sixth, Unanimity.

Of all which personages, Genius and Thamesis were the only speakers, Thamesis being presented by one of the children of Her Majesty's Revels, Genius by M. Alleyn,[12] servant to the young Prince; his gratulatory speech (which was delivered with excellent action and a well-tuned audible voice) being to this effect:

That London may be proud to behold this day, and therefore, in name of the Lord Mayor and Aldermen, the Council, commoners, and multitude, the heartiest welcome is tendered to His Majesty that ever was bestowed on any king, etc.

Which banquet being taken away with sound of music, there ready for the purpose, His Majesty made his entrance into his Court Royal. Under this first gate, upon the battlements of the work, in great capitals was inscribed thus:

LONDINIUM

And under that, in a smaller but not different character, was written,

CAMERA REGIA
The King's Chamber

Too short a time (in their opinions that were glued there together so many hours to behold him) did His Majesty dwell upon this first place; yet too long it seemed to other happy spirits that higher up in the Elysian Fields awaited for his presence.

4
From *Troia-Nova Triumphans*[13]
(Thomas Dekker, 1612)

In returning back from the Guildhall to perform the ceremonial customs in Paul's Church, these shows march in the same order as before; and coming with the Throne of Virtue, Envy and her crew are as busy again, Envy uttering some three or four lines toward the end of her speech only, as thus:

Envy Fiends and furies that dwell under,
  Lift hell-gates from their hinges; come
  You cloven-footed brood of Barathrum,[14]
  Stop, stony[15] her, fright her with your shrieks,
  And put fresh blood in Envy's cheeks.
Virtue On, on, the beams of Virtue are so bright,
  They dazzle Envy: On, the hag's put to flight.

This done, or as it is doing, those twelve[16] that ride armed discharge their pistols, at which Envy and the rest vanish, and are seen no more.

When the Lord Mayor is, with all the rest of their triumphs, brought home, Justice, for a farewell, is mounted on some convenient scaffold close to his entrance at his gate,[17] who thus salutes him.

The Speech of Justice

My this-day's-sworn-protector, welcome home,
If Justice speak not now, be she ever dumb.
The world gives out she's blind, but men shall see
Her sight is clear, by influence drawn from thee.
For one year, therefore, at these gates she'll sit,
To guide thee in and out; thou shalt commit,
If she stand by thee, not one touch of wrong,
And though I know thy wisdom built up strong,
Yet men, like great ships being in storms [are] most near
To danger, when up all their sails they bear.
And since all magistrates tread still on ice,
From mine own school I read thee this advice:
  Do good for no man's sake, now, but thine own,
Take leave of friends and foes; both must be known
But by one face; the rich and poor must lie
In one even scale; all suitors, in thine eye,
Welcome alike. Even he that seems most base,
Look not upon his clothes but on his case.
Let not Oppression wash his hands i'th'tears
Of widows or of orphans; widows' prayers
Can pluck down thunder, and poor orphans' cries
Are laurels held in fire;[18] the violence flies
Up to heaven gates, and there the wrong does tell,
Whilst innocence leaves behind it a sweet smell.

Thy conscience must be like that scarlet dye:
One foul spot stains it all; and the quick eye
Of this prying world will make that spot thy scorn.
That collar, which about thy neck is worn
Of golden esses,[19] bids thee so to knit
Men's hearts in love and make a chain of it.
That sword is seldom drawn, by which is meant,
It should strike seldom — never the innocent.
'Tis held before thee by another's hand,
But the point upwards (heaven must that command);
Snatch it not then in wrath; it must be given,
But to cut none, till warranted by heaven.
The head, the politic body must advance,
For which thou hast this cap of maintenance,
And since the most just magistrate often errs,
Thou guarded art about with officers,
Who knowing the oaths of others that are gone,
Should teach thee what to do, what leave undone.
Night's candles lighted are, and burn amain.
Cut therefore here off thy officious train,
Which love and custom lend thee. All delight
Crown both this day and City; a good night
To thee and these grave Senators, to whom
My last farewells in these glad wishes come:
That thou and they, whose strength the City bears,
May be as old in goodness as in years.

5
From *Monuments of Honour*[20]
(John Webster, 1624)

I fashioned for the more amplifying the show upon the water two eminent spectacles in manner of a sea-triumph. The first furnished with four persons: in the front Oceanus and Thetis,[21] behind them Thamesis and Medway, the two rivers on whom the Lord Mayor extends his power as far as from Stanes to Rochester. The other show is of a fair terrestrial globe, circled about, in convenient seats, with seven of our most famous navigators, as Sir Francis Drake, Sir John Hawkins, Sir Martin Frobisher, Sir Humphrey Gilbert, Captain Thomas Cavendish, Captain Christopher Carlisle, and

Captain John Davis. The conceit of this device to be that in regard the two rivers pay due tribute of waters to the seas. Oceanus in grateful recompense returns the memory of these seven worthy captains, who have made England so famous in remotest parts of the world. These two spectacles, at my Lord Mayor's taking water at the Three Cranes,[22] approaching my Lord's barge, after a peal of sea-thunder from the other side the water, these speeches between Oceanus and Thetis follow.

Oceanus and Thetis

Thetis What brave sea music bids us welcome, hark!
 Sure this is Venice, and the day St Mark,
 In which the Duke and Senate their course hold,
 To wed our empire with a ring of gold.
Oceanus No, Thetis, y'are mistaken, we are led
 With infinite delight from the land's head,
 In ken of goodly shipping and yon bridge.
 Venice had ne'er the like; survey that ridge
 Of stately buildings which the river hem,
 And grace the silver stream, as the stream them:
 That beauteous seat is London, so much famed,
 Where any navigable sea is named;
 And in that bottom[23] eminent merchants placed,
 As rich and venturous as ever graced
 Venice or Europe. These two rivers here,
 Our followers, may tell you where we are;
 This' Thamesis, that Medway, who are sent
 To you, most worthy Praetor,[24] to present
 Acknowledgement of duty ne'er shall err,
 From Stanes unto the ancient Rochester.
 And now to grace their triumph, in respect
 These pay us tribute, we are pleased to select
 Seven worthy navigators out by name,
 Seated beneath this globe; whose ample fame
 In the remotest part of earth is found,
 And some of them have circled the globe round.
 These you observe are living in your eye,
 And so they ought, for worthy men ne'er die:
 Drake, Hawkins, Frobisher, Gilbert, brave knights
 That brought home gold and honour from sea-fights;
 Ca'ndish, Carlisle, and Davis, and to these

So many worthies I could add at seas,
Of this bold nation, it would envy strike
Ith' rest o' th' world, who cannot show the like.
'Tis action values honour, as the flint
Look[s] black and feels like ice, yet from within't
There are strook sparks which to the darkest nights
Yield quick and piercing food for several lights.
Thetis You have quickened well my memory, and now,
Of this your grateful triumph I allow;
Honour looks clear and spreads her beams at large,
From the grave Senate seated in that barge;
Rich lading swell your bottoms, a blest gale
Follow your ventures that they never fail;
And may you live successively to wear
The joy of this day, each man his whole year.

This show, having tendered this service to my Lord upon the water, is after to be conveyed ashore and in convenient place employed for adorning the rest of the triumph. After my Lord Mayor's landing and coming past Paul's Chain, there first attends for His Honour, in Paul's churchyard, a beautiful spectacle called the Temple of Honour, the pillars of which are bound about with roses and other beautiful flowers, which shoot up to the adorning of the King's Majesty's arms on the top of the temple.

In the highest seat, a person representing Troynovant or the City, enthroned in rich habiliments; beneath her, as admiring her peace and felicity, sit five eminent cities, as Antwerp, Paris, Rome, Venice and Constantinople. Under these sit five famous scholars and poets of this our kingdom, as Sir Geoffrey Chaucer, the learned Gower, the excellent John Lydgate, the sharp-witted Sir Thomas More, and last, as worthy both soldier and scholar, Sir Philip Sidney, these being celebrators of honour and the preservers both of the names of men, and memories of cities above, to posterity.

I present riding afore this temple, Henry de Royal, the first pilgrim or gatherer of quarterage[25] for this Company; and John of Yeacksley, King Edward the Third's pavilion-maker, who purchased our Hall in the sixth year of the aforesaid king's government. These lived in Edward the First's time likewise, in the sixth of whose reign this Company was confirmed a guild or corporation by the name of Tailors and Linen Armourers, with power to choose a Master and Wardens at Midsummer. These are decently habited and hooded according to the ancient manner. My Lord is here saluted with two speeches, first by Troynovant in these lines following.

The Speech of Troynovant

History, truth, and virtue seek by name
To celebrate the Merchant Tailors' fame;
That Henry de Royal, this we call
Worthy John Yeacksley, purchased first their Hall;
And thus from low beginnings there oft springs
Societies claim brotherhoods of kings.
I Troynovant, placed eminent in the eye
Of these admire at my felicity:
Five cities, Antwerp and the spacious Paris,
Rome, Venice, and the Turk's metropolis.
Beneath these, five learned poets, worthy men,
Who do eternize brave acts by their pen;
Chaucer, Gower, Lydgate, More, and for our time,
Sir Philip Sidney, glory of our clime.
These beyond death a fame to monarchs give,
And these make cities and societies live.

... These passing on, in the next place my Lord is encountered with the person of Sir John Hawkwood in complete armour, his plume and feather for his horse's chamfron[26] of the Company's colours, white and watchet.[27] This worthy knight did most worthy service in the time of Edward the Third in France, after served as general divers princes of Italy, went to the Holy Land, and in his return back died at Florence, and there lies buried with a fair monument over him. This worthy gentleman was free of our Company. ... After him follows a triumphant chariot with the arms of the Merchant Tailors, coloured and gilt in several places of it, and over it there is supported, for a canopy, a rich and very spacious pavilion, coloured crimson, with a lion passant; this is drawn with four horses (for porters would have made it move tottering and improperly). In the chariot I place for the honour of the Company (of which records remain in the Hall) eight famous kings of this land that have been free of this worshipful Company.

6
From *The Triumphs of Health and Prosperity*[28]
(Thomas Middleton, 1626)

... More to encourage the noble endeavours of the magistrate, His Lordship and the worthy Company is gracefully conducted toward the Chariot of Honour. On the most eminent seat thereof is Government illustrated, it being the proper virtue by which we raise the noble memory of Sir Henry Fitz-Alwin,[29] who held the seat of magistracy in this City twenty-four years together, a most renowned brother of this Company. In like manner, the worthy Sir John Norman,[30] first rowed in barge to Westminster with silver oars, under the person of Munificence. Sir Simon Eyre,[31] that built Leadenhall, a granary for the poor, under the type of Piety, etc. This Chariot, drawn by two golden-pelted lions, being the proper supporters of the Company's arms, those two that have their seats upon the lions presenting Power and Honour, the one in a little streamer or banner bearing the arms of the present Lord Mayor, the other the late, the truly generous and worthy Sir Allen Cotton,[32] Knight, a bounteous and noble housekeeper, one that hath spent the year of his magistracy to the great honour of the City, and by the sweetness of his disposition and the uprightness of his justice and government hath raised up a fair lasting memory to himself and his posterity forever; at whose happy inauguration, though triumph was not then in season (Death's pageants being only advanced upon the shoulders of men), his noble deservings were not thereby any way eclipsed.

Est virtus sibi marmor, et integritate triumphat[33]

The Speech of Government

With just propriety does this City stand,
As fixed by fate, ith' middle of the land;
It has, as in the body, the heart's place,
Fit for her works of piety and grace;
The head, her Sovereign, unto whom she sends
All duties that just service comprehends;
The eyes may be compared (at wisdom's rate)
To the illustrious counselors of state,
Set in this orb of royalty to give light
To noble actions, stars of truth and right;

The lips, the reverend clergy, judges all,
That pronounce laws divine or temporal,
The arms, to the defensive part of men;
So I descend unto the heart again,
The place where now you are. Witness the love,
True brotherhood's cost, and triumph, all which move
In this most grave solemnity, and in this
The City's general love abstracted is;
And as the heart, in its meridian seat,
Is styled the fountain of the body's heat,
The first thing receives life, the last that dies;
Those properties experience well applies
To this most royal City, that hath been
In former ages as in these times seen,
The fountain of affection, duty, zeal,
And taught all cities through the commonweal,
The first that receives quickening life and spirit
From the king's grace, which still she strives to inherit,
And like the heart will be the last that dies;
In any duty toward good supplies
What can express affection's nobler fruit,
Both to the kings, and you, his substitute.

7
From *Britannia's Honour*[34]
(Thomas Dekker, 1628)

Our third presentation is called *The Glory of Furs*. This is a chariot triumphant, garnished with trophies and armours. It is drawn by two lucerns,[35] the supporters of the Skinners' arms. On the two lucerns ride two antics,[36] who dance to a drum beating before them, there aptly placed. At the upper end of this chariot, in the most eminent seat, carrying the proportion of a throne, are advanced a Russian prince and princess, richly habited in furs, to the custom of the country.

1. Under them sits an old lord, furred up to his chin in a fur cloak.
2. By him, a lady with marten skins about her neck and her hands in a muff.
3. Then, a judge in robes furred.

4. Then, an university doctor in his robes furred.
5. Then, a *frau* in a short furred cassock, girt to her.
6. Then a skipper in a furred cap.

In all these persons is an implication of the necessary, ancient, and general use of furs, from the highest to the lowest.

On the top of the throne, at the four corners, are erected the arms of the City in four pendants. On the point of the forefront, a large square banner plays in the wind, which Fame, who is in this chariot, holds in her hand as she stands upright, *being the speaker.*

Fame's turn is now to speak, for who but Fame
Can with her thousand tongues abroad proclaim
Your this day's progress, rising like the sun,
Which through the yearly zodiac on must run.
    Fame hath brought hither from great Moscow's court
(The seven-mouthed Volga spreading the report)
Two Russian princes, who, to feast their eyes
With the rich wonders of these rarities,
Ride in this glorious chariot. How amazed
They look, to see streets thronged, and windows glazed
With beauties, from whose eyes such beams are sent,
Here moves a second starry firmament.
    Much, on them, startling admiration wins,
To see the brave, grave, noble citizens,
So streamed in multitudes, yet flowing in state,
For all their orders are proportionate.
    Russia now envies London, seeing here spent
Her richest furs in graceful ornament,
More brave and more abounding than her own;
A golden pen she earns,[37] that can make known
The use of furs, so great, so general;
All men may these their winter armours call.
    Th'invention of warm furs the sun did fret,
For Russians lapped in these slighted his heat,
Which seen, his fiery steeds he drove from thence,
And so the muff has dwelt in cold ere since.
    What royalties add furs to emperors, kings,
Princes, dukes, earls, in the distinguishings
Of all their several robes? The furs worn here,
Above th' old Roman state make ours appear;
The reverend judge, and all that climb the trees

Of sacred arts, ascend to their degrees,
And by the colours changed of furs are known;
What dignity each corporation
Puts on by furs, witness these infinite eyes.
    Thank, then, the bringers of these rarities;
I wish, grave Praetor, that as hand in hand
Plenty and bounty bring you safe to land,
So health may be chief carver at that board
To which you hasten; be as good a lord
I' th' eyes of heaven as this day you are great
In Fame's applause: hie to your honoured seat.

8
From *London's Jus Honorarium*[38]
(Thomas Heywood, 1631)

Then Time maketh a pause and, taking up a leafless and withered branch, thus proceedeth.

See you this withered branch, by Time o'ergrown?
A city's symbol, ruined and trod down,
A tree that bore bad fruit: dissimulation,
    Pride, malice, envy, atheism, supplantation,[39]
Ill government, profaneness, fraud, oppression,
Nelgect of virtue, freedom to transgression.
Obedience here with power did disagree,
All which, fair London, be still far from thee.

The second show by land is presented in the upper part of Cheapside, which is a chariot. The two beasts that are placed before it are a lion passant and a white unicorn in the same posture, on whose backs are seated two ladies, the one representing Justice upon the lion, the other Mercy upon the unicorn. The motto which Justice beareth is *Rebelles protero*;[40] the inscription which Mercy carrieth is *Imbelles protego*.[41] Herein is intimated that by these types and symbols of honour, represented in these noble beasts belonging to His Majesty, all other inferior magistracies and governments, either in commonweals or private societies, receive both being and supportance.

The prime lady seated in the first and most eminent place of the chariot representeth London, behind whom, and on either side, divers others of the chief cities of the kingdom take place: as Westminster, York, Bristol, Oxford, Lincoln, Exeter, etc. All these are to be distinguished by their several escutcheons. To them London, being speaker, directeth the first part of her speech as followeth.

> You noble cities of this generous isle,
> May these my two each ladies ever smile,
> Justice and Mercy, on you. You, we know,
> Are come to grace this our triumphant show,
> And of your courtesy, the hand to kiss
> Of London, this fair land's metropolis.
>   Why, sister cities, sit you thus amazed?
> [Is't] to behold above yon windows glazed
> With diamonds 'stead of glass, stars hither sent
> This day to deck our lower firmament?
>   Is it to see numerous children round
> Encompass me, so that no place is found
> In all my large streets empty? My issue spread
> In number more than stones whereon they tread?
> To see my temples, houses, even all places,
> With people covered, as if tiled with faces?
>   Will you know whence proceeds this most fair increase,
> This joy? The fruits of a continued peace,
> The way to thrive, to prosper in each calling,
> The weak and shrinking states to keep from falling,
> Behold — my motto shall all this display,
> Read and observe it well: serve and obey.
> Obedience, though it humbly doth begin,
> It soon augments unto a magazine
> Of plenty; in all cities 'tis the ground,
> And doth like harmony in music sound;
> Nations and commonweals by it alone
> Flourish; it incorporates many into one,
> And makes unanimous peace, content, and joy,
> Which pride doth still insidiate[42] to destroy.
> And you, grave Lord, on whom right honour calls,
> Both born and bred i' th' circuit of my walls,
> By virtue and example have made plain
> How others may like eminence attain.

Persist in this blest concord; may we long
That cities to this City still throng
To view my annual triumphs, and so grace
These honoured praetors that supply this place.

Notes

1. Trumpeters, from waits or watchmen equipped with horns for sounding alarms.
2. Armed attendants, or pikemen, charged with holding back crowds for processions.
3. For the inauguration of Sir Wolston Dixi, Skinner.
4. A lynx, emblem of the Skinners Company.
5. Wagon.
6. The words that follow describe the pageant float itself.
7. A Spanish pony.
8. From the time of Richard I, the barons, or chief burgesses, of the Cinque Ports had served as a coronation order, carrying the canopy over the monarch's head.
9. Ben Jonson, the poet involved in the preparation of the Fenchurch or Londinium arch, wrote his own lengthy account of it, *B. Jon: His Part of King James His Royal Entertainment* (1604). It has seemed preferable, however, to present here the briefer account of Thomas Dekker, who was involved in the preparation of several of the other arches.
10. Side-gate.
11. A terminal figure, a bust or statue rising out of a column.
12. Edward Alleyn, the actor.
13. For the inauguration of Sir John Swinnerton, Merchant Taylor.
14. A deep ditch behind the Acropolis, into which malefactors were thrown.
15. Astonish.
16. Twelve persons representing the Twelve Great Companies rode before the Throne of Virtue.
17. Either the gate to the Lord Mayor's home or the city gate nearest his house.
18. The laurel was said to resist lightning and fire.
19. The collar of SS, a symbol of allegiance, was used by the Lancastrian kings and restored by Henry VII.
20. For the inauguration of Sir John Gore, Merchant Taylor.
21. A sea goddess, chief of the Nereids.
22. See Introduction, pp. 337.
23. Ship (of state).
24. The Mayor.
25. In the early years of the Merchant Taylors, the gatherers of quarterage, or charges, were called Wardens, and the Master was called the Pilgrim.
26. Frontlet of an armoured horse.
27. Pale blue.
28. For the inauguration of Cuthbert Hacket, Draper.
29. London's first Lord Mayor, 1190–1211.
30. Lord Mayor, 1453; 'the first Mayor that was rowed to Westminster by water, for before that they rode on horseback' (Stow).

31. See 10.4.
32. Lord Mayor in 1625, a plague year when no pageant was performed.
33. Virtue is like marble itself and triumphs through its soundness.
34. For the inauguration of Sir Richard Deane, Skinner.
35. Lynxes; see note 4 above.
36. Grotesque clowns.
37. Longs for.
38. For the inauguration of Sir George Whitmore, Haberdasher.
39. Rebellion.
40. I crush rebels.
41. I shield the peaceful.
42. Lie in wait.

BIBLIOGRAPHICAL REFERENCES

Note: In cases where multiple issues or editions appeared in a single year, I have added the STC number to indicate when my copy text is not the first one listed in the STC.

Chapter 1

1. *The White Book of the City of London*, ed. H.T. Riley (London: John Russell Smith, 1862), p. 54.
2. *Itinerarium Britanniae*, in *Two Italian Accounts of Tudor England*, trans. C.V. Malfatti (Barcelona, 1953), pp. 32-7.
3. *Relatione ... dell 'Isola d'Inghilterra*, ed. Charlotte A. Sneyd (London: Camden Society, 1847), pp. 42-3, 45.
4. *The First Boke of the Introduction of Knowledge* (1548), sig. B.
5. *The Debate Betwene the Heraldes of England and Fraunce* (1550), sig. L2–L2v.
6. *A Description of England and Scotland* (Paris, 1558), in *The Pleasures of London*, ed. W.H. Quarrel (London: Witherby & Co., 1940), pp. 58–9.
7. *Civitates orbis terrarum* (1572), sig. A; editor's translation.
8. *The Historicall Description of the Islande of Britayne*, in Holinshed, *Chronicles* (1577), sig. C4.
9. *Journey Through England and Scotland Made by Lupold von Wedel in the years 1584 and 1585*, ed. Gottfried von Bulow, *Transactions of the Royal Historical Society*, n.s. 9 (1895), pp. 228, 229, 230, 267.
10. *Britannia* (1586), trans. Philemon Holland (1610), pp. 421, 422, 435.
11. 'A True and Faithful Narrative of the Excursion [of] Frederick, Duke of Wirtemberg ... by his Private Secretary', in *England as Seen by Foreigners in the Days of Elizabeth and James the First*, ed. W.B. Rye (London: John Russell Smith, 1865), pp. 7-8.
12. *Speculum Britanniae. The firste parte* (1593), pp. 9, 12, 47.
13. *A Survay of London* (1598), sig. E7v–E8.
14. *Travels in England*, trans. Clare Williams (London: Jonathan Cape, 1937), pp. 153-7, 166-7, 170-1, 175-6; reprinted by permission.
15. *A Journey into England in the Year 1598*, trans. Horace Walpole, in *Aungervyle Society Reprints*, I (1881), p. 29.
16. *Diary of the Journey of Philip Julius, Duke of Stettin-Pomerania, through England in the Year 1602*, ed. Gottfried von Bulow, *Transactions of the Royal Historical Society*, n.s. 6 (1892), pp. 7, 11-13.
17. Letter Dedicatory to Sir Henry Rowe, in John Stow, *Abridgement of the Chronicles of England* (1611), n.p.
18. *The Theatre of the Empire of Great Britaine* (1676), fol. 29A–29B.
19. *An itinerary written by F. Moryson, Gent.* (1617), sig. Kkk4.
20. *The Glory of England* (1618), pp. 258, 259, 261.
21. *London and the Countrey Carbonadoed* (1632), sig. B–B2v.
22. *Cosmography* (1652), p. 270.
23. *Londinopolis* (1657), p. 404.

Chapter 2

1. In John Stow, *A Survay of London* (1598), sig. G2v.
2. MS. Cotton Vespas. B, xvi, fol. 4r, in *Political Poems and Songs* (Rolls Series), ed. Thomas Wright (London, 1859–62), II, 256.
3. MS. Vitellius A XVI, ed. C.L. Kingsford, *Chronicles of London* (Oxford: Clarendon Press, 1905), pp. 253-4.
4. *Concordance of Histories* (1516), sig. AA–AAv.
5. *Cygnea Cantio*, in *Naeniae in mortem Thomae Viati equitis incomparabilis* (1542), sig. C–Cv; trans. in *Chronicles of Old London Bridge* (1827), pp. 321-2.
6. *The Will and Testament of Isabella Whitney*, in *A Sweet Nosegay and Pleasant Posye* (1573), sig. E3v–E5.
7. *A Light Bondell of Lively Discourses called Churchyardes Charge* (1580), sig. D4–D4v.
8. William Camden, *Britannia*, trans. Philemon Holland (1610), p. 437.
9. *The Faerie Queene* (1590), III.ix.45-6, p. 540.
10. *The Faerie Queene* (1596), IV.xi.27-8, pp. 163-4.
11. *The Pleasant Walkes of Moore-fields* (1607), sig. C2–C2v.
12. *Pimlyco, Or Runne Red-Cap. Tis a mad world at Hogsdon* (1609), sig. B2.
13. *Londons Artillery* (1616), pp. 54-5, 60-5, 77-80.
14. *Poems* (1619), sig. Zv.
15. MS. Rawl. 62, in Thomas Randolph, *Poems*, ed. John Jay Parry (New Haven: Yale University Press, 1917), p. 231; reprinted by permission.
16. *The Pepys Ballads*, ed. Hyder Edward Rollins (Cambridge: Harvard University Press, 1929), III, 220-1; reprinted by permission.
17. *Trinobantiados Augustae sive Londini Libri VI* (1636), sig. A4–A4v; editor's translation.
18. *Panegyricon inaugurale* (1637), sig. B2v; editor's translation.
19. *London, King Charles His Augusta, or, City Royal* (1648), p. 12.
20. *The Pepys Ballads*, ed. Hyder Rollins (Cambridge: Harvard University Press, 1929), III, 217-22; reprinted by permission.

Chapter 3

1. *Of Gentylnes and Nobylyte*, sig. A–Av, A2.
2. *Cyvile and uncyvile life* (1579), sig. A4v, B2v–B3, Ev, G2, L4–Mv.
3. *An Apologie of the Citie of London*, in John Stow, *A Survay of London* (1598), sig. Gg7v–Gg8.
4. Ibid., sig. Hhv–Hh2.
5. *De Republica Anglorum* (1583), sig. D2v, C2, C3.
6. *The Anatomy of Abuses* (1583), sig. L3v–L4.
7. *A Touchstone for the Time*, in *A Mirour for Magestrates of Cyties* (1584), sig. I, I2v.
8. *The Description of England*, in Holinshed's *Chronicles* (1587), sig. P2v, P3, P6v.
9. *Christs Teares over Ierusalem* (1593), sig. X3–X3v.
10. *The State of England, Anno. Dom. 1600*, ed. F.J. Fisher, *Camden Miscellany*, 3rd series 52 (1936), p. 21; reprinted by permission.
11. *A Survay of London* (1603), sig. G2v–G3.
12. *An itinerary written by F. Moryson, Gent.* (1617), sig. Rrr2.
13. *Hobsons Horse-load of Letters* (1617), sig. K.
14. *The Glory of England* (1618), p. 318.
15. *The Cities advocate, in this case ... whether Apprenticeship extinguisheth Gentry* (1629), sig. Kv.

Chapter 4

1. *A Notable Sermon of the Reverend Father Master Hugh Latimer, Which He Preached in the Shrouds at St. Paul's Church in London, on the xviii Day of January 1548* (1548), sig. Blv–B3v.
2. *A Sermon made in the Chappel at the Gylde Halle in London, the .xxix day of September, 1574* (1575), sig. C3, C4v.
3. *A Sermon Preached at Pauls Crosse in Trinity Sunday, 1571* (printed 1576), n.p.
4. *A Sermon Preached at St Mary's Hospital,* in *XCVI Sermons* (1629), sig. A6–A6v; printed by permission.
5. *Abraham's Suit to Sodom: A Sermon Preached at Paul's Cross on August 25th, 1611* (1612), sig. D4, D6v–D7v.
6. *Eirenopolis: The City of Peace* (1622), sig. H4–H8.
7. *The White Devil, or the Hypocrite Uncased* (1613), sig. E2v, F2–F2v.
8. *The Righteous Mammon. An Hospital Sermon* (1618), pp. 52-4, 97-9.
9. *Londons Warning, by Jerusalem. A Sermon Preached at Pauls Crosse* (1619), pp. 8-9, 33.
10. *A Sermon at Paul's Cross, on Behalf of Paul's Church* (1620), pp. 43-7.
11. *The Kings Towre, And Triumphal Arch of London. A Sermon preached at Pauls Crosse, August 5, 1622,* sig. F5v–F7v.
12. *XXVI Sermons* (1661), sig. Qqq–Qqqv.

Chapter 5

1. *A C. Mery Talys* (1525), sig. D3.
2. Ibid., sig. Ev.
3. *Tales and quicke answeres, very mery, and plesant to rede* (1535), sig. A4.
4. *The Sack-Full of Newes* (1673), p. 20.
5. Ibid., p. 21.
6. *The First and Best Part of Scoggins Jests* (1626), sig. A2.
7. *The Whole Life and Death of Long Meg of Westminster* (1582), pp. 2-3.
8. Ibid., pp. 11-12.
9. Ibid., pp. 23-4.
10. *The Pleasant Conceites of Old Hobson the merry Londoner* (1607), sig. A3.
11. Ibid., sig.A4.
12. Ibid., sig. Cv.
13. Ibid., sig. E2.
14. *Tarltons Jests* (1638), sig. B8v.
15. Ibid., sig. Cv.
16. Ibid., sig. C2.
17. *Pasquils Jests, mixed with Mother Bunches Merriments* (1609), sig. Dv.
18. Ibid., sig. Dv–D2.
19. *Baconiana, Or Certaine Genuine Remains of St Francis Bacon* (1684), pp. 54-5.
20. *Taylors Wit and Mirth* (1629), sig. B4.
21. Ibid., sig. C2.
22. *A Banquet of Jests, or Change of Cheare* (1633), sig. F9.
23. *Conceits, Clinches, Flashes, and Whimsies* (1639), sig. D.
24. Ibid., sig. E2v.
25. Ibid., sig. G2.
26. *A New booke of Mistakes* (1637), pp. 25-6.
27. Ibid., pp. 226-7.

Chapter 6

1. BM Harleian 367, ed. Eleanor P. Hammond, *Anglia*, 20 (1898), pp. 411-19.
2. *The Roxburghe Ballads*, ed. William Chappell (Hertford: The Ballad Society, 1872), II.i.24-8.
3. *Melismata. Musical phansies, fitting the court, citie and countrey humours* (1611), sig. D.
4. *A Pepysian Garland*, ed. Hyder Rollins (Cambridge: Cambridge University Press, 1922), pp. 31-4; reprinted by permission.
5. *The Pepys Ballads*, ed. Hyder Rollins (Cambridge, Mass.: Harvard University Press, 1929), III, 52-4; reprinted by permission.
6. *A Pepysian Garland*, ed. Hyder Rollins (Cambridge University Press, 1922), pp. 223-8; reprinted by permission.

Chapter 7

1. *The Lamentacion of a Christian against the Citie of London made by Roderigo Mors* (1542), sig. A2–A2v, A3, B3–B3v.
2. *The Poems of Henry Howard, Earl of Surrey*, ed. Frederick Morgan Padelford (rev. edn, University of Washington Press, 1928); reprinted by permission.
3. *One and Thyrtye Epigrammes* (1550), sig. A7v–A8.
4. *Christs Teares Over Ierusalem* (1593), sig. M3–M4.
5. *Poems, by J.D.* (1633), pp. 327-8.
6. *Virgidemiarum* (1597), sig. E7v–E8.
7. *Skialetheia* (1598), sig. D4–D5v, D7–D7v.
8. *The Scourge of Villanie* (1599) [17486], sig. E7–E7v, F3v–F4v.
9. *Micro-cynicon. Sixe Snarling Satyres* (1599), sig. Bv–B2, B3, B3v.
10. *Englands Helicon* (1600), sig. Aa4.
11. *The Seuen deadly Sinnes of London* (1606), sig. F–Fv, F2–F2v.
12. *Abuses Stript, And Whipt* (1613) [25894], sig. S8–S8v.
13. *Epigrammes*, in *The Workes of Beniamin Jonson* (1616), pp. 815-18.
14. *Poems with the Tenth Satyre of Juvenal Englished* (1646), sig. B7v.

Chapter 8

1. 'An Exhortation, or Rule, sett downe by one Mr Norton, sometyme Remembrauncer of London, wherebie the L. Maior of Lo. is to order himselfe and the Cittie', ed. J.P. Collier, *Instructions to the Lord Mayor of London* (1866), pp. 1-4, 11-12, 16.
2. *The othe of euery fre Man* (1580) [16762].
3. STC 8122.
4. MS. Lansdowne 44, art. 38, ed. H. Ellis, *Original Letters* (1824), II, 296-8.
5. John Nichols (ed.), *The Progresses and Public Processions of Queen Elizabeth* (1823; rpt. New York: Burt Franklin, n.d.), p. 255.
6. STC 8523.
7. *The Articles of Charge of the Wardmote Inquest*, part of *An Acte for Reformation of Divers Abuses in the Wardmote Inquest* (1617) [16727], sig. B5–C9.

Chapter 9

1. *The Orchard of Repentance*, in *The Rock of Regard* (1576), sig. O2–O2v.
2. *The Second Part of Cony-Catching* (1591), sig. C3v–C4.
3. *A Treatise of the Plague* (1603), sig. C3v–C4v.
4. *Lanthorne and Candle-light. Or, The Bell-Mans second Nights-walke* (1609), sig. D4–D4v.
5. *The Guls Horne-booke* (1609), sig. D3v–D4, E.
6. *Advice to his Son*, ed. G.B. Harrison (London: Ernest Benn, 1930), pp. 112-13; reprinted by permission.
7. *A Strange Foot-Post* (1613), sig. G4v.
8. *The Art of Thriving. Or, the plaine path-way to Preferment* (1635), pp. 75-82.
9. *An Essay of Drapery: or, the Compleate Citizen* (1635), pp. 85, 136-8.
10. *The Worth of a Penny* (1677), sig. D2v–D3v.
11. *The Art of Living in London* (1642), sig. Av, A2, A3, A3v–A4, A4–A4v.

Chapter 10

1. *An Epitaph of Maister Fraunces Benison, Citizene and Marchant of London, and of the Haberdashers Company* (1570).
2. *The Nine Worthies of London* (1592), sig. A2, A4, B3–Cv.
3. BM Harleian MS. 7368, ed. Rev. Alexander Dyce (London: Shakespeare Society, 1844), pp. 24-32.
4. *The Shoemakers Holiday. Or The Gentle Craft* (1600), sig. E4v–Fv. H3v–H4v.
5. *The Second Part of, If you know not me, you know no bodie. With the building of the Royall Exchange* (1606), sig. C4–Dv, Fv–F2v.
6. *A Crowne-Garland of Golden Roses* (1612), sig. B5–B7v.

Chapter 11

1. Trans R. Hayman, *Quodlibets*, sig. Civ.
2. *Londinopolis* (1657), p. 407.
3. T.R. Hayman, *Quodlibets* (1628), p. 33.
4. *Divers Centuries of New Sayings*, in *Paroiemiologia* (1660), p. 5.
5. Trans. Timothe Kendall, *Flowers of Epigrammes* (1577), sig. N1.
6. *The Life, Letters, and Writings of John Hoskyns*, ed. Louise Brown Osborn (New Haven: Yale University Press, 1937), p. 171.
7. *The Pleasant Conceits of Old Hobson the Merry Londoner* (1607), sig. A4v.
8. *A Survay of London* (1598), sig. Klv.
9. *Epigrames* (1604), sig. C6.
10. *Epigrams*, in *The Workes of Beniamin Jonson* (1616), p. 790.
11. *The Furies* (1614), sig. D.
12. *Epigrams* (1608), sig. Gv.
13. *Wits A.B.C.* (1608), sig. B4.
14. *Wit's Bedlam* (1617), sig. A8v.
15. *The Furies* (1614), sig. B6v.
16. *Thalia's Banquet* (1620), sig. C7.
17. *Rubbe and a great Cast* (1614), sig. F4v.
18. *More Fooles Yet* (1610), sig. C4.
19. *The Furies* (1614), sig. B3.

20. *The Nipping or Snipping of Abuses*, in *All the Works* (1630), p. 264.
21. *Thalias Banquet* (1620), sig. B8.
22. *Wits Recreations* (1640), sig. L6.
23. *Epigrams* (1608), sig. A4v.
24. *The Furies* (1614), sig. B8.
25. *Skialetheia* (1598), sig. B2.
26. *Works* (1562), sig. Dd.
27. *Barnabae Itinerium* (1608), sig. L3.
28. *Rubbe and a great Cast* (1614), sig. B3.
29. *Epigrammes and Elegies by J.D. and C.M.* (1590), sig. A4v.
30. *Skialetheia* (1598), sig. A7v.
31. *Epigrammes and Elegies by J.D. and C.M.* (1590), sig. G1v.
32. Ibid., sig. D2.
33. *Humours Ordinarie* (1604), sig. B.
34. *Humors Looking-Glasse* (1608), sig. D3.
35. *Skialetheia* (1598), sig. B6–B7v.

Chapter 12

1. *Songes and Sonettes Written by the ryght honorable Lorde Henry Haward late Earle of Surrey, and Other* [Tottel's Miscellany] (1557), sig. L1.
2. *Epitaphes, Epigrams, Songs and Sonets* (1567), sig. K6–K6v.
3. *An Hundreth sundrie Flowres* (1573), pp. 372-3.
4. *Howell His Devices* (1581), sig. D2v–D3.
5. *Emblemes and Epigrames* (MS. 1600), ed. F.J. Furnivall (London: EETS, 1876), p. 80.
6. *A Pleasant Comedie, called Summers last Will and Testament* (1600), sig. Iv.
7. Westmoreland MS., printed in Edmund Gosse, *The Life and Letters of John Donne* (London: Heinemann, 1899), I, 82.
8. *Rubbe and a great Cast* (1614), sig. Kv.
9. *Songs of 3. 4. 5. and 6. parts* (1622), sig. Dv.
10. *Latin and Italian Poems of Milton Translated in English Verse* (1808), pp. 9-13.
11. *Castara* (1634), sig. K4.
12. *Poems, with the Muses Looking-Glasse* (1638), sig. I2v–I4.
13. *Hesperides: or The Works both Humane & Divine* (1648), sig. Bb3–Bb4.
14. Ibid., sig. T6v–T7.
15. *Several Discourses by Way of Essays, in Verse and Prose*, in *The Works of Mr Abraham Cowley* (1668), sig. M4.

Chapter 13

1. *Songes and Sonettes, Written by the ryght honorable Lorde Henry Haward late Earle of Surrey, and other* [Tottel's Miscellany] (1557), sig. M3.
2. *A Handefull of pleasant delites* (1584), sig. D5–D6.
3. *Epitaphes, Epigrams, Songs and Sonets* (1567), sig. D1–D1v.
4. *Syr P.S. His Astrophel and Stella* (1591), CIII, sig. G2.
5. *Pierce Pennilesse His Supplication to the Deuill* (1592) [18373], sig. C2v–C3.
6. *A Quip for an Upstart Courtier* (1592), sig. F3v.
7. *Christs Teares ouer Ierusalem* (1592), sigs. V1, V2, V3–V4.
8. *Poems, by J.D. with Elegies on the Author's Death* (1633), sig. S4–S4v.

9. *Idea. In Sixtie-Three Sonnets,* in *Poems* (1619), sig. Kk4.

10. Osborne MS b93 (Beinecke Library, Yale University), pp. 19-20; printed by permission.

Chapter 14

1. *Eastward Ho* (1605) [4971], sig. A2–A4.

2. *The Knight of the Burning Pestle* (1613), sig. B–B2v.

3. *A chast mayd in Cheap-side* (1630), sig. B4v–C2v.

4. *Bartholomew Fayre* (1631), in *The Workes of Beniamin Jonson* (1640), sig. D–D2v, D4v–E2.

Chapter 15

1. *English Villainies ... discovered by Lanthorne and Candle-light* (1632), sig. K2–K3.

2. *New and Choice Characters* (1615) [18908], sig. J6–J6v.

3. Ibid., sig. K7v–K8.

4. *The Good and the Badde* (1616), sig. Dv.

5. *Cures for the Itch,* sig. A2–A3.

6. *Micro-cosmographie. Or, A Peece of the World Discovered; in Essayes and Characters* (1629) [7442], sig. C3–C4v.

7. Ibid., sig. G9–G11v.

8. Ibid., sig. H2–H3v.

9. Ibid., sig. M12v–Nv.

10. *Picturae Loquentes. Or Pictures Drawne forth in Characters* (1631), sig. D9v–D11.

11. *Characterismi: Or, Lentons Leasures* (1631), sig. E3v–E4v.

12. *London & The Countrey Carbonadoed and Quartered into Severall Characters* (1632), sig. G6–G7v.

13. Ibid., sig. G7v–G8v.

14. *The Poetical Works of William Strode,* ed. Bertram Dobell (1907), pp. 111-14.

Chapter 16

1. *The Quenes maiesties passage through the citie of London to Westminster the day before her coronacion* (1558, i.e. 1559), sig. A2v–A3v, C2–C3v.

2. *The Deuice of the Pageant borne before Woolstone Dixi LORD Maior of the Citie of London* (1585), sig. A2–A2v.

3. *The Magnificent Entertainment ... upon the day of his Maiesties Triumphant Passage ... through ... London* (1604), sig. B4–C2.

4. *Troia-Noua Triumphans. London Triumphing* (1612), sig. C4v–Dv.

5. *Monuments of Honour. ... Celebrated in the Honorable City of London, at the sole Munificent charge and expences of the ... Merchant-Taylors* (1624), sig. A3v–Bv, B2–B2v.

6. *The triumphs of Health and Prosperity ... at the Inauguration of ... CUTHBERT HACKET, Lord Mayor* (1626), sig. Bv–B2v.

7. *Britannia's Honor ... to Celebrate the Solemnity of the Right Honorable Richard Deane, at his Inauguration into the Majoralty* (1628), sig. B3–B4.

8. *Londons Ius Honorarium. Exprest in sundry Triumphs ... at the Initiation ... of the Right Honourable George Whitmore* (1631), sig. B3v–B4v.

SELECT BIBLIOGRAPHY
of works consulted and
recommended for further reading

Introduction

Ashton, R., *The City and the Court, 1603–1643* (Cambridge University Press, 1973)
Borer, M.C., *The City of London: A History* (Constable, London, 1977)
Braudel, F., tr. Miriam Kochan, *Capitalism and Material Life, 1400–1800* (Harper & Row, New York, 1975)
Brett-James, N.G., *The Growth of Stuart London* (George Allen & Unwin, London, 1935)
Clark, P. and Slack, P., *English Towns in Transition* (Oxford University Press, London, 1976)
Davis, E.J., 'The Transformation of London', in R.W. Seton-Watson (ed.), *Tudor Studies Presented ... to Albert Frederick Pollard* (Longmans, Green & Co., London, 1924), pp. 287-314
Foster, F.F., *The Politics of Stability: A Portrait of the Rulers in Elizabethan London* (Royal Historical Society, London, 1977)
Glanville, P., *Tudor London* (Museum of London, London, 1979)
Gray, R., *A History of London* (Taplinger, New York, 1979)
Harrison, M., *London Growing: The Development of a Metropolis* (Hutchinson, London, 1965)
Holmes, M., *Elizabethan London* (Praeger, New York, 1969)
Johnson, D.J., *Southwark and the City* (Oxford University Press, London, 1969)
Mumford, L., *The Culture of Cities* (Harcourt Brace Jovanovich, New York, 1970)
Patten, J., *English Towns, 1500–1700* (Dawson, Folkstone, 1978)
Pearl, V., 'Change and Stability in Seventeenth-Century London', *The London Journal* 5 (1979), pp. 3-34
—— *London and the Outbreak of the Puritan Revolution* (Oxford University Press, 1961)
Power, M.J., 'The East & West in Early-Modern London', in E.W. Ives, R.J. Knecht, and J.J. Scarisbrick (eds), *Wealth and Power in Tudor England: Essays Presented to S.T. Bindoff* (Athlone Press, London, 1978), pp. 167-85
Priestly, H., *London: The Years of Change* (Frederick Muller, London, 1966)
Ramsay, G.D., *The City of London in International Politics at the Accession of Elizabeth Tudor* (Rowman & Littlefield, Totowa, N.J., 1975)
Rasmussen, S.E., *London: The Unique City* (1934; rev. edn. The MIT Press, Cambridge, Mass., 1982)
Reddaway, T.F., 'The Livery Companies of Tudor London', *History* 51 (1966), pp. 287-99
—— 'London and the Court', *Shakespeare Survey* 17 (1964), pp. 3-12
Unwin, G. *The Guilds and Companies of London* (2nd edn Methuen, London, 1925)

Chapter 1

Gransden, A., 'Realistic Observation in Twelfth-Century England', *Speculum* 47 (1972), pp.29-51

Hyde, J.K., 'Medieval Descriptions of Cities', *Bulletin of the John Rylands Library* 48 (1966), pp. 308-340

Williams, C. (trans.), *Thomas Platter's Travels in England, 1599* (Jonathan Cape, London, 1937), Introduction, pp. 15-142

Chapter 2

Burgess, T., *Epideictic Literature* (University of Chicago Press, Chicago, 1902)

Chapter 3

Cressy, D., 'Describing the Social Order in Elizabethan and Stuart England', *Literature and History* 3 (1976), pp. 29-44

Hexter, J.H., *Reappraisals in History* (University of Chicago Press, Chicago, 1961)

Lang, R.G., 'Social Origins and Social Aspirations of Jacobean London Merchants', *Economic History Review*, 2nd series 27 (1974), pp. 28-47

Laslett, P., *The World We have Lost* (3rd edn Methuen, London, 1983)

Palliser, D.M., *The Age of Elizabeth: England Under the Later Tudors, 1547–1603* (Longman, London, 1983)

Stone, L., *The Crisis of the Aristocracy* (Oxford University Press, London, 1967)

Youings, J., *Sixteenth-Century England* (Penguin, Harmondsworth, 1984)

Chapter 4

Blench, J.W., *Preaching in England, 1450–1600* (Basil Blackwell, Oxford, 1964)

Carey, J., 'Sixteenth and Seventeenth-Century Prose', in C. Ricks (ed.), *English Poetry and Prose, 1540–1674* (Barrie & Jenkins, London, 1970)

MacClure, M., *The Paul's Cross Sermons, 1534–1642* (University of Toronto Press, Toronto, 1958)

Morgan, I., *The Godly Preachers of the Elizabethan Church* (Epworth Press, London, 1965)

Owst, G.R., *Literature and the Pulpit in Medieval England* (Cambridge University Press, 1933)

Seaver, P., *The Puritan Lectureships: The Politics of Religious Dissent* (Stanford University Press, Stanford, 1970)

Chapter 5

Kahrl, S.J., 'The Medieval Origins of the Sixteenth-Century Jest-Books', *Studies in the Renaissance* 13 (1966), pp. 166-83

Paulson, R., *Popular and Polite Culture in the Age of Hogarth and Fielding* (University of Notre Dame Press, Notre Dame, Ind., 1979)

Pätzold, K.M., 'Deloney and the English Jest-Book Tradition', *English Studies* 53 (1972), pp. 313-28

Wilson, F.P., 'The English Jest-Books of the Sixteenth and Early Seventeenth Centuries', in *Shakespearian and Other Studies* (Clarendon Press, Oxford, 1969), pp. 285-324

Chapter 6

Burke, P., 'Popular Culture in Seventeenth Century London', *London Journal* 3 (1977), pp. 143-62
Collison, R.L.W., *The Story of Street Literature* (J.M. Dent, London, 1973)
  de Sola Pinto, V. and Rodway, A.E. (eds), *The Common Muse: An Anthology of Popular British Ballad Poetry* (Chatto & Windus, London, 1957)
Fowler, D.C., *A Literary History of the Popular Ballad* (Duke University Press, Durham, N.C., 1968)
Shephard, L., *The Broadside Ballad: A Study in Origins and Meaning* (Herbert Jenkins, London, 1962)
—— *The History of Street Literature* (David & Charles, Newton Abbot, 1973)
Waage, F.O., 'Social Themes in the Urban Broadsides of Renaissance England', *Journal of Popular Culture* 11 (1977), pp. 730-42

Chapter 7

Elliott, R.C., *The Power of Satire: Magic, Ritual, Art* (Princeton University Press, Princeton, N.J., 1960)
Gransden, K.W. (ed.), *Tudor Verse Satire* (Athlone, London, 1970)
Jensen, E., 'The Wit of Renaissance Satire', *Philological Quarterly* 51 (1972), pp. 394-409
Kernan, A., *The Cankered Muse: Satire of the English Renaissance* (Yale University Press, New Haven, 1959)
Peter, J., *Complaint and Satire in Early English Literature* (Clarendon Press, Oxford, 1956)
Powers, D.C., *English Formal Satire: Elizabethan to Augustan* (Mouton, The Hague, 1971)
Selden, R., *English Verse Satire 1590–1765* (Allen & Unwin, London, 1978)

Chapter 8

Williams, G.A., *Medieval London, From Commune to Capital* (Athlone, London, 1963)

Chapter 9

Clark, S., *The Elizabethan Pamphleteers* (Athlone, London, 1983)
Wright, L.B., *Middle-Class Culture in Elizabethan England* (University of North Carolina Press, Chapel Hill, N.C., 1935)

Chapter 10

Barron, C.M., 'Richard Whittington: The Man Behind the Myth', in A.E.J. Hollaender and W. Kellaway (eds), *Studies in London History Presented to Philip Edmund Jones* (Hodder & Stoughton, London, 1969), pp. 197-248
Heninger, S.K., 'The Tudor Myth of Troynovant', *South Atlantic Quarterly* 61 (1962), pp. 378-87
Kendrick, T.D., *British Antiquity* (London, 1950)
Riggs, D., *Shakespeare's Heroical Histories* (Harvard University Press, Cambridge, 1971)

Stevenson, L., *Praise and Paradox: Merchants and Craftsmen in English Renaissance Literature* (Cambridge University Press, 1984)

Chapter 11

Hudson, H., *The Epigram in the English Renaissance* (Princeton University Press, Princeton, N.J., 1947)
Whipple, T.K., *Martial and the English Epigram* (University of California Publications in Modern Philology, Berkeley, 1925)

Chapter 12

O'Loughlin, M., *Garlands of Repose: The Celebration of Civic and Retired Leisure* (University of Chicago Press, Chicago, 1968)
Williams, R., *The Country and the City* (Oxford University Press, London, 1973)

Chapter 13

Shugg, W., 'Prostitution in Shakespeare's London', *Shakespeare Studies* 10 (1977), pp. 291-313
Stone, L., *The Family, Sex and Marriage in England, 1500–1800* (Weidenfeld & Nicolson, London, 1977)
Thompson, C.J.S., *Love, Marriage, and Romance in Old London* (Heath Cranton, London, 1936)

Chapter 14

Brown, A., 'Citizen Comedy and Domestic Drama', in J.R. Brown and B. Harris (eds), *Jacobean Drama* (Edward Arnold, London, 1960)
Gibbons, B., *Jacobean City Comedy* (rev. edn. Methuen, London, 1980)
Knights, L.C., *Drama and Society in the Age of Jonson* (Chatto & Windus, London, 1937)
Legatt, A., *Citizen Comedy in the Age of Shakespeare* (Toronto University Press, Toronto, 1973)
Wells, S., 'Jacobean City Comedy and the Ideology of the City', *English Literary History* 48 (1981), pp. 37-60

Chapter 15

Aldington, R. (ed.), *A Book of 'Characters'* (Routledge, London, 1924)
Bush, D., *English Literature in the Earlier Seventeenth Century, 1600–1660* (Oxford, 1945)
Routh, H.V., 'London and the Development of Popular Literature', in *The Cambridge History of English Literature* (Cambridge University Press, 1932), vol. IV, pp. 316-63

Chapter 16

Bergeron, D.M., *English Civic Pageantry, 1558–1642* (Edward Arnold, London, 1971)

Kipling, G., 'Triumphal Drama: Form in English Civic Pageantry', *Renaissance Drama* 8 (1977), pp. 37-56

Leinwand, T.B., 'London's Triumphing: The Jacobean Lord Mayor's Show', *Clio* 11 (1982), pp. 137-50

Wickham, G., *Early English Stages, 1300–1600* (Routledge & Kegan Paul, London, 1980)

Williams, S., 'The Lord Mayor's Show in Tudor and Stuart Times', *The Guildhall Miscellany* 10 (1959), pp. 3-18

INDEX